History and Uses of Limestones and Marbles;

History and Uses

OF

Limestones and Marbles

BY S. M. BURNHAM

WITH FORTY-EIGHT CHROMO-LITHOGRAPHS

Boston
S. E. CASSINO AND COMPANY
1883

PREFACE.

IT was not the design of the author of Limestones and Marbles to write a treatise on geology, nor is the book intended for scientific readers as such, since it makes no claims to new investigations, nor offers any new theories on the subject; it only presents the facts and speculations of original explorers and writers, so selected and arranged as to illustrate the value of limestones in some departments of geology, but more especially their use in the mechanic and the fine arts, and their history in civilization Technical terms have, generally, been explained so that an unscientific reader may be able to understand them without reference to a text-book.

Calcareous rocks are of great value in determining the age of strata, on account of the large number and variety of organic remains which they enclose, while they largely contribute to the diversified and picturesque scenery of the globe. Limestones are, in one sense, a link between the mineral and the animal kingdoms, since most of them have an organic origin and possess, on that account, an interest above that of most other rocks. The adaptability of marbles to the purposes of art have made them indispensable to man in the higher department of sculpture and architecture

There is no work exclusively devoted to limestones and marbles known to the writer, who has been compelled to gather facts from various sources; and any deficiency of such facts in regard to the limestones of some countries is due, probably, rather to the lack of geological knowledge than to any failure of supply.

The authors consulted for scientific truth, or what claims to be truth, include some of the most prominent geologists of this country and Europe, as well as those of less note ; but, as is well known, there is a difference of opinion among them on many geological questions   In regard to the age of a formation and some other points they are likely to differ or change their opinions, and the theories of to-day may be abandoned to-morrow, while the essential character of the rocks remain as unquestionable facts   An illustration of this subject is afforded in the Red Ammonite and the Carrara marbles of Italy, which modern geologists have changed in chronological rank many times.   This may be an extreme case, but other formations have acquired, in some degree, the same doubtful character.

To give the subject continuity and completeness it has been sometimes necessary to refer to other formations combined and interstratified with calcareous strata, forming series, groups, and systems

In the classification of the animal kingdom the general arrangement has been followed, and in the descriptions of fossiliferous limestones an antiquated name may have been occasionally retained   Prominence has been given to the color of marbles and other ornamental stones, because this quality, combined with a capacity for polish, is of primary importance   The Latin names of the "Antique Stones" have been mentioned as far as they are known, since they occur in classic writings, while their corresponding Italian names, by which they are recognized by modern antiquaries, are used in preference to their English equivalents, which, in many instances, are absurd or fanciful.

INTRODUCTION.

A BEAUTIFUL statue, a fine monument, a magnificent building, or any other grand and pleasing object in stone, naturally
suggests inquiry as to the nature of the substance composing
it, the place where it was obtained, its age, importance in art,
and various other facts connected with its history ; for most
rocks have a history extending far back through geological
eras beyond human computation   A knowledge of the nature
and origin of limestones, a rock that contributes so largely to
works of art, enhances the pleasure these productions afford,
and awakens admiration for the wonderful laws of Nature, and
the methods by which she has brought to perfection the
abundant materials of her immense laboratory, and placed
them at man's disposal to be applied by his energy and genius
to his use and the gratification of his æsthetic tastes.

The perfect adaptability of marble to statuary and the more
ornamental parts of architecture had, undoubtedly, an important influence in the creation of the beautiful works of
those nations that have attained the highest excellence in the
fine arts, the Greek and Latin races, in whose countries are
found an abundance of the best material for sculpture. How
far the superiority of Greek art was due to the native production of Greece is a question no one can decide, but there
can be little doubt that the excellence of Parian and Pentelic
marbles had an influence in the development of the Attic taste

for sculpture, and stimulated the Greek artists to aim at the highest results in execution

Marbles rank next to precious stones for beauty and elegance in decoration, but, unlike them, they are very abundant and of an almost unlimited variety   Under the general term of marble, are often classed other stones used for artistic purposes, which for beauty, diversity of colors, and fine polish are suitable for decoration; such as alabaster, aragonite, gypsum (all calcareous), serpentine, porphyry, labradorite, basalt, and some others, whose constituents are essentially different   All marbles, properly speaking, are limestones admitting a polish, whether crystalline or uncrystalline.

Stratified rocks embody the geological records of the globe, and these important memorials are, to a great extent, preserved in calcareous strata, therefore they are the most significant and interesting among all strata for scientific study.

Limestones constitute a large part of the rocks of the earth, being found in every period from the oldest to the most recent. A difference of opinion exists among geologists in regard to their formation, some maintaining the theory that they are all, or nearly all, of organic origin, while others believe that a large proportion were formed by precipitation resulting from chemical reactions. It is probable that both processes effected the result, but by far the greater part, even of those that have undergone metamorphism, were composed largely of the remains of living beings, inhabiting marine and fresh waters   Shells, either entire or in comminuted fragments, small particles of older calcareous rocks broken off and reduced to fine sediment, were precipitated to the bottom of the ocean, and, gradually accumulating, constituted beds of limestone, in some instances of very great thickness; those of organic origin were formed in a similar manner, in fresh and inland waters   It can hardly be doubted that some limestones were the result of precipitation, as water, charged with carbonate of lime, in dropping through small crevices, and depositing the lime, would in time produce masses of pure limestone, as in the case of stalagmites and stalactites, and, perhaps, those marbles called calcareous alabasters.

Various. causes operated to consolidate the sediments forming limestones, whether composed of shells or pulverized rocks. The agents were carbonate of lime in the nature of cement, great and long-continued pressure, and water of a high degree of temperature, when the process occupied a very long time. As the materials of limestones, in some instances, have been worked over many times, passing from "sand to rock, and from rock to sand, in ever recurring cycles," their growth must have been exceedingly slow.

They contain more organic remains than any other rock, and by their general distribution afford proof that the waters of the earth, in past eras, as they are now, were inhabited by an unlimited number and diversity of organized beings. A very large number of the living species that have contributed to the formation of limestones were extremely minute, affording an admirable illustration of the wonderful economy with which Nature carries on her operations. These innumerable beings, the necessity of whose existence might have been questioned by human presumption, yielded their stony skeletons for the structure of rock material ages before the creation of the human race.

The oldest rocks known are the Laurentian, a formation of great thickness, including calcareous strata, thus proving the extraordinary age of limestones It was formerly supposed there was no organic life during this remote era, the mythological period of geology, but as the chemists say that the presence of graphite indicates organic matter, and as this mineral is found among the Eozoic rocks, the inference would seem to follow that there existed vegetable and probably the lower forms of animal life during this period; at least, this is the argument of those who maintain the theory.

Although limestones have had a long chronological history, they are to be found among the youngest rocks, and are in process of formation at the present time.

CONTENTS.

CHAPTER I.

DIFFERENT CLASSES OF LIMESTONES.

CHAPTER II.

FOSSILS.

CHAPTER III.

GENERAL DIVISIONS OF GEOLOGICAL TIME.

CHAPTER IV.

LIMESTONES OF THE UNITED STATES.

ATLANTIC REGION.

CHAPTER V.

LIMESTONES OF THE UNITED STATES—*continued.*

THE MISSISSIPPI BASIN.

CHAPTER VI.

LIMESTONES OF THE UNITED STATES — *concluded.*

ROCKY MOUNTAINS AND PACIFIC COAST

CHAPTER VII.

LIMESTONES OF BRITISH AMERICA AND THE WEST INDIA ISLANDS.

BRITISH AMERICA.

WEST INDIA ISLANDS

CHAPTER VIII.

LIMESTONES OF MEXICO AND SOUTH AMERICA.

MEXICO

SOUTH AMERICA.

CHAPTER IX.

LIMESTONES OF GREAT BRITAIN

CHAPTER X.

LIMESTONES OF FRANCE

CHAPTER XI.

LIMESTONES OF BELGIUM, GERMANY, AND THE NETHERLANDS

BELGIUM

CHAPTER XII.

LIMESTONES OF SWITZERLAND AND THE ALPS.

CHAPTER XIII.

LIMESTONES OF THE AUSTRIAN EMPIRE, DENMARK, SCANDINAVIA, AND THE POLAR REGIONS.

AUSTRIA.

DENMARK.

SCANDINAVIA.

POLAR REGIONS

CHAPTER XIV.

LIMESTONES OF THE SPANISH PENINSULA AND ITALY.

SPAIN AND PORTUGAL

ITALY.

CHAPTER XV.

LIMESTONES OF GREECE.—GREEK ART.

CHAPTER XVI.

LIMESTONES OF THE RUSSIAN EMPIRE AND CHINA.

THE RUSSIAN EMPIRE.

CHINA.

CHAPTER XVII.

LIMESTONES OF THE TURKISH EMPIRE.

CHAPTER XVIII.

LIMESTONES OF ARABIA, PERSIA, AFGHANISTAN, BELOOCHISTAN, AND INDIA.

ARABIA.

CHAPTER XIX.

LIMESTONES OF JAPAN, AUSTRALIA, AND AFRICA.

CHAPTER XX.

ANTIQUE MARBLES.

CHAPTER XXI.

ANTIQUE ALABASTERS, SERPENTINES, BASALTS, GRANITES, AND PORPHYRIES.

CHAPTER XXII.

ANTIQUE STONES AND WORKS OF ART IN MODERN ROME.

CHAPTER XXIII.

ANTIQUE STONES USED TO DECORATE ROMAN CHURCHES.

APPENDIX.

LIMESTONES AND MARBLES.

CHAPTER I.

DIFFERENT CLASSES OF LIMESTONES.

LIMESTONES may be classified and named according to their difference of origin, fossils, age, structure, texture, color, uses, locality, and other distinctive features. Many of them are fragmental, consisting of particles broken from older strata and deposited as sediment, hence they are called sedimentary rocks. When changed from a sedimentary to a crystalline condition, they are said to be metamorphic. Limestones, when formed at the bottom of the sea, are called marine formations; when deposited by the waters of lakes and rivers, fresh-water formations. They are crystalline when the carbonate of lime assumes the form of regular crystals. The crystallization may be of different kinds, coarse-grained, when the crystals are large and distinct; or fine, with the appearance of loaf-sugar, when it is called saccharoidal. A limestone is fossiliferous when it encloses organic remains, or the traces of organic remains, either vegetable or animal. A smooth, fine-grained limestone, of a dull or splintery fracture, is called compact, and when made up of angular pieces of rocks, either of the same or of different kinds, cemented by lime it is known as a breccia. Some of the most beautiful variegated marbles are of this class. A limestone composed of spheroidal masses, larger or smaller, passes under the name of concretionary. The terms "concretionary" and "nodular" are used very indefinitely, sometimes as synonymous, and again as of different signification, even by the same writer. Concretions are formed of aggregations of matter around a centre, sometimes a shell or other foreign substance constituting the nucleus; they may be solid or hollow, and of a concentric or radiated internal structure. When lined with crystals, they are called geodes. With concretions of the size of a pea, the limestone is called pisolitic; and oolitic when the concretions are no larger than the roe of fishes. These small concretions are known to have several concentric coats, and are sometimes hollow, at other times enclosing minute particles. The Oolite makes a desirable building-stone, on account of its color and the facility with which it may be worked in any direction.

Hydraulic limestone is used for the manufacture of hydraulic lime; bituminous or carbonaceous limestone is formed partly of decayed organic matter, and yields black marbles; fetid limestone, when struck with a hammer, emits sulphuretted hydrogen, the result of the decomposition of animal substances.

Many fossiliferous limestones are designated by some typical shell, as Nummulitic, Gryphite, Orthoceratite; other varieties are named for the place where they are specially developed, as Trenton, Eifel, Alpine; while others are known by the geological period in which they were formed, as Carboniferous, Triassic, Jurassic.

Some varieties of limestones consist of nearly pure carbonate of lime, while others have a large admixture of foreign substances, as clay, sand, iron oxide, when they receive the distinctive appellation of argillaceous, siliceous, or ferruginous; by a modification of their structure or texture they may become schistose, shaly, friable, or porous. Chalk is limestone of a friable texture.

The difference in color is occasioned by the presence of foreign substances: limonite, or hydrous oxide of iron, imparts a brown or brownish-yellow; glauconite, hydrous iron-silicate, colors different greens; and red oxide of iron, the shades of red. Carbonaceous substances cause the blacks and deep-browns. Other minerals have contributed to the color of marbles and limestones, a quality upon which much of their beauty and value depend.

Dolomite, or magnesian limestone, consists of the carbonate of magnesia united to the carbonate of lime, but it does not differ materially in appearance from pure limestone, and sometimes can be distinguished from it only by chemical analysis. Dolomite does not so readily effervesce in acids, crumbles more easily, and is less compact, but is generally highly crystalline and often granular. The crystals are very small, yet distinct; the rock presents the aspect of a fine sandstone. The colors range through shades of reddish-brown or yellow, white, gray, and black, and it varies in structure like common limestone, being sometimes concretionary, with nodules of the size of cannon balls: botryoidal, with concretions like clusters of grapes; and not unfrequently oolitic. Like pure limestone, dolomite is found in all geological periods, and is of continental extent, embracing a large part of the calcareous rocks of the globe, including many kinds of white statuary and colored architectural marbles. It was employed for antique sculpture to a considerable extent, though its composition is a modern discovery, made in 1791, by Dolomieu, a French geologist, for whom it was named. Dolomite often constitutes the veins and spots of variegated stones, as the yellow veins of the marble called Porto Venere, or the "black and gold" of marble-workers. It is extensively used in England for buildings, but is liable to decay in the moist and smoky atmosphere of that country, as may be seen in the Houses of Parliament, which were built of this stone. It is very abundant in Spain, and has been employed in the construction of Madrid; it is found in the United States and British America, where it is of considerable economical value for the excellent lime it affords. True dolomite has nearly the following chemical composition: carbonate of

lime, 54.35 ; carbonate of magnesia, 45 65 ; but these propor-
tions vary in the dolomites of different localities on account
of the presence of foreign substances.

The Oolite, the great Jurassic formation in Great Britain,
including many varieties, is composed of small, round concretions composed of different substances cemented by lime. It
is soft and uniform in texture and of light colors, — white,
gray, drab, and cream-color.

In contrasting the Great Oolite with the Portland stone,
both members of the Jurassic formation, Hull says that the
former is especially adapted to the delicate chisellings of the
Gothic style, while the latter is better fitted for the massive
and more uniform structures of classic and Italian architecture.

The Caen stone, from the northern part of France, is a
Jurassic limestone very generally used for interior decorations,
for which it is unrivalled in color and texture. It is said to
hold the same rank in architecture that is held by Carrara
marble in sculpture. The quarries have been worked for
centuries, and it is still in great demand for a building
material

The Calcaire grossier of the Paris basin belongs to the Tertiary period, consequently is of more recent origin than the
Jurassic limestones. The Eocene, or lower Tertiary, in England, includes the London basin, and appears again across the
Channel throughout the valley of the Seine, constituting the
most important formation of what is called the Paris basin.
The strata of this basin are of both marine and fresh-water
origin.

The Calcaire grossier, employed in building, is of a light-
buff color, particularly adapted to an atmosphere free from
fog and smoke. Much of the beauty of Paris, where it is
generally used, is due to the excellence of this stone for
architectural purposes, its light and delicate tint imparting a
fresh and cheerful aspect to the city. It has been used in the
buildings of other cities with similar effect : Marseilles, Mont-

pelier, Bordeaux, and Brussels in Belgium afford instances. The Louvre in Paris, and the cathedrals of Rouen and of Amiens are examples of edifices built of this limestone from the Paris basin.

The quarries of the Calcaire grossier extend along the Seine and under a large part of Paris; it was quarried here for building from a very early period until the seventeenth century, but subsequently these caverns were used for burial places, and at the present time, the Catacombs, as they are called, form an intricate labyrinth under the city.

The Nummulitic limestone receives its name from the coin-shaped Rhizopod, which constitutes a large part of the rock. Geologically it belongs to the middle Eocene, and is largely developed in southern Europe, Asia, and northern Africa. In Europe this formation extends over a large part of the Pyrenees, the Alps, constituting summits eleven thousand feet above the sea, the Apennines and the Carpathians. It ranges through Algiers, Morocco, Asia Minor, the Caucasus, Persia, the mountains of Afghanistan, India, on the southern slope of the Himalayas, sometimes attaining the height of 16,500 feet in Western Thibet, and reaches to the borders of China; it also occurs in the islands of Japan, Java, and the Philippines. It furnished material for some of the Pyramids, particularly that of Cheops, the Great Pyramid, which was built upon the native limestone, the four corner-stones set into the rocky mass constituting the foundation of the most remarkable structure ever erected. Nummulitic limestone was employed in the buildings of Baalbec, Aleppo, and some of the cities of the Holy Land, and was largely used as marble in Verona, Padua, and other cities of northern Italy.

Travertine is a porous, concretionary limestone, formed by the precipitation of carbonate of lime held in solution by the waters of particular springs and streams. Among the most remarkable examples are those of Tivoli near Rome, and Gardner's River in the Yellowstone Park, Wyoming. The phenomena of Gardner's River present many interesting

features. The water in its descent has formed a series of
parapets at different stages, enclosing beautifully ornamented
basins, over the edges of which it falls, leaving a calcareous
deposit in the form of exquisite sculptured decorations. The
large masses of travertine at Tivoli, near the Arnio, Italy,
were deposited in a lake which once occupied the spot. This
stone was called by the ancient Romans *Lapis Tiburtinus,*
and it was used in early times, as it has been since, for buildings in Rome and other Italian cities. It is white or light
yellowish, sometimes with wavy lines; soft when first quarried,
but on exposure it becomes harder, and in the clear atmosphere of Italy is very durable. The Emperor Augustus employed travertine in connection with Carrara marble, to construct the architectural monuments which embellished ancient
Rome. The exterior of the Colosseum, the Tomb of Hadrian,
now the Castle of St. Angelo, the Quirinal Palace, St. Peter's
of the Vatican, and the walls of nearly all the other churches
of Rome are built of this stone. The travertine of Tivoli is
a recent formation and affords beautiful pendants like stalactites The walls of the deep chasm into which the water is
precipitated, consist of thick beds four hundred or five hundred
feet in depth, while a precipice with a sheer descent of four hundred feet has been formed under the temples of Vesta and the
Sybil, with spheroids six or eight feet in diameter, consisting
of thin concentric layers. The calcareous tufa, used for building in Naples, is composed of a deposition of volcanic matter
in a former bed of the sea, but it is inferior to that of Tivoli
Travertine is found in the ruins of Pompeii, and was used in
the construction of the Temple of Paestum. A volcanic tufa,
called Peperino, is a coarse, hard stone of a gray color, often
enclosing small pebbles.

Satin spar is a variety of fibrous limestone with a silky
lustre, and is used for inlaid work; it differs from the satin
spar of gypsum in its superior hardness and readiness to yield
to the action of acids.

Agaric mineral, a very pure carbonate of lime, frequently

Plate II.

VERMONT, REDDISH-BROWN AND WHITE.

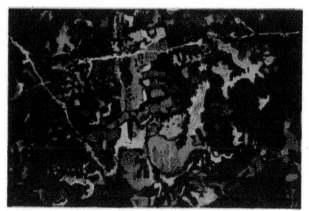

TENNESSEE, DARK.

ARMSTRONG & CO. LITH. BOSTON.

passing into calcareous tufa, is white and soft, easily crumbles, and is sometimes deposited in caverns.

Forest, ruin, or fortification marble is an argillaceous limestone, presenting when polished, representations of trees, ruins, temples, and fortifications, caused by the infiltration of oxide of iron, and is used with beautiful effect in mosaic work

Alabaster. — There are two kinds of alabaster, calcareous and gypseous True or Oriental alabaster is a carbonate of lime, like marble in its chemical properties, but differing from most marbles in origin, being produced by precipitation and not from organic and sedimentary deposits. It has a greater translucency than marble, and takes a fine polish, constituting one of the most agreeable ornamental stones, ranking next to gems, it was extensively used for decoration by the ancients. A very white, translucent alabaster was used in Assyria for the sculptures in bas-relief, taken by Mr. Layard from the supposed palace of Sennacherib, whose reign has been assigned to about 700 B C, and deposited in the British Museum.

The beautiful onyx marble of Mexico is a calcareous alabaster, similar to the ancient and modern onyx marble of Algeria, extensively used in France for ornamental purposes since the quarries were rediscovered

The name alabaster has been given to massive gypsum, a hydrous sulphate of lime, a stone much softer than calcareous alabaster, when highly crystalline and translucent it is called Selenite, when fibrous it becomes the satin spar used in making ornaments.

Gypsum occurs in most formations from the Silurian to the Tertiary, but is most abundant in the Triassic and Carboniferous beds It is quite largely developed in some parts of England, and is found in many other countries to a greater or less extent The principal gypsum quarries of France, from which the stone is obtained that affords the best plaster of Paris, are at Montmartre, near Paris Beds of limestone are sometimes changed into gypsum by the penetration of water charged with sulphuric acid.

Serpentines. — Though serpentine is not a limestone, yet for decorative uses it is classed with marbles, and for the beauty and vivacity of its colors, the excellent polish it receives, and the facility with which it is worked, it holds an important rank among ornamental stones.   In a pure state it is a hydrous silicate of magnesia, but it is never truly crystalline, and when crystals do occur they are pseudomorphs, or those which have borrowed the crystalline form from other minerals   Massive serpentine is frequently mixed with dolomite, calcite, and other substances, and is compact, not granular, but sometimes fibrous and greasy to the touch.   There are several varieties, dependent on structure, as massive, lamellar, foliated, and fibrous.   It is a metamorphic rock, developed in all the older geological formations, and distributed quite generally through-out the countries of both hemispheres.

Serpentines used for ornamental purposes are selected for their rich and beautiful colors, including different shades of green to yellow, white, red, brown, and even black ; they are often brilliant with crystals of diallage, mica, and calcite. Noble serpentine is translucent and usually of a light yellow-ish-green

The celebrated Verde antique marble, or Ophiolyte, is ser-pentine combined either with magnesia or carbonate of lime ; the Vermont Verde antique is said to have no lime, or less than the European, and is harder, fine-grained, and compact, with great crushing power.

The serpentine of the Vosges mountains encloses diallage, olivine, iron, and garnets, of various colors from blood-red to green

It is very abundant in France, and yields many fine varieties. The Moors of Spain employed the serpentine of the Sierra Nevada for decorating their remarkable buildings, and it is proved that the ancient Romans used it for the same purpose, since it is found in the ruins of their cities.

The most ancient serpentine, geologically, is the Laurentian of Canada, said to enclose the Eozoon Canadense, the earliest known fossil.

Metamorphism. — Since this term has been used in connection with limestones it needs some explanation. As employed in geology, it is applied to the change of sedimentary rocks into a crystalline state, as limestone into marble. The process has sometimes been called "plutonic," from the supposition that it occurred in the depths of the earth The causes of metamorphism are, perhaps, not very well understood, but the agents are thought to be heat, water, and pressure as a secondary cause, with alkalies, and perhaps some other substances.   Water alone at 752° Fahr. reduces nearly all rocks to a paste, and its solvent power is greatly increased by the presence of alkali.   The amount of heat required to melt rock material without water is from 2,000° to 3,000°; with water and alkali combined, it requires only from 300° to 400°.

It is generally admitted that the interior of the earth, though solid, is in a heated condition, and the great mass of sedimentary strata is penetrated by water from above and by heat from beneath, which combine to produce certain molecular changes and chemical reactions resulting in crystallization.   This change in great masses of rocks takes place far below the surface, but many of the metamorphosed rocks have been brought within the sphere of observation by the denuding power of water, or by some violent internal disturbance. There may have been a long period between the formation of a rock from sediments and its crystallization, and it is probable that metamorphism is going on continually in the buried sedimentary strata.

That some crystalline rocks contain fossils, seems to indicate that a high degree of heat was not always essential to metamorphism, otherwise all traces of organic remains would be obliterated, as they are, to a great extent, in altered strata

CAVERNS. — Water possesses great dissolving properties, especially when containing carbonic acid, and becomes a powerful agent in disintegrating rocks, as has been stated; it produces a marked effect upon limestone, eroding compact masses, often leaving immense cavities; and sometimes the work of erosion is expedited by the addition of other acids, as sulphuric, and those formed by decomposed organic remains. Besides these chemical agents, sand and pebbles, borne along by subterranean rivers, and igneous disturbances, have, in some instances, contributed a mechanical force in rock destruction, and assisted in the formation of those wonderful and beautiful subterranean palaces which seem like the weird and grotesque phantasms of dreams.

Caverns occur in nearly all countries, and though generally found in limestone formations, they sometimes exist in other rocks, as, in granite, in Norway and Sweden; in lava, in France and Iceland, and in porphyry, near Quito Among the best known caverns are the Mammoth Cave in Kentucky, the largest explored; Wier's Cave in Virginia; Adelsberg, in Carniola, Austria; Antiparos, in Greece, Elephanta and Ellora, in India. A large number of others are known, and the discovery of new caverns is of frequent occurrence.

Stalactites and stalagmites, found in limestone caves, are formed in the following manner: The water from the strata above, charged with carbonic acid, percolating the superincumbent mass, finally reaches the limestone, some of which it dissolves, holding the lime in solution A part of this lime is deposited on the roof of the cave, while another drop of water trickles down, leaving its stolen particle of lime beside its companion. The process is continued age after age, until the deposit assumes the form of a pendant stalactite of greater or less size Returning to the first drop of water, which deposited only a portion of the lime on the roof, let us follow its course. It reaches the floor of the cavern, where it leaves the remainder of its plunder, followed by succeeding drops, which distribute a part of the lime to the work on the roof, and a part to that on the floor, until the stalagmite is built up, often joining its kindred stalactite above, the two united making a complete column If the water follows fissures in the roof, the stalactites and stalagmites, when meeting, form sheets, as in Wier's Cave, where they are so thin as to become translucent, and when struck, produce a ringing sound.

The deposits in caverns assume a great variety of forms, some grotesque, others quite perfect imitations of various objects. They are of different colors, pure white, yellow, or gray, according to the presence and nature of foreign substances. Fossils are sometimes found in stalactites, as the latter will form around any object left on the floor.

The stalactites of Ball's Cave, in New York, are of the purest white. In the recently-discovered cavern of Big Saltpetre, in Missouri, which is thought to rival the Mammoth Cave in size, the beautiful spar assumes a great diversity of figures. The Cave of Adelsberg is remarkable for the variety of its stalactites, some of which represent curtains, and some columns, arranged as trees in a forest, while others form long colonnades, verandas, and cascades.

A new cave was discovered, in August, 1878, in Paige County, Virginia, and named Luray Cavern. It was at first supposed to be in the Sub-carboniferous strata, a formation in which many remarkable caverns have been found, but it has since been referred to the Silurian. In this region the limestone has been fissured, and the seams filled with various minerals which have served for coloring matter. The limestone is partly magnesian, very fine grained, with color varying from light brown to deep blue and black, traversed by veins of white spar. The strata are folded and wrinkled, hence the cave does not afford the immense domes, rooms, avenues, and navigable rivers found in some other caverns, where the limestone is horizontal and homogeneous. The interior of Luray Cavern is divided into a large number of rooms, of different dimensions; corridors, galleries, amphitheatres of immense magnitude, brilliant with stalactites of different hues, columns of all shapes and sizes, transparent curtains, and a hundred other subterranean marvels sculptured by the hand of Nature. One enchanting room, covered by a dome supported by columns with walls of green and orange, and ceiling of the whiteness of snow, would seem, from the description given by an eye-witness, to have sprung into being at the touch of some magician's wand. A flight of stairs in the solid rock descends thirty feet to a series of apartments, in which are different simulated forms, some fanciful, others majestic; here is seen a petrified cascade, there a garden of alabaster flowers; alabaster pillars shooting upwards, graceful drapery frozen into stone: some objects are pure as snow, others are of translucent brown with agate bands, and one fluted column of pure white marble, of the finest grain, is thirty feet high.

It is said to be difficult to determine the size of cavernous rooms from sight merely, for the reason that it is not easy to produce sufficient illumination to judge with accuracy; there being no particles floating about to reflect the rays, the tendency is to exaggerate the magnitude of subterranean objects and space. Making due allowance for this fact, and for the effect which these magical structures have upon the imagination, they are still among the most wonderful productions of nature which diversify our globe.

CHAPTER II.

Classification of Fossils found in Calcareous Strata.

THE following synopsis of organic remains does not include all genera found in calcareous rocks, but those that are most characteristic and best known, and that have contributed most largely to their structure.

VEGETABLE KINGDOM.

Cryptogams. —

Campylodiscus (a Diatom).
Coccoliths (seed-stone).
Corallines (having jointed stems).
Desmids.
Diatoms (siliceous). } Protophytes.
Fucoids (leathery sea-weed).
Nullipores (without pores).
Charae (calcareous).
Gaillonella (siliceous).

Algae, or Sea-weed.

ANIMAL KINGDOM.

1. *Sub-Kingdom.*

Protozoans.
Sponges.
Regarded also as forming the Sub-kingdom Porifera.

Receptaculite.
Stromatopora. } Sponge, or Rhizopod.
Scyphia.
Siphonia.
Ventriculite.

Infusoria.

Both plants and animals.

13

Rhizopods ;
including
Foraminifers
and

Radiolaria.

Amphistegina (found in the Vienna Basin).
Fusilina.   Orbitolites.
Globigerina.   Orbulina.
Nummulina.   Peneroplis.
Orbitoides.   Textularia.
Orbitolina.

Polycystines (siliceous Foraminifers).

2. *Sub-Kingdom.*

Radiates.

Polyps, or
Zöophytes.

Polyps include Ac-
tinoid and Alcyo-
noid Corals.

Acervularia.
Actinia (Sea-anemone).
Alveolites.
Astræa.
Calceola (doubtful).
Columnaria (basaltic form).
Favosites (honeycomb coral).
Gorgonia (sea-fan).
Halysites (chain-coral).
Lithostrotion.
Madrepora (branching coral). The Madre-
    pores include many species.
Meandrina (brain-coral).
Syringopora.
Strombodes (cup-coral, Cyathophylloid).
Tubipora (organ-pipe coral).
Zaphrentis (cup-coral, Cyathophylloid).

Acalephs.

Hydroids.

Chaetetes. (?)
Graptolites (allied to Sertularia).
Millepores.

Echinoderms
include Cystoids.

Crinoids, having
stems.

Blastoids.

Cystids (bladder-shaped).
Comatula (Feather-star).
Crinid, or Encrinite.
Marsupite.
Pentacrinus.
Pentremites.

Asteroids. { Asteria (Star-fish).

Echinoids. { Cidaris.
Echinus.
Hemicidaris.
Spatangus.

3. *Sub-Kingdom.*

Mollusks.
Molluscoidea, or
Brachiate Mollusks.
Bryozoans, or
Polyzoans.

Archimedes.   Flustra.
Fenestella.   Retepora.

Brachiopods.
Bivalves. ──

Athyris.   Orthis.
Atrypa.   Pentamerus.
Chonetes.   Producta.
Crania.   Rhynchonella.
Discina.   Spirifer.
Leptæna.   Stringocephalus.
Lingula.   Strophomena.
Obolella.   Terebratula.
Obolus.   Waldheimia.

Mollusks Proper.

Acephals.
(Lamellibranchs.)
Bivalves.

Anomia.   Cyprina.
Arca.   Cyrena.
Astarte.   Cytherea.
Avicula.   Diceras.
Aviculapecten.   Donax.
Caprina.   Exogyra.
Caprotina.   Gervillia.
Cardiola.   Grammysia.
Cardium.   Gryphæa.
Cardita.   Haploscapha.
Chama.   Hippurite.
Chiton.   Inoceramus.
Conocardium.   Lima.
Corbis.   Lithodomus.
Crassatella.   Lucina.
Cyclas.   Mactra.

Mollusks Proper.

Modiola.
Modiolopsis.
Myrtilus.
Nucula, or Leda.
Orthonota.

(Lamellibranchs.)

Ostrea.

Bivalves.

Pandora.
Pecten.
Pentunculus.
Perna.
Pholas.
Pinna.

Posidonomya.
Radiolite.
Saxicava.
Solen.
Spherulite.
Spondylus.
Tellina.
Teredina.
Trigonia.
Unio.
Venus.
Venericardia.

Cephalates.
Univalves.

Conularia.
Hyalea.
Theca.
Tentaculite.

} Hyolites.

Pteropods.

Gasteropods.

Ampullaria.
Ancillaria.
Ancylus.
Buccinum.
Bellerophon.
Beloptera.
Bulla.
Cancellaria.
Cassis.
Cerithium.
Chiton.
Conus.
Cypræa.
Euomphalus.
Fusus.
Harpa.
Helix.
Litorina.
Litorinella.
Lymnea.
Maclurea.

Melania.
Mitra.
Murex.
Murchisonia.
Nassa.
Natica.
Nerinaea.
Nerita.
Neritina.
Oliva.
Ovula.
Paludina.
Planorbis.
Pleurotoma.
Pleurotomaria.
Pupa.
Purpura.
Physa.
Pterocera.
Pyrula.
Rostellaria.

	Scalaria.	Turbo.
	Solarium.	Turritella.
Gasteropods.	Strombus.	Voluta.
	Terebra.	Vermetus.
	Trochus.	

	Ammonite.	Hamite.
	Ancyloceras.	Lituite.
Cephalopods.	Bacculite.	Nautilus.
	Belemnite.	Orthoceras.
Dibranchiata.	Belemnitella.	Scaphite.
Tetrabranchiata.	Ceratite.	Sepia.
	Clymenia.	Spirula.
	Crioceras.	Toxoceras.
	Cyrtoceras.	Turrilite.
	Goniatite.	

4. Sub-Kingdom.

Articulates.

Crustaceans.

{ Cancer (crabs).
Cypris, or Daphne (Ostracoides, bivalves).
Limulus.
Trilobites.

Worms.

{ Serpula (having calcareous tubes).

DESCRIPTION OF FOSSILS.

Many limestones are largely made up of organic remains, and some knowledge of these remains is important in the study of fossiliferous rocks.

Lyell defines a fossil to be "any organic body, animal or vegetable, or the traces of any body, which has been buried in the earth by natural causes." Fossils afford unequivocal proof that the land and sea of former geological periods teemed with living beings, and the remains they have left are of vast importance in determining the age of strata.

Though other fossils are sometimes enclosed in limestones, testacea and corals are the most characteristic, and have contributed most largely to the beauty and value of marbles Often entire masses of rock are composed of aggregations of shells, more especially of the lower animals, which, says Dana, are the best rock-makers, because they consist very largely of calcareous matter.

Fossil shells are found in strata in different conditions: 1. When the substance has not been changed. 2. When the form of the shell is preserved, but the substance petrified; as in limestone it assumes the appearance of calc spar. 3. When fossils have left casts or impressions.

To understand the language of geology in regard to fossils, a general knowledge of the classification of the animal kingdom is necessary.

Most naturalists arrange all living creatures, according to their structure, in five divisions or sub-kingdoms, namely, Protozoans, Radiates, Mollusks, Articulates, and Vertebrates.

PROTOZOANS.

These "first animals" are mostly microscopic, and include Sponges, Infusoria, and Rhizopods, or animals with "root-like feet." The sponges are regarded by some naturalists as forming a sub-kingdom called Porifera

Sponges. — Fossil sponges are numerous in the Cretaceous period, sometimes constituting entire layers of rocks, and are found in calcareous strata, as in the Kentish Rag and Portland stone, and in flint and pebbles. Sponges are regarded as compound animals of different forms, cup-shaped, tubular, branched, and others, and some are borers, penetrating shells and even solid rock.

The earlier paleontologists classed them as Alcyoniae, which were described as animals assuming vegetable forms either fleshy, gelatinous, or spongy. A species with a finely-reticulated structure is popularly called "Dead man's fingers," and another species shows a curious instinct for enveloping the

Plate III.

VERMONT, GRAY SHELL.

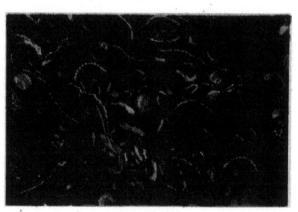

LUMACHELLA NERA.

ARMSTRONG & CO. LITH. BOSTON.

Nerita, a small Gasteropod found in the chalk of northern Italy. A peculiar sponge resembling a cucumber is found in a dense, siliceous limestone of an ash-gray and straw color.

Rhizopods. — These animals, called Foraminifera, because their shells are perforated by pores, and important in the formation of calcareous rocks, began their existence at the dawn of animal life, and are found in the deposits of modern seas.

The genus Orbulina has only one globular cell while the Nummulite presents a succession of cells or chambers divided by transverse septa, and varies from a size nearly microscopic to one and one half inches in diameter; the colors are white, shades of brown, red, and bluish.

The Fusilina, a univalve allied to the Nummulite, resembles a grain of wheat, and was abundant in some countries in the Carboniferous age. The fossil Receptaculite has been called a Rhizopod, though it resembles a Coral in some of its characteristics. It is the predominant fossil in the Receptaculite limestone of Missouri, and is found in the German Eifel and other foreign calcareous deposits.

RADIATES.

This sub-kingdom comprises animals with a radiated structure, or parts arranged around a centre like the petals of a flower. They include Polyps, Acalephs, and Echinoderms.

Polyps. — These have a cylindrical body with a mouth at one extremity, and are permanently united at the base; when stony, they are called corals, which are only aggregated polyps. The framework is secreted by the animal tissues as bones are, and not by "the conscious power" of the polyps. The Actinoid polyps form ordinary corals, and the Alcyonoid polyps, the Gorgonia and Alcyonium corals; the red variety used in jewelry is the stem or axis of the Alcyonoid. Some of the most valuable limestones and the most beautiful marbles were formed entirely or partly by polyps, the most ingenious and indefatigable rock-builders in existence, whose constructive powers are constantly in active operation.

Not until the beginning of the eighteenth century was the true character of the Coral understood. Some naturalists previous to that time placed it with plants, others ascribed to it a dual nature, partly animal and partly vegetable, while a third class held that it was made by the polyp, somewhat as a bee constructs its comb.

Corals, says Dana, are made by four different organisms: 1. Polyps, the chief architects of coral reefs. 2. The Hydroids forming the corals called Millepores, on account of the minute cells seen covering the surface. Some of the Graptolites — feather stone — named from its plumose appearance, are probably included in this class. They are prevalent in the older rock strata, particularly in the Quebec group. 3. Bryozoans — moss animals — called by this name from the moss-like coral they secrete. Algae, plant-corals which produce calcareous secretions, as Corallines with jointed stems, Nullipores without cells, and Coccoliths — seed-like stones. Nullipores are very solid and strong; Corallines are more delicate, and broken up, form thick calcareous deposits.

The Actinoid polyps, which secrete the ordinary coral, are exceedingly curious and interesting The genus Actinia, or Sea-anemone, includes animals with a sub-cylindrical body and a disk at the top, with radiated structure internally and externally. Its stomach can be distended to swallow its prey, which it seizes with its myriad arms, thrown out with the rapidity of lightning. Actinoids vary in color and size, and are propagated by ova or buds.

The Zoophytes — plant animals — or polyps, form groups or compound animals from one germ, each polyp, however, having a separate mouth, stomach, and tentacles. When any portion of the coral is broken off, their vital energy is such that they can restore the lost fragment, which also has the power of becoming a new zoophyte.

Ordinary corals are largely calcareous, containing from ninety-five to ninety-eight per cent of lime, and form immense beds of hard, compact limestone, frequently constituting entire islands or *atolls*.

The growth of coral reefs is exceedingly slow, not more, it is believed, than five feet in 1,000 years, therefore at that rate, some of the Pacific Ocean reefs must have required hundreds of thousands of years to attain their present size; shell limestone deposits were of still slower growth, because corals are, to a large extent, calcareous. The great depth of coral formations is due to the gradual subsidences of the land upon which they grew.

The author of "Corals and Coral Islands" says that such islands are really monuments erected over departed lands, and, by the evidence of these records, it has been discovered that the Pacific has its deep-water mountain chains, or lines of volcanic summits, thousands of miles in length, as the Hawaiian Islands, which extend under water 2,000 miles. The Coral island subsidence has a length of more than 6,000 miles and a breadth of 2,500, but had there been no growing coral the history of this subsidence would have passed into oblivion

There are evidences that this process is still going on, and that not subsidences only, but elevations, are occurring, some islands having already reached a height of 600 feet above sea level.

The Coral reef at the Loo Choo Islands, east of China, is thus described: When the rock has been left dry for some time, it appears to be a hard, compact, rugged mass, but as the sea washes over it the polypi protrude themselves from holes before invisible. They are of a great variety of shapes, colors, and sizes, and in so prodigious numbers that in a short time the rock appears to be alive and in motion until the water ceases to cover it, when the animals die.

The islands of the Polynesian Archipelago were formed of corals, and in the Indian Ocean, southwest of Malabar, one chain of reefs and islets has been built up extending 480 geographical miles, another 700, and a third 600 miles. It has been stated that the whole bed of the Red Sea is a submarine garden of exquisite verdure, interspersed with various species of Sponges, Corals, and shells in luxuriant abundance.

The fauna of the Red Sea is different from that of the Mediterranean, being essentially calcareous. In 1869, McAndrew and Fielding found in this sea, more than 800 species of Mollusks, numerous Echinoderms, Corals, and Crustaceans Upwards of 350 species of the Mollusks had not been known before their discovery, as inhabitants of the Red Sea, while 53 species and three genera were new to science.

The varieties of Corals are numerous, but will not be here mentioned with the exception of some families and genera entering into the composition of limestones and marbles.

The Cyathophyllum, composed of two words meaning cup and leaf, is the name of a family called "cup-corals," which began in the Lower Silurian and disappeared in the Permian period. They are often of large size; some Cyathophylloids of the Devonian age have been found six or seven inches across the top These fossils, abundant in the Corniferous period, are enclosed in some of the most beautiful marbles of Devonshire, England.

The Favosites, or honeycomb coral, belonging to the Madrepores or "branching" group, originated in the Lower Silurian, attained their climax in the Devonian, and disappeared in the beginning of the Sub-carboniferous, according to Dana; but Mantell says they are found in the Jurassic limestone.

The Lithostrotion was named by Da Costa from lithostron, pavement, because these fossils were supposed to exist in loose masses in the strata of other rocks like a mosaic pavement

The columns have five, six, or seven sides, are frequently one inch in diameter, and when cut transversely present the interstertial appearance of a spider's web One species presents a columnar structure, and another is floriform, having the appearance of clusters of flowers The Lithostrotion is abundant in the Carboniferous era, and yields a variety of beautiful marbles, generally of an ash-gray

The Tubipore, called Tubiporite in a fossil state, is an organ-pipe coral, resembling the living Tubipora musica. Tubipores enclosed in a marble of Derbyshire, give to the rock a reddish tint, while a limestone of the Mendip Hills and a black marble of Wales enclose white varieties of this fossil.

The Halysites — chain-coral — resembles a series of links forming a chain, and is enclosed in the Eifel limestone.

The Meandrina — brain-coral — is marked by foldings like the convolutions of the brain, and is found in the West Indies frequently from ten to fifteen feet in diameter.

One kind of madrepore is proliferous, sending out a fresh series of stars from the centre disk of previously existing ones.

The Madrepora turbinata is a top-like fossil varying from the size of a bean to three or four inches, and is seen in a rare marble of Blankenburg.

Another species, called the Porpital or shirt-button madrepore, affords a beautiful variety consisting of transparent, calcareous spar, enclosed in a limestone of Gothland, a region abounding in coral.

A beautiful variety of stellated madrepore exists in Transylvania, in which the stars form separate cylinders with elevated margins.

Parkinson mentions a fossil coral named the Spider's stone, supposed to be the production of spiders, which was formerly used as a charm against some diseases; it is called by this author the Madrepora arachnoides, and is found in a light-brown limestone of Wiltshire.

The Madrepora truncata, with cup-shaped body and stellated surface, is enclosed in the blue limestone of Sweden and the M. stellaris with stars of numerous rays is found in Gothland.

This variety at Steeple Ashton, England, is exceedingly curious in regard to the manner of its growth.

When the lowest terrace of the polypean town was covered with dwellings, a colony began a settlement on a more elevated area, until several new terraces, one above another, were all occupied by the teeming population; when the highest site was fully covered, the enterprising denizens constructed castles in the clouds, by throwing into the air perpendicular structures which assumed graceful forms of foliage, and upon these the little ambitious creatures built their star-shaped dwellings.

An organ-pipe coral, probably one of the Syringopora, with tubes joined by membranes, is found in a fossil state on the shores of the Baltic, and another species, enclosed in the blue limestone of Sweden, is similar to that found in St. Vincent's rock, a dull pinkish marble, near Bristol, England.

A coral with stars varying in number, composed of pale yellow spar, is seen in a fine, compact, light-brown marble found in Switzerland and Sardinia, and another species in which silica has replaced the coral, forming a semi-pellucid, flint-like rock, similar to the Indian agate, affords beautiful marble of different shades of gray tinged with red; a variety of this species is called in Wiltshire, England, Feather-stone, on account of its plumose appearance.

A reed-like coral, composed of small Zoophytes, occurs in a British marble, with a reddish-brown foundation and light-colored fossils.

The Black Kilkenny is a coral marble with rather large, white, or light-gray fossils, the beautiful black color being partly due to animal charcoal.

The Chaetetes, classed both with Corals and Acalephs, occurs in strata from the Lower Silurian to the Permian, often in solid masses forming hemispheres, and the Columnaria, a basaltic coral, predominant in the Black River limestone, is often found in enormous masses.

The Stromatopora, also classed with Protozoans, is a massive coral with very small pores, and is thought to be allied to the Eozoon; it occurs in the Eifel and other Paleozoic limestones.

Acalephs. — The second class of Radiates is the Acalephs, or nettle-animals, and includes jelly-fishes with a body nearly transparent which, in this state, are seldom found in strata, but a polyp-like species called Hydroids, is very common as fossils.

Echinoderms. — Of this class of Radiates, receiving their

name on account of their spines, — skin like a hedgehog, — Crinoids are very numerous and important in limestone strata. They are arranged in three families: Crinids or Encrinites, lily-shaped; Blastids, bud-shaped; and Cystids, bladder-shaped.

The Encrinites — flower animals — are furnished with arms extending from a disk, and a stem, as a means of support or attachment to the bottom of the sea, which consists of a series of rings either oval or circular, and when separated are called Trochites, wheel-shaped   These rings have been called by different names according to their fancied resemblance to some object, as beads, raystones, coin of St. Boniface, petrified giants' tears, cheese-stones, mill-stones, bushel-measure, barrel-measure, wheel-stones, screw-stones, pulley-stones, fairy-stones, and St Cuthbert's beads.

When these bones form a column they are styled Entrochi, — in a wheel, — and often form the principal constituent of Entrochal marbles.   Trochites, forming beautiful varieties of marble, consist of a sparry substance with flat or convex surfaces of various markings, with a central opening like a bead; the markings are in the form of rays diverging from a centre, and sometimes the margins are crenated.   The colors vary, ranging through white, yellow, gray, greenish, reddish-brown, and pale red.   The Lily encrinite, Encrinus liliiformis, is very curious and remarkable.   When the flower is unfolded the arms are divided into what may be called hands, with two fingers each, and from the hands are extended articulated tentacles, the whole capable of folding up like a lily.   The number of bones in a single individual of this species is said to be from 26,000 to 27,000   Limestones enclosing portions of the Lily encrinite are very generally distributed in many countries, but it is not usual to find the fossil entire except in the Muschelkalk of Germany, which yields a harvest of Sea-lilies, either intact or in fragments. The species of Encrinites are numerous, to which have been applied peculiar names to designate some quality, usually the form, as Pear encrinite, dark-gray and purple, forming a variety of marble ; Nave encrinite, so called from its resemblance to the hub of a wheel with arms thrown out like spokes, found in France and Germany; Tortoise, Straight, Bottle, Clove, Stag's-Horn, and some others The Clove species has been found in great abundance in Zurich and Schaffhausen, Switzerland.

The Pentacrinites are those Crinoids which have pentagonal stems and five bases, and arms divided into innumerable smaller branches, giving them a plumose appearance. The separate bones of the pedicel, which correspond to the Trochites of the Encrinites, have sometimes been called "star stones." They are flat, and ornamented with a star of five rays corresponding to the five sides. A species which Parkinson designates "Briarean," very abundant in Great Britain, is characterized by vertebral processes extending from 'every part of the stem, and perhaps resembled the Caput Medusa. Mantell says the Pentacrinite contains more than 150,000 joints or bones.

These fossils are prevalent on Lassington Hill, near Gloucester, England, where they are called Lassington stones ; as they are often found about brooks, they have sometimes suggested names for streamlets, as "Fairy-stone Brook" Some writers include Encrinites and Pentacrinites in one genus.

The Blastids or Bud-Crinoids, according to Dana, have an ovoidal body without arms, and five petal-like plates meeting at the top, resembling the folded leaves of a bud. Mantell calls the Pentremite a pear-shaped Encrinite, forming a link between the Sea-lily and the Sea-urchin. They are numerous in a limestone of Kentucky and in the Carboniferous limestone of Illinois, called Pentremital limestone

The Comatula Crinoids — resembling hair — are not attached by a pedicel, while one curious genus, the Saccocoma, has a purse-shaped body with jointed, spiny arms or tentacles, arranged like coils of hair, which may not inaptly be compared to purse-strings. The name is derived from *saccus*, purse, and *coma*, hair.

Crinoids began in the Primordial period and extend through a large part of geological history, but were in the most flourishing condition in Paleozoic time, especially in the Carboniferous period, during which enormous limestone strata were deposited.

The Echinite or fossil Echinus is one of the most common of the Echinoderms, which are very numerous in the Chalk formation, the genus Cidaris is prevalent in the Oolite of Calne, England.

MOLLUSKS

These animals, with soft bodies, are arranged in three divisions: 1. Molluscoidea or Brachiate mollusks, with arms having no regular gills, including Bryozoans and Brachiopods. 2. Ascidian mollusks, not found in a fossil state. 3 Mollusks proper, comprising Acephals, headless Mollusks; Cephalates, having heads; and Cephalopods.

MOLLUSCOIDEA.

Bryozoans.— These Mollusks, called also Polyzoans, are minute creatures with hair-like organs, and secrete corals resembling sprays of moss, or cup-shaped flowers with fringed petals; they comprise the genera Flustra, Retepora, Fenestella, and Archimedes

Brachiopods. — The name implies arm-like feet, given on account of the fringed appendages like arms coiled up in the shell, which serve on occasions for support. There is often an aperture in the beak through which a kind of pedicel is extruded to fix the animal to some foundation, as is seen in the Lingula.

Brachiopods comprise several families with many genera, each characterized by some distinctive feature. The Terebratula, "bored or pierced," is so-called on account of the foramen or perforation in the beak; it includes the genera Waldheimia and Stingocephalus, sometimes called a sub-family, and very abundant in the Eifel limestone. The Spirifer family has a watch-spring apparatus, or arms coiled up in the form of a spiral, and comprises the Athyris, a genus very common in the Devonian rocks

The Rhynchonella comprises the Pentamerus, a genus which is very abundant in the Silurian formations, and the Atrypa, classed by Nicholson with the Spirifers. The Producta, or Productus as it is usually written, characteristic of the Carboniferous limestone, is furnished with projections called ears; to this family belongs the Chonetes, with the hinge of one valve bristling with spines   The genera Strophomena and Leptaena belong to the Orthis family, and the Obolus and Obolella to the Lingula family, characterized by a small ovate shell, supported by a stem like the handle of a spoon   The Lingula is found in the Cambrian rocks, and has maintained its existence until the present time.

The Calceola has been classed with Brachiopods, Lamellibranchs, and Corals, while the Calceola sandalina, "little slipper," has met with worse treatment   Cuvier called it an oyster; Lamarck classed it with the Rudistes; Davidson considered it a Brachiopod, and Suess and Lindstrom styled it Zoantharia rugosa, generally regarded as a coral, but even the Rugosa has been separated from the true polyp, and thought to be more nearly allied to the Hydrozoa than to the Anthozoa. "This seems," as an English naturalist facetiously remarks, "like the game 'Hunt the slipper.'"

MOLLUSKS PROPER.

Acephals. — They are all included in one group, the Lamellibranchs or Conchifers, bivalves with lamellar gills   In ordinary Lamellibranchs, the valves cover the right and left sides. They appear in the older formations, and have continued to exist until the present time; one of the oldest genera, the Conocardium, is enclosed in the Newfoundland limestone, and others are found in the Quebec, Chazy, Trenton, Niagara, and several European formations.   The Devonian and Carboniferous limestone contain several species, and the Triassic several of the Trigonia family, while in the Jurassic, new genera make their appearance. The Gryphaea incurva, of the oyster family, forms the characteristic fossil of an extensive limestone formation of the Lias, and a very large species of the same family is found in the Cretaceous period.

Not unfrequently, fossil oysters are of gigantic size, in some instances more than-twenty inches in length and two in thickness. The Ostrea carinata, found in France, has crenated edges and resembles the striking Crista Galli, "cock's comb," with its serrated crest.

The Gryphée virgules, of the French geologists, is abundant in the Upper Oolite of France, and the Exogyra, a genus of the oyster family, frequently occurs in the Gryphite formation

The Diceras, a peculiar fossil with spiral beaks turned in opposite directions, is so abundant in the Middle Oolite of the Alps, that a limestone of this formation has been called Calcaire à dicerates.

The Avicula margaritifera, with an elegant, grooved, and striated shell, furnishes the pearl oyster, the beautiful Trigonia, covered with bosses arranged in radiating lines, is abundant in the Portland stone, and occurs as siliceous, translucent fossils, in the whetstone pits of Devonshire; it is generally distributed throughout both hemispheres and occurs in the Cretaceous formation of the United States, between the Mississippi and the Pacific.

The Rudistes, a family of Lamellibranchs, include the genera Hippurites, Radiolites, Spherulites, and some others.

The Hippurites, meaning horse-tail, peculiar in structure as well as in name, have been regarded as bivalves by some, and as univalves by others, but later geologists class them with the bivalves. They have a straight, conical, lower valve, sometimes a foot or more in length, shaped like a horn, and closed by a perforated upper valve, which serves the purpose of a lid; the shell is composed of two distinct layers, the outside covering exhibiting prisms with annular markings. These remarkable fossils occur in the Cretaceous limestones of the south of Europe, Africa, and North America; the Hippurite Texanus of the United States is often of gigantic size, and a specimen of the Haploscapha, supposed to be one of the Rudistes, enclosed in the Niobrara group, had a diameter of twenty-six inches.   Radiolites and Spherulites, closely allied to Hippurites, from six to ten inches in diameter, have been found in some Southern States.

The Pinna, a wedge-shaped fossil, occurs in the Chester limestone of Illinois and the Oolitic limestone of England. A species of the Pinna is found in the Calcaire grossier; and a large species of the Perna is abundant in the Atherfield clay of England.

The Pecten flourished in the more recent geological periods, and is easily distinguished from other bivalves.   Some of the species are fine, as seen in the Pecten Poulsoni of the Vicksburg group, with channelled and scalloped shell, and the P. Mortoni, nearly globular and with fine striae ; but the most interesting is the P. Jacobeus, the scallop shell represented in the Mediterranean by the famous scallop worn by the pilgrims to the Holy Land.   The fossil is frequently very large, some specimens measuring six inches or more in length, and constitutes solid limestone strata in Sicily, found at a great elevation above the sea

The Myrtilus includes the true mussels, and occurs in the Devonian era ; the Lithodomus and Pholas genera of this family have the instinct of boring, and their operations assist in the disintegration of wood and rocks   When the channels made in wood by Pholades are filled with different colored spar, beautiful specimens of petrifaction result   The perforations in the columns of the Temple of Jupiter Serapis, near Naples, were made by modern Lothodomi.

The Unio, a river mussel, forms beds of compact limestone of a dark-colored ground with white shells ; strata in Derbyshire enclosing this fossil are called "musselband."

The Cardium comprises the cockles, and is found in the Rhaetic beds and the Portland stone.

Of all the bivalves, the Venus family, says Nicholson, is the

most highly organized, and comprises some of the most beau-
ful examples of Lamellibranchs. They originated in the Oolitic
period, were abundant in the Tertiary, and are found among
living fauna The genus bearing the family name comprises
about 150 species, and the Cytherea, now extinct, comprised
100. The Venericardia, another genus, is an elegant shell of
large size, found in Italy and in England.

The Cardita planostica, of the Cyprina family, is a beautiful
species found in the Tertiary, and the Cyclas and Cyrena,
genera of the Cyclas family, are fresh-water fossils of the
Wealden A single genus of the Lucina family affords between 200 and 300 species; the Posidonomya, written also
Posidonia, is abundant in the Carboniferous strata, and is
found west of the Rocky Mountains.

The Caprina, a very odd-shaped fossil, having one valve in
a spiral form, is characteristic of a limestone formation in
Texas, and the Caprotina has given the name to another
Texan formation. The Donax, found in Tertiary limestone, is
frequently of very large size, measuring eight or nine inches
in length, and as many in width.

The remains of Lamellibranchs are very abundant and of
great importance in determining the age of strata, since they
cover a long period, beginning at the Lower Silurian, and
increasing in species and individuals to the present time

Cephalates. — This division consists of Mollusks with heads,
and includes two groups, — Gasteropods and Pteropods. The
Gasteropods are univalves, generally locomotive, moving on a
soft, flattened disk or foot, whence the name "stomach-feet,"
and carrying their shells on their backs, as the snail; they
are marine, fresh-water, or terrestrial The shell is usually
cone-shaped, with an apex more or less elongated, often with
whorls, the typical form, and is said to be turreted, truncoid,
or turbinated, as the whorls pass more or less obliquely around
the axis, called columella The Gasteropods with indentations
in the margin of the aperture were carnivorous; those with
smooth margins were vegetable feeders. The class has been

traced back to the Cambrian period, and includes many orders, families, genera, and species.

The Strombus, though very rare, is contained in the Cretaceous and Tertiary rocks of Spain and Italy; and the remarkable Rostellaria, with a very long, sharp beak or spur, occurs in the Devonshire formation and the Barton clay of England. The Pterocera — scorpion shell — was furnished with long, pointed claws, which gave the animal so formidable a look that, as has been said, he must have been the terror of the Jurassic seas

The Murex, conspicuous for its spines, found in England and in the Paris basin, has its modern representative in the Mediterranean, used for the celebrated, beautiful Tyrian dye.

More than fifty species of the spindle-shaped Fusus, have been found in the Paris basin; the shell of the F. contrarius, called also the Trophon antiquum, is reversed, that is, the whorls incline from right to left, instead of left to right, which is their usual direction

The Buccinum comprises the whelks; the beautiful Cassis, — helmet-shell, — is met with in Spain and Italy, the Purpura, in the Red Crag of England; the small Oliva in the Balderberg of Belgium; the elegant Conus in France; the Nassa in California; the Pleurotoma and Ancellaria in the Barton clay.

The Cypraea, with convoluted, enamelled shell, comprises the living representatives called Cowries.

One of the most interesting genera of Gasteropods is the Cerithium, exhibiting a spiral, turreted shell, often highly decorated, as in the C. hexagonium, which may be styled for its ornamentation the Gothic species of the class   The C. Portlandicum is sometimes called the Portland screw, on account of its resemblance to that mechanical power; the C gigantea, remarkable for its immense size, yields specimens nearly twenty-four inches in diameter and thirty in length.   The shells, in the form of winding, turreted pyramids, translucent and yellowish-brown, occur in light-gray limestones of France.

The Nerinaea is so abundant in one of the limestones of

the Jura, corresponding to the Middle Oolite, that this formation has been called Calcaire à nérinées

The true Periwinkles are classed with the Litorina, having a thick shell, in form like a top. The Solarium ornatum is ornamented with a delicate tracery like fine embroidery ; the Paludina, abundant in the Wealden, and the Neritina, are generally fresh-water shells, and the Nerita, found in the Great Oolite, is one of the most characteristic fossils of the Lits coquilliers, of France.

The Turbo family includes several genera, mostly confined to the Paleozoic rocks, and are found in limestone of Silurian and Carboniferous age. The Chiton, rare as a fossil, is a peculiar shell, being composed of eight plates, and the Bulla comprises the Bubble-shells.

The Heteropoda, sometimes called the mariners of the Gasteropods, are adapted by their organization to an existence in the open sea, being furnished with a tail and central fin which enables them to swim. The Bellerophon and the Maclurea, belonging to this order, were furnished with a shell into which they could retire ; they flourished in the Paleozoic era. The Maclurea, remarkable for its peculiar shell, constituted the most characteristic fossil of a Chazy limestone in Tennessee.

The Helix and the Pupa embrace Land snails, and the Lymnia, Pond snails. Parkinson says only one species of the Lymnia is found in the Paris basin, while the Melania, which resembles it, frequently occurs there.

The Physa is one of the few univalves with spirals arranged in a direction opposite to the general method; the Ancylas comprises the river Limpets, the Planorbis is found in the Bembridge and Headen strata of the Tertiary period

The Pteropods are pelagian and furnished with appendages for swimming. A part of this class is supplied with shells and no distinct head, and a part is without shells but has a distinct head; the species are few, but the individuals numerous and of variable size, some specimens attaining colossal dimensions.

The best-known genera are Hylea, Theca — the Hyolites of America — Tentaculites, and Conularia. The Tentaculites have been called Annelids, but most paleontologists place them with the Pterepoda, the shell is a cone-shaped tube closing in a point at the end, and with a circular opening at the other end. It is a Silurian fossil, very abundant in a limestone of the Waterlime group.

The Conularia, the most remarkable genus of the Pteropods, is a four-sided cone, generally truncated, found in the Devon. shire limestone of England, and the Trenton and Niagara of America.

Cephalopods. — Of all Mollusks the Cephalopods are the most highly organized and the most interesting in their structure; they are included in two orders, one with external shells and the other without them. They have eight or more arms furnished with suckers, which are arranged around the head, as the name implies, and used for walking on the bed of the sea. The shells, called chambered shells, are divided into several apartments or chambers by transverse partitions, and connected by a tube or siphuncle passing through the entire length of the shell, whether coiled or straight By means of suckers these animals, of which the Cuttle-fish of modern times furnishes a good illustration, can fasten themselves to any object with remarkable tenacity. Most Cephalopods now existing, except the Argonaut and the Nautilus, have no external shells, and the remains of those in a fossil state consist principally of the mandibles or jaws, usually called Rhyncholites, skeletons, and sometimes the ink-bag.

The manner in which chambered shells are built up is exceedingly curious The creature begins his existence at the small end of the shell, and occupies a room suitable for his modest wants; as he grows, he makes preparation for a more spacious chamber, by running a partition, called a septum, from one side of the shell to the other, thus forever closing his first apartments, to which he cannot, of course, return. The same method is pursued with other rooms, as his propor-

Plate IV.

STELLARIA.

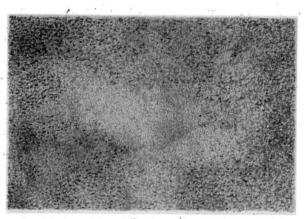

BAALBEC.

tions increase in size, until he has built a large mansion of several stories, all connected by the siphuncle passing through perforations in the partitions; the last spacious room, which has an open door, enabling the occupant to communicate with the outside world, constitutes his dwelling-place. Some of these hidden chambers are beautifully decorated with pearly nacre and ornamental markings, often assuming the form of graceful curves which, when they appear on the outside of the shell, are called sutures.

The Nautilus, the most interesting of the Cephalopods, on account of its great antiquity and its curious organization, is frequently found in a fossil state, with the outside covering decomposed, leaving exposed the resplendent pearly coating, which gives to the marble enclosing these shells a remarkable brilliancy and beauty. The Nautilus is found fossilized in septaria on the Island of Sheppy, at the mouth of the Thames, and in the rocks of Somersetshire.

The Spirula, a genus of the Nautilus family, having a shell with the coils not in contact, is found in a reddish marble of Mecklenburg, Normandy, and Switzerland, and in a German gray marble, but they occur in the greatest numbers in Gothland and Oeland. The Clymenia, with a flat, discoidal shell, is abundant in the Devonian rocks of Germany, constituting the representative fossil of the Clymenia limestone.

Orthoceratites, characterized by a straight shell resembling a horn, frequently grow to a remarkable size, specimens from ten to fifteen feet in length being found in the Trenton limestone They are very numerous in Paleozoic strata, and occur in such masses in Sweden and other countries of the Baltic, that the rock enclosing them has been styled the Orthoceratite limestone, a formation yielding the Marble of the Baltic. Orthoceratites are found in the marbles of Blankenburg, in Switzerland, in Siberia, and a species of pearl white has been enclosed in the strata of the Apennines, near Siena.

Barrande discovered in the Silurian strata of Bohemia more than 500 species of the Orthoceratite, and about 250 species of the Cyrtoceras, which differs from the Orthoceras, in having a curved, instead of a straight shell

In the Ammonites, the septa are foliated on the edges, while in the Nautilus family they are only curved; they first appeared in the Silurian and disappeared in the Cretaceous, therefore, as far as is known, there are no existing species. The Ammonite received the name from its likeness to the horns of Jupiter Ammon, an Egyptian deity represented by the figure of a ram. Curious opinions have been entertained by the illiterate concerning the character of Ammonites, some supposing them to be jointed snake-stones. The genus Ammonite includes more than 500 species, varying in size from a few inches to the diameter of a coach-wheel; sometimes the shell is crenated or scalloped, and in the Cornu Ammonis the nacrous covering is very brilliant.

The Goniatite, a very ancient genus of the family, constitutes the distinctive fossil of the Goniatite limestone of Indiana; and the Ceratite, a characteristic fossil of the Trias, occurs in the Muschelkalk of Germany, like the Goniatite it has a disk-like shell, but the sutures are crenated

Hamites, with hook-like shells, are abundant in the Cretaceous period; Bacculites, having a straight shell and indented sutures, occur in the Faxoe and Maestricht beds   Turrilites, with spiral, turreted shells, are rare and elegant fossils, found in the Cretaceous rocks of France and North America

Belemnites—darts—or "thunder stones," have been the subject of many curious and absurd ideas as to their origin. They consist of a conical or spindle-shaped body ending in a point at one end, and at the other in a broad cavity termed the guard or rostrum, in which are placed a series of chambers with curved septa and siphuncle; it is this internal skeleton or osselet that is usually found in a fossil state   The broad, conical end of the bones often expands into a feather-shaped extremity which corresponds to the pen of the Calamary or Squid.

It is said that specimens of Belemnites have been found

which afford evidence that the animal was furnished with two fins, an ink-bag, eight arms, tentacles provided with suckers, and a mouth with jaws. If supplied with all these weapons he must have been a very formidable creature considering the size to which some of the species attained. They are numerous in the Jurassic limestones, and are in some specimens translucent, of different shades of brown, many of the dark-brown marbles of Switzerland are chiefly formed of these remains.

The shells of the higher orders of Mollusks consist of calcite with a small proportion of animal matter, and in the Pholades, the carbonate of lime assumes the character of aragonite, which is harder than limestone.

ARTICULATES.

These animals have jointed bodies consisting of a series of rings, and include three classes: 1. Insecteans, or Insects, Spiders, and Myriapods, having the body in three parts. 2. Crustaceans, with the body in two parts, and covered by a thin, crust-like shell. 3 Worms, with body not divided; they comprise the Serpula, with a calcareous tube, and Annelids.

VERTEBRATES.

They are characterized by vertebrae, and are divided into four classes: Fishes, Reptiles, Birds, and Mammals; the last three are warm-blooded and air-breathing.

VEGETABLE KINGDOM.

Nullipores and Corallines secrete lime, like most corals, but Diatoms, generally regarded as plants, secrete siliceous shells, and form large masses of rocks. Ehrenberg, with a powerful microscope, discovered in the earth called tripoli, used in polishing marble, the shells of the Gaillonella, a genus of Diatoms so minute, that a single grain in weight enclosed about 187,000,000 of these microscopic organisms. These infinitesimal bodies were propagated with astonishing rapidity, hence the great masses of strata they were able to produce.

The Paris basin, so well known to paleontologists for the variety and abundance of its organic remains, affords a large number of fossil shells, several genera of which have already been described. Among bivalves are found the Pholas, Pandora, Saxicava, Teridina, Mactra, Tellina, Chiton, Nucula, Solen, Chama, Lima, and others. Species of the Lucina and the Cytherea often occur of large size, and those of the Venericardia are often beautifully ornamented with markings. Specimens of the Perna and Cardium are found measuring four and five inches in length, and some species of the Ostria are very striking.

The Univalves include the Ampularia, Scalaria, Pyrula, Harpa, Terebra, Ovula, Beloptera, Lymnia, Melania, with other genera, each including several species. The Cerithium comprises a great number of species, fifty, if not more having been found in the environs of Paris, varying in size from almost minute to two feet in length

The species of the Turritella, with a long-pointed shell, bear a close resemblance to one another.

The Solium is similar in appearance to the Nummulite; the Pleurotoma, with a long beak like a stem, includes nearly eighty species.

The very peculiar Rostellaria includes a species of gigantic size, sometimes measuring from eight to nine inches in length. The Cassis is characterized by a wide aperture, and the Strombus displays an ornament like a ruffle at one side of the opening.

To those already mentioned may be added the Fusus, Cancellaria, Voluta, Trochus, Pleurotomaria, Paludina, Bulla, Helix, Planorbis, Physa, Ancylus, Nerita, Conus, Natica, and Cypraea.

Plate V.

AFRICAN BLACK AND WHITE.

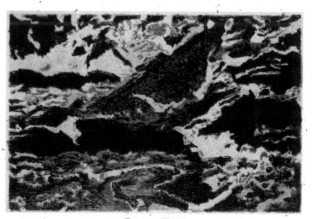

BIANCO E NERO.

CHAPTER III.

THE history of the earth is written in its rocks, therefore the arrangement of strata in chronological order is of vast importance For greater convenience, geological time is divided into different eras, ages, periods, and epochs, each including an indefinite number of years, while some of these divisions are of inconceivable length. This classification depends upon the relative age of strata, which is determined in three ways: By order of superposition ; by the lithological nature of rocks ; and by fossils   The last is the best method, and the one most frequently employed.

Rocks, in regard to their age, may be studied either by beginning with the most recent and passing to the oldest, which is the better method for investigation, and the one adopted by Lyell ; or by following the order of their occurrence, and, beginning with the oldest, pass to the youngest formations, which is the better method for studying the laws of evolution, and the one generally adopted in America.

As limestones are largely fossiliferous, they become of very great value in determining geological periods.

The oldest known rocks are those of the Archaean or Eozoic era — dawn of life — the twilight of geological time, and very little positive knowledge in regard to their origin has yet been obtained. This era is thought to be of inconceivable length, probably exceeding any other in the earth's history, and, perhaps, all others combined. The Eozoic rocks are of immense thickness, and, for the most part, meta-

39

morphic, but on account of the absence of fossils, or their extremely limited number, the order of succession of strata cannot be decided with the precision of succeeding eras. They have been divided by the most recent classification into Taconian, Montalban, Huronian, Norian, and Laurentian ages.

The formations of this system, first established in America, are found in various parts of this continent and in the Eastern Hemisphere, and include the great iron-ore beds of New Jersey, Missouri, Lake Superior, and Sweden Among the series are found serpentines, dolomites, limestones, and some of the most extensive marble beds, including those of the Green Mountains, formerly referred to the Silurian.

According to the divisions of time made by most American geologists, the next in order is the Paleozoic era, — ancient life, — including Lower and Upper Silurian, Devonian, and Carboniferous ages. Instead of Upper and Lower Silurian, some writers use the terms Cambrian and Silurian.

The comparative quiet of the long Silurian age was favorable for the development of the great limestone formations which characterize it, as the Chazy, the Trenton, the Niagara, and the Helderberg, with many smaller divisions

A large part of the calcareous rocks of the United States were deposited during the Trenton period of the Lower Silurian ; they are widely distributed, and cover extensive areas in this country and in British America, where they constitute the mass of rock through which the Montmorency River has cut a channel.

The Trenton limestones, so called from Trenton Falls, N.Y , are interesting for the great number and variety of fossils they contain, ranging from the lowest forms of Protozoans to Articulates. The Radiates and Mollusks afford examples of their largest specimens ; some Orthoceratites have been found measuring from ten to fifteen feet in length Crinoids and Corals contributed to the embellishment of "the marine gardens " of the Silurian age, for, as remarked by Dana, there were no other flowers of Paleozoic time. Large masses of limestone during this period were formed of corals

It has been estimated that a large part of the Appalachian rocks, one-third of those of Tennessee, and five-sixths of those of Illinois and Missouri are Lower Silurian.

The Niagara period of the Upper Silurian constituted another long time for the formation of limestones, which are spread over a broad region, covering extensive tracts in the centre of the continent, stretching from New York towards the south and west on the eastern coast, and in British America on the north, reaching to the Arctic regions.

The formation received its name from the Niagara Falls, at and near which it is well-developed, forming the upper part of the precipice over which the water flows   It can be traced through the northern part of Vermont, New Hampshire, and Maine to Eastern Canada, and includes the Guelf or Galt limestone of West Canada, and the Le Clair of Iowa. The Coralline limestone of New York, with fossils characteristic of the formation, and the Meniscus limestone of West Tennessee, enclosing a moon-shaped sponge, for which it is named, are believed to be of the same age

The Niagara limestone is dark-gray or drab, sometimes concretionary, and filled with cavities holding dog-tooth and pearl spar, fluor-spar, gypsum, and celestite. Sometimes this limestone breaks into smooth, vertical columns, affording a structure called Stylotites.   Both the Trenton and the Niagara limestones yield mineral oil, and both are highly fossiliferous. . Corals, Crinoids, and Trilobites characterize each formation, but the fossils of the Niagara surpass in beauty those of the Trenton.   Among the corals of the former, are Favosites, or honeycomb, Halysites, or chain-coral, and Cyathophylloids, or cup-corals   The Clinton limestone of the Niagara period encloses the Pentamerus oblongus, a large bivalve, and the singular fossil called Graptolites   The largest display of the Niagara limestone occurs in New York and in the Mississippi Basin.

The Lower Helderberg group of the Upper Silurian, named for the Helderberg Mountains in the eastern part of New York, include limestone strata of considerable thickness. They spread over a large tract towards the west, and appear in Ohio, Indiana, and Illinois, towards the south along the Appalachians to the Potomac, and are supposed to extend northeastward to Cape Gaspé The lower beds, designated Water-lime, because used for hydraulic cement, consist of a drab-colored or bluish limestone, characterized by the Tentaculite, and sometimes called Tentaculite limestone. Besides the Water-lime, the series includes a Pentamerus, the Catskill or Delthyris, and an Encrinal limestone.

The Helderberg limestones surpass even those of the Trenton and Niagara periods in the abundance, size, and beauty of their fossils More than three hundred species have been already recognized in the formation, some of which belonged to former epochs.

The Oriskany limestones, in the latest series of the Upper Silurian, are not very extensively developed ; they occur in New York and in the Mississippi Basin, and are thought from the presence of their characteristic fossils, to exist in Northern New England and British America, extending to the Gulf of St. Lawrence. The formation was called for Oriskany, New York, a State which has supplied names for nearly all representative Silurian limestones of America.

It has been seen that the Silurian was a great limestone-producing age, that marine life was exceedingly abundant, that, on the whole, it was a season of comparative quiet, and that it was a period of inconceivable length, since sedimentary limestones were deposited with extreme slowness.

In taking leave of the Silurian age, with its teeming population of marine life, we are introduced to new genera and species of fauna, whose remains largely contributed to the formation of calcareous strata. The Corniferous of the Devonian age, was one of the great limestone periods of North America, and from the remarkable abundance of corals, it has been styled the Coral-reef period of the Paleozoic era. Some of the Devonian corals are of very large size, masses often measuring five feet in diameter.

At the Falls of the Ohio, near Louisville, the Corniferous limestone is almost entirely composed of corals of different forms and sizes, of bright and variegated colors; some of the cup-corals are six or seven inches in diameter. The limestone is variable in color, sometimes with an oölitic structure, and frequently including horn-stones, from which the name Corniferous is derived. The formation is found in other States of the Mississippi Basin, in New York, and in Canada.

Several notable oil-wells have their source in this formation, as those at Terre Haute, Indiana, which are nearly 2,000 feet deep; the shells and the cells of the corals enclosed are often filled with oil.

The limestones of the Hamilton period are represented by thin beds, including an Encrinal, and the Tully limestone of New York

In the West, the Devonian rocks are mostly limestone, while in the East, they consist largely of shales and sandstone

The Carboniferous age, a great coal-producing time, closes the Paleozoic era, and is divided into Subcarboniferous, Carboniferous, and Permian periods; the former is remarkable for immense limestone deposits both in Europe and America. The Subcarboniferous limestones of the United States constitute the principal rocks of the vast central region, where it reaches, in certain places, 1,200 feet in thickness.

The predominant fossils of any geological age, differ from those of any preceding or succeeding age; in the Silurian, Brachiopods, Crinoids, and Corals are about equally distributed; in the Devonian, Corals are the most abundant, while the Carboniferous yields a great number and variety of Crinoids.

The Carboniferous limestones, including a great diversity in color, black, gray, blue, yellow, and red, are largely developed in the West, extending beyond the Rocky Mountains,

and, to a limited extent, in Pennsylvania, comprising the
Pittsburg, while on the Potomac, their thickness is considerable.

The Permian limestones of America are prevalent in the
Continental Basin west of the Mississippi. They are generally impure and magnesian, soft and irregular in structure.

Mesozoic or medieval time succeeds the long Paleozoic era,
and includes the Triassic, Jurassic, and Cretaceous periods.

As a considerable portion of the continent was dry land at
the beginning of this era, Mesozoic rocks are not universally
distributed, but are confined to the Atlantic and Pacific
borders and the Rocky Mountain region. In the United
States, the Triassic affords no important limestones, while in
Europe, it is represented by the great Muschelkalk formation.

In consequence of the absence of fossils, the lines of de-
markation are not distinctly drawn on the Atlantic coast
between the Triassic and the Jurassic formations, but the
latter has been fully identified in the western region and on
the Pacific slope; the strata are only partly calcareous, while
the Jura of Europe is largely a limestone formation.

The Cretaceous period on the Eastern Continent yields vast
beds of Chalk, whereas in North America it is rarely found;
it is said a large bed in Western Kansas is the only one known
in this country. The formation is represented by limestones,
sometimes compact, and sometimes with the particles loosely
held together, when they are called "rotten limestones"
Those of Texas are firm and compact; those of Mississippi
and Missouri include a soft, chalky variety, and a hard, white
limestone, containing Glauconite or Green earth, in Tennessee
and Alabama, they consist of shell or rotten limestones, and
New Jersey develops a fossiliferous limestone of this period.
The Cretaceous groups of Texas receive different names, as
Caprotina and Caprina, from their characteristic fossils, and
Washita and Austin from their locality

The last great division of geological time is the Cenozoic, —
recent life, — including the Tertiary and Quaternary ages.

The Tertiary embraces the Eocene, Miocene, and Pliocene epochs, a distinction not strictly marked in America. This formation has a thickness of from 3,000 to 4,000 feet in California; and in Florida, South Carolina, Alabama, and Mississippi it is represented by coral and shell limestones.

The Vicksburg group encloses the Orbitoides, a coin-shaped Rhizopod resembling the Nummulite, the representative fossil of the most remarkable formation of the Tertiary in the Eastern Hemisphere.

The Infusorial beds of Virginia, an accumulation of the siliceous remains of microscopic organisms, mostly Diatoms, now regarded as plants, and the Mauvaises Terres or Bad Lands of the West, are of the Tertiary age. By the aid of the microscope, Ehrenberg discovered about one hundred species of Diatoms in the Infusorial earth of Richmond.

The principal rocks of the Quaternary period, of chemical origin, are stalactites, stalagmites, and travertines or calcareous tufas; others are formed of organic remains, including coral-reef formations, and some shell limestones.

CLASSIFICATION OF CALCAREOUS STRATA, ARRANGED IN CHRONOLOGICAL ORDER, AFTER DANA, LE CONTE, AND OTHER AMERICAN GEOLOGISTS.

ERAS.	AGES.	PERIODS.	EPOCHS.
5. Psychozoic	Age of Man	Human.	Recent.
4. Cenozoic	Age of Mammals.	Quaternary	Terrace, Champlain, Glacial.
		Tertiary	Pliocene, Miocene, Eocene.
3. Mesozoic (Secondary)	Age of Reptiles	Cretaceous	Chalk, Green Sand.
		Jurassic	Wealden (?) Oolite, Lias.
		Triassic	Muschelkalk Formation.
2. Paleozoic, (Primary)	Carboniferous, Age of Acrogens and Amphibians,	Permian	Permian, Zechstein Formation.
		Carboniferous	Coal Measures.
		Sub-Carboniferous	Mountain Limestone.
	Devonian, Age of Fishes,	Catskill, Chemung. Hamilton, Corniferous,	Hamilton, Corniferous.
	Silurian, Age of Invertebrates	Oriskany	*U. Silur.* { Oriskany. Lower Helderberg.
		Lower Helderberg	
		Salina.	
		Niagara	Niagara, Clinton. }
		Trenton	*L. Silur.* { Cincinnati, Trenton. Chazy, Quebec, Calciferous.
		Canadian	
		Primordial or Cambrian	Potsdam. }
1. Archaean, or Eozoic	Taconian. Montalban. Huronean. Norian. Laurentian.	Not divided into periods and epochs.	Green Mt. Marbles. Eozoon Canadense.

CHAPTER IV.

LIMESTONES OF THE UNITED STATES.

THE limestone areas of the United States may be classed in three general divisions. The Atlantic region, including the States east of or on the Appalachian chain, the Mississippi Basin, embracing the region between that chain and the Rocky Mountains ; and the Pacific slope, reaching from these mountains to the sea.

New England. — Although limestones are found to some extent in nearly every State, yet there are certain sections where they constitute the characteristic rock, and become of great economic value. The western slope of the Green Mountain chain in Vermont and Massachusetts, affords an example of the most extensive limestone formation in New England, and one of the most important in the United States.

The Green Mountain marbles, formerly regarded as Silurian, are now classed with the Eozoic rocks.

The Stockbridge limestone has been named by Hitchcock, the Eolian, from Mt Eolus in East Dorset, Vermont, where it is largely developed. The formation, says this geologist, is the most remarkable in New England, extending fifty miles, varying in thickness from 1,000 to 3,000 feet, and containing some very large caverns. One of the peaks of Mt. Eolus displays 2,000 feet of white and gray marble, which is considered the most extraordinary exhibition of the kind in the country

The Vermont marbles have been classed as the Eolian, the Winooski, the Variegated Plymouth, and the Isle La Motte. These classes include a great variety, many different kinds being often found in the same quarry. Those of West Rutland, the most extensively worked in the State, often exhibit gray, white, mottled, saccharoidal, compact, friable, and laminated marbles in close neighborhood.

The blue-gray mottled marble of Sutherland's Falls, Rutland, has been compared to the Italian Bardiglio. The two marbles are similar in color, but differ in several other particulars; the Italian is fine-grained, of firm texture, with very distinct clouding, and is capable of excellent polish, while the Vermont is coarsely granular, hard, enclosing mineral particles, and with a more blended shading.

The Brandon marble is generally pure white, and somewhat translucent, but it is not used, to any extent, for statuary marble. Swanton yields a magnesian, dove-colored marble, and Sudbury a white variety, of nearly pure carbonate of lime

The Winooski marble is named for a river in the western part of Vermont; it is dolomitic and affords a great variety in color, composition, and structure. The prevailing tint is a dull-red in blotches of various forms and shades, affording, in some specimens, a ground of blackish-green, with spots of bright pink and reddish-brown, while in others the red color is wanting. A brecciated variety called "Mosaic," has been used for ornamental work.

The Plymouth marble is a dolomite, but, unlike most dolomites, it is said to weather well. In some respects it differs in appearance from any other American marble The ground color is a bluish-gray, covered with long, white figures or stripes; it is susceptible of a good polish, yet it is not in demand, and is used for quicklime, known as "Plymouth white lime "

The Isle La Motte marble is developed in the Champlain valley, and in the island of the same name in the lake. It is fossiliferous, solid, black, and capable of a high polish, and is used largely for tiles of floors. Though black is the prevailing tint, yet there are other colors, as gray, and different shades of brown, from light to dark. It is said to be the first marble worked in Vermont, and has been used in several of the public buildings of Burlington and for construction in various other places. It was employed with excellent effect in the fine, new, Congregational Church of St Johnsbury, Vermont, and for the Victoria Bridge on the Grand Trunk Railway.

Seams of crystalline hydro-mica schist, of delicate green or blue, occur in nearly all the light-colored marbles of Vermont, especially the Rutland varieties. The white, statuary marble in this State has been compared to the Carrara of Italy, but any marble-worker knows that the latter is greatly superior to the former for art purposes It is softer, more translucent, and freer from siliceous and other foreign substances.

The limestones of Stockbridge and North Adams, Mass., belong to the Eolian or Stockbridge formation, of the Green Mountain chain, therefore they are Eozoic in age. The marble of North Adams is formed largely of perfect crystals of calcite, sometimes of a large size, while that of Mt. Eolus is highly granular. The variety called "sparry," encloses veins of white calcareous spar, which give it a checkered appearance. The Eolian or Stockbridge marble was used in the construction of Middlebury College, and for the columns of Girard College, Philadelphia. An Eozoic limestone of Newburyport, Mass., is believed to enclose the Eozoon Canadense.

Serpentines form a large element in the Green Mountain system of rocks, and afford a variety of beautiful ornamental stones. When they enclose some other minerals, they constitute a variety called ophiolite, which passes under the commercial name of Verde antique marble. It ranges through various shades of green, from whitish to greenish-black, and is developed in many different localities. It receives a good polish, and is believed to compare favorably with the antique.

The Green Mountain serpentines present a great variety of structure, comprising massive, brecciated, laminated, fibrous,

and some others. They often contain diallage, and sometimes actinolite and garnet. The dark variety, found at Roxbury, Vermont, has nearly the same composition as the dark-
colored European, there being a slight preponderance of silica,
magnesia, and water in the former, and of protoxide of iron in
the latter, while in the light-colored varieties the difference is
greater.

Fine species of serpentine are found in Oxford, Vermont,
including a sub-translucent variety of deep olive-green with
blush veins and even texture, and another of a mottled greenish-gray tinged with purple.

Although the limestones of the Green Mountains are the
most extensive and important in New England, and yield the
largest quantity of marbles, yet there are other calcareous
formations in this section which develop marbles and material
for building purposes.

In New Hampshire, where the characteristic rocks are of
the granitic class, limestone strata are found of considerable
extent in the northern section, and are occasionally interstratified with the White Mountain gneissic rocks

A large part of the limestones of New Hampshire are referred to the Corniferous period of the Devonian age, while
some others are Lower Helderberg, Upper Silurian. A Crinoidal limestone occurs at Lisbon, and at Littleton, a Coral
limestone enclosing Zaphrentes and Favosites.

Eozoic rocks occupy a large space in New Hampshire,
Massachusetts, Connecticut, and Rhode Island. In the latter
State, they cover an area in the northwest, while the Carboniferous system, including conglomerates, slates, and limestones, occupies most of the southeast

At Fort Adams, in Newport Harbor, are displayed beds of
compact limestone considered very old, perhaps Eozoic,
variegated with red, green, brown, or buff, and the same formation appears on Lime Island, east of the fortifications.
The quartz conglomerate constitutes one of the most striking
features of the scenery in the vicinity of Newport.

A part of Connecticut is intersected by a series of limestone valleys considered Eozoic, developing a rock suitable for
marble. In the northwest the formation crosses Berkshire
Co, Mass., and passes into New York ; but the most extensive limestone strata are seen at Kent Hollow in the valley
of the West Aspetuck. White marble may be obtained from
the limestones of Danbury ; and the quarries of New Preston,
in the time of Percival, had long been worked

A range of limestones in the south part of the State, has
yielded, says the poet geologist, the New Haven and the
Milford marbles. The latter is described as of fine grain, and
variegated with green, blue, and yellow, enclosing talc, epidote,
and sometimes black serpentine with veins of light tints
which give it the appearance of Verde antique. The New
Haven marble is a variety conspicuous for its yellow tints.

These marbles used in Percival's day may not, at the
present time, be employed for ornamental purposes

The most remarkable trap ridges in New England occur in
the western part of this State, combined with limestones

While granite, gneiss, and other non-calcareous rocks are
characteristic of Maine, limestones, often yielding marbles,
are abundant in many parts of the State. The Niagara and
Lower Helderberg in the north, comprise limestones, while on
Passamaquoddy Bay, the L Helderberg is represented by
slates and sandstones, and to the southeast of this region a
fossiliferous limestone is met with, either Niagara or L.
Helderberg. The Oriskany strata, principally limestone,
occur between Moosehead Lake and Vermont.

The limestone of Thomaston, partly magnesian, has been
extensively quarried for lime and building, and appears to be
inexhaustible.

The Owl's Head limestone is penetrated by trap, and at
Philipsburg Basin, where it is largely developed, it encloses
garnets and various other minerals.

Calcareous rocks are well represented in the interior, along
the Atlantic coast, and in the west, some of the strata being

magnesian, as the white dolomite of Union, which affords marble. Some of the limestones of Maine are Eozoic.

The later formations are composed of fossiliferous sands and clay enclosing the Saxicava and the Leda.

Deer Island, in Penobscot Bay, yields a beautiful serpentine, enclosing asbestos and yellow or olive-green diallage, constituting a desirable ornamental stone.

New York. — Limestones, marbles, and serpentines, are abundant in New York, and some of the marbles are of considerable commercial value. What are called primitive limestones, the Eozoic, resemble those of the same age in New England and Canada, and when free from foreign substances, are said to form a marble of fair quality, but are inferior to those of Vermont.

The Trenton limestone, loaded with organic remains, comprises a dark-colored variety capable of yielding marble, and a light, sparry rock forming the upper layers at Trenton Falls.

The Bird's Eye and the Black River are of the same epoch; the former marked by Fucoids, — Paleozoic seaweeds, — which are frequently replaced by calcite or other mineral substances, is mostly confined to the Mohawk valley, while the Black River prevails in the northwestern part of the State. Both varieties afford marbles of agreeable tints.

The Niagara limestone, Upper Silurian, is distinguished by a fine, granular texture with numerous shining points of vitreous lustre, magnesian in composition and often nodular.

The Water-lime or Hydraulic limestones of the Lower Helderberg are spread over an extensive area, but are most conspicuous in the southeast, where they form the isolated eminence called Becraft's Mountain, near the Hudson, which Dana thinks is the remnant of a great formation once existing in that region. The limestone near this mountain is full of Encrinites, and, when polished, forms a beautiful reddish-gray marble, comparing favorably, it is claimed, with the Derbyshire shell marble of England.

The granular limestones east of the Hudson afford vast

mines of marble, varying in color and texture, including the Dover, a fine-grained, pure white or clouded variety, resembling the Stockbridge

The calcareous formations of Columbia and Dutchess Counties, belonging to different epochs, appear on the west side of the Hudson, in New Jersey.

Marble beds are found in West Chester County, in the south part of the State, but those of Sing Sing and Kingsbridge are the best known   The crystalline white marble of East Chester is suitable for columns and cornices of buildings; those of Putnam County are dove-colored, reddish, and variegated.   In this county occurs a conglomerate of gray and white limestones with pebbles of other rocks, the mass resembling the Potomac breccia   On the west bank of the Hudson a white, Eozoic limestone is seen, resembling in portions calcareous spar, and near Lake George it is pierced with caverns

Gray limestones with numerous fossils, in the central part of of the State, were used in the construction of the Erie Canal.

The Onondaga Crinoidal limestone, of a bluish-gray, makes an excellent building-stone   The Onondaga marble is characterized by the Pentamerus, while the dark Seneca limestone consists largely of the Brachiopod, Strophomena lineata

The Tully limestone displayed at Tully's Corners is an extensive deposit, though it does not exceed sixteen feet in thickness   It is very fossiliferous, of a uniform character, fine, compact, and a light bluish-gray color, but is not well adapted for construction

Several varieties of marbles are developed on the southern shores of Lake Ontario; that at Lockport, enclosing fragments of organic remains, forms a beautiful ornamental stone, and a dove-colored marble is found in the region of Lake George. The fine black marble in the north part of the State, probably similar to the Isle La Motte, takes a good polish and has been compared to the Irish black.   The black fossiliferous marble of Glenn's Falls, derived from the Trenton limestone, has been used for mantels, and the Island of New York furnishes limestones which have been used for different purposes.

The serpentines are abundant, and form the main ridge of hills on Staten Island. They present many elegant varieties, with colors ranging from white to black, and various shades of green. The beautiful green and white variety, called Verde antique, forms a desirable ornamental stone, and that of Syracuse is said to resemble the Tuscan.

Beds of travertine are deposited in several places; from Tully's Corners, in the direction of Syracuse, the hills are covered with an immense deposit of gypsum, abounding with beds of calcareous tufa.

New Jersey.—It is asserted by G. H. Cook that the rocks of New Jersey range through nearly every period of geological time, from the earliest to the most recent, the only important member wanting is the Coal formation.

The Eozoic strata cover a large area in the north, and include crystalline and metamorphic limestones, which constitute a portion of the rocks of Marble Mountain.

Paleozoic limestones are largely represented, and are classed by this geologist in the following manner: 1. Magnesian, a name sometimes applied to the Calciferous sandstone of New York, older than the Trenton. 2. Trenton or Fossiliferous. 3. Delthyris, named for its predominant fossil, of the Lower Helderberg. 4. Pentamerus, L. Helderberg. 5. Water-lime, represented by what is locally called the Ribbon limestone, characterized by laminæ of different shades. 6. Onondaga, a Devonian limestone occupying a very inconsiderable place.

The Lower Helderberg limestones afford several varieties of limited distribution, locally known as "Fire Stone," a solid, fossiliferous rock, resisting in a remarkable degree the action of heat; "Peth Stone," an argillaceous limestone, of a light blue color; "Old Quarry Stone," and "Quarry Stone;" the limestone last named contains fossils.

The Magnesian limestone, a true dolomite, has a larger development in this State than all the others combined, and

Plate VI.

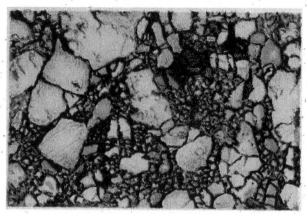

Breccia Corallina.

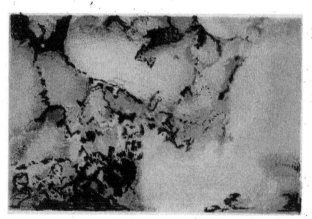

Pavonazzetto.

Armstrong & Co. Lith. Boston.

on account of its texture and color makes a desirable building-stone. The white, crystalline limestones are regarded as marbles.

A calcareous conglomerate and the Red Sandstone belong to the Triassic period, while the Cretaceous and Tertiary are represented by clays, marls, and sand. The Cretaceous Green Sand, valuable as a fertilizer, the most characteristic formation of the State, is loaded with marine fossils. The Terebratula Harlani bed, ninety miles in length, one mile in width, and from two to three feet in depth, is made up of the remains of this species of Brachiopod, pressed closely together.

The Gryphaea beds, directly below the Terebratula Harlani, enclose some individuals of the Exogyra costata, weighing from three to four pounds

The serpentine of Hoboken is similar to that of Staten Island, and probably belongs to the same formation. It is thickly covered with drift and boulders, except on the eastern side, where it presents an outcrop rising forty or fifty feet. The walk to the Elysian Fields was cut in this rock.

Pennsylvania —The great Appalachian chain, running in a northeasterly direction from Georgia to the Gulf of St Law-rence, a distance of 1,500 miles, and 50 miles in width, consists of several parallel ranges, embracing anticlinal and synclinal ridges and valleys, affording remarkable instances of folded strata.

Lyell says that no European chain presents so striking an illustration of the persistency of such flexures, extending continuously for long distances. This chain, completed at the close of the Paleozoic era, is, quoting from Le Conte, the monument of the greatest revolution which has taken place in the geological history of America. The Appalachians include Eozoic rocks, found in the Blue Ridge, in the High-lands of the Hudson, and the Adirondacks of New York. The Green Mountains, belonging to this great chain, were formed before the Silurian age, but the Alleghanies were not complete until the end of the Carboniferous period.

The thickness of the Paleozoic rocks in the Appalachians is enormous, the greatest being 55,000 and the average 40,000 feet, in Pennsylvania they reach 45,000 feet. It has been stated that if the Appalachian strata were now resting as they were deposited, the mountains of this chain would equal in height the Himalayas with the Alps atop, whereas, their greatest height does not reach 7,000 feet, and their mean altitude is only about 3,000. Of this prodigious mass of rock only one-fourth consists of limestones, while in the Mississippi Basin they comprise two-thirds of all the Paleozoic strata.

In Pennsylvania, limestone formations attain great thickness and considerable extent, though sandstones and shales exceed, by far, the calcareous deposits, the Black shale varying in thickness from 10,000 to 20,000 feet. H. D. Rogers, who has named the various formations of Pennsylvania according to the natural divisions of the day, a nomenclature not generally adopted, has included in his "Auroral" series a part of the Calciferous, the Chazy, and the Black River of New York, equivalent to the Blue limestone of the Western States.

The "Auroral" strata consist largely of magnesian limestone, found throughout the entire length of the Appalachian chain, reaching in places a thickness of from 3,000 to 6,000 feet. It is variable in character, and in Pennsylvania is generally light-blue or bluish-gray, constituting the principal rock of the valley of the Schuylkill, in Montgomery and Chester Counties, a region diversified by woodland tracts and cultivated farms, watered by numerous streams, bordered by flourishing villages and busy factories. In the valley of the Lower Susquehanna, and on a branch of the Antietam, it appears as white limestone, capable of being used as marble. The upper members, corresponding to the Chazy and the Black River limestones, are replete with fossils.

The Trenton limestone, or "Martinal" of Rogers, is not found south of the Kittatinny Valley, but appears and disappears at intervals from the Delaware to Maryland. It is from 300 to more than 500 feet thick, and full of organic remains, the prevailing types being Chaetetes, Leptaena, and Bellerophon.

The Clinton, or "Surgent," and the Niagara, essentially a limestone formation in other States, include only thin beds of this rock in Pennsylvania. The Water-lime group comprises a massive limestone, full of fossils, corals predominating, while above this formation rests a mottled stone convertible into marble. The upper member of the L. Helderberg, "Pre-Meridian," a massive, fossiliferous limestone, is nearly everywhere present west of the Susquehanna

The Corniferous series of the Devonian era, interesting for its fossils, and constituting one of the most extensive formations of New York and the Northwest, covers but an insignificant area in this State.

The rocks of the Subcarboniferous period are, for the most part, limestones in the Mississippi Basin ; here they include only a few calcareous strata in the southeast, but in the southwest they become independent formations.

The blue and black Pittsburg limestone of the Carboniferous period, enclosing Crinoids, is twenty-five feet thick ; the Great limestone of the same age, spreading from Pittsburg to the borders of Virginia, is non-fossiliferous and extremely variable in thickness and composition. It is blue, black, or yellow, and very hard; the yellow being susceptible of polish, may be used as marble. The Great limestone covers the highest hills and forms the escarpments along the streams of Alleghany and Westmoreland Counties; it is valuable for construction and as a fertilizer.

Maryland and Delaware — Paleozoic rocks are represented by a massive limestone of the Water-lime group, which, on the Potomac, is 500 feet thick. It encloses few species of fossils, but numerous individuals, Crinoids constituting the most prevalent type.

The Triassic system appears in sandstones and calcareous conglomerates, while the Cretaceous is represented by limestones which cross Delaware and Maryland between Annapolis

and Baltimore, stretching towards the southwest into Virginia.
In the northern counties, the limestones are largely magnesian,
and in Baltimore and Ann Arundel counties they are capable
of yielding marbles.

The calcareous rocks at Harper's Ferry assume a distinctive
character, passing from ordinary blue limestone to fine-grained
marble of variable colors, which furnished the material for the
conglomerate on the banks of the Potomac, known as the
"Potomac marble," used in the colonnade of the House of
Representatives and other parts of the National Capitol.
White marble, considered equal to statuary, is met with in
some localities.

The Maryland limestones, like those of other regions, present considerable variety in color, texture, and composition.
The term "alum limestone" has been applied by some geologists to a very fine variety containing much calc spar.
Those of Maryland include both "alum" and magnesian limestones, either crystalline or compact, and white, light-tinted
or darker-colored.

The strata east of Antietam yield marbles, and those on the
west are peculiar in composition, furnishing the soil of the
region known as the "Salisbury tract" which, it is stated,
cracks and freezes, rendering it unsuitable for vegetation at
some seasons of the year.

The prevailing rocks of Delaware belong to the granitic
group, while limestone covers a small extent compared with
gneiss. At Pike's Creek, near the State line, it is largely
developed, yielding both coarse and fine marbles, generally
white, but occasionally of a bluish tint.

There is a small mass of light and dark green serpentine
displayed near Wilmington, and another near Baltimore. A
very white, coarse-grained marble, used in the construction of
the Washington Monument, is known as the "Baltimore
Crystal."

Virginia and West Virginia. —The oldest rocks in Virginia
are the Eozoic, found in the Blue Ridge, extending to Rich-

mond, and in West Virginia.; but the great valley between the Blue Ridge and the Alleghanies develops, on a grand scale, Paleozoic strata largely calcareous, including limestone, dolomite, gypsum, and shale. The Niagara formation, one of the most widely-diffused on the continent, is, in this region, 1,500 feet thick.

The Carboniferous limestones increase in extent towards the southwest, reaching to Alabama and Mississippi. The Chester limestone of the Sub-carboniferous period, and some thin beds of Carboniferous among the Coal Measures, are developed in West Virginia, but the largest display of Paleozoic. limestones are seen on the Ohio River. An impure limestone occurs on the Potomac, which, in extending towards the west, gains in thickness from 80 to 800 feet

The Cretaceous rocks of the Atlantic border cross the Potomac and are seen extending towards the south for some distance, when they are lost to view, but they reappear with a small development in North and South Carolina. On the upper course of the Potomac, limestone cliffs of great height form a marked feature of the landscape

The Tertiary of Virginia occupies a wide area on the Atlantic, and is remarkable for accumulations of fossil remains. Besides the Infusorial beds, in some places thirty feet in thickness, there are other deposits consisting almost entirely of fossil shells. A series of these beds enclosing the Pecten, Ostrea, Chama, and Venus, some of large size, occurs at one locality on the James River, and more are found in other places. These aggregations of the flora and fauna of the Tertiary period in this State, afford interesting studies for the paleontologist.

The Virginia limestones, comprehending, according to W. B. Rogers, nearly forty varieties, yield many different marbles, some of which are fossiliferous. A white marble, shaded with pink and sometimes green, is obtained from a talcose limestone; and a granular, sparry variety of blue and gray, tinted with rose, is found on the Rapidan. A very delicate

salmon-colored marble, and another of a dark slate color may
be added to the list of Virginia marbles

The Carolinas —The rock systems of North Carolina have
been assigned by Emmons to the Recent or Quaternary, the
Tertiary, the Cretaceous, the Permian being doubtful, and,
Dana adds, the Triassic and the Archaean or Eozoic; the
latter are found in the Blue Ridge. The Triassic system
forms a band from eight to eighteen miles in width, crossing
the State from north to south through the central part.
Granite, gneiss, mica schist, and Taconic slates form a large
part of the rocks, while limestones have only a limited development and are destitute of fossils; it is therefore difficult to
determine their geological age. The limestone of King's
Mountain is of a dark color, that of Lincoln County is white,
fine, and even-grained, suitable for statuary marble

The Eozoic and Triassic rocks of North Carolina have
penetrated South Carolina in the north, central, and western
portions, and the Cretaceous occupy a narrow strip along the
Atlantic coast. Limestones, in this State, have a larger
development than in North Carolina. A white or blue crystalline limestone occurs on the Saluda, in the western part, but
the best known and most extensive beds of this rock are
found in the Spartanburg District, in the northwest. On the
frontier, near King's Mountain, it forms a beautiful blue
marble with veins of white calcite marked with gray and reddish bands, and is suitable for an ornamental stone The
Spartanburg limestone, or marble, varies in thickness from
30 to 300 feet, but it is not easily accessible The Santee
beds of the Tertiary, found near Charleston, include thick
layers of white limestone; in this region also occurs the
Buhrstone formation.

Georgia and Florida. —It is said that no rocks have been
found in Florida older than the Vicksburg group, Upper
Eocene, and the peninsula is thought to be a prolongation of
the limestones of Georgia, where the Middle and Upper
Eocene beds, corresponding to the Alabama period, are

extensively developed. From Macon, Georgia, the great · southern Cretaceous formation passes into the Mississippi Basin.

The Orbitoidal limestone of the Vicksburg group, is the prevailing rock of Florida, according to E A. Smith, and is everywhere in this State, as it is in Mississippi and Alabama, covered with the Orange sand and a yellow loam It is exposed along the banks of streams, in ravines, and sometimes it outcrops upon level ground near the numerous boiling springs, and is characterized by "sink holes," ponds, and lakes. In 1871, says this geologist, the outlet of a small creek becoming closed, a lake was formed several miles wide and from fifteen to twenty feet in depth.

In Jackson County, in the northwestern part of the State, this formation lies near the surface, giving to the soil a very fertile character, and is used for construction in this and other places. It is thought the limestone underlies nearly all the western, middle, and southern counties, though not developed on the surface, and as it occurs on the southwestern and southern borders of Okefinokee Swamp, in Georgia, the probability is that it extends over the whole region, and, it is possible, the Everglades of Florida.

All the coast of East Florida is calcareous, and the most characteristic formation is the Coral reef, still in progress of construction.

CHAPTER V.

VALLEY OF THE MISSISSIPPI. — Many of the extensive formations of the Atlantic border have crossed the Appalachians, and appear in the Mississippi basin under new titles, without change in their general features.

Ohio — The Lower Silurian is represented by the Cincinnati group, abounding in fossils, and the Blue limestone, extensively quarried for building.

The Niagara limestone, the great representative formation of the Upper Silurian, includes, in this State, the Guelph, a name borrowed from the Canadian, the Springfield, the West Union, and the Dayton The Niagara group, which abounds in fossils in other regions, is comparatively deficient in remains, in Ohio. The Clinton of the same period includes a larger number of fossils, and is especially rich in Corals and Crinoids, which often constitute the mass of rock. This formation is valuable for the petroleum it yields.

The Water-lime, a magnesian rock, includes several varieties, and covers a large area; it abounds in "sink-holes," or caves with the roof fallen in, as may be seen in Put-in-Bay Island, whose whole surface appears to be honeycombed by subterranean galleries.

The limestone is employed for hydraulic lime, and in the western part of the State for architectural purposes.

The Oriskany group, which is mostly sandstone in New York, is partially represented by limestones in this and other States of the Mississippi basin. What is called the Cliff limestone includes strata belonging both to the Niagara and the Lower Helderberg.

The limestones of the Devonian system appear in the Hamilton and the Corniferous series, forming a group of considerable importance. The Corniferous affords one of the most extensive formations in the State, and is exceedingly interesting to the paleontologist, being a vast storehouse of organic remains, comprising corals, shells, fishes, and land-plants.

The limestone includes the varieties Columbus, which is white; and the Sandusky, sometimes exhibiting a dark-gray, and sometimes a light color, quarried under the name of "Sandusky stone." It has been used for buildings in Sandusky, Toledo, and other western cities

A Crinoidal limestone, occupying a place between the coal beds, is very important for determining the age of strata on account of the large number and variety of its fossils.

The Carboniferous or Mountain limestone, formerly supposed to be wanting in Ohio, is best displayed in the central part of the State, where it receives the name of Maxwell limestone. It is a gray, magnesian, compact rock, with few fossils, badly preserved. The Waverly group, which supplies the well-known sandstone so extensively used in building, is rich in the fauna of the Carboniferous types.

The Hanging Rock District develops a great variety of limestones, bearing different local names and varying in color, texture, composition, and other characteristics. The Shawnee or Buff is quite pure, consisting of ninety-three per cent of lime, while the Cambridge or Black is one of the most persistent

Ohio is well supplied with excellent building materials, consisting largely of limestones and sandstones. The "Berea Grit," quarried as "Amherst stone," makes a desirable architectural stone for its durability, texture, and color

Indiana. — One of the most valuable properties of a building stone is the power of resistance to crushing weight, which varies from about 16,000 to 6,000 pounds, or less, to the square inch.

The North Vernon Blue stone of Indiana, of the Hamilton epoch, is nearly pure carbonate of lime, and, according to Cox, will sustain a weight of 15,750 pounds to the square inch, while a cubic foot weighs 165.43 pounds   It is evident, therefore, that as a building stone this limestone forms a valuable acquisition to the mineral resources of the State.

The power of resistance of the St. Louis limestone is much less than that of the North Vernon, being 7,500 pounds, but is superior to that of the magnesian limestone of England, extensively used in building, which is stated to be 5,219 pounds ; it also surpasses the Portland stone in strength and density. This formation affords immense blocks nearly as long as the longest found at the ruins of Baalbec, in the Turkish Empire.   Mr. Cox saw at the Bedford quarry, in this State, a block sixty-six feet in length, while others of sufficient size to duplicate Cleopatra's Needle, as he remarks, might be cut from the same place.

• Most of the Carboniferous limestones of Indiana are identical with those of Missouri, where they received their names.

The St Louis is oolitic, of the Sub-carboniferous period, varying from grayish to chalk-white, and has been called "Cavernous limestone" from the number of caves it contains, among these the Mammoth in Kentucky, and Wier's in Virginia.   The Carboniferous limestones form many of the noted caverns of other countries, a fact illustrated by the Kirkdale of England, Antiparos in Greece, and those of Franconia

The beautiful White Oolite of the St. Louis group, thought by some to be a chemical deposit on account of its brilliancy, structure, and capacity for polish, makes a valuable ornamental stone.

The light-gray Baalbec marble, recently brought into notice, belongs to this group and is very pure, averaging nearly ninety-seven per cent. of carbonate of lime, with a crushing strength of 11,750 pounds, and a weight of 146 56 pounds to the cubic foot. The stone is very hard and admits of a high polish.

The Keokuk group includes several varieties of limestones, but is best known for the Geode beds.

Geodes, one of the curiosities of geology, are balls of rock, with a rough exterior, and the interior filled with crystals of quartz, calcite, or some other mineral. The cavities are supposed to be formed by the decay of animal or vegetable matter, and subsequently filled with water holding in solution silica or calcite, which crystallizes on the evaporation of the water.

The Chester group is represented by the Archimedes or Kaskaskia limestone, loaded with fossils.

Nearly every State presents some phenomena which form a peculiarity in its geological history One of the features of Indiana is its caverns. Borden Cave, recently discovered in Harrison County, includes only a few apartments which have been explored, but the Wyandotte Cavern, in Crawford County, is one of the most extensive and remarkable in the country.

The history of caves affords an illustration of the wonderful power they exercise over the imagination, as do most things that belong to the realms of mystery, darkness, stillness, and immensity. The chill atmosphere, the overpowering silence, the ghost-like forms, strike the visitor with awe and hold him spell-bound.

Caves are not peculiar to any one country, but are found in nearly all regions, and have been used as dwellings, temples, sepulchres, and retreats from enemies Ancient records allude to them, they are mentioned in the Bible, and classic writers have made them the resort of divinities whence oracles were delivered.

The limestones of the Sub-carboniferous formation, in which many of the caverns occur, are, in the United States, of great thickness, from 1,000 to 1,200 feet, therefore the caverns are on a grand scale.

The rocks of Wyandotte Cave, formerly called Salt Petre, consist of a gray limestone, enclosing the fossil Archimedes, the White Oolite, and an Encrinal limestone. In this mass of strata have been formed numerous large cavities, assuming the appearance of halls, arches, flights of steps, corridors, avenues, bridges, chasms, all differing from one another in size, beauty, and magnificence. One of the apartments, called Bandit's Hall, is frescoed with starry gypsum; on the pavement lies a solid cube of limestone, twenty feet square, which was detached from the roof ninety feet above. Ascending several steps and passing through various apartments, another hall is reached two hundred and ten feet long, with walls of solid limestone supporting a dome, whose crown, adorned with heavy mouldings, is eighty feet from the floor. On one hand is represented a phantom ship, with " sails unfurled and rudder set," and on the other a marble cascade, with its noiseless, motionless fall

The room called the Senate Chamber, is a vast ellipse, six hundred feet in the longest diameter, and one hundred and fifty in the shortest, enclosing a mountain of white, lustrous spar, from whose top arises a fluted column, called the Pillar of the Constitution, twenty-five feet in diameter, reaching to the centre of the dome Near the Pillar hangs Independence Bell, which, it is said, when gently struck, gives out a clear, musical note; the Chair of State is enveloped in snowy curtains of marble folds. Sprigs, leaves, tendrils, and mosses, are exquisitely wrought in marble and gypsum, some pearly white and flecked by the iridescent nacre of sea-shells A part of the chasms and avenues are filled with beds full of the fossils characteristic of the Carboniferous formation.

More than two miles from the entrance, says the writer from whom these facts were gathered, at the utmost limit of the cavern, occurs a dark, gloomy apartment called Pluto's Regions The entire length of the galleries of Wyandotte Cave is reckoned twenty-five miles, and it is thought to be equal in size to the Mammoth Cave of Kentucky. The largest 'room is two hundred and forty-five feet in height and three hundred and fifty in length.

Illinois. — The Eozoic, Triassic, Jurassic, and Cretaceous formations are not developed in Illinois, but Worthen thinks the oldest rocks, though not brought to the surface, may underlie the whole area. There are only few places in the State that exhibit indications of metamorphism, and these occur in the southern part.

The limestones of Illinois, which constitute a large part of the rocks, are largely Sub-carboniferous, having an aggregated thickness of about 1,500 feet. They are arranged in several groups · the Chester, St Louis, Keokuk, Burlington, and Kinderhook, all of which are found in other States of the Mississippi basin.

The Chester limestone, the most recent of the group, is from five hundred to eight hundred feet thick, and includes several distinct beds. It is gray, coarsely granular, and full of fossils, some of the Cephalopods being of very large size. It furnishes good building material and a fertile soil, sustaining some of the finest peach-orchards in the southern part of the State. The " Pentremital," and "Upper Archimedes " or Kaskaskia, are included in the group.

Below the Chester limestone occurs the St Louis group, comprising very pure limestones of light-gray and dark colors, sometimes affording a fine, compact, black marble. It presents so great a variety that it can be recognized only by its remains, the most characteristic, from northern Illinois to Alabama, being the coral genus Lithostrotion The beds at Warsaw, on the Mississippi, contain great numbers of the remarkable Bryozoa called Archimedes Wortheni. The group yields excellent building-stone, and some varieties are suitable for marble, particularly portions of the oolitic beds, but it contains numerous " sink holes," which once formed entrances to caves, now filled with sediments and covered with small ponds.

The Keokuk group embraces the Geode beds, the gray

limestone of Keokuk and Nauvoo, and some chert beds, and affords more important minerals than are found in any other group in the State. The geodes, which have been sent to nearly all the cabinets of the world, are filled with crystals of quartz, calcite, dolomite, zinc, blende, and other minerals. Fossil shells and corals of great beauty and variety are numerous in the Keokuk limestone, which also furnishes a great number of vertebrates It has been used in construction, as in the Mormon Temple at Nauvoo, and the Custom-Houses at Galena and Dubuque.

Immediately under the Keokuk, lies the Burlington limestone, which has a remarkable development in Burlington, Iowa. It is exceedingly rich in fossils, especially Crinoids or Sea-lilies, and affords, as stated by Worthen, a greater number of species and individuals than all other Paleozoic rocks on this continent combined. This formation has an equivalent in what is called the Quincy limestone.

The Kinderhook, named for the place where it was first examined, including the Chouteau and a lithographic limestone, is of variable character in regard to fossils, which are sometimes abundant, at other times rare; this is also true of the Devonian limestones of Illinois.

A mass of yellow limestone, three hundred feet thick, partly Devonian and partly Silurian, forming the bluffs on the Mississippi, in the southern part of the State, is known by the name of the Clear Creek limestone.

The Niagara limestone, Upper Silurian, occupies a large area in Northern Illinois, and forms the fundamental rock. In some places it presents a brown or buff dolomite variety, while in others it is a yellowish, concretionary, or brecciated stone. Near Chicago it is charged with petroleum, which gathers in pools or floats on the water, filling the old quarries. It is stated that though the rock is completely saturated with the oil, yet in consequence of its compact texture, this formation cannot be used as an oil-producing deposit. At Athens, the Niagara yields a gray, compact limestone, susceptible of a fine polish, called the "Athens marble," and is used for an ornamental stone at Chicago and other places. The Joliet, belonging to this formation, affords an excellent stone for building and flagstones.

The Trenton group of Illinois comprises the lead-bearing Galena, and a blue and buff-limestone. The Galena is the most important formation in the State for its valuable ore, affording lead and zinc mines, and is described by Prof J. D Whitney as a thick-bedded, light-gray, or yellowish-gray dolomite, of crystalline texture inclining to granular, but sometimes compact. The streams of northwestern Illinois and Iowa are bordered by cliffs composed of this rock, which present the appearance of ruined towers and castles, notably in the vicinity of Dubuque and Galena; most of its fossils are in the form of casts. The Trenton limestone, found in the southern part of the State, is light-gray, semi-crystalline, taking a fine polish and used for an ornamental stone. In Missouri it is quarried under the name of Cape Girardeau marble.

The Calciferous or Lower Magnesian limestone, considered the oldest rock yet discovered in the State, rests immediately below the St. Peter's sandstone, a formation of great importance in the manufacture of glass. It is almost pure silica, and is the equivalent of the "saccharoidal sandstone" of Missouri, employed at the Pittsburg glass-works.

Michigan. — The Eozoic rocks are represented by crystalline limestones found in the Menominee, iron region of the Upper Peninsula, and the Lower Silurian are represented by the Chazy and the Trenton limestones, including the Black River and the Bird's Eye varieties. The Trenton group, very similar to that of New York, underlies a considerable part of this Peninsula, where it yields fewer fossils than in some other places, but they include the great diversity usually found in this formation. The Chazy affords a variety of limestones, including coarse-grained, white, dolomitic, oolitic, arenaceous, and nodular varieties, with large masses of the Stromatopora.

A nodular kind of either the Chazy or the Trenton is called "Wedge-shaped" limestone. The Cincinnati affords a dark bluish-gray limestone, enclosing the fossil Chaetetes, with stems of Crinoids crystallized by calc spar, and occasionally by violet fluor spar.

Nearly all the southern part of the Upper Peninsula is covered by the Niagara group, which is essentially limestone, mostly magnesian, embracing several varieties, some of which are pure limestones. The formation is highly fossiliferous, and on Drummond's Island, in Lake Huron, there is a large accumulation of organic remains, while at Point Delane they form almost the entire mass of rock. In the corals replaced by silica, the polyps have been preserved in a nearly perfect state; beautiful specimens are found on Whitney Bay.

The white marble-like deposits between the lower strata of the Burnt Bluff region are almost pure carbonate of lime.

The Clinton group, Upper Silurian, appears in Michigan with peculiar fossils, and the Lower Helderberg of the same period is recognized by gray and blue limestones and dolomites of fine crystalline structure.

The Corniferous, of the Devonian period, occupying the southeastern part of the State, embraces a light-colored limestone with concretions of hornstone, and numerous fossils not well preserved   The Hamilton group in New York is essentially a shale formation, but in Michigan it is, to a great extent, calcareous, and represented by limestones crowded with fossils, especially corals, and a light-gray dolomite   Portions of these beds are capable of yielding a decorative stone, but the mass of the rock is not sufficiently compact to be used for marble.

The Carboniferous formation is very unequal in its development and characteristics in this State, the upper part consisting of a limestone similar to the Sub-carboniferous found throughout the Mississippi valley, while the lower beds are gypseous, and have been called the Michigan salt group.

The calcareous rocks of this period are variable in color

Plate VII.

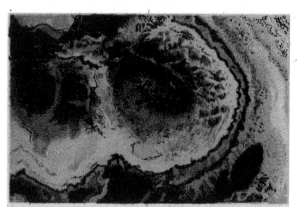

ROSE ALABASTER.

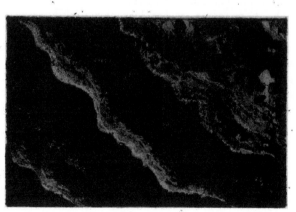

CALIFORNIA ALABASTER.

ARMSTRONG & CO. LITH. BOSTON.

and structure, and are replete with fossils characteristic of the formation. At Grand Rapids, the gypsum beds are quarried for ornamental stone.

Michigan yields a rich harvest of Paleozoic remains, especially Corals, where Favosites are largely represented, and Alveolites, Halysites, Syringopora, Columnaria, Cyathophyllum, Lithostrotion, Zaphrentes, and many other genera are more or less abundant.

From the " Reports of Rominger," we learn that the entire surface of the Lower Peninsula, with few exceptions, is covered with drift deposits, resting on Paleozoic rocks

Travertine is sometimes found in large masses on the sides of hills abounding in springs, while the bottom of some inland lakes are covered with white marl, composed of the shells of fresh-water Mollusks and carbonate of lime, affording an instance of a lacustrine limestone in its early stages of formation.

Wisconsin. — Limestones form no inconsiderable part of the rocks of the Upper Mississippi, embracing the States of Wisconsin, Iowa, and Minnesota. The central and north central areas of Wisconsin are covered with Eozoic rocks, both Laurentian and Huronian, principally the former, embracing granites, porphyries, and quartzites, while trap is displayed in high escarpments on the St. Croix Silurian calcareous strata, both Lower and Upper, have their types in this State, though frequently appearing with local names.

The formation called the Calciferous sandstone in New York has been designated by Owen the Lower Magnesian, a name adopted throughout the West. Though enclosing organic remains, these are so imperfect that the rock was formerly believed to be unfossiliferous. The mass, in some localities, according to Hall and Whitney, is concretionary or brecciated, and usually of a grayish-white or ash-color, finely-crystalline and compact, yielding minerals and metallic ores. This limestone occurs in massive walls, often fissured, and presents everywhere the most picturesque scenery, frequently simulating ruined castles and fortifications. It has not the grandeur, says Owen, often seen in other formations'; there are no lofty peaks, no dark, narrow gorges with rushing torrents, no precipitous defiles, no contorted strata, but with walls and rounded towers are found steep cliffs and crystal streams, with clumps of trees as ornaments to the pictorial landscape.

St. Peter's limestone, receiving its local name from St. Peter's River, has no great thickness, but is rich in organic remains of the Lower Silurian type. The Chazy has not a well-defined character, either in this State or the West generally; the Trenton group, so persistent in other States, appears in Wisconsin as Blue, Buff, Cliff, and Galena limestones; the latter covering a large portion of the State. The Cincinnati, and an impure limestone called Mendota, form a part of the Lower Silurian series.

The Niagara limestone occupies a large area, extending north and south two hundred miles, and is quite uniform in its character. It forms the upper portion of the "mounds," and from that circumstance has been called the Mound limestone It includes the Guelph, Racine, Waukesha, and Mayville beds. The Racine limestone is yellowish, friable, and readily decomposes by exposure to the air, hence it is worthless as a building-stone. The Waukesha, identical with the Le Claire of Iowa, is a tough, compact, magnesian rock of a gray or buff color. The Niagara is, everywhere in the West, essentially a coralline limestone, but in Wisconsin, nearly all fossils are in a very imperfect condition.

Iowa. — The Transition or Paleozoic limestones of Iowa, beginning at the Mississippi, extend in a succession of bands towards the northwest The most southerly of these bands is the Carboniferous series, which has a large development at Burlington, including the Encrinal or Burlington, the Keokuk or Archimedes, the Warsaw, the St. Louis, and the Kaskaskia or Pentremital limestones. The Burlington limestone yields a rich harvest of fossils, more than three hundred species having been discovered, which are important to the paleontologist, it is claimed, in forming important links in the great chain of organic life. This limestone, which has not been recognized beyond Iowa, Missouri, and Illinois, in some of the beds, consists of nearly pure carbonate of lime capable of a polish, and is extensively quarried for building purposes

The Carboniferous group, including the Geode beds and a magnesian limestone, is of economic value for building and lime.

Proceeding north, the Devonian strata form the next band, taking the same direction as the Carboniferous formation. The Niagara group of the Upper Silurian follows, embracing the Le Claire limestone, having the same general trend but vanishing about one-third the distance; then the Niagara, with a much more extensive distribution, while the Galena and the Trenton of the Lower Silurian, covering a smaller area, form the most northerly zone of Paleozoic rocks.

The Le Claire limestone, of a gray or whitish color, developed at the Rapids of Le Claire, rests upon the Niagara.

The superficial area covered by the Devonian rocks in Iowa is inconsiderable; they are calcareous, comprising limestones of great purity, generally light-colored, and in texture resembling lithographic stone, including both concretionary and brecciated varieties. The Devonian strata of the Cedar and the Iowa valleys comprise what are called the lower coralline beds, the shell beds, and the upper Coralline limestone. In the lower beds occurs the coral Acervularia, the characteristic fossil of the Iowa marble, a limestone seldom found in masses of sufficient size for commerce; but a cream-colored limestone of Cedar River has been employed for monumental stone On the Iowa River, Carboniferous limestone forms elevations resembling immense roofs with sloping sides.

The rocks of Iowa, as well as of other western States, are deeply buried beneath a rich, black soil of drift, overspread with thick prairie grass, and are seldom brought to the surface

except in the deep cuts of the streams; hence the examination of strata is attended with great difficulty. The investigation of the organic remains enclosed in the Sub-carboniferous
beds is highly important in searching for the coal-measures,
since certain fossils are always found below and never above
them.

Missouri. — Some of the oldest rocks are developed in Missouri, including the "Marble beds" in Madison County in the
southeastern part of the State, which have been referred to
the Laurentian series by some, and to the Primordial by
others.

The Paleozoic limestones of this section include some of the
varieties of other States, with a few bearing local names with
or without equivalents.

Magnesian limestones have a large development and are
divided into four classes. The First magnesian limestone,
characterized by the fossil Cytherea, is generally buff color,
thick, even-bedded, and suitable for buildings   The Second
magnesian encloses fossils analogous to those of the Calciferous rocks of New York, which would place it in the Lower
Silurian, and it is often lead-bearing. The Third magnesian
limestone of the Lower Silurian is an important member,
being the chief lead-producing rock of the central and south-
central region, and forming the hills of lead ore in this part
of the State   It is gray and crystalline, with numerous fissures
filled with Galena, and is from three hundred to six hundred
feet thick. The Fourth magnesian limestone resembles the
Third   ·

The Galena limestone of Illinois and Iowa, of the Trenton
group, is wanting in Missouri, but its place is supplied by the
Receptaculite limestone, which receives the name from the
predominant fossil enclosed   The Trenton, Black River, and
Bird's Eye limestones are found here; the last two mottled
with drab and reddish colors, frequently yield marbles

The Upper Silurian is represented by the Niagara, and a
Spirifer or Delthyris limestone. The Cape Girardeau lime-

stone or marble has been placed both in the Upper and the Lower Silurian.

The Devonian system appears in the Onondaga limestone with a very limited development, while the Carboniferous limestones, including Sub-carboniferous, afford a greater variety in this State than those of any other era. The Chester limestone is almost entirely wanting, but the St. Louis group, including the Warsaw and a sandy limestone with Archimedes and Pentremites, constitutes the entire mass of calcareous rocks at the city of St. Louis, where it reaches a larger development than in any other part of the State. The Keokuk group is very generally distributed in the southwest, and yields lead

The Burlington or Encrinital limestone, long used in Missouri for building material, has effectually resisted the disintegrating influence of the atmosphere, thus proving its excellence for such a purpose.

The Kinderhook group, comprising a coarse limestone and a fine compact variety called Lithographic stone, is better developed in Missouri than in Illinois and Iowa Other varieties of Carboniferous limestones are represented by Fusilina, Chaetetes, and Rhomboidal limestones. The Chaetetes is found projecting from the sides of hills, and is valuable in determining the position of coal.

The Permian, Triassic, Jurassic, Cretaceous, and Tertiary formations are said to be wanting in Missouri

The Marble beds, from eight to twenty feet thick, found in the south part of the State, are variable in color and texture, presenting species of gray, buff and gray, red variegated with buff and white, red and white banded, and unicolored with dolomitic veins, most of them enclosing crystals of calcite, and sometimes quartz. The beds are interstratified with porphyries and serpentines.

Paleozoic limestones yield some excellent marble; the Silurian afford the Cape Girardeau and the McPherson; the Devonian, the Cooper marble of the Onondaga limestone, a fine, compact variety, enclosing spar; and the Carboniferous; several varieties, including a beautiful oolitic marble from the Keokuk or Archimedes limestone, a white crystalline marble from the Encrinital, a fine, bluish-drab variety from the Lithographic, and the Fort Scott marble. A magnesian limestone develops a light-drab marble tinted and clouded with peach-blossom, forming a very pleasing stone for decoration.

Tennessee. — Tennessee, the great marble-producing State of the Mississippi basin, possesses invaluable resources in this commodity, where immense bands of marble, extending many hundred feet in width, are cut by streams and railways, thus affording an easy and economical means of transportation. The marbles are embraced in many varieties of different geological periods, including Silurian and Carboniferous, and are extensively distributed throughout the State. They are generally fossiliferous, Crinoids and Corals being the characteristic remains.

Where marbles are abundant there must be, of course, a large development of limestone formations, and these, with the marbles they yield, may be grouped as East, Middle, and West Tennessee limestones.

In East Tennessee, the Calciferous and Quebec formations, Lower Silurian, include from 3,000 to 4,000 feet of limestone; the Trenton, of the same era, embraces the lower beds of the Nashville group, and a blue and dove-colored limestone from which marbles are obtained. The upper strata of the Nashville are placed with the Utica and Cincinnati, the most recent members of the Lower Silurian. The Chazy is represented by the Maclurea limestone, taking the name from its characteristic fossil, a large Gasteropod, and a blue and drab concretionary rock of a thickness varying from fifty to six hundred feet. A Quebec, dolomite limestone, enclosing Trilobites, breccia marbles and conglomerates, are comprised in the limestones of this section of the State.

Most of the marbles of East Tennessee are Lower Silurian, usually heavy-bedded, and dipping at an average angle of 45°, while those of Middle and West Tennessee are horizontal.

Safford arranges the marbles of Tennessee in the following classes: 1. Variegated fossiliferous; 2. Grayish-white fossiliferous; 3. Magnesian; 4 Black; 5. Brecciated. The Variegated is the most important, and is found in all three divisions of the State, but is most abundant and of the best quality in Hawkins County, East Tennessee. Blocks of the Variegated, sent as a contribution to the Washington Monument, says Safford, induced the Building Committee to employ this Tennessee marble in the extension of the National Capitol

The Grayish-white is only a species of the Variegated, and on account of its great number of Corals and Crinoids, is sometimes called Coralline or Encrinal marble. It is below the Variegated, and forms a mass of light-gray, sparry limestone or marble, mottled with pink and red; sometimes it is white. It is worked at Knoxville, and in commerce is often called Knoxville marble These two varieties are, undoubtedly, of the Trenton period.

The quarries of East Tennessee are numerous and scattered over a large region, and the marble obtained from the mines offers some variety. One kind is argillaceous with few organic remains, of a dull grayish or brownish red, sometimes of a greenish tint, arranged in no definite form; but the best and . most important variety called, *par excellence*, Marble of East Tennessee, is purer and more fossiliferous, of more lively colors, and with more distinct clouds and spots than the argillaceous.

The Sub-carboniferous or Mountain limestone forms an extensive bed of blue and light-blue rock, occasionally oolitic, forming the base of the Cumberland table-land separating East from Middle Tennessee.

The Lower Silurian of Middle Tennessee has its representatives in a blue limestone of the Trenton period, and those of the Nashville group. The limestones of the latter are generally bluish-gray, sometimes nearly black, frequently enclosing green particles, presenting a gray marble with crystals of spar. Some of the beds are full of fossils, and receive a good polish, others are crossed by mineral veins. The central basin of this section is mostly covered by Silurian limestones, generally blue or dove-color; that of the Lower Helderberg appears in the form of a gray, Crinoidal limestone

The lower group of the Sub-carboniferous, includes Lithostrotion or Coral beds, equivalent to the St. Louis, while the upper member consists of the blue Mountain limestone; both groups are also found in East Tennessee. The marbles of Middle and West Tennessee are similar to those of East Tennessee, and are developed generally from the same formations.

The Niagara formation is represented by the Meniscus limestone of West Tennessee, and a light-blue variety of the Lower Helderberg.

Though the magnesian limestones of this State yield marbles, usually light-gray and pink, they are less valued than those derived from pure limestones

Most of the limestones of Tennessee are Paleozoic, but the Cretaceous formation, which crosses the State west of the Tennessee River, displays calcareous rocks in the form of Rotten limestone, with a thickness from two hundred to three hundred and fifty feet. The Tertiary system is represented by beds of lignite and the Quaternary by drift deposits, which occur along the tributaries of this river.

Kentucky. — Kentucky as well as Tennessee, is a limestone region, but its marbles are less in quantity and variety. Most, if not all, of the calcareous formations, belong to the older sedimentary rocks, or those of the Paleozoic era , the secondary formations have a limited range in the State, being represented by the Cretaceous, which crosses the western part from the State of Tennessee to the mouth of the Ohio Beds of lignite belong to the Tertiary, and the Quaternary consists of loam, marl, clays, and gravel enclosing Pleistocene mammal remains of gigantic size.

The oldest limestone of Kentucky and the oldest known formation in the State, according to Owen, is the Blue limestone of the Lower Silurian, predominating in what is called the Blue-grass counties in Middle and North Kentucky. This formation, extending along the Ohio to the Cumberland, one of the most important in the State, has a thickness of five hundred feet, embracing many varieties full of organic remains It varies in color, but the prevailing tint is bluish-gray with much calc spar, which gives it the appearance of marble, and when polished it is suitable for uses to which marble is applied. The region in which this formation is developed is celebrated for fertility, and is considered the garden of the State Some of the varieties of the Blue limestone are the Bird's Eye, of a dove-color, smooth texture, with specks of spar, and yielding marble; a gray Leptaena limestone, named from the predominance of a fossil of the Orthis family; the Trenton, of dark color and fine grain; Bellerophon, with a light gray color and granular texture; magnesian, of a gray color; and some other varieties characterized by the usual Lower Silurian fossils.

The Kentucky marble, as it is called, is derived from the Bird's Eye limestone, of a light bluish-gray or dove-color, mottled with dark or light-buff, and generally interstratified with magnesian limestone. In the bold escarpments on the Kentucky, near the mouth of Duck's River, occur, says Owen, some of the finest expositions of this formation seen in the romantic cliffs of marble forming a deep gorge crossed by the suspension bridge of more than twelve hundred feet, at an elevation of four hundred feet above the river A variety of the Lower Silurian limestone yields the Murchisonia marble, so called from the characteristic fossil Gasteropod.

The Coralline or Falls limestone, corresponding to the Corniferous and Chemung of New York, of the Devonian era, is peculiar for the Cup-corals, Cyathophylloids, and the Honeycomb corals, Favosites, which are so abundant as to present the similitude of a petrified coral reef. It is about fifty feet in depth, and has its largest development in the valley of the Ohio, and yields a soil only a little less productive than that of the Blue limestone. Its widest belt is in Jefferson County, on the Ohio, where it is eight miles in width, and covered by a large growth of timber.

The Upper Magnesian or Cliff limestone, in the same county, probably corresponds to the Cliff limestone, Upper Silurian, found in Ohio. Beds of magnesian limestone form the surface stratum in this region, and they furnish shell and argillaceous limestones. A locality in Bullitt County is celebrated for Encrinites, and an Encrinital limestone is developed in Shelby, Trimble, and Franklin Counties. A variety of the Niagara epoch is exposed in the southern counties, but yields a soil inferior to that of either the Blue or the Falls lime-, stone.

The Blue-grass region, from the Ohio to Virginia and Tennessee, is traversed by a belt of cone-shaped hills, arranged in groups called "knobs," composed of slates, shales, and grit of the Devonian age, frequently capped by limestones enclosing shells and corals, the whole called the Knobstone formation; above this rests the Sub-carboniferous strata, composed chiefly of alternate beds of white, gray, and buff limestones. Notwithstanding the copious springs issuing from between these beds, the valleys are comparatively dry, says the State geologist, because the streams are engulfed by the numerous "sink holes" peculiar to this formation. In the southeastern part of the State the Carboniferous system appears in a line of bluffs and hill-slopes.

The Sub-carboniferous limestone on the Ohio is, in places, four hundred or five hundred feet thick, and includes a reddish-yellow limestone enclosing Archimedes and Pentremites, and an oolite limestone affording cream-colored marble; some of the Pentremites are nearly three inches in length. The largest of the caverns which are frequent in this formation is

the celebrated Mammoth Cave. The platform constituting
the entrance to this cavern, consisting of limestone with some
sandstone, is two hundred and thirty-two feet above the bed
of Green River. The cave itself is eleven miles in length,
with more than one hundred and fifty miles of rooms and
passages, many of the apartments being enormously high, one
of them nearly three hundred feet   These gigantic excavations in solid rock, forcibly illustrate the eroding power of
water, an agent supposed to produce in part these marvellous
results.

The upper division of the Sub-carboniferous formation is
composed of the Archimedes and Pentremital limestones,
while below are the Lithostrotion beds, or the Barren limestone group. What is called the Barrens includes a tract of
land which was destitute of trees when the State was first
settled, but has since been covered by a growth of forest vegetation, and forms a fertile table-land consisting principally of
the St. Louis limestone of this period.   The Barren limestones
vary in color from light-gray or cream-color to very dark,
approaching black ; they often include hydraulic limestones,
and sometimes a compact variety resembling the lithographic
stone of Solenhofen, but without the uniform texture for
which the latter is celebrated   This formation encloses extensive deposits of oxide of iron, to which is due the red tints
of the Barren lands, and in some localities it yields lead.   The
Keokuk or siliceous, the Chester, and perhaps some others,
occur among the Sub-carboniferous limestones of Kentucky.

Fayette County yields an unfossiliferous, light-gray limestone used for building, and the homogeneous, magnesian
limestone employed for construction in Lexington, which
furnished the block for the Washington Monument. Marble
Hill, on the Ohio, affords a granular limestone or marble, of
a warm or drab-gray, enclosing fragments of the Murchisonia
and corals, having the cavities filled with beautiful transparent
spar, sometimes colorless and sometimes pink or brown, constituting a rock susceptible of a good polish and appropriate

for ornamental uses; it may be identical with the Murchisonia marble.

The limestones of the Carboniferous period consist of thin
beds between the Coal, extending over limited areas, and
embracing what is locally called the Carthage limestone.   The
lower Coal beds yield only two kinds of limestones of any
note, including variegated and a black variety, thought to be
capable of yielding marble.   Prof. Shaler, speaking of the
flora of Kentucky, says that a change in formation produces
immediate and marked effects on timber, but this change is
less perceptible where the Keokuk or siliceous group has
furnished the soil.

Mississippi. — Only four of the geological periods, according
to Hilgard, are represented in Mississippi, — the Carboniferous, Cretaceous, Tertiary, and the Quaternary.   Though
limestones are not the predominant rocks, yet they are developed in different parts of the State, to a greater or less
extent, seen in a gray, crystalline limestone of the Carboniferous era, a dark-colored hydraulic limestone forming the bold
tops of the hills on the Yellow Creek, a gray fossiliferous
and a black limestone without fossils, displayed at Cypress
Pond, and the Rotten limestone of the Cretaceous period,
found also in other States   The latter is a soft, chalky-white
or pale-blue rock, enclosing a variety of fossils peculiar to the
Chalk formation, which attains in Mississippi a great thickness.   The Ripley group, Cretaceous, extending from this
State into Alabama, is very fossiliferous, including white,
crystalline limestones frequently with glauconite; one member
of the series is called Turritella limestone, from the prominence of that elegant univalve.

With the exception of the Orange Sand, the Tertiary
deposits, said to occupy by far the greater portion of the State,
embrace clays with lignite, sandstones, and limestones with
organic remains.   The Vicksburg group of the Upper Eocene,
first studied at Vicksburg, is the youngest of the marine formations of Mississippi, and comprises lignite beds, a ferruginous

rock of Red Bluff, full of fossils, and a compact limestone eighty feet in thickness, called Orbitoidal limestone, bearing some analogy to the Nummulitic limestone of the Eastern Continent. The Vicksburg limestone, which is quite pure, has been used in building the town of Vicksburg.

The Orange Sand, of the Quaternary period, the characteristic formation of the State, consists of siliceous sand, usually of an orange or ochre yellow, but sometimes white, rose, crimson, purple, and other tints, enclosing fossils of different periods, and frequently gems of the quartz family.

Alabama. — The extreme southern limit of the Silurian system in Alabama is thought to be about the latitude of 33°, terminating in a limestone formation at Centreville, on the Cahawba, a branch of the Alabama. The group contains various limestones, both crystalline and compact, yielding marbles of variegated colors, comprising gray with red veins; red and yellow; a variety with greenish veins; a buff with fossils; white clouded with red, black with white, and a magnesian marble of soft-gray.

A limestone well-adapted for architecture, developed in the valley of the Talladega River, yields a gray and a fine white crystalline marble, said to compare well with Italian, which have been quarried for mortuary monuments

The largest display of Carboniferous limestones are seen north of the Tennessee River.

At Huntsville, the Sub-carboniferous series consists principally of gray limestones which, with some beds of shale, are nine hundred feet thick. A part of the formation encloses Chester fossils, and a part those of the St. Louis group of Missouri Some of the limestones of this vicinity display black and yellow colors, with beds yielding a yellow marble with black spots.

The Cretaceous rocks of the Atlantic coast thin out in South Carolina, but farther inland, beginning at Macon, Georgia, they pass into the Mississippi Basin and are seen at Montgomery, Alabama. In this State they are two thousand feet thick, and from nine hundred to eleven hundred feet, according to Dana, consist of the Rotten limestone.

The Tertiary system is very prevalent in this State, and is, perhaps, better known than any other, on account of its numerous and interesting organic remains. What is called the Alabama period of the Tertiary, includes the Eocene, and is extensively developed in Georgia, Mississippi, and Alabama. The Middle Eocene is represented by the Claiborne beds, on the Alabama River, in the southwestern part of the State, and the Upper Eocene includes the Vicksburg group, met with in the southwest, constituting the limestone bluff at St. Stephens, on the Tombigbee. Sir Charles Lyell, who visited this State, says, four hundred species of marine shells, with numerous Echinoderms and teeth of fishes, were found in the Claiborne beds. Among the shells, the Cardita planostica is very abundant, which fact led this geologist to assign them to the Middle Eocene, making them contemporary with the Calcaire grossier of the Paris Basin. Above the Cardita beds rests the Orbitoïdes limestone superimposed by the White limestone, a very pure and compact rock, enclosing peculiar species of the Coral. It is in the White limestone that the Zeuglodon, a gigantic mammal of the whale tribe, has been found, some specimens with a vertebral column being nearly seventy feet in length.

Orbitoidal limestones are quite free from foreign constituents, being composed of more than ninety-five per cent. of carbonate of lime, and have been employed for building purposes

Louisiana —The geology of Louisiana is mostly included in the recent periods, but a ridge of Cretaceous rocks, consisting of gray limestones, traverses the State from northwest to southeast One variety of this formation, remarkably pure, with a granular, banded structure, and free from fossils, has received the name of St. Landry marble. A crystalline limestone, in some portions consisting of pure white and yellow calcite, forms a hill near Winfield, but on account of its brittle nature it. cannot be used for marble. The Tertiary limestones are generally impure, but those of the Vicksburg group are the freest from foreign elements.

The varieties found in the county of Calcasieu, in the southwestern part of the State, include a nodular variety resembling the Vicksburg, and a white, crystalline limestone. Gray and black limestones of the Tertiary are displayed at Sabine Bayou in the southwest, but no later marine Tertiary beds are recognized than the Upper Eocene.

The Port Hudson group of Mississippi and Louisiana consists of the Orange Sand and the bluff loam, loess or alluvium, forming what is called the Bluff formation, and containing carbonate of lime, partly in concretions, covered by a thin deposit of yellow loam. The loess of the Mississippi encloses numerous fresh-water shells, and south of New Orleans it contains also marine fossils

Texas — Eozoic rocks, as stated in the surveys of the State, are found in the western part along with Paleozoic strata, while the Llano Estacado Mountains, between four thousand and five thousand feet in height, consisting of granite, are capped by Potsdam limestone of the Cambrian period.

The hills of this region display high, irregular walls of gray limestone of different shades, alternating with red, gray, and yellow sandstones, of different ages. Mount Llano is composed in part of fossiliferous limestones, while in that region and in San Saba and Burnet Counties, the Calciferous sandrock is associated with a magnesian limestone called Burnet marble, constituting a formation several hundred feet in thickness, penetrated by veins of saltpetre.

The limestones of this series differ in color and composition, and afford good material for building-stone, while some of the beds yield white, gray, and drab marbles suitable for monumental uses. The rocks in the western part of the State contain iron ore and the precious metals, and Paleozoic and Cretaceous pebbles, enclosing characteristic fossils, are scattered over a large tract south of Austin. Carboniferous limestones are met with in nearly all the counties, harder than those of the Cretaceous period, and generally of different shades of gray.

Near Comanche Peak in the north, the Gryphæeae, characteristic fossils of the Lias of the Jurassic period, are very abundant, forming a mass two or three feet thick, and are remarkably well preserved. This eminence is six hundred feet above the bed of the Brazos River, and presents two summits with truncated cones. The upper part of the northern hill consists of a Hippurite limestone of the Cretaceous period overlying a gray limestone, both resting upon a Gryphite bed of the Lias, and on the south side of the peak, the Gryphite formation is two hundred feet thick. The Cretaceous limestones are very widely disseminated and differ in texture, a part being hard and compact, and a part soft and friable with nodules, and nearly as pulverulent as chalk; the color varies from dark-gray to yellowish-white. It is thought that the Cretaceous formation, which is very fossiliferous in Texas, enclosing species of corals and other remains, may be fifteen hundred feet thick.

The Tertiary formation, including limestones, occurs near Austin and the Trinity River; the Austin limestone has been used in the buildings of Austin, and for public edifices in some of the counties of the State. The marbles of Burnet, Llanos, and San Saba Counties, including white, black, flesh-color, and variegated, are of fair quality, but not the best.

Arkansas — Like most other States in the Mississippi Basin, Arkansas yields limestones, including a great variety in color, age, and composition, and of greater or less economic value.

The strata covering the northwestern part of the State, between the Black and Arkansas Rivers, have been classed by Owen, in three principal formations: the Millstone grit, Subcarboniferous limestone, and Lower Silurian magnesian limestone, each with associated rocks; the latter contain the lead and zinc ores of the State. Between the Sub-carboniferous

Plate VIII.

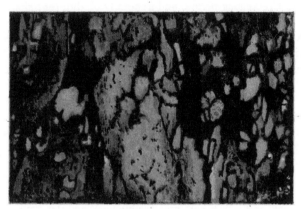

VICTORIA RED.

WARRICK, N. Y.

ARMSTRONG & CO. LITH. BOSTON.

and the magnesian, occur Encrinital and variegated limestones or marbles which may be Devonian.

The Millstone grit, Carboniferous, is the most prevalent, covering the entire area of eight, and portions of six other counties.

There are only few instances of the Sub-carboniferous limestone being found south of the Arkansas River, but the distinction between them and those of the Carboniferous formations, is not always clearly indicated in the rocks of Arkansas, except where the fossils are well preserved. The Oil Trough Ridge, consisting of limestones, includes the Archimedes, important as a guide to coal-mining, and the Producta limestone, seventy-five feet thick, of a fine black and capable of a good polish; it is probable that this formation furnished the black marble found in Independence County. On the White River, the Carboniferous limestones are well developed, associated with varieties belonging to a different period. A cherty limestone, with white and yellow sands, forms the variegated cliffs on this stream, known as Calico Rock. The magnesian formation is displayed in the White River valley frequently in bluffs, presenting pink, white, gray, and red variegated limestones or marbles. In Marion County, the marble is similar to the Cooper marble of Missouri, which is thought to be of the age of the Onondaga, Devonian, and underlying these beds are three hundred feet of magnesian limestone containing lead and zinc ores. This county is very rich in limestones capable of yielding marble, comprising a variety of light color, called Cotton rock.

The lead-bearing rock in Carroll County is two hundred or two hundred and fifty feet thick, embracing about thirty feet of Encrinital marble, and on the Little Red River in Van Buren County, limestone cliffs displaying the Archimedes, the Keokuk, and the Burlington limestones, all Sub-carboniferous, yield red, white, and pink marbles of a compact texture, corresponding to those of Marion and Carroll Counties.

The Cretaceous limestone extends from the eastern part of

the State through the centre, spreading out towards the south-west, passing at Ultima Thule into the Indian Territory. The formation in Hempstead County, including marls and lime-stones, enclosed most of the fossil bones found in the early settlement of the State, which were secured for the Museum at Berlin, Prussia. Some of the Cretaceous beds are entirely made up of shells cemented by lime, the most characteristic fossil being the Exogyra costata

The so-called Chalk Bluffs on the St. Francis River, con-sisting of potter's clay resembling white chalk in color, some-times variegated and suitable for ware, is considered a Quater-nary deposit, covering the Orange sand ; yellow ochre, lignite, and amber have all been found in the region.

The block sent to the National Monument, obtained from the corner of Newton and Carroll Counties, in the northwest-ern part of the State, was taken from a bed of gray marble, mottled and clouded with liver-colored spots.

Kansas. — The oldest known formation in Kansas is the Carboniferous, which passes on its western border into the Permian, and in New Leavenworth it yields a variety of lime-stones from which the material was quarried for the govern-ment buildings. Nearly one-fourth of the Carboniferous strata is limestone, and a portion of it affords marbles of various colors except black and white, receiving a fair polish, and comparing favorably with those of, New York and New Eng-land. The best marble is obtained from the Lawrence lime-stone, in Leavenworth and Atchison Counties, of different shades of buff, inclined to brown, of a beautiful mellow tint, and is quarried for buildings. Other varieties enclosing the Fusilina, Spirifer, Producta, Pinna, Crinoids and other fossils exist in the State.

The Permian system, limited in extent in the United States, is believed to exist in Kansas, Nebraska, and the Indian Terri-tory, including limestones in Kansas suitable for construction. The Triassic rocks cross the Republican and Smoky valleys, but the fossils are so badly preserved that they cannot always be distinguished from those of the Jurassic, a misfortune which occurs in other regions of this country.

The Cretaceous formation has a large development, including an extensive bed of chalk, while the Loess or Bluff formation, seen on the Missouri, encloses the bones of the Mastodon.

CHAPTER VI.

The Region of the Rocky Mountains and the Pacific Coast.—— The geological systems of this section have not been so thoroughly investigated as those of the Atlantic Border or the Mississippi Basin, and, though much has been achieved in that direction within a few years, extensive tracts yet remain which may richly compensate the future scientific explorer.

By the surveys of King, we are made acquainted with the geology of a vast territory crossed by the Union Pacific Railroad, covering a belt one hundred miles from north to south, and fourteen degrees from east to west, reaching from the Great Basin to the Borders of California. The rocks included within this area are of an immense thickness, and of nearly every geological period from the oldest to the youngest.

The Eozoic formations, comprising limestones, marbles, dolomites, porphyries, and serpentines, are found throughout the Rocky Mountains, the whole covered by volcanic rocks of great thickness.

The Humboldt Range of the Rocky Mountain system, rising from near the centre of the Nevada plateau, twelve thousand feet, offers a bold and rugged mass of Eozoic and Paleozoic rocks. The former includes limestones which are in places changed to coarse marble. The top of Mount Bonpland of this range, says King, is covered with marble. The Eozoic limestone of the Humboldt Range is a compact dolomite from fifty to sixty feet in thickness. Southeast of

90

the Washoe Mountains the same formation comprises a white, crystalline dolomite, yielding a pure, fine-grained marble of granular texture, closely allied to the limestone of the Humboldt Range. It rests under a Carboniferous limestone, and at some places is intercalated with porphyry. In the West Humboldt Range, occurs a limestone formation characterized by the fossils of the St. Cassian beds and the Alpine Trias

The Paleozoic rocks are not well displayed in the Rocky Mountains, being covered with Mesozoic and Tertiary deposits, yet, it is stated, they form a continuous sheet over the whole area, and have a special development in the Uinta Range. The limestones of the whole series, thirteen thousand feet in thickness, are largely Carboniferous, more than one-half containing fossils characteristic of the formation. A blue-gray limestone of this period, conspicuous for the fossil Bellerophon, is found in the Uinta Mountains. The Transition or Paleozoic limestones include those of the Silurian type. The Ute-Pogonip limestone, charged with Primordial fossils, reaches, on the Ute Peak, in Nevada, a thickness of two thousand feet. It is light-colored, crystalline, with peculiar cloudings, and is considered analogous to the Quebec of the Lower Silurian. It is not metamorphic, though the remains are in the usual imperfect condition of those found in most western strata; it extends through the entire group of the Wahsatch Range, and includes, in the regions of the Cotton-wood, fragmental masses of white marble

The Wahsatch Range of Utah and Nevada, from eleven thousand to twelve thousand feet in height, constitutes one of the most important and complicated of the Rocky Mountain chains. All the principal formations, reports King, from the Eozoic to the latest Tertiary, are here represented on a magnificent scale. This immense mass of rock is "twisted and folded like cords and sheets of paper."

The Wahsatch affords a very large development of limestones reaching many thousand feet in thickness and belonging to different formations, from the Cambrian to the Tertiary.

The Jurassic series is of great thickness along the base of the range; both this and the Triassic series are associated with gypsums.   These limestones are very generally distributed over Utah and Nevada, and present some exceedingly grand views, displayed in cañons from six thousand to seven thousand feet in depth.

The Paleozoic limestones of this region afford great diversity of colors,—blue, gray, pink, buff, sombre and brilliant reds, and white, and are equally variable in texture and composition.

Near Star City, a limestone encloses the remains of Saurians; at Star Peak, the Triassic limestone rises several hundred feet in a nearly vertical direction; and in the Augusta Mountains, it is covered, in some places, by a whitish, concretionary calc spar.

The Eocene, Tertiary, affords a concretionary, and the Miocene, a saccharoidal limestone, enclosing fresh-water mollusks; the Cheyenne limestone of Wyoming belongs to this period

The Cretaceous formation includes only a few limestones in the regions between the Wahsatch and the Rocky Mountains.

The strata, from the bottom of the Cambrian to the top of the Tertiary, in the section explored by King, were about seventy-seven thousand feet thick, comprising nearly twenty thousand feet of limestone, and a small proportion of calcareous shales

The recent deposits include travertine   At Pyramid Lake, Nevada, occur the Tufa Domes, consisting of calcareous masses of light-brown or gray color, generally from fifty to sixty feet in height; one of these domes, called the "Pyramid," attains a height of four hundred feet.   These pyramidal accumulations, as well as the banks of the lake, are encrusted with gay-lussite, or as the explorer calls it, thonolite, consisting of carbonate of lime, carbonate of soda, water, and sometimes silica.   This deposit of gay-lussite varies in depth from twenty to one hundred and fifty feet, and extends over hundreds of miles.

Colorado. — The fossiliferous strata of Colorado, including Paleozoic, Secondary, and Tertiary deposits, have a maximum thickness of between twenty-four thousand and twenty-five thousand feet.

The Silurian rocks, scattered in various parts in small masses, hold a subordinate rank, they afford some limestones of the Trenton and Quebec epochs. In Southern Colorado, occurs an extensive development of massive blue limestone of the Devonian era.

The distinct lines separating the periods of the Carboniferous era in the eastern part of North America, are not so well-defined in the western regions The rocks of this formation, consisting largely of limestones more or less fossiliferous, but with the fossils not always well-preserved, include compact and blue-gray limestones. In this State, as in some other regions of the West, the Triassic strata cannot always be distinguished from the Jurassic, dolomites are interstratified with the former, and limestones, embracing blue, red, pink, and white varieties, with the latter. The Cretaceous formation covers a large area in the South and Southwest, where the beds are nearly horizontal. Tertiary and Quaternary deposits, though of far less extent than the Cretaceous, occupy no inconsiderable territory, while volcanic and eruptive rocks form a characteristic feature in the geology of the State. Colorado, remarkable for its mineral wealth, affords also many interesting natural and archæological features. Of the former are the cañons, with their perpendicular sides, hundreds and thousands of feet in depth; remarkable monuments of stone carved by the hand of Nature, rising, in some instances, from three to four hundred feet far above the forest trees, and walls of natural rock many hundred feet in height.

The famous "monuments," or pillars of native rock, caused by denudation, are generally of sandstone, or with base and column of shale capped with sandstone; some of them resemble the ruins of castles, with turrets and battlements.

The most remarkable objects found in this State and New Mexico are the cave and cliff dwellings, containing relics of a civilization superior to that of the present native races. Possessing a human interest, they excite the imagination more powerfully than any merely natural phenomenon can.

The cliff-houses or fortresses were constructed generally of stones on the elevated projections of massive rocks, often steep, and apparently inaccessible. The most extensive ruins in Colorado are said to be found at Aztec Springs. The stone for the dwellings was taken from an outcrop of fossiliferous limestone at the base of the Mesa Verde, a mile from the ruins.

Territories west of the Mississippi. — The Territories west of the Mississippi yield an abundance of limestones and gypsums, differing in age, color, and constitution, as may be learned from the valuable and interesting reports of Hayden, Powell, Ives, Newbery, and others. In Idaho and Wyoming, are found nearly all the formations, from the lowest to the most recent period. Of Paleozoic strata, the Calciferous, Lower Silurian, the Niagara, Upper Silurian, Carboniferous, and Sub-carboniferous limestones are recognized. The Carboniferous is of a blue color, massive and abundant ; the Sub-carboniferous is mostly magnesian. The Triassic strata, developed to a very limited extent, include a semi-crystalline limestone with Natica, and the Jurassic are represented by marls and limestones. The Tertiary strata afford drab, blue, and gray limestones ; some of the Idaho and Wyoming varieties are susceptible of a polish, and can be used as marble

The lower Triassic beds contain great quantities of gypsum of light red, gray, or yellow color, resembling alabaster in texture, and sometimes they are fibrous, yielding satin spar ; many of these gypsums are suitable for ornaments. Beds of hematite, affording red paint, form a deposit under the Sub-carboniferous limestones and dolomites.

The Eocene beds of Wyoming enclose gigantic vertebrates. The Cretaceous formation occupies extensive areas, and attains considerable thickness.

The gypsum deposits constitute the most conspicuous feature of the geology of the Indian Territory and New Mexico. They are placed between the Permian and Cretaceous periods, and are thought to represent a part of the Permian, the Triassic, and the Jurassic of Europe   The most magnificent display of this rock, perhaps, occurs in New Mexico   It is fossiliferous, and presents a great diversity of character and of remains.   The "Red Beds" of the gypseous series near Santa Fé, from one thousand five hundred to one thousand six hundred feet thick, are a very striking feature of the scenery.   Limestones form a large proportion of the rocks of the Santa Fé Mountains, including several varieties enclosing fossils characteristic of the Carboniferous period. Limestone with Fusilinæ (Rhizopods allied to the Nummulite), and of wide distribution, but found only in Carboniferous strata, occur in this region.

The bed of the Arkansas River is composed chiefly of white or cream-colored limestones.   The Tertiary strata of the Arkansas Basin are thought to resemble the fresh-water deposits of the Paris Basin, and the Mauvaisses series of the Upper Missouri, they contain masses of porous scoria   The Cretaceous deposits of New Mexico are on a grand scale; they embrace light-blue, compact limestones, charged with the Inoceramus, the Gryphaea, and other characteristic fossils

Perhaps there is no grander scenery in this region than that along the banks of the Colorado River, which has its source at an elevation of ten thousand or twelve thousand feet above sea level.   This stream once flowed, through five thousand miles of its course, over a table-land rising from five thousand to eight thousand feet; in the lapse of ages, its rapid waters cut a channel several thousand feet in depth through the mass of rocks, forming immense walls of solid masonry on either side

The Grand Cañon, one of the most magnificent gorges in the world, is six thousand eight hundred feet above sea level and five thousand five hundred above the Colorado.   The

upper strata consist of Carboniferous limestone, the lower of
granite, while between are beds of Silurian and Devonian
limestones, sandstones, and shales. The limestones found in
the valley of the Colorado present many varieties, some of
which are developed into marble. The Carboniferous forms
the surface rock, and the base upon which the San Francisco
Mountain rests. Its numerous and well-preserved fossils
render it a reliable guide in geological researches between the
Colorado and Mississippi Rivers.

Limestones of various colors, — variegated, crimson, yellow, cream-colored, light-blue, lemon-yellow, and bluish-gray,
— are developed in the Cañon of Cascade River, and those
of Marble Cañon afford beautiful marbles of white, gray, pink,
purple, and crimson colors.

In the Yellowstone valley, in Montana, several varieties of
limestones are developed, Silurian, Carboniferous, and Jurassic, including . brown, red, yellow, and blue, compact and
crystalline.

California. — Though celebrated for its mineral resources,
California is no less remarkable for its lofty mountains,
arranged in two principal groups, with several branches, —
the Coast Range, following the shore of the Pacific, and the
Sierra Nevada, forming the eastern barrier of the State. The
southern branch of the Coast Range is the Mount Diablo
Range, including several groups reaching to the Bay of San
Francisco on the northwest, and made up of a series of
mountains and valleys very formidable to explorers. The
Contra Costa Hills, one of the group, rising from the Bay,
are composed of Cretaceous and Tertiary strata, but little
changed by metamorphism ; the Cretaceous rocks are full of
organic remains

Mount Hamilton, one of the highest peaks of the Mount
Diablo Range, consists principally of metamorphic sandstones,
jasper, and serpentine, enclosed on all sides by strata unchanged   The jaspers, says Prof. J. D. Whitney, form the
characteristic rock, and with their brilliant red and light-green

colors, present a beautiful effect Argillaceous limestones are developed among the Cretaceous group on the north side, enclosing numerous fossils.

The Cretaceous and Tertiary systems are found in the environs of San Francisco, but the fossils are less abundant than in the Mount Diablo Range, and it is claimed that the Tertiary rocks have an extensive development towards the north.

A few miles from Santa Cruz, the sandstone assumes the picturesque form of the remains of buildings, bearing a resemblance to columns, capitals, and other architectural members, the whole known as the Ruined City.

Cinnabar ore is found in different formations, but the Cretaceous, according to Whitney, yields the best mines, it is developed in the Tertiary of the Coast Range. The mine of New Almaden ranks next to the Almaden of Spain, and the second in the world.

Limestones are not the characteristic rocks of California, yet they exist in many localities. At the summit of Black Mountain, an elevation of three thousand feet, occurs an outcrop of a hard, compact limestone like that seen in many different localities ; it has been quarried for lime, and portions of it enclose fossil fishes

The Cañon of St. Andreas displays a heavy mass of limestone several hundred feet in thickness, while a belt of limestone between the San Andreas and the San Mateo creeks, runs out to the ocean, forming headlands. The band of metamorphic limestone north of the Bay of San Francisco, appears to be a continuation of the San Andreas belt

Nearly the entire peninsula on which Benicia is built consists of low Cretaceous hills, on which rest Post-Tertiary deposits. Beds of hydraulic limestone have been extensively quarried near Benicia, enclosing the Trigonia, one species of which, as stated by Prof. Whitney, is a very characteristic and widely-distributed fossil, of the Lower Cretaceous, found on the Pacific coast, from Central California to Vancouver's

Island. The Suisun marble occurs in the Cretaceous strata of the Pelevo Hills, south of the Suisun valley, for which it was named. This marble, or more properly alabaster, is a deposit from calcareous springs, of a deep brownish-yellow color, with a banded structure, and is an elegant ornamental stone, but unfortunately does not exist in large masses. It is much to be regretted that it should ever have been burned for quicklime. Travertine is deposited at a short distance from the quarry.

. In the San Luis Range, a zone of compact limestone was deposited, enclosing numerous fossil oysters, often of a gigantic size; and beds of crystalline limestone containing graphite form one of the constituents of the San Antonia Hills. Metamorphic limestone is abundant in some parts of the Gavilan Range and forms the culminating points; a similar variety is found near Fort Tèjon. A deposit of calcareous tufa has been formed at Tuscan Springs, which is finely banded, and bears a close resemblance to the Suisun marble and the limestones on the west side of Monte Diablo.

Prof. Whitney advances the opinion that the Coast Ranges were uplifted since the Cretaceous period, while the Sierra Nevada were elevated before that time. He says a belt of marine Cretaceous and Tertiary deposits runs along the base of the Sierras, while vast masses of fresh-water strata cover a considerable portion; they include the gold-bearing deposits, consisting largely of metamorphic slates and sandstones.

The grand Sierra Nevada group rivals the Alps in extent and height; the culminating peak, Mount Whitney, the loftiest known in this country, reaches a height of fifteen thousand feet, while some of its cañons are cut to the depth of two thousand or three thousand feet. It is said that from Mount Tyndall, one of the peaks, may be seen five mountains more than fourteen thousand, and fifty more than thirteen thousand feet high. Mount Shasta, an extinct volcano, composed of lava, crowned with *red* snow, is nearly four thousand feet higher than Mount Etna.

Though granite is the prevailing rock of the lofty Sierras on the western flanks, yet limestones are more or less extensively developed in their numerous ranges. On the northern foot-hills, beds of calcareous deposits, called Pence's Ranch limestone, extending several miles, are capable of being worked for gray marble. The fossils, consisting of Crinoids, the Producta, and the Spirifer, assign it to the Carboniferous period. A white crystalline limestone with graphite, and penetrated by dikes of basalt, occurs at Fremont's Pass, and another with dark bands, affording a beautiful stone, is found on the Kern River.

In Tuolumne County, occur Tertiary and Post-Tertiary deposits, remarkable for the remains of the Mastodon, the Elephant, and other Mammals The Sierra limestone, well-developed in this county, is more or less crystalline, of various shades of gray passing into white, but is destitute of fossils, so far as is known; on the north fork of the Merced River, it forms the picturesque grotto called Bower Cave. Trees more than one hundred and thirty feet in height are flourishing at the entrance, forty feet below the stream. The Tuolumne formation is distributed over considerable territory, and is intersected by numerous trap-dikes, and throughout its whole extent this limestone is considered a productive area for placer-mining In some localities it is quarried for monumental and architectural purposes, but it does not well bear exposure to atmospheric influences

At Texas Flat, on the Stanislaus River, travertine has been deposited in cliffs similar to coral-reefs enclosing the remains of Mammals and fresh-water shells.

The most striking feature of this county is Table Mountain, a mass of basalt which flowed for forty miles down the slope of the Sierra, in a stream from one hundred and forty to one hundred and fifty feet deep, and in portions of its course nearly two thousand in width. From its homogeneous character, Prof Whitney thinks it may have been poured out at one eruption.

The limestone at Murphy's Creek, where it affords a grand and picturesque view, is dark-gray, with large veins of quartz, yielding gold, copper, and cinnabar. The copper mines yield masses of beautiful malachite. This limestone, at Cave City, forms an extensive cavern, with long, winding passages, chambers, stalactites and other forms of calcareous deposits peculiar to caves. The limestone of Tuolumne and Calaveras Counties extends into Amador as far as Volcano, where it is seen as a white, saccharoidal marble with blue clouding, resembling that of Sonora. Like the Tuolumne limestone it is cavernous, and encloses auriferous deposits. The Sierra limestone occurs in detached masses in Placer County, in Marble Valley of El Dorado County, and other localities. A zone of crystalline limestone with a few imperfect fossils, probably the stems of Crinoids, has been laid down in the Genesee valley.

At Bass's Ranch, near the Upper Sacramento River, is a locality said to be the only one known in the State where any considerable number of fossils have been found in the Sierra Nevada limestone. The rock is a peculiar grayish-blue color, and is characterized by great masses of pyrites, some of them being several cubic feet in size, and enormous crystals of garnet. The limestone has a large development forming the hills called Gray Mountains or Marble Mountains, two thousand feet in height; the fossils are those of the Carboniferous period. Whitney discovered fourteen species belonging to eleven different genera, six of the species being considered new.

Marble and gypsum are found in Owen's Mountains, one of the Sierra Nevada group.

Limestones constitute the principal rock in the Great Basin extending over the southeast part of California, forming entire groups of lofty and rugged mountains. This region is the only one yet explored, on or near the Pacific Coast, where limestones cover any considerable territory.

The Temescal Range contains a heavy mass of porphyry,

passing from gray into dark-green and chocolate-brown, interspersed with crystals of white feldspar, making a very beautiful stone resembling the best Swedish porphyry.

The Cretaceous system is developed in Oregon east of the Cascade Range ; marine Tertiary beds occur along the Pacific Coast. The Miocene Tertiary, near Astoria on the Columbia, and on the Willamette River, consists of shale and sandstone. It is said that no northern drift is found in Oregon, though very thick deposits of this character occur in some regions, both stratified and unstratified.

CHAPTER VII.

LIMESTONES OF BRITISH AMERICA AND THE WEST INDIA ISLANDS.

I. *British America.* —The Eozoic rocks are distributed over the entire globe, but not in every country are they so fully represented as in Canada. Including the Laurentian and the Huronian they have, probably, an aggregate thickness of fifty thousand feet. With few exceptions they are meta-, morphic, and include granitic and hornblendic rocks, lime-stones, dolomites, porphyries, serpentines, and the beautiful opalescent labradorite.

The Laurentian series in Canada is supposed to cover an area of two hundred thousand square miles, but from the absence of fossils the chronological order of the series remains undetermined. The rocks yield rare and valuable metals and minerals, one of the rarest being the sulphuret of molybdenum, useful as a chemical reagent, and as a blue dye for silk and cotton fabrics, while among the more common products are magnetic iron, plumbago, mica, and other minerals.

The composition of the Laurentian limestones, it is said, makes them of considerable scientific importance, affording more essential aid in deciding the structure of the series than do those rocks whose different strata more closely resemble one another, though there is, to a greater or less extent, a similarity in the lithological character of these limestones.

These rocks are easily disintegrated, constituting a very productive soil, and possess the qualities for making excellent lime   They are generally highly crystalline, coarse-grained,

Plate IX.

ENGLISH SERPENTINE.

GRIOTTE.

ARMSTRONG & CO. LITH. BOSTON.

sometimes saccharoidal, but not fine enough to be called compact, in color they are commonly white, but sometimes gray, salmon, red, blue, yellow, dark-green, dove-color, or purple, with a banded appearance, produced by the distinct arrangement of the light and dark colors. •The marble is not suitable for statuary, but has been used for architectural purposes, as in the Parliament buildings at Ottawa. A white marble, marked with spots and patches of green serpentine, has been obtained near the Rouge River.

Although the Laurentian rocks have been considered Azoic, yet Mr. McMullen discovered what were thought to be fossil remains in a limestone at Grand Calumet When first discovered, the fossil was believed to be a coral resembling the Stromatopora rugosa, but it has since been classed with the Rhizopods, and called the Eozoon Canadense. The same fossils have been detected in dark-green serpentine with crystalline dolomite.

The porphyries of the Laurentian series are of a superior quality for ornamental uses ; they present harmonious contrasts of color, comprising a variety of dark-gray or black ground, with deep flesh-red crystals, capable of receiving a brilliant polish, and a hard, compact, green porphyry, with red, brown, and black spots, the green often passing into olive or chocolate brown

Labradorite often constitutes mountain ranges, and great boulders of this rock, with iridescent portions, are frequently met with The opalescent varieties, used for ornament, occur as cleavable masses enclosed in a fine-grained paste of the same mineral character, and when thickly disseminated, render the stone useful for decoration. The best specimens are found near Abercrombie, where the rock is lavender-blue, fine-grained, with opalescent spots, producing a play of gold-green, bronze-green, and ultramarine-blue

Serpentines are found in Eozoic and Paleozoic strata, and though they have been considered by some geologists intrusive rocks, it is claimed that the Laurentian and the Paleozoic

serpentines of Canada, are sedimentary and stratified.   The
Laurentian are paler in color and more tender than those of
the Green Mountains, therefore less valuable for decoration.
A variety occurs of oil-green or sulphur-yellow masses in a
white, crystalline base, presenting a banded appearance, and
another of pale-green with clouds of rich brown, green, and
red.

In the Quebec group, Lower Silurian, serpentines constitute
the mass of rock, they are generally dark-colored and better
for ornament than the Laurentian.   Much of the formation is
distinctly stratified, and it is frequently clouded with red and
brown   The serpentine of Eastern Canada is mixed with
dolomite, like the European, and resembles the serpentine of
Roxbury and Cavendish, Vermont, which is called Verde
antique.

The great Silurian formations of New York are traced, by
an identity of fossils, through Canada and other parts of
British America   Of the Lower Silurian, the Calciferous,
Chazy, Bird's Eye, Black River, and Trenton are represented.
The Calciferous formation yields a few beds of magnesian
limestone, the Chazy some, while the Bird's Eye, Black River,
and Trenton limestones are fully developed, but the distinctions between these groups in Canada, are less definite than in
New York.

In the vicinity of Montreal, the Chazy limestone abounds
in the Rhynchonella plena, in the valley of the Bonne-Chère
River, this formation, combined with the Black River and the
Trenton, displays nearly fifty beds differing in character and
thickness   Some varieties are afforded by the Utica and Cincinnati groups

The River St Lawrence flows through a region of fossiliferous strata of the Silurian age, consisting, in great part, of
limestones of different tinted grays and various kinds of
structures, and all more or less charged with organic remains.

The Chazy and Trenton limestones, replete with shells,
afford brown, light, and dark-red, and dove-colored marbles,

while the Trenton alone develops a black and a fine gray mottled with red and yellow.   The gray limestones in the vicinity of Montreal are sometimes used as marble, but they are of dull colors and do not polish well, two radical faults in marble.   A fine-grained, compact limestone, suitable for lithographic purposes, is afforded by the Bird's Eye and the Black River formations.   The Trenton limestone forms a broad belt of considerable extent, ranging from the Gulf of St. Lawrence to Western Canada ; it forms a part of the rocks at the Falls of Montmorency, and is developed near the cities of Ottawa and Montreal   It is quarried at the latter place, and has been used for some of the fine buildings and other structures of the city, especially the excellent quays and canal docks ; it is gray, with a granular structure owing to the crystalline texture of the organic remains   The Trenton is employed for building-stone at Quebec, where the tint is more inclining to yellow than that of Montreal, and bears better exposure to the weather.

Several new genera of Silurian fossils have been discovered in the Canadian rocks, including Crinoids, Cystids, Astrias, Brachiopods, Gasteropods, Cephalopods, and Crustaceans. Most of these recent discoveries were made in the Trenton and the Chazy limestones of Ottawa and Montreal, in the Black River series, and the limestones of Anticosti and the Mingan Islands. .

The extensive Quebec group, Lower Silurian, older than the Chazy, is especially Canadian, since it was first recognized by the geologists of Canada, and because all the series are well represented there.   The group has a thickness of about seven thousand feet, and yields a variety of limestones of different colors, from white to black, with red and white dolomites containing geodes.   Some of the Quebec limestones afford fine-grained, white, black, greenish, and dove-colored marbles.

At Point Lévis, near Quebec, dolomites and limestones occur, the latter frequently forming masses many feet in thickness, without any visible marks of stratification or of organic remains. They are compact, conchoidal, sub-translucent, with a banded structure, which leads to the conclusion that they are chemical deposits from water, or travertines ; they are pure carbonate of lime and of different shades of pearl-gray, sometimes pale green. Interstratified with these travertines, are found beds of fine, granular limestone with Orthoceratites, Trilobites, and other fossils of a marine character, affording an instance of alternate subsidences and elevations. Besides these travertines and limestones, there occurs at Point Lévis a conglomerate of a peculiar character.

The Anticosti series of rocks extends through the Upper Silurian and Devonian into the Carboniferous, embracing in the group a large development of limestones. They were deposited in a quiet sea, in uninterrupted succession, and enclose fossil fauna hitherto unknown in North America, hence they are highly important and interesting. The upper layers consist of white limestones, crowded with the remains of large Crinoids, but enclosing few other fossils. The south side of the island is generally low, the most elevated points consisting of cliffs on Jupiter River, from eighty to one hundred and fifty feet in height, but the whole of the north side is a succession of ridge-like elevations from two hundred to five hundred feet, while Macastry Mount attains the height of one thousand four hundred feet. The masses of limestone contributing to form these elevations are more or less fossi- liferous and varied, grays forming the predominant color. A coarse, granular limestone, of a yellowish white, is displayed at West Point, on the island, which forms a good building- stone, and was used for the construction of the lighthouse at this place. The limestones of Anticosti are regularly strati- fied, forming nearly horizontal beds two thousand three hundred feet thick. Those of the Mingan Islands, a chain of very small islands north of Anticosti, are similar, and include the Bird's Eye, Black River, and Trenton groups ; the Anticosti series is also found in western Canada.

The Gaspé limestones, named for Cape Gaspé, of Eastern Canada, a variable formation, are classed with the Upper Silurian or Devonian; they are widely disseminated, and consist of beds aggregating two thousand feet. The yellow, red, and green jaspers, frequently of brilliant colors, called Gaspé pebbles, are found in these limestones.

The Guelph formation, Upper Silurian, wanting in New York, is largely magnesian, containing light-drab, compact dolomites and a buff-colored coralline limestone. Those of the Lower Helderberg, Upper Silurian, including the Tentaculite, Pentamerus, Spirifer, Encrinal, and Hydraulic varieties, are all represented. Many of the Pentamerus beds attain considerable thickness. The limestones of the Niagara group are found in British America as well as in the United States, while the Corniferous and Hamilton of the Devonian, including Encrinal limestones, cover a large extent of territory, the former six thousand or seven thousand square miles Excellent building-stone is afforded by the Niagara, the Guelph, and the Corniferous groups The limestones thought to be Devonian, yield a great variety of marbles, comprising a cream-colored, with ochre-yellow veins, a dark-gray and yellow breccia with yellow veins, resembling the Porto Venere of Italy, not only in appearance but in composition.

When the limestones of the solid strata of the Thames, in Ontario, are smoothly polished, they present the appearance of red and yellow marble crossed with lines of white, forming a natural mosaic pavement. In some of the coral limestones of Canada, the fossils project in masses several feet in diameter, and from one to five feet from the rock, covering the surface with large, irregular protuberances

A limestone enclosing the Spirifer, a characteristic fossil of the Hamilton group, is developed on the shores of Lake Huron. Cape Breton Island affords gray and white marbles, and variegated marble of the Carboniferous period occurs north and west of Plaister Cove. Serpentine, and a pure white marble with a variety of purple and green, of the Upper Silurian, are found at Fire Islands.

The Hudson Bay territory is chiefly composed of Upper Silurian limestones, thought to be littoral deposits, and Silurian limestones extend along the western side of the granitic chain from Lake Winnipeg to the mouth of the Mackenzie, and from the edges of the continent to the Arctic Sea. The Lake Winnipeg limestone contains gigantic Orthoceras and Receptaculites

II. THE WEST INDIA ISLANDS — *Cuba* — Madrepore limestone, enclosing marine shells, constitutes the principal rock near Havana, where it is quarried and has been employed in the construction of the city A singular breccia prevails in the northeastern part of the island, composed of white marble, or a kind of stalagmitic limestone, with numerous cavities filled by calcareous deposits of a brick-red, the shells of several species of land snails, marine univalves, and the bones of quadrupeds

This peculiar conglomerate, deposited in caves remote from the shore, has been accounted for in the following ingenious manner: Quadrupeds and land snails resorted to these caverns, where they left their bones and shells, the red portions of the rock were formed by the coprolites of bats, which also frequent such places; and the well-known habits of the hermit-crab account for the presence of marine fossils The crabs resort to the sea-shore, appropriate the shells of other animals and bear them away to these mountain retreats. All these materials, collected by different agencies, were cemented by carbonate of lime deposited by the water percolating the crevices, in the manner of stalactites, forming solid beds of marble elevated several feet above the sea

Jamaica — The coast ranges of Jamaica rise on all sides, either directly from the shore or at some distance inland The eastern portion of the island is mountainous, the western, hilly, affording the sources of more than one hundred rivers.

with numerous tributaries   The sub-structure appears to consist everywhere of igneous rocks, superimposed by limestone, which form the principal surface strata.

The White limestone and the Coast limestone constitute a Tertiary formation, reaching a depth of more than two thousand feet, and covering five-eighths of the island.   It encloses land shells, and is compact, brecciated, or of a cellular structure, due to the solvent power of water.

The White limestone has a large development, forming the northern coast range, and the capes and promontories extending beyond the influence of freshwater   In places it is elevated several thousand feet, and where washed by the sea, it exhibits a coral structure.   By some geologists this limestone is considered the equivalent of the Calcaire grossier of the Eocene, while others assign it to the Miocene   It encloses Rhizopods, Lamellibranchs and Gasteropods, similar to those now living in the adjacent waters, and appears to have been deposited "slowly and steadily in the bed of a tranquil sea "

The beds at Port. Royal Parish are said to resemble the Jurassic limestones in mineral characteristics.

The Coast limestone has less extent, is never seen at great elevation, is rarely found inland, and is of recent origin   The White and the Coast limestones produce two different kinds of soil, one white, resembling chalky marl, the other red ; the latter, from its superior fertility, is appropriated to the cultivation of coffee.   The brecciated variety of this formation is well-displayed in a place called the Devil's Hole, where it is one thousand feet in thickness, resting upon five hundred or six hundred feet of laminated limestone , it is also found on the summits of hills two thousand or three thousand feet above sea-level.   The compact variety of the series is characterized by large fissures and caves

Below the White limestone occurs the Yellow limestone formation of Miocene age, five hundred feet thick, and comprising numerous interstratified thin beds essentially marine. This limestone, during an epoch of subsidences, sank to great depths, in places, more than one thousand feet, affording room for the great coral formations, which, in turn, contributed the débris for the enormous White limestone strata deposited during an almost inconceivably long period of time. The Yellow limestone is variable, full of fossils, and portions of it yield marbles This formation is superimposed by a compact variety with Orbitoides.

The Cretaceous system includes a Hippurite limestone, and other species which have lost their fossiliferous character by metamorphism. The lower strata include a compact, massive limestone with large Radiolites, occasionally seven feet in length, and is of variable color, sometimes light, sometimes dark-blue or black. The Cretaceous group is of the same age as the Hippurite of the south of Europe, and differs from the Cretaceous of the other West India Islands. The beds are separated by very fine lines of decomposed green or purple shale, producing colored bands in the rock The more calcareous part is not finely granular, like statuary marble, but yields a compact, crystalline limestone, capable of a good polish and of being used as marble. The group is often crossed by copper veins.

Jamaica is well supplied with building stone from the finest marble to the coarsest sandstone. Marbles are abundant along the southern base of the central chain of the eastern mountains, and a great variety occurs in other localities, including black, white, green striped with gray, and white with brown and red. A chalk of sufficient firmness for building was used in the church at St. Antonio, the best specimen of architecture, it is said, in Jamaica. Besides marbles this island yields serpentines, porphyries, granites, travertines, and various colored ochres, all serviceable for domestic use or as articles of commerce.

Coral limestones cover six-sevenths of the Island of barbadoes, including a siliceous variety.   A part are hard, compact, with conchoidal fracture, and are quarried for building-stone, while those of a porous texture are used for infiltration

A conglomerate formed of basalt, peridot, titanic iron, and spar, cemented by yellow limestone, is found in the Sandwich Islands, and is used by the natives for disks employed in games.

CHAPTER VIII.

I. *Mexico.* — The great chain of the Andes, passing through the Isthmus of Panama and traversing Central America and Mexico, presents in these countries many of the features that characterize it in South America. In both regions the range comprises volcanic peaks, elevated table-lands, and rock systems similar in character. Some of the limestone formations found in one country occur also in the other; thus a variety, called by Humboldt the "Alpine," which he considers similar to the Zechstein, Permian, but which is regarded Jurassic by some other European geologists, extends along the Cordilleras of Mexico, constituting the native rocks of many of the rich silver mines of this region

The great table-land of Mexico, rising from seven thousand to eight thousand feet, is largely porphyritic, some of the strata enclose garnets and the beautiful fire-opal, so much admired as a gem A coarse, granular limestone of the so-called Alpine formation is, in some localities, associated with the porphyry It occurs in immense masses near the salt lake Tuspa, and is sometimes found with compact, specular gypsum of a bluish-gray, with calcite veins, and frequently passes into a white, compact rock, resembling the limestones of Pappenheim of the Jurassic period. It is seen in different places, often forming caverns.

A limestone formation with the upper layers whitish and the lower grayish, with large masses of calc spar, occurs near Mazatlan and Chilpansingo.

The vast table-land between Alto de las Caxones and Mus-cala, is composed of limestones, gypsums, and sandstones.   A bluish-gray limestone, found throughout a considerable extent of territory, enclosing few fossils, generally compact, with occasional white, granular beds, underlies a formation re-sembling the "Alpine"; this limestone is remarkable for its caverns

We are indebted to the reports of Mr A Rémond, edited by Prof J. D Whitney, for the geological investigation of Northern Mexico, including the States of Durango, Chihuahua, Sinaloa, and Sonora.   He says that the oldest sedimentary rocks belong to the Carboniferous series, represented in Sonora by parallel ridges of massive limestone following the general direction of the Sierra Madre.   It is bluish in color, fine-grained, enclosing flint nodules, and with associated schists reaches, probably, five thousand feet in thickness   At Her-mosillo, the rock is converted into white, saccharoidal marble, and at La Cruz and some other localities it encloses Crinoids; the fossils of this limestone are generally well-preserved The formation contains argentiferous veins, and above it rests the Triassic: it is doubtful whether the metamorphic slates and limestones, which include the richest gold placers of Sonora, belong to this or to the Jurassic period, as the fossils are too imperfect to leave no doubt on the subject.

The beds considered Jurassic, though their age cannot be determined beyond doubt, contain layers of variously colored limestones entirely made up of fossils   An argillaceous lime-stone, loaded with shells, occurs at a hill called "Cerro de las Conchas," or "Shell Mountain," and constitutes a depository of Cretaceous fossils of great interest.

The most beautiful and interesting formation of Mexico is the so-called Onyx marble, a calcareous alabaster, the result of chemical agencies, which equals, if it does not surpass, in beauty, the antique Onyx marble of Algeria.   Its translucency, its soft, delicate lines of stratification, its deep orange and light green spots or clouds, and its exquisite polish, render it one of the most attractive of ornamental marbles.

The Isthmus of Tehuantepec, in Southern Mexico, presents but little variety in geological formations, and but few mineral productions, compared to the rich and varied re. sources of other parts of this country. In his Surveys of the Isthmus, R. W Shufeldt, U. S. N., says that there are two limestone belts running nearly parallel with the Atlantic and the Pacific, whose synclinal valley between the ranges forms the table-land or mesas of Tarifa and Chivala. The northern or Masahua Range appears to be the continuation of the Cordilleras, and forms the dividing ridge between the two oceans; the southern is the Majada Range. The nucleus of these ridges is blue limestone, which forms everywhere the summits and highest peaks of the belts.

Coarse, yellowish chalk deposits denote the presence of the Cretaceous system, and the Tertiary is represented by a soft and a compact blue limestone. Calcareous tufas and breccias, dolomites, marbles, porphyries, and granites form a part of the rocks of this region.

II. *South America.* — The most characteristic geological feature of South America is the great chain of the Andes, extending the entire length of the American Continent, and remarkable for its lofty peaks, the highest exceeding twenty-five thousand feet, its precipitous western slope of an ascent from one hundred to one hundred and fifty feet to a mile, and its elevated passes, varying from more than twelve thousand to more than sixteen thousand feet above sea-level. The enormous mass constituting this extensive range presents interesting alternations in the composition of the strata. In portions of the chain, granite forms the fundamental rock; in others clay slates, of which entire mountains are composed; then porphyries, which, perhaps, predominate; trachytes, sandstones, limestones, gypsums, and serpentines have also contributed to the framework of this mountain system, traversing two continents through their entire length of seven thousand or eight thousand miles.

It is the opinion of Hartt that the fundamental rock of the

whole Brazilian plateau is gneiss, which forms the mountain chains along the Atlantic Coast.   Earlier geologists believed that no fossiliferous strata older than the Cretaceous were found in this region, but recent investigations have made it nearly certain that Eozoic and Paleozoic rocks are represented ; and that on the Amazons, fossil series embrace Carboniferous, Devonian, and Upper Silurian strata.   In regard to the age of the Brazilian rocks, Agassiz says there is no sequence, as in North America, of Eozoic and Paleozoic strata, though fossils have been detected here and there peculiar to the latter ; that the oldest trustworthy data are of the Cretaceous period, and its strata formed the basin of the Amazons, with extensive deposits of recent age ; but it was his belief that there were no remains of Tertiary beds.   Throughout the extent of the basin, this naturalist traced three distinct formations ; a stratified sandstone formed the lowest, superimposed by laminated clays, presenting a variety of colors, pink, orange, crimson, yellow, gray,-blue, black, and white, affording pigments to the native Indians ; then a ferruginous sandstone with quartz pebbles ; and above this a drift formation of reddish, sandy clay   This series is very extensive, reaching from the Atlantic to the foot of the Andes, and constitutes a peculiar feature.

Somewhat conflicting with the above statements are the views of Hartt, who writes that the metamorphic rocks of the Amazonian region include crystalline limestone, probably Laurentian, and Carboniferous strata very rich in organic remains, including numerous species of Corals, Echinoderms, Bryozoans, Brachiopods, Lamellibranchs, Gasteropods, and Trilobites   On the authority of Dana, the Jurassic system is found in many regions of the Andes, from their northern limit to Tierra del Fuego.

In South Brazil limestones are very rare.   A bed of white marble occurs at Barra, which is of a coarsely crystalline texture and bluish tint, and encloses green serpentine ; in some places it contains what resembles the Eozoon

The table-land of Brazil is crossed by a limestone chain, excavated by numerous caverns, in which have been discovered human remains and the bones of extinct animals. Lund claims to have found these remains in six of the six hundred caverns of this formation, but in only one were the human remains mingled with those of extinct animal species.

The Tertiary system is largely represented in Brazil, and includes a calcareous tufa, or limestone called "Tosca," and the extensive formation called Pampas, composed of red clayey earth, with calcareous concretions and numerous fossils, some of extinct and others of recent species. It is said by Darwin that the whole area of the South American Pampas is one wide sepulchre of gigantic quadrupeds. More than one hundred species, now extinct, have been discovered in this formation.

W O Crosby, who has visited this region, says that Guiana and Venezuela are mainly composed of crystalline rocks. The Tertiary basin of Venezuela, connected with the vast Tertiary plain of the Amazons, includes limestones, combined with serpentine, supposed to enclose the Eozoon, and are probably Laurentian   There occur other crystalline limestones of great thickness, varying in color from white to nearly black. A compact limestone, resembling the Trenton, is very fossiliferous, enclosing bivalves resembling the Nucula, and univalves like the Murchisonia.

Among the limestones of the extensive plains of Venezuela, beds of gypsum are developed, and in the eastern part the surface is overspread with pebbles of ribbon jasper, called "Egyptian pebbles," while in the northern part Cretaceous rocks occur.

Limestones are developed in the Andes of Ecuador, associated with gypsum and rock-salt, and on the table-land of Quito appears a white limestone resembling Carrara marble, alternated with a banded, translucent marble, employed by the inhabitants for statuary, and the windows of chapels and convents   This formation, displayed on the banks of the Llano de Tarqui, resembles in its banded structure, alabaster, and was probably a travertine deposit, analogous to the Mexican onyx.

Bluish-gray granular limestones with particles of quartz are found in New Grenada.

A limestone of the Andes is frequently mentioned by Humboldt under the name of " Alpine" limestone, on account of the resemblance he noted between its fossils and those of this formation in Europe, but the name is inappropriate for a formation on the Western Continent, and is not very generally adopted here. The limestone thus designated is grayish, bluish, and occasionally reddish, often passing from compact to fine granular, intersected by small veins of calcite, which gives the stone great brilliancy ; sometimes it is bituminous, and the source of mineral pitch and hydrogen vapors.

In Peru, it includes immense beds of flint, and veins of red and gray silver, and is found at an elevation of more than thirteen thousand feet, enclosing Gryphites, Terebratulae, and Ammonites, fossils of the Jurassic and Cretaceous periods, while in Venezuela and Mexico this formation is highly crystalline.

Porphyry of a columnar structure forms a very characteristic rock in this country, constituting mountains of considerable height   One species exhibits numerous large crystals of hornblende, forming a stone similar to the Porfido verde of the ancients   Among other species, are a green porphyry, a variety enclosing black mica, and another of hard, fine texture, and black color, resembling the stone of many of the Egyptian statues, formely supposed to be basalt.

The mounds or " shell-heaps," the work of the early inhabitants, form an interesting feature in the geological history of Peru, inasmuch as they prove the upheaval of the coast. These mounds, some being sixty metres high, were undoubtedly made near the sea, but they now occupy a place from eighteen to twenty miles inland. They enclose shells of the Venus, a living species, and two species of the Corbula, not now found on the coast.

One of the most characteristic geological features of Chili are the terrace-plains, consisting of shingle or rolled pebbles and gravel.

The rocks sliding down from the precipitous sides of the Andes, and forming immense masses in the valleys, include porphyries of great thickness, red sandstones, conglomerates, limestones, and clay slates, passing into vast beds of gypsum, while the base and sides of the hills are covered with bright red and purple porphyry. The marine shells on the summits of mountains, at an elevation as high as fourteen hundred feet, lying scattered about or embedded in the soil, show that the coast has been raised to that extent above its original level.

The calcareous rocks of Chili include limestones, marbles, and gypsums. The limestones are variable in color and texture, and yield marbles, including white statuary, black, green, yellow, gray, and parti-colored, as gray with white, yellow and blue veins; and green with black and brown. The latter has been quarried at San Fernando, and is held in high esteem. It is said there are two mountains in this country which consist principally of marble zones of various colors, and that marble is very abundant in the lower Andes. In the plains near Coquimbo, there are beds of a white marble, of the nature of a lumachelle, more than three miles in extent, with an average thickness of two feet. Pinkerton says that the Chilian marbles are generally of good quality, and susceptible of a fine polish. It is stated that Muscovy glass, a kind of mica, is found in this country in great perfection, both as regards color and the size of the crystals; it is used for glazing and in the manufacture of artificial flowers.

The Tertiary formation east of the Andes, including the concretionary limestone called Tosca, and covered by the Pampas, is very extensive, reaching to Tierra del Fuego. Patagonia, one of the least attractive regions of the continent, and of which little is known save the fabulous tales told by Magellan and his crew, of the gigantic stature of the natives, has a geological interest above that of some more favored

Plate X.

CAMPAN VERT.

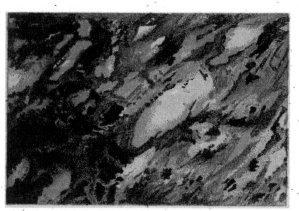

VERDE ANTICO.

countries. One great deposit, writes Darwin, extending for five hundred miles along the coast, consists of Tertiary shells of extinct species, the most characteristic being·a gigantic oyster; this formation is covered by a peculiar soft, white stone, enclosing gypsum, which resembles chalk, and is composed largely of marine infusoria. :· At Port St. Julian, in the southeast, the formation is eight hundred feet thick. Above it rests a mass of gravel remarkable for its extent, covering an area of six hundred or seven hundred miles from north to south, and perhaps two hundred miles in width; its greatest depth is believed to be two hundred and its average fifty feet. The pebbles of this shingle, consisting of older rocks, were rolled and transported subsequently to the formation of the white strata, and both after the Tertiary, proving the inconceivable duration of geological eras. The plains of Patagonia rise one above another like terraces, the lowest having an elevation of ninety feet, the highest nine hundred and fifty; the shells covering the plains still retain, to a considerable degree, their natural colors In the south of Patagonia, occurs a great basaltic platform.

The limestones of Patagonia, referred to the Tertiary, are of several varieties, including a marly limestone with dendrites found near the Negro River.

Limestones are found in the valley of the Uruguay, though granite is the rock of most frequent occurrence Serpentines similar to those of Saxony are developed near Caraccas and Venezuela.

The Island of Trinidad, forming one of the British West Indian islands, is, by its geographical position and its geological structure, intimately connected with the mainland, from which it is separated by a channel only a few miles in width, that is gradually filling up with alluvial or other deposits. The coast line of Venezuela, thus extended, may eventually take in the entire area of this large island. . The rocks constituting the mountains of Trinidad are identical with those of the coast from the Orinoco to Caraccas, and consist of Paleozoic, Tertiary, and recent deposits; the Cretaceous formation is said to occur in portions of the llanos of Venezuela.

Crystalline limestones in large masses, including many varieties of color, with numerous fossils whose distinctive characteristics are partially obliterated, are found in Trinidad. They have been referred both to the Devonian and Carboniferous periods, but W. O. Crosby considers them Taconic of the Eozoic era; the newer beds, however, resemble the Trenton limestone of the Lower Silurian.

CHAPTER IX.

In his Manual of Geology, Mr. J. B. Jukes makes the following statement: "The structure of the British Islands is better known than that of any other part of the globe of equal size, and they contain a more complete series of rocks in a small space than are found in any other district."

For an investigation, classification, and naming of the rocks of the Silurian system in Wales and the west of England, the geologist is indebted to Sir R I. Murchison, though his grouping has been somewhat modified by subsequent writers.

The representative limestones of the Lower Silurian best developed in Wales are, the Bala, twenty-five feet in thickness, including the Hirnant, ten feet more, and the Caradoc In Merionethshire, in the northwest part of Wales, are the town and lake of Bala, where the group named for this locality is best displayed; a few miles from Bala, the Hirnant valley gives its name to a subordinate limestone belonging to the same group. On account of their impurities, the Bala limestones are no longer quarried. Towards Shropshire, or Salop, the Bala limestones pass into a sandstone enclosing calcareous beds called the Caradoc, from Caer or Camp Caradoc, a hill bearing the name of the king of the ancient Silures whom his Roman conquerors designated Caractacus.

Carnarvonshire in the northwest is pervaded by associations of historical interest, and abounds in scenes of natural beauty and grandeur. Near the ancient town of Bangor, stands Penrhyn Castle, built of gray Mona or Anglesey marble

obtained from the Island of Anglesey, erected on the site of
the old palace of Mochwynog, Prince of Wales, in 720, the
Penrhyn slate quarries are not far from here. Beaumaris
Castle, with its Moorish towers and beautiful canopied niches,
was erected on Anglesey by Edward I.; and not far from the
ruins are the quarries from which the Anglesey marble, used
in constructing many of these strongholds, was mined *

The Castle of Carnarvon, built by this conquering prince
and celebrated as the birthplace of Edward II., is an immense
pile, with walls ten feet thick, defended by thirteen towers.
The Romans, during their occupation of the country of the
Silures, built the town of Segontium, the remains of which
are still to be seen near the present Carnarvon.

In this interesting region rises the highest mountain south
of the border, the Snowdon, a name made classic by the great
Scottish bard. It is composed mostly of slate, remarkable
for hardness and fineness of texture, and a calcareous ash or
volcanic tufa, the representative of the Bala limestones resting
upon igneous rocks which sometimes penetrate the strata,
causing " dislocations and ruinous heaps of disjointed beds."
Including all the contemporaneous rocks, the Bala beds are
from ten thousand to twelve thousand feet thick, but of this
immense mass only a small portion is limestone   The fauna
of this group is extensive, enclosing, says Sir C. Lyell, five
hundred and sixty-five species, three hundred and fifty-two of
them being peculiar to the series ; Brachiopods predominate,
while Trilobites attain their maximum

It is believed that the group, including Orthoceratite and
Maclurea limestones, is developed in Scotland from Dumfries
to the Lammermuir Hills   The Wrae limestone of Peebles-
shire is a Lower Silurian formation.

The Bala and Caradoc groups, with some bands of limestone, occur in the counties of Wicklow, Wexford, and Water-

* Besides the gray Anglesey, this island develops a black, and a green and
white serpentine marble of the Cambrian period which may be analogous
to the Irish Connemara.

ford, Ireland, while in the "Chair of Kildare," hills west of Dublin, the calcareous rocks abound in the characteristic fossils of this formation.

The mountains known as the "Bins of Connemara" are Lower Silurian, the green and white crystalline rock, called Connemara marble, or Serpentine, is of the same age.

The typical limestones of the Upper Silurian are the Woolhope or Barr, the Wenlock or Dudley, and the Aymestry or Ludlow.

The Woolhope or Barr forms the western declivity of the Malvern Hills, famous in literature for the vision of Piers Ploughman. On one side lies the valley of the Severn, on the other, flows the "sylvan Wye" between its picturesque banks. The scenery of this region is delightfully varied by commanding summits, wooded banks, shaded glens, and bold escarpments of red and purple rocks.

The towns of Wenlock and Dudley gave the name to a fossiliferous, concretionary formation quarried for its limestone, which, says Lyell, forms a continuous ridge extending twenty miles, nearly parallel with a similar escarpment of the Aymestry limestone, a mile distant. The rock often encloses large masses of carbonate of lime called "Ball stones" sometimes eighty feet in diameter, quarried for smelting iron. The limestone is crowded with corals and other fossils. North of Dudley, it rises in domes with the particular names of "Castle Hill," "Wren's Nest," and others, affording a superior kind of limestone quarried by subterranean galleries.

The Ludlow or Aymestry group was called for towns of the same name, the former in Shropshire or Salop, the latter in Herefordshire.

The Ludlow encloses numerous fossils and a great variety of minerals; the central portion consists of a dark-gray limestone, on which Ludlow Castle, a border Welsh fortress is built of the same rock. The poet Milton spent some time at or near this castle, and a deep depression of the Ludlow promontory, since called "Comus Woods," is the scene of his

"Masque of Comus." The Aymestry limestone liable to subsidences is developed in Hereford, Salop, and Stafford Counties,
and is quite extensively quarried.

. The Pentamerus is the characteristic fossil, although ·the
Orthoceratite is abundant, eleven species having been discovered in the strata.

It is stated by Murchison that the Silurian series in Great
Britain reaches the enormous depth of fifty-six thousand feet,
or more than ten miles.

In the southwest part of England, are the counties of Cornwall and Devon; the latter gave the name to an extensive
series of rocks, the Devonian, which occur in nearly all regions
of the globe. In Great Britain, the formation is best studied
in these counties, but it also occurs in South Wales, Herefordshire, in Scotland along the side of the Grampians across the
southern part, and in Ireland. The representative rock in
most of the English Devonian is the Old Red Sandstone;
limestones are not a feature of the series except in Cornwall
and Devonshire, where the great Devon or Plymouth limestone
becomes the type. The limestones of Ilfracomb and Comb
Martin of Devonshire, the Cornstone of Wales, and varieties
with Clymenia and Posidonomya, have been classed with the
Devonian or Plymouth. It is a formation characterized by an
abundance and variety of fossils, Corals and Trilobites being
very conspicuous. The Devon in England and the Eifel of
Germany are the great representative limestones of the period
in Europe.

The largest development of British marbles occurred during
the Devonian and Carboniferous periods

The great typical formation of the Sub-carboniferous period
in Great Britain is the Mountain limestone, abundant in
England and Ireland, and developed, to a certain extent, in
Scotland and Wales A grand display of pure, compact limestone of this variety, of one thousand or one thousand five
hundred feet, is seen in the north of England, and in Derbyshire it is cut into picturesque valleys and bold cliffs, afford-

ing some grand scenery. One of these cliffs called "High Thor," on the Derwent River, rises four hundred feet in a mass of shell limestone in which are numerous cavities filled with spar, while in a contiguous cliff, occur masses of fluor spar called "Blue John." Opposite High Thor, is displayed a cream-colored limestone called "Dun-stone" Mantell mentions calcareous, petrifying springs as occurring at Matlock Dale, on the Derwent, where travertine is deposited ; and high up in the Masson Hill Range, he says, a thick bed of tufa, of a nature suitable for buildings, covers a large area.

In Nottingham, on the Trent, the Mountain limestone is called the Great Scaur or Scar ; the word in this sense meaning a precipitous bank or rock. It is more than one thousand one hundred feet thick, extending from the valley of Eden across the country to the mouth of the Tyne ; in Scotland it has less thickness, and is seen in several subordinate bands, including a variety identical with the Scaur of Durham.

In no European country, says Jukes, is this formation so well developed as in Ireland, where it has a maximum thickness of three thousand feet ; in the south may be seen, probably, one of the largest displays of limestone in the world. In this island it often occupies low, undulating ground, but along Galway Bay, it rises in ridges of hills from one hundred to one thousand six hundred or one thousand seven hundred feet high, of solid limestone, for the distance of twenty miles. The hills are very picturesque, especially when the most exquisite tints are brought out by the magical effect of the setting sun.

The centre of Ireland is a great plain of Carboniferous limestone encircled by groups of lofty hills of older rocks, where the strata are covered by comminuted sand and pebbles called "Limestone sand," often containing large blocks, used for the manufacture of lime.

The "Ekers" are long banks or ridges with steep sides, formed of limestone, sand, and gravel, often extending for miles.

Throughout its whole extent, the Mountain limestone of Great Britain is penetrated, more or less, by igneous rocks, and is everywhere charged with marine fossils, largely made up of Corals, Crinoids, and Mollusks Of Corals the Lithostrotion is most abundant, while the Bryozoa are best represented by the Fenestella ; the Crinoids by the Pentremites ; the Brachiopods by the Producta, Spirifer, and Terebratula ; and the Gasteropods by the Bellerophon The Productæ are so numerous that the formation is sometimes styled the Producta limestone Sea-lilies once grew here in great abundance, often forming beds of solid limestone one thousand feet thick.

The Encrinital limestones of Derbyshire, of this formation, yield many beautiful varieties of marbles used for the manufacture of ornamental tables, sideboards, chimney-pieces, and other decorative articles.

The general type of the Mountain or Carboniferous limestone is bluish-gray with pure white organic remains, though some varieties are pale-red and others nearly black, with fossils of a deep ochre-yellow.

The Carboniferous group in the Lowlands of Scotland include fresh-water limestones. According to Hibbert, the formation of " Birdie House," near Edinburgh, is of this character. It is very fossiliferous, enclosing innumerable microscopic Crustaceans of which the Cypris is the most abundant, and the Unio, a bivalve, fresh-water shell, with ferns remarkably well-preserved This writer says the quarries had been worked for half a century before their fossil treasures were made known to science.

The great Carboniferous formation in the British Islands, remarks one of their geologists, affords, probably, the best example in the world of a continuous series. He says the Lower and Upper Silurian and the Carboniferous may be taken as three tolerably complete and consecutive groups of rocks forming isolated volumes of the world's history, while the Devonian and Permian records are but a few torn and half-obliterated leaves from lost volumes that may, perhaps, never be recovered.

The Magnesian limestone is the representative of the Permian period in England, as the Zechstein is that of Germany. The former is greatly diversified in structure, texture, and composition, but less in color One variety encloses concretions from the size of grapes to that of cannon-balls, while another is oolitic; sometimes it is compact, at other times it is cellular. The proportion of magnesia varies, giving to the rock, in some instances, the character of a true dolomite, while in others it falls below the standard. Occasionally it is very fossiliferous, but the evidences of life at this period are meagre and unsatisfactory. The tint is generally yellowish, though sometimes red or brown.

In England, the Magnesian limestone is found along the borders of the coal regions, which are most largely developed in the north, where, in Durham County, it reaches six hundred or seven hundred feet in thickness, while in the central and southern counties it is wanting. The Permian and a part of the Triassic beds were formerly called the "New Red Sandstone."

The Triassic period is well represented on the Continent, in the Muschelkalk of Germany, the Hallstatt and St Cassian beds of Austria, and the Calcaire coquillier of France, in the British Isles it is recognized by the New Red Sandstone, with few fossils, and the nearest approach to a limestone formation in the English Trias is the dolomitic Conglomerate of Bristol, found in the region of the Severn. It consists of the fragments and pebbles of older rocks cemented by a red or yellow dolomite. Many of its fossils are deceptive, having been borrowed from the Mountain limestone upon which the Conglomerate, in part, rests Bone beds are found near the top of the series, both in England and Germany. The Rhaetic beds, including cream-colored limestones without fossils, corresponding to the Koessen beds of Austria, are called, in England, the Penarth beds, from Penarth in the south part of

Wales, where they reach a thickness of fifty feet; the principal member of the group has been styled the Avicula contorta
bed, from the great abundance of that fossil.

The Jurassic or Oolitic period is represented in England
by the oolitic limestones : on the Continent, the rocks constitute the chain of mountains and hills on the northwest frontier
of Switzerland known as the Jura, and hence are called
Jurassic   If limestones were barely represented in the British
Trias their deficiency is made up in the Jurassic or Oolitic
system.   The series representing this great formation are the
Portland or Upper Oolite; the Oxford or Middle Oolite, and
the Bath or Lower Oolite.

In the ascending order, first comes the Lower Oolite, which
includes, 1. Inferior Oolite; 2. Stonesfield Slate; 3. Great
Oolite; 4. Cornbrash and Forest Marble.

The lower member, or Inferior Oolite, includes the Rag-
stone, a brown, sandy, incoherent limestone ; Freestone, a fine-
grained, pale, oolitic or shelly limestone ; Pea Grit, a pisolitic
limestone , and the Collyweston beds, erroneously called
slates.   Some of the characteristic fossils of the Inferior
Oolite are Terebratula, Rhynchonella Ostrea, Pleurotomaria,
Trochus, and Ammonite.

Above the Inferior Oolite is the Stonesfield Slate, which is
a shelly limestone, not a slate, celebrated for its fossils of
terrestrial reptiles.

The next of the series is the Great Oolite, one member of
which, called the Bath Oolite, is an excellent building-stone.
The Great Oolite consists of blue limestones, white oolitic
freestone, and flaggy limestones, sometimes called slates   It
is abundant in Crinoids and Corals, the most prominent of
the latter being a species of Eunomia, often found in large
masses.

The upper division of the Lower Oolite consists of Cornbrash and Forest Marble.   The Cornbrash, easily broken and
useful for corn land, whence the name, is a rubbly, nodular,
cream-colored limestone, each concretion being covered with

a deep-red coating. The Forest Marble, named from Wych-wood Forest, is an argillaceous limestone replete with marine fossils.

The representative member of the Middle Oolite is the Coral Rag, formed of continuous beds of corals, sometimes fifteen feet thick, and of a variable character, found in the south and north of England It corresponds in age to the Nerinaean limestone of the Jura, and the Lithographic slate or limestone of Solenhofen The Corals embedded in this rock generally retain their natural position, and resemble the reef-building polyps of the Pacific. The Kelloway Rock is a sandy limestone developed in Wiltshire and in the north of Wales.

The Portland beds of the Upper Oolite consist of sandstone below and oolitic limestone above. The celebrated Portland stone, well-known as a building material, is a light-colored, oolitic limestone enclosing about fifty species of Mollusks, some of the Ammonites are of large size, and the Cerithium Portlandicum or Portland Screw, a very common fossil in this rock, nearly always occurs as a cast.

Portland, a part of the time an island and a part a peninsula, is a bold headland projecting for four and one-half miles into the English Channel, terminating in the Portland Bill, a rocky promontory on which are two lighthouses and the remains of a castle of the time of Henry VIII. In this semi-island is quarried the Portland Stone, which was not extensively used until the middle of the seventeenth century.

That employed in St. Paul's Cathedral and many of the churches of Queen Anne's reign is said to be more durable than the stone quarried from more recent mines. It is capable of being cut with a smooth and equal surface, which increases its value for building purposes.

East of Portland, is an island ten miles long and seven broad, formed by the River Frome and the English Channel, called Purbeck Isle, with a southern projection named St. Alban's Head; here is developed the Purbeck formation classed by Lyell with the Upper Oolite, divided into Upper, Middle, and Lower beds, each characterized by peculiar species of fossils. The Upper strata, about fifty feet in thickness, are exclusively of fresh-water origin, and made up, to a great extent, of shells, the Paludina and Cypris being very abundant ; the Purbeck marble belongs to this series. The Middle Purbeck contains beds of limestone partly of fresh-water and partly of brackish water origin, enclosing fossil mammalia, while the Lower Purbeck strata include fresh-water limestones. Between the layers of the Purbeck beds occur what are called " Dirt Beds," with petrified trees which, in some instances, constitute fossilized forests. Some of the trees are erect, with trunks broken off three or four feet from the root ; others are prostrate.

The Purbeck formation has a limited extent, but is important for the three distinct classes of fossils it contains. In the Upper - Purbeck are the fresh-water genera Physa, Limnaea, Paludina Planorbis, Cyclas, Unio, and the Cypris, which is characteristic of the formation ; in the Middle, besides Mammals, are the marine fossils Pecten, Modiola, Avicula, Ostrea, and the Hemicidaris, and below the Middle Purbeck occur fresh-water shells.

Purbeck marble was quite generally employed in the architecture of the Middle Ages, and formed a part of the decorations of the churches of that period   A fine example is seen in the column of the Chapter House of Westminster Abbey, the columns of the nave of the Abbey, and in the Church of the Knights Templars   The marble is a brown color without lustre, and owes its attraction to the shells of which it is composed.

The Jurassic or Oolitic period yields a rich harvest of organic remains, some of the Lias beds having been compared to a pavement made entirely of the Belemnite ; other beds display a solid mass of Ammonites, which have been found in Ireland from the size of a pea to a foot in diameter. Probably as many as six hundred species of Ammonites have been named by paleontologists, and a majority of these occur in the Jurassic series.

The Wealden Beds. — Lyell classes the Wealden with the Cretaceous system ; Jukes follows the same method, but questions the correctness of this arrangement ; while Dana and Phillips assign it to the Jurassic.   It is a fresh-water formation, consisting of clay, sand, and some beds of limestone called " Sussex Marble," and, though the strata rest between marine beds, they contain only fresh-water and land organic remains The system received the name of Wealden from weald or wold, Anglo-Saxon for forest, because the group is developed in the Weald of Kent, Surrey, and Sussex, where formerly existed, it is supposed, a river since obliterated   The most common fossils are the Paludina, Cyrena, Cyclas, Unio, Melania, and Melanopsis fresh-water genera, though some of the beds enclose shells of brackish and sea-water origin.   The gigantic Iguanodon, an extinct terrestrial reptile, is characteristic of the formation.

The Wealden extends along the northern shore of the English Channel and is found again in the southern part of France, and in Hanover and Westphalia.   It is estimated that its maximum thickness is two thousand feet

The Sussex or Petworth marble, belonging to this formation, consists largely of the Paludina, a fresh-water snail, with the shells frequently decomposed, leaving nothing but their casts ; in the compact masses, the fossils have been changed into spar, affording a beautiful marble of various shades of gray, blue, and ochre, mixed with pure white ; some of the Sussex beds enclose the fossil Cypris, no larger than a pin-head.   The Sussex marble has been called, from the abundance of its shells, " Lumachelle à Paludines."   The Sussex and the Purbeck marbles, both belonging to fresh-water formations, appear to be closely allied in origin and in the character of their fossils, and were formerly arranged in the same group.   The Paludinæ of the Purbeck are much smaller than those of the Sussex, which encloses myriads of Cyprides, both formations are characterized by the Cyclas, a fresh-water bivalve.

The white Chalk is the most characteristic rock of the English Cretaceous system; though it differs from the Carboniferous limestone in texture and hardness, the face of the country in the chalk regions is similar to that produced by the Mountain limestone. The hills of both formations have broad, undulating, grassy downs, smooth in the Chalk, but cut into steps in the Carboniferous, while the valleys of both are equally marked by scaurs, torrs, and pinnacles. The Chalk is literally filled with organic remains, Echinoderms, Crinoids, and Marsupites predominating.

In the neighborhood of Neufchatel, there are beds including limestones called Neocomian, the Latinized name of this Swiss town, considered the marine equivalents of the Wealden. The name has been applied by English geologists to the Lower Green Sand, occupying the lower beds, while the Chalk formation, twelve hundred feet thick, occupies the Upper Cretaceous.

On the Continent, the Maestricht of the Netherlands, the Faxoe of Denmark, the Hils conglomerate and Mittelquader of Germany, the Hippurite of the Pyrenees, the Scaglia of Italy, and the Pisolitique of France, are representative Cretaceous formations.

The Tertiary beds form isolated districts in the hollows of the Chalk formation, including the Hampton and the London Basins, on the north side of the Channel, and the Paris Basin on the south.

The Tertiary strata of England are classed as Lower, Middle, and Upper Eocene — recent dawn; 'Lower and Upper Miocene — less recent, or with fewer number of recent species; Pliocene — more recent, or with a larger number of recent species; and Pleistocene — most recent, or the largest number

Limestones form but a small and insignificant part of the English Tertiary, while in other countries they become, in some instances, representative, as in the great Nummulitic formation and the Calcaire grossier

The Lower Headon series, M. Eocene, developed at White-cliff Bay, near Headon Hill, and Alum Bay in the Isle of Wight, includes a limestone from sixty to eighty feet thick. The Bembridge series, U. Eocene, displayed in the Isle of Wight, with a thickness of one hundred and twenty feet, yields a compact limestone charged with fossils similar to those of the Headon group

The Pliocene is represented by the Red Crag and the White or Coralline Crag of Suffolk. The latter is a soft, marly, white sand with occasional bands of limestone, composed principally of ·broken shells and the remains of Bryozoa, sometimes constituting a rock suitable for building ; some of the numerous species of fossils are peculiar, and belong to extinct genera. Both the White and the Red Crag are used in agriculture for fertilizers. The Pleistocene is represented by glacial deposits, erratic blocks, boulders, clay, till, etc.

The Liassic and Oolitic limestones of Great Britain are frequently too soft to receive a good polish, but the Oolitic group affords immense quantities of building-stones. They were extensively used in mediæval architecture, as may be seen by examination of the buildings erected during the reigns of Henry VII., Henry VIII., and Elizabeth. The Bath stone of the Great Oolite was employed in the restoration of Henry VII 's Chapel in Westminster Abbey. It has a warm tint and is well-adapted to architectural ornament, but suffers from exposure to the moist atmosphere of England.

The Kentish Rag, a hard, siliceous limestone, and the Magnesian or dolomitic limestone, are largely used for architectural purposes ; the latter is employed in the manufacture of carbonate of magnesia and Epsom salt.

There is no white statuary marble, in any considerable quantity, in Great Britain, but colored marbles are very abundant and beautiful, the largest development occurring in the Devonian and Carboniferous eras. The Mountain or Carboniferous limestone yields an abundance of valuable marbles in Derbyshire and Staffordshire, in the north central region, and the Devonian formation in the south. The marbles of both regions are well-adapted for ornamental work, and are made into various articles for household decoration.

The Derbyshire and Staffordshire marbles enclose Encrinites, and display a great variety of brown colors, while those of Devonshire are of more brilliant hues. One of the rarest and most beautiful of the former is the Rosewood, having the ground of a dark, reddish-brown, marked with light-brown layers, imitating so perfectly the fibres of the wood that the marble might easily be mistaken for genuine rosewood.

In the south of England, the Devonian limestones afford many varieties of beautiful variegated marbles, enclosing corals, and known as Madrepore marbles. The group exhibits colors as brilliant as those of the Giallo antico of the ancients ; the green shades are feebly represented in the English marbles, there being only one variety of that color in the fine collection seen in the Geological Museum, London.

The monolithic shafts of the forty columns of the National Provincial Bank of England, were cut, says Hull, from a reddish, Devonian Madrepore marble, one single block affording eighteen columns ; the bases are of black marble from Ireland, and the capitals of cream-colored stone.

The Ipplepen and Babbicomb limestones of Devon yield very fine varieties of variegated Coral marbles, while those of Plymouth, though less brilliant in color, include some valuable kinds.

The picturesque rocks that line the Avon, on which the city of Bristol is situated, present, in their bold outlines, several varieties of fossiliferous marbles of the Carboniferous era, called Bristol marbles. A Forest marble near Bradford was formerly used for small ornaments, and a beautiful brown marble, with light-yellow shells of the Ammonite, is found in Somersetshire.

Plate XI.

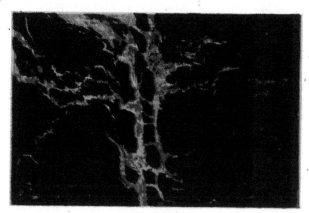

Rosso Levantino.

Belgian.

The Isle of Man, with its groups of picturesque mountains, yields limestones affording various kinds of marbles Some of the Manx marbles are a black, Carboniferous variety; a dark and light breccia; and a marble used in architecture, which has been quarried for more than two hundred years.

The Welsh marbles include a brown, yellow, and purple breccia of Glamorgan, and the Mumbles marble of Swansea, with dark ground covered with light-yellow spots and veins What is called St Vincent's Rock of Bristol, is a gray and reddish-brown marble resembling alabaster.

The peculiar marble from Tiree, a small island belonging to the Hebrides, displays a base of light-pink or pinkish-yellow, with small masses of dark-green or red augite, which gives the stone a porphyritic appearance The Strathdon marble of Aberdeen presents different greens, and the Glen Tilt of Perthshire combines dark colors and white

The Scotch marbles are neither numerous nor remarkable, but in Ireland, marbles of the Carboniferous period are very abundant, embracing pure white statuary, black, and colored varieties. The " Irish Green " or the Connemara serpentine marble of Galway, is very conspicuous for its colors and the forms of its clouds, and affords several varieties.

It is said that the fine color of the Black Kilkenny is liable to injury by exposure to the air This unrivalled marble is mottled with white corals in the form of calcareous spar, resembling sometimes nebulæ of stars, and sometimes lace-work, constructed of the cells of polypi Near the Kilkenny, appears a beautiful red and white marble.

The white marble of Connemara cannot be found in large blocks without impurities, while the white Donegal is too coarse for fine work

The best varieties of the " Irish Siena," found near the Shannon Harbor, is veined and mottled with distinct colors, and takes a fine polish.

From Limerick are obtained pink and white, and brown and gray varieties, while those of Clonomy are generally of different browns, marked sometimes with peculiar veins or spots.

Cork yields black and white marbles, and the islands in the Kenmare River furnish marbles of various colors, some of the combinations being black and white; purple, white, and yellow; and a variety resembling " bloodstone "

The Galway black marble takes a fine polish, and was employed, it is said, in the construction of Hamilton Palace, Scotland.

The Serpentines of Great Britain are very numerous, varied, and beautiful, but perhaps none surpass the Lizard Point serpentines in richness and elegance   There is a fine display at a cave near the Lizard, where they have been polished by the waves, their dark, variegated colors forming a bold contrast to the white sands of the beach.   The Potsoy serpentines of Scotland are generally light and dark-green, red, and white, and yield an excellent stone for decoration.

The Alabasters of Great Britain, not generally beautiful, are light-yellow or yellowish-brown, with the colors diffused in irregular, cloud-like markings.

See Appendix C.

MARBLES OF THE BRITISH MUSEUM.

The antique marbles of the British Museum afford an interesting study in ancient art and history, and illustrate the use of marble and alabaster in sculpture and architecture, and for decorative purposes, by the early nations of the world.

The Elgin Marbles, as is generally known, are portions of the sculptures from the Temple of Minerva, called the Parthenon, built 438 B. C., at Athens.   They were brought to England by Lord Elgin and purchased by the government in 1816.   They include the fifteen metopes from the south side of the Temple, representing the battle of the Athenians and the Centaurs, sculptured in the marble taken from Mount Pentelicus, north of Athens.

The Phigalian Marbles, purchased for the Museum in 1814, were brought from the ruins of the Temple of Apollo Epicurius, built at about the same date as the Parthenon, at Phigalia, in Arcadia. They are covered with a series of sculptures representing the battles between the Greeks and the Amazons, and the Centaurs and the Lapithae. It is not known whence the marble was obtained, but probably from some of the mines near the city, as marbles were very abundant in Greece. A copy of the Diadumenos, "the Crowned," of Polycletus, is in Pentelic marble.

The marbles from Halicarnassus, in Caria, Asia Minor, belonging to the celebrated Tomb of Mausolus, contain reliefs on the frieze, the subject, a favorite one for the Greek chisel, being the battle of the Greeks and the Amazons. The colossal statues, one of which is supposed to be that of Mausolus, are of Parian marble, while the columns and other portions are of a different kind. The marble from the Temple of Diana of Ephesus, another of the World's Wonders, encloses large bluish-white crystals, and has the appearance of being clouded It was undoubtedly from some near locality, since Asia Minor, as well as Greece, produces a great abundance of marble. Among the numerous relics of ancient art are a head from the Temple of Nemesis, at Rhamnus, in Attica, and a torso of Æsculapius, from his Temple at Epidaurus The battle of the Centaurs was sculptured on the metope of this building, and the great Pantheaic Festival on the inner frieze. An Ionic capital from the Temple of Minerva Polias, at Priene, Caria, in Asia Minor, was cut from a coarsely granular marble, probably from some of the beds found in that region

The Lions from the "Sacred Way" leading from the Temple of Apollo to the seashore, in Branchidæ, Caria, dating 580 B C., are especially interesting from their great antiquity. They are said to be the oldest known specimens of Greek sculpture in marble. Some of the reliefs on the Harpy Tomb which stood on the Acropolis of the city of Xanthus, in Lycia, are in the British Museum.

The marbles from Assyria and Egypt are of much older date than those from Grecian cities, and include a series of slabs, of a hard, fossiliferous limestone with sculptured figures representing the battles of Assurbanipal, the grandson of Sennacherib, 668 B. C. The sculptures in the palace of the latter monarch, 700 B. C., are on gypseous alabaster, and represent the king at Lachish.

Besides the above, are inscriptions of the campaigns of Tiglath Pileser II. against Babylon, 720 B. C. ; inscriptions of Merodach Baladin I., King of Babylon, 1320 B. C. ; a black marble monument of Shalmaneser II , 850 B. C., and contemporary with Hazael, King of Syria, and Jehu, King of Judah.

In the Egyptian department, are a Bacchus in a yellowish translucent stone, with large, brilliant scales resembling Parian marble ; another specimen of a white, waxy, statuary marble of coarse texture; and a third of a bluish tint, with large, crystals. The inference is fair that all these varieties were found in the ancient quarries of Egypt.

The collection of marbles in the Museum of Liverpool includes twenty-nine varieties from the ancient quarries of Numidia, Africa, recently discovered by Signor G. B. Del Monte, and presented to the Museum by Signor G. Fontana, 1876.

These marbles are conspicuous for their red and yellow colors, and in some of their varieties, bear a striking resemblance to the Giallo antico, also a Numidian marble. It is possible, then, that the marbles of Del Monte are of the same species as the antique.

CHAPTER X.

LIMESTONES, marbles, serpentines, porphyries and granites are very generally distributed throughout the eighty-six departments of France, though the marbles most widely known are limited to certain regions, the largest number of varieties being in the south.

Limestones employed for construction or as marble have been grouped in the following classes : Nummulite, Gryphite, Hippurite, Miliolite, Calcaire grossier, Calcaire moellon, Calcaire polypiers, Calcaire coquillier or Muschelkalk, Calcaire siliceux, Calcaire de la Beauce, Oolite, Caen Stone, Pisolitic limestone, Visé and Givet limestones, and limestone of Bailly, besides the Faluns and Molasse, which are, in part, calcareous.

All these varieties are later than the Paleozoic era, except the Givet, Devonian, and the Visé, Carboniferous; some geologists refer the Griotte marbles to the Devonian period.

The Nummulitic limestone, a Tertiary formation, with a most remarkable development throughout the Eastern Hemisphere, is well represented in the southeast part of France, and constitutes, it is said, in the French Alps, one of the most interesting features of European geology. It furnishes building-stone, and was employed in the city of Bayonne, which has its foundation laid on the native rock; and in the Pyrenees, where it has been upturned, it yields crystalline marble.

The Gryphite limestone, a name sometimes applied to the

whole Liassic series from the prevalence of the Gryphæa
incurva, belongs to the Lias of the Jurassic period, consequently is older than the Nummulite.

A large area, of which Paris is the centre, is encircled by
Jurassic strata, largely represented by limestones of a uniform character, covering the surface of the interior of France
with the exception of the mountains, which are nearly all
granite, gneiss, or porphyry. They are divided into Lias or
Gryphite, and Lower, Middle, and Upper Oolite, each group
being separated, the one from the other, by clay beds and
each characterized by different fossils.

The plains composed of the Jurassic rocks are unproduc-
tive and monotonous, except where they are intersected by
steep cliffs and deep valleys cut by numerous quarries. The
series, on the banks of the Rhone, rests upon dolomites
and oolitic jaspers, and furnishes material for building,
and marble for the manufacture of tables, consoles, and other
articles of furniture.

Normandy, one of the old divisions of France, is occupied
by the modern departments of Calvados, Eure, Manche, Orne,
and Lower Seine. This historical region abounds in Jurassic
limestones, celebrated for their economic value as building
material, and for supplying geological specimens, mostly
obtained from the quarries of Moutiers, near Caen. The rock
here is loaded with fossils, affording in many places proper
lumachelles

The Lower Oolite includes the famous Caen Stone of Normandy, enclosing Ammonites, Belemnites, and other fossils
corresponding to those of the Great Bath of England. This
limestone, sometimes exhibiting an oolitic structure, and at
other times compact, with small spathic scales, is soft, easily
cut, and of a delicate tint, qualities which render it a valuable
building-stone. A variety called Calcaire Marbre of Caen,
destitute of fossils, exhibits other colors, as yellowish clouded
with rose, gray, and sometimes a lively red. A narrow band
of Caen Stone, about nine feet thick, has supplied for a long

time, and still supplies, not only France, but other countries, with this desirable commodity; it was employed in the construction of the Tower of London, Westminster Abbey, Canterbury Cathedral, and other celebrated buildings.

The Calcaire polypiers, made up of an aggregation of polyps, and remarkable for its fossil plants, is quarried in the neighborhood of Caen for a building-stone, and has been called the "limestone of the hills," while the Caen Stone has been called the "limestone of the plains."

In the department of Côte d'Or, the Gryphite limestone encloses Ammonites of large size, some specimens being nine feet in circumference, and in the department of Yonne it yields a blue-black marble called by miners "Blue Stone," and another variety of a grayish-white named "White Stone." In the valleys of the Moselle and Meuthe Rivers, the Gryphite is quarried for hydraulic lime, and the well-preserved fortifications and fine arcades of Joug-aux-Arches, built by the Romans, prove its excellent quality for cement. The citadel of Sedan, in Ardennes, is built upon a series of beds enclosing this variety.

There occurs in some localities a limestone colored by a brilliant red oxide of iron — eisenrahm, iron mould — called Pierre Rouge, a lumachelle in which eisenrahm occupies the place of the lost shells. The red tint is exceptional in lumachelles, brown and black being the usual colors. Pierre du Serpentine is a lumachelle found near Armay-le-Duc.

The department of Ardennes, in which is situated the celebrated forest, the Ardenna Silva of the Romans, is based upon slate rocks with a limited proportion of limestones; of the latter, one species of dark color clouded with white supplies several varieties of beautiful Crinoidal marbles. A granular quartz of this region resembles in appearance the gray and white marbles of Belgium.

The abrupt sides of the valley of the Meuse display the Givet limestone or marble, named for the town on its banks, where the rock rises into a mountain or hill on both sides of the stream; on the top of the Belgian hill was built' the town of Charlemont, overlooking Givet. The marble, quarried by the inhabitants of both cities, is uniform from the base to the summit of the mountain, of a blue-gray color, hard, and susceptible of a fine polish.

The limestone of Glageon furnishes several varieties of beautiful marbles known as Glageon Fleuri, Glageon Mêle, and Glageon Mouchête, called also the marble of St. Anne, which is said to rival the Belgian marbles. The quarries of Hon Hergies near Bavay, comprise black, gray, and white varieties

The city of Montbard, in Côte d'Or, built upon an isolated mountain, was the native place of Buffon, the naturalist, and in 1744, while residing at this place, he began his famous explorations in the clay beds on the side of the mountain, which led to important discoveries. The ancient chateau occupied by Buffon is on an island of Entrochal limestones, rising from the valley of the Brienne, possessing, in some of the beds, the qualities of marble. The "Great Fountain" of Côte d'Or was formed, by subterranean and pluvial waters in the interior of the massive limestone.

Burgundy, including Côte d'Or, Saone et Loire, and Yonne, does not yield marbles equal to those of Languedoc in the south Though Guettard, the geologist, recognized more than fifty Burgundian varieties, Buffon regarded the greater part of them inferior to marbles in color and susceptibility to polish.

The old city of Langres, in Upper Marne, considered of great importance during the Roman occupation, was built upon a high promontory of Entrochal limestone, which was used in its construction.

At Nancy the Calcaire polypiers is seen in a fine-grained rock, covered with yellow calcite resembling alabaster, with the cavities vacated by fossils filled with calc spar and ochre. Some beds of this formation, upon which the Fortress of Verdun is built, are quarried as the "Marble of

Nancy," which is not very valuable in consequence of its cavities

The Great Oolite, corresponding to the English, was employed for the buildings of Nancy, and is noted for its numerous grottoes. A very white, chalky limestone, of an oolitic structure, is used in the department of Meuthe for building and for the manufacture of glass. This chalky stone was used for the Cathedral of the city of Toul, on the Moselle River, which is here crossed by a fine bridge

The large masses of oolitic limestone in the wild and picturesque valley of the Cure appear in the form of caves, obelisks, columns, and numerous other shapes more or less fantastic. Near the village of Arez, occurs a series of grottoes supported by columns of stalactites, and supposed to be ancient quarries, but abandoned so long ago that all traces of human labor have been obliterated One apartment found in these caverns is twelve hundred feet long, forty wide, and eighty-five feet high. The limestone in which they occur furnished the material for the Cathedral of Auxerre

The Oolitic limestone in the valley of the Serain is celebrated for the excellence, beauty, and size of the blocks; it was quarried for the statues and columns of the chapel of the Chateau of Versailles, built in the reign of Louis XIV, and yields the marbles of Bailly and of Bris.

The representative rock of the Vosges Mountains is sandstone, which receives the specific name of "Vosges Sandstone" The highest rock on Mount Donon, one of the range, affording, it is said, one of the finest and most extensive views in France, is a natural monument, interesting for the legends to which it has given rise Blocks of the rock scattered at the base, covered with rude sculptures in bas-reliefs, are regarded as the ruins of a Druidical temple, or a monument of one of the early French kings On the German side of the Vosges, apartments have been cut in the rock, with steps, halls, chambers, battlements, platforms, and small windows with Gothic ornaments. It is due to the firmness of the Vosges sandstone that the old chateaux and castles, which render the views of this region charmingly picturesque, have been so well-preserved.

Limestones, though not the fundamental rock, are found in this range, of different colors, furnishing, in some of their varieties, beautiful marbles, among them a Cipolin marble with veins of serpentine and mica of a copper lustre, a fine blue and white variety, and a gray marble capable of resisting, to a great degree, atmospheric influences. Sometimes a Crinoidal limestone of the Vosges, of a white, rose, or violet color, and veined with schist, mica, and feldspar, is quarried for marble.

The limestones of the department of Nord develop a great variety of marbles valued for their strength and suscepti-bility to polish. One species, with dark base, and small white spots occasioned by fossils, is called "Petit Granit," on account of its resemblance to granite. The beds of the Nord marbles extend into Belgium, where they preserve the same characteristics Encrinital marbles of Marbaix are similar to the "Petit Granit."

The Visé limestone, corresponding to the Mountain lime-stone of Great Britain, and more properly a Belgian formation, is represented in the northeast of France by a deep-blue marble with fossils.

The Visé and Givet formations, yielding gray, fossiliferous marbles, and an oolitic limestone quarried under different names, for building, are found near Bas-Boulonnais, in the north of France; in this section occurs the variety called Marbre Napoleon, enclosing fossils identical with those of the English Chalk.

Between the confluents of the Brienne, Lozain, and Loze, rises Mount Auxois, on which the town of Alesia, famous in the wars of Julius Cæsar, was built. The hill is composed of an Entrochal, marly limestone, surrounded by valleys on three sides. Where these valleys unite, an elevated plain composed of this rock, is spread out, and it was on this plateau that the battle between the Frank and the Roman cavalry was fought, which decided the fate of Gaul. Various relics of the struggle, in the form of marbles, nails, brick, and pottery, have been found in the vicinity. From the south side of Mount Auxois, issues the Fountain of Sainte Reine, renowned for its supposed medicinal qualities

In the valley of the Seine, is developed a limestone or Coral Rag, yielding large quantities of shell marbles or lumachelles, valued for their beauty and high polish, known as Brocatelle de Bourgogne. A hard, compact rock of iron-gray spotted with light-gray, composed of a mass of small mussel-shells, is called the Marble of Argonne ; and another of similar character found near Pay-de-Bray is known as the Marble of Beauvais, or Hircourt.

The Calcaire coquillier, corresponding to the Muschelkalk of Germany, forming the middle member of the Trias in France, is a compact, smoke-gray limestone crowded with fossils, but is not uniform in character. Like the German Muschelkalk, it encloses the Encrinus liliiformis, together with the bones of Saurians. It frequently happens that the exterior of the rock is yellow, while the interior is blue ; and in some places it presents a vertical columnar structure, yielding yellow marbles crossed by veins of calcite   The name Crapaud is sometimes applied to a breccia associated with this limestone ; Gypsum, used for ornamental work, often occurs with this formation.

The Indusial limestone of Auvergne, a remarkable freshwater formation of the Miocene epoch, is composed mostly of the cast shells or hollow cases called "indusia," of the Caddis-worm, deposited in a shallow lake, which it is supposed existed here in former ages.

The remains of Tertiary Birds of the Miocene beds, in the department of Allier alone, comprise seventy species, many of them being tropical ; a fresh-water formation, with Helices, is found in the same department. The Mountains of Forez furnish limestones used in construction, and a light or white saccharoidal marble, with numerous joints and fissures which render it unsuitable for sculpture.

Provence, famous in the literature of France, and celebrated for its delightful and salubrious climate, is occupied by the southeastern departments on the east side of the Rhone. The strata composing this section, including a great variety of limestones, marbles, and lumachelles, of different colors, and enclosing numerous fossils, form a plateau which extends from Provence to the Alpine table-lands.

The celebrated Campan marbles of the Pyrenees are composed of calcareous nodules, consisting, in most varieties, of the Nautilus and Clymenia cemented by green schist, the mass presenting an amygdaloidal structure.

Shelly limestones, both marine and fresh-water, enter into the composition of the Black Mountains, but it is in Languedoc, covering eight departments lying on the west side of the Rhone, and along the Mediterranean, that the most noted and most beautiful French marbles are to be sought; and of all the quarries in this province those of Caunes, near Black Mountains, are the most important The Languedoc formation comprises a clear, blue-gray or white limestone, combined with green fossiliferous schist, forming a rock similar to Cipolin marble, while in some of the beds it resembles the "Turquin."

The Caunes limestones are of considerable thickness, and comprise two kinds, compact and schistose ; the latter affords several rich and beautiful varieties of the Griotte shell marbles The schist in some species is sombre red, while the carbonate of lime is lively red mingled with white ; the concretions bear traces of organized beings, the Nautilus, in the kind known as Oeil-de-Perdrix, being very distinctly visible. This variety sometimes passes to a red schist, forming an imperfect marble, while the green schist is changed to a limestone similar to Campan marble.

Griotte marbles, found in the Pyrenees, enclose the Goniatite, Cardium, and other Devonian fossils.

A rich Caunes marble of a rose-yellow, with spots of deep-red, crystalline corals, called Couleur-de-Chair, was quite extensively used in France during the reigns of Louis XIV. and Louis XV., as may be seen by examination of the monuments of that period

Associated with these beds are those of Marbre Cervelas, sausage, enclosing concretions of calc' spar and brown iron, but few fossils. A gray marble with Encrinites, belonging to the Caunes group, resembles the Belgian marbles, in its organic remains.

In Herault, on the Mediterranean, molasse forms the hills, and a fresh-water limestone the valleys, with the exception of the Calcaire moellon, which is marine, while a lacustrine breccia of yellow, reddish, and gray marble, extends from Montpellier to the department of Gard.

Saint Loup, an elevation nearly two thousand feet above sea-level, crowned by the Hermitage of St. Loup, consists of Gryphite, Oolite, and other varieties of limestones of the Jurassic period. In the department of Var, the mountains of Marnes and Esterel, interesting for their geological structure, are encircled by a band of limestone.

The table-land between the Loire and the Seine is founded upon a fresh-water limestone called Calcaire de la Beauce, which constitutes the summits of the hills about Paris, and appears south of the Loire in Cantal and Puy de Dome. The department of Vendée, celebrated in history for the brave resistance of the inhabitants to the armies of the revolution of 1793, develops the Jurassic limestones, and east of Vendée, a fine, white variety yields a desirable building-stone.

Poitiers, the theatre of the memorable conflicts between Charles Martel and the Saracens in the eighth century, and King John and the Black Prince in the fourteenth, is in the region of the Oolitic formation, which constitutes the cliffs and the numerous caverns along the banks of the river Clain near the city.

In several of the departments where the Jurassic limestone

predominates, the valleys are deep, with abrupt precipices caused by rents made in the rocks.

·The limestone of the coal region, between Nantes and Angers, is a fine, black, fossiliferous rock, while that covering the schist on which the latter city is built, at the confluence of three rivers, is of the same color and encloses Crinoids. Entrochal limestones of a reddish tint ·yield some beautiful marbles and excellent building-stone.

The limestones of the five departments in the' northwest, occupy the peninsula of ancient Brittany, and afford a marble of deep-black, crossed by veins of white spar, forming a variety similar to the highly-prized St. Anne marble.

The upper Chalk beds of France form a pure white mass, generally too soft for building, though sometimes sufficiently hard to be used for this purpose.

THE PARIS BASIN.

The basin of the Seine, or what is called the Paris Basin, includes a territory about one hundred and eighty miles from north to south, and ninety miles from east to west, as stated by Lyell   It affords a series of marine and fresh-water strata of the Tertiary period, comprising a very great variety and abundance of organic remains in the character of shells, bones of Mammals, Birds, Reptiles, and Fishes.

The shells are remarkably fresh and natural, comparing well with living species except in color.   The Miocene strata abounds in the remains of quadrupeds, about fifty species having been discovered.

The Tertiary beds present a diversity of rocks, including gypsum, sandstone, and a variety of limestones; of the latter the Calcaire grossier is one of the most important members, making a desirable building-stone on account of its compactness and light, cheerful color.   It is interstratified with green marls and abounds in organic remains.   The most characteristic fossil is the Cerithium, an elegant Gasteropod, of which there are one hundred and thirty-seven species in the Paris Basin, and nearly all of them represented in the Calcaire grossier, which is quarried at Mount Meudon and Vaugirard This formation occurs in other parts of France, as at Rennes and Bordeaux.

The Miliolité limestone, largely made up of the microscopic shells of Foraminifers, is found with the Calcaire grossier, and is used for construction.

A siliceous limestone, quite distinct from the others, with numerous cavities and very few organic remains, is called the Calcaire siliceux, or lower travertine.

The gypsum, from which the celebrated Plaster of Paris is manufactured, is obtained from Mounts Valerian, Chaumont, and Montmartre. At the latter place, Cuvier began his interesting studies on fossils, which subsequently gave him so much fame as a comparative anatomist.

The Paris Basin contains one of the largest, most interesting, and most important collections of organic remains to be found in any geological period, and for Tertiary fossils it is, perhaps, unsurpassed Nature has her great paleontological museums, whose rich collections amply repay the patient investigator with valuable and interesting facts, and such a repository is found in this locality. A list of some of the more important genera of shells is given in another place.

The serpentines of France are abundant, and make beautiful ornamental stones, one of the most striking being found in the south, in the department of Tarn, where it is traversed by the Aveyron. The scenery of the deep gorge through which the river flows is grand and picturesque.

Molasse, a term applied in Switzerland to the Miocene formation, both marine and fresh-water, in this country consists of a shelly, incoherent, greenish sandstone, while in France the rock is composed of quartz, mica, clay, and shells cemented by lime; that of marine origin is very solid, and serviceable where great strength is needed.

A coarse, soft, and porous kind of limestone, made up of shells, corals, and sand loosely agglutinated by lime, employed for agriculture and building, is called "Falun."

A list of the numerous ornamental stones, including from one hundred to two hundied different specimens of marbles, serpentines, porphyries, and granites, exhibited at the Paris Exposition of 1878, is furnished in the Appendix B.

Plate XII.

African Red.

Rosso Antico.

Armstrong & Co. Lith. Boston.

CHAPTER XI.

I. *Belgium.* — Some of the limestone formations of Belgium are identical with those of the northeast of France ; especially is this true of the Givet, Devonian, which takes the name of a French town, and the Visé, Carboniferous, called for a Belgian town, while both are classed with the limestones of the two countries.

The Eifel, the great Devonian formation of Germany, is represented in Belgium by a coralline rock, partly dolomitic, upon which the ancient citadel of Huy, on the Meuse, is built.

The Givet limestone is sometimes called the Stringocephalus, from a characteristic fossil, a name also applied to another formation, which causes some confusion in regard to their identity. A subordinate limestone, combined with schists, encloses both Devonian and Carboniferous fossils.

The city of Chimay rests upon the Givet formation. The limestone in this locality is used for building material and for marble, while near Rance it develops gray marbles and a black variety veined with white, like that of Chimay. In this vicinity a red and white marble enclosing calc spar and Encrinites, and interstratified with the Psammites of Condroz, is quarried for ornamental uses.

The Carboniferous system is well displayed by its grand masses of limestone, including the Visé and the Tournai; the former is sometimes dark, affording the black marble of Theux, and has its representative in the black schistose limestone of Hoyoux, and the black marble of Gobzienne.

The Visé limestone is penetrated several times by the Meuse between Namur and Dinant, and in some places it affords a beautiful lumáchelle analogous to the " Petit Granit;" in others, a fine, black marble resembling that of Dinant.

Along the valley of the Less, a branch of the Meuse, in the caverns of the Carboniferous limestone, are found human bones along with those of other *mammals*, supposed to be of the Paleolithic or Old Stone Age, and contemporary with the Mammoth.

Between the limestone of Givet and the Conglomerate of Burnot, a characteristic rock of Belgium, rests the Grauwacke of Rouillon, a limestone analogous to the German Grauwacke. It is very thick, and passes into a fine-grained dolomite of a black, brown, or gray color veined with calcite.

Psammites or red schists are abundant in Belgium, and those of Condroz are used for paving-stones The name has given rise to what is called by Dumont the Condrusian system, which includes a Crinoidal limestone of the Carboniferous period, similar to that of Hainault, on the borders of France, quarried under the name of " Petit Granit." This formation is worked for its valuable stone, at Tournai, an important town in the southwest, and furnishes excellent material for building and hydraulic lime.

The Miocene, of the Tertiary, has an extensive distribution in this country ; the Lower Miocene, called by Dumont the Rupelian system, from the Rupel, a branch of the Scheldt, includes clay used for tiles, and an argillaceous limestone ; the formation is very fossiliferous, the Leda or Nucula being one of the most characteristic shells At Mons the Tertiary limestone is very fertile in organic remains

The beds of Kleyn Spawen, a few miles from Maestricht, enclose, says Lyell, about two hundred species of Testacea, besides Foraminifera and the remains of fishes.

The Upper Miocene comprises the beds of the Bolderberg, a hill near Hasselt, with fossils corresponding to those of the faluns of France

Belgium, like most other countries, yields limestones and marbles not directly traceable to any of the great formations having a general distribution, belonging to this class of rocks are a compact breccia formed of white, ash-colored, and reddish marble fragments, quarried at Dourlers, a black, shell limestone, and a black coral marble enclosing crystals of dolomite, between Chimay and Trélon

In the valleys of the Meuse and the Awirs, are found limestones exhibiting varieties in color, structure, and fossils, some of them are quarried under the name of granite. A limestone near the coal basin of Namur is related, by its fossils, to the Givet, and a variety enclosing the Lima, Ostria, Trigonia, Pecten, and Belemnite, is oölitic; a species with polyps is called the "Limestone of Barjosien," and is associated with that of Boussu, on the borders of France.

There are also fresh-water limestones in Belgium, including Cretaceous and Tertiary

Though the Duchy of Luxembourg belongs to the Netherlands politically, it has a geological affinity with Belgium and France   In this Duchy, the Calcaire coquillier of the Trias encloses rolled pebbles of sandstone, and a variety mined for lime and plaster is so arenaceous that miners say, "It is a lime that carries its own sand"

The Calcaire grossier is represented in some places by a gray or yellowish crystalline rock, and the valley of the Sambre affords tufa of a concretionary, cellular, or stalactitic structure

With the numerous ornamental rocks of Belgium may be classed serpentines, though they are less known and less abundant than those of Great Britain and France

The marbles of Belgium, as is well known, are valued for their excellence and beauty, and have become an important article of commerce.   The Belgian black of Namur, unrivalled for its beautiful color and exceedingly bright and sparkling lustre, has a fine, compact texture, not distinctly granular, and takes a remarkable polish, it is thought to resemble the

Nero antico, but its color is deeper. A blue marble is found at Namur and other parts of Belgium and in Holland. Da Costa describes this marble as possessing an agreeable, uniform, bluish color, compact, solid, and of brilliant fracture, taking an excellent polish. It encloses corals and entrochi like snow-white spar, affording a beautiful stone. The same writer says it was extensively used, in his day, for the steps or stairs of buildings in Holland, where it is called "Blue Stone." Namur affords a red marble variegated with white, which has been known as Marble of Charlemont, and a variety with dark ground, and large, black and white spots resembling porphyry, called Breccia de Florennes. A red, figured with black and white, is found at Mons. A white marble, veined and clouded with different colors, is said to be used in the construction of the Stadthaus of Amsterdam.

With other Belgian marbles, there was exhibited at the Paris Exposition of 1878, a very showy breccia of black, white, dark-yellow, and green, in large and small fragments, crossed with fine veins of different colors.

II *Germany and the Netherlands* — The great representative limestones of Germany are the Eifel of the Devonian, the Zechstein of the Permian, the Muschelkalk of the Triassic, the Jura of the Jurassic, and the Planerkalk of the Cretaceous period. The Grauwacke, a term of no significance as applied to the age of a formation, is generally a gray, compact, fossiliferous limestone, widely distributed, and classed among the older Paleozoic rocks

The Eifel limestone, which has given the Devonian rocks a prominent character on the Continent of Europe, was named for the Eifel Mountains, near the Rhine, in Western Prussia, where it has a large development

The Calceola, the most characteristic shell of the formation, is very abundant in the Calceola schiefer, which is contiguous to the limestone. This fossil is so peculiar in structure that naturalists have been at a loss where to place it, some regarding it as a Coral, others as a Brachiopod. Above the Eifel rests the Stringocephalus limestone, a name sometimes incorrectly applied to the Eifel

The Zechstein, a magnesian limestone, is the chief member of the Permian series in Germany, the name signifies "mine stone," so called because it is cut through to reach the copper below. This limestone has its representative in Switzerland, Russia, Spain, England, and on the Western Continent On the high mountains it is generally a simple formation, but in the plains it consists of several subdivisions, including the Lower Zechstein, a gray and white limestone, the Middle called Smoky limestone, and the Upper or Platten dolomite Under the-Zechstein is the formation, consisting of red sandstone, breccia, and igneous rocks, called Rothliegendes, or "red lyers" The compact limestone often passes into a fine, granular variety enclosing calc spar, which often gives it brilliancy. The Zechstein has been carefully studied to determine the relative age and succession of strata.

The Trias, which received its name in Germany, consists of three members, of which the middle one is a limestone called the Muschelkalk, corresponding to the Calcaire coquillier of France and the Guttenstein Kalk of the Alps The limestone is from one thousand to one thousand two hundred feet thick, and occupies a large area in Hanover and Westphalia, and passing over the table-land between Hanover and Stuttgart, reaches the chain of the Vosges on the French frontier It is rich in organic remains, and important as representing the life of the Triassic period The Gervillia is a very prominent fossil, but the Encrinus liliiformis, which in this formation is often found entire, is the most interesting. Mantell refers to a place in Brunswick, near the village of Erkerode, where this fossil is obtained from a cream-colored limestone, one of the members of this formation. The lower beds of the Muschelkalk are called Wellenkalk, "wavy layers;" the upper strata form an Encrinital limestone, and in Northern Germany, a member composed almost entirely of the Terebratula vulgaris, is styled Terebratula limestone. The Jurassic formation is very complex, comprising a variety of limestones covering a large extent of country from the Alps to the centre of the Empire ; one member of the group receives in Germany the distinctive name of Jura limestone.

The Alpenkalk is a name given by Humboldt to a formation in the south of Europe, called Alpine limestone, different from the white or grayish rock of Jurassic age.

The Planerkalk of Saxony, Hanover, and Westphalia is a grayish-white, marly limestone with shells belonging to the Cretaceous period.   A Serpulite limestone of Westphalia, corresponding to the Wealden of England, and the Hils-conglomerate of Hanover and Westphalia, a formation composed of grains of quartz cemented by calcareous marl, are of the same age as the Planerkalk.

The Carboniferous period affords a series of limestones in Germany as in other countries, but here they do not constitute any of the most characteristic formations, unless the "Culm " of the Rhenish Provinces be considered such.

The famous Maestricht beds of the Chalk era are located at St. Peter's Mount, a few miles from Maestricht, in the south part of Netherlands.   Lyell reckons that about one hundred feet of calcareous rock, with very peculiar fossils, are underlaid by ordinary white chalk enclosing flint; below the strata are fifty feet of fine, soft, yellow limestone, which has been quarried a long time for building-stone   The entire beds form an elevated escarpment, washed by the Jaar on one side and by the Meuse on the other ; the banks of the latter are composed of fine, white sand with Madrepores, while those of the Jaar are calcareous, with the shells in excellent preservation, exhibiting, in some instances, their natural colors.   Among the great number of remains are found fossils varying in size from small oolitic concretions to the Mososaurus, a marine reptile supposed to be twenty-four feet long.

The Zoophytes contained in the rocks are exceedingly interesting for their beauty and structure; one elegant fossil may be compared to a star-shaped flower with six petals. The remains comprise petrifactions, casts, and impressions

The Thuringian Forest, covering a considerable extent in Central Germany, occupies a part of the ancient Hercynian Forest of the Roman period. The rocks are, for the most part, Silurian, including dolomites, porphyries, melaphyres, and the best roofing and pencil slates; the limestones are represented by the "Aphrite," which holds a large place in the Muschelkalk of this region. In advancing westward, nearly all traces of the Silurian rocks of Bohemia, Saxony, and Thuringerwald are lost, while deposits of the Devonian and Carboniferous ages increase vastly in extent

In the Hartz Mountains, "the shrine where poets have worshipped," the Devonian formations include limestone, porphyry, labradorite, serpentine or schiller-rock, and compact fluor-spar, while the Brocken, "the giant of the chain," venerated for many a legend, is composed of granite. Near Altenberg, Saxony, occurs a granular limestone with mica, forming a Cipolin.

Devonian and Carboniferous limestones occur in Weimar, and the former are found in Franconia. The picturesque gorge of the Saale, near Saalfeld, Bavaria, displays a magnificent mass of Cypridinæ limestone, while the Zechstein covers the terrace. Between Eichstadt and Ratisbon or Regensburg the ancient Castra Regia, a variety of cavernous limestones are observed, including a species similar to the Solenhofen. Amergau, celebrated for the "Passion plays," yields dolomites, limestones, and a red marble resembling the Ammonite in grain and color.

The lithographic slates of Solenhofen, near Pappenheim, Bavaria, used in lithography, are a fine-grained, cream-colored limestone of the Upper Oolite, enclosing organic remains which afford a remarkable illustration of the preservation of the more delicate parts of plants and animals These remains include Crustaceans, Fishes, Reptiles, Birds, and Insects, in the form of impressions, showing in the feathers of birds the veins and shafts, and in the wings of insects the delicate, gauze-like tissues. A Bavarian serpentine of Eozoic age is supposed to enclose the Eozoon Bavaricum, similar to the Eozoon Canadense.

Beds of calcareous rocks, developed in the basin of May-ence, on the Rhine, are recognized as Paludina, Litorinella, and Cerithium limestones, named for characteristic fossils ; and a Westphalian species, abounding in cavities, is called " Ant Stone," from the fact that ants use these holes for their nests. The slaty, convoluted, Carboniferous strata, crowned with ruined castles, the monuments of baronial times, form the chief feature of the gorges of the Rhine.

On the authority of Roemer, Silesia gives a group of lime-stones of different geological periods ; Mountain or Carbon-iferous limestone, Muschelkalk, Triassic, a species resembling Solenhofen slates, called the stratum of Exogyra virgula, Nerinæan limestone, the Rhynchonella beds, one hundred and fifty feet thick, and the Ammonite beds The Jurassic strata resemble those of South Germany, and the Tertiary is repre-sented by a limestone from five hundred to seven hundred feet thick, corresponding to the Leitha, near Vienna.

The ancient Grauwacke, in the mountains of Breslau, have passed into crystalline schists and marbles ; at Waldenburg, southeast of Breslau, Devonian limestones are found.

The Rauch-wacke of Germany, composed of the fragments of other rocks cemented by lime, forms a breccia identical with the Nagelfluhe of Switzerland, but the Rothliegende is the characteristic conglomerate. Von Cotta describes the conglomerate of St. Loretta, in the Leitha Mountains, enclos-ing hollow limestone pebbles, as exceptional in character. It is formed of the bones of animals, which are very white, cemented by a brick-red, calcareous paste, the combination forming a dull red marble mottled with white, used as an or-namental stone.

A fresh-water formation of great thickness, composed of

siliceous infusoria, is spread over a considerable area in the vicinity of Berlin.

'Those parts of Germany abundant in limestones afford, says Bischof, numerous deposits of calcareous tufa, sometimes from twelve to fifteen feet thick: it was formed in the Roman Aqueduct, from the Eifel Mountains to Cologne, in such masses that it has been used for columns in churches. These tufas, with fresh-water limestones of the Tertiary period, form an element in the rock system of Wurtemberg

Germany has its limestone caverns, affording the beautiful and peculiar phenomena seen in the caves of other countries. In the one called Foster's Kohle, the stalactites appear like pellucid alabaster, while the top of the cave resembles a richly-fretted Gothic roof with pendent corbels.

Agates form so considerable a majority of the ornamental stones of Germany that a brief notice of them may not be irrelevant. The most celebrated are those of Oberstein on the Nahe, in the Rhenish Provinces, which are quarried from an amygdaloid rock. The roofs of the numerous mines are kept constantly wet, while the water, holding silica in solution, dropping through, collects in hollows, — important conditions in the formation of agates. They are artificially colored in layers arranged one above another, and this process of coloring proves that siliceous matter can be penetrated by liquids.

The varieties of German marbles are very numerous, on the authority of Da Costa, but it is probable that some species used in his da are not quarried at the present time. A list of these marbles is given in the Appendix.

This sketch would be incomplete without some reference to the antiques now in the possession of the government, at Berlin.

The Old Museum contains the Gallery of Original Sculptures, about one thousand objects in all, some of which are considered of great merit. The collection embraces the marble statues and busts of the gods, heroes, and emperors of the later Roman Empire.

Assyrian art is represented by sculptures in alabaster, taken from the palaces of Calah and Nineveh, erected between the ninth and tenth centuries, before the Christian era.

Besides original marbles, the Museum has a valuable collection of casts of sculptures found, since 1875, on the site of the national shrine of the Greeks at Olympia, but the most interesting antique relics are the marbles of Pergamos, which the German Government has recently purchased of Turkey, with the design of reproducing, at Berlin, the entire structure of which they formed a part.

Pergamos, the modern Pergama or Bergama, is in Asia Minor, on the Caicus, about twenty miles from the sea It was built on the slopes of two hills, in one of the most beautiful and fertile valleys of the world. The ruins of the Acropolis of the old town are still to be seen, consisting of a theatre, amphitheatre, stadium, temples, etc. The origin of the city is lost in the traditions of a remote antiquity, but it became an important place after the conquest of Alexander the Great, on account of its celebrated library, which rivalled that of Alexandria, and as the centre of a great school of literature, and the seat of one of the Christian churches of Asia.

The Germans have made some interesting discoveries near the Acropolis of the old city. By excavating they found a thick wall adorned with reliefs, which proved to be the exterior wall of a colossal altar. A structure of this kind forty feet high, with sculptures representing the battles of the gods, is mentioned by ancient writers ; Pausanias refers to the altar of Pergamos as similar to the one at Olympia.

Continuing the excavations, a quadrangular structure, one hundred feet square, was unearthed, with groups of statues arranged around it, some broken, and their fragments strewn on the ground On the east side were two groups, one representing the battle of Athene, the other, Jupiter darting his thunderbolt at a giant. It is believed by German archæologists, that the altar was erected nearly two hundred years before the present era, to commemorate the victories of one of the kings over his enemies.

When re-erected the altar will be forty feet high and four hundred in circumference, with a sculptured frieze. An inner marble staircase will lead up to the offering altar, also carved, and surrounded by a hall of columns. The collective sculptures of the altar are intended to represent the giants storming Olympus.

Besides the principal groups of Zeus and Athene, there were found several minor groups and statues; a head of Medusa resembling the Medusa of the Villa Ludovisi, Rome, affording evidence that the two pieces of sculpture were of the same period in art. It is claimed that the torso of Poseidon resembles that of the Vatican, and one of Apollo that of the Belvedere.

The marble is of coarser grain than the kind used for Greek and Roman sculpture generally, and was probably obtained from some neighboring quarry.

CHAPTER XII.

THE Alpine chain, like most other lofty ranges, belongs to the youngest of the mountain systems, having been elevated during the Tertiary period ; hence the deposits are of different ages, from Paleozoic to recent.   The Alps, including the Jura, covering the greater part of Switzerland and portions of the adjacent countries, are divided into various groups or ranges, each characterized by some distinctive feature.

The Eastern Alps consist of an axis of Paleozoic rocks, with the exception of the Permian, which are not well represented in Southern Europe, flanked by zones of calcareous strata enclosed by Tertiary deposits.   The fossiliferous limestones of Gratz, of the Styrian Alps, the eastern range of the chain, belong to the older Paleozoic formations, but as they extend westward into Switzerland their fossils have been nearly obliterated by metamorphism.

The Trias has a remarkable development in the St Cassian beds, elevated more than five thousand feet above the sea, which, on account of their importance, are sometimes called the Alpine Trias   The limestones of this formation are very abundant in the Tyrol, and often appear in vertical walls superimposed by Jurassic dolomites

Though the Trias is abundant in the Tyrol, it exists only to a limited extent in the Central Alps, but occurs in the northern groups, and includes a large variety of limestones known by different names.

The Liassic formation, constituting the lower member of the Jurassic, is called, by some geologists, the Alpine lime-

162

stone. In the Salzburg Alps, it is separated into two great masses by shales, sandstones, and salt-deposits, in other places it is represented by grayish limestone, with very few fossils; while in Germany, France, and England it includes a large number and variety

The Jurassic limestones of the Eastern Alps differ in character from those of the Western; the former are generally light-colored, and include great masses of dolomite penetrated by porphyry and other igneous rocks, while the limestones of the latter are dark or black, passing into gypsum, which sometimes forms entire mountains   The regions about Mont Blanc, Mont Cénis, and the gorges of the Maurienne are considered zones, along which the transformation of limestone into gypsum has taken place.   In the South Tyrol, the Red Ammonite limestone forms the summit of the Jurassic strata.

Dolomite, corresponding to the Lower Lias, forms a characteristic rock of the Northern Alps; that found at St Gotthard is associated with fluor-spar, and that of the Binnen Thal is remarkable for its phosphorescence and the great variety of minerals it encloses

The Cretaceous formations embrace the Inoceramus limestone, equivalent to the Chalk, and the Neocomian, forming the lower member, and by far the thickest.

In the Venetian Alps, the Cretaceous limestone is white with fossils and bands of flint; in Austria, it comprises Hippurite limestone and gray, pink, and yellow marble, in Savoy, some beds of this formation are used for marble.   The Cretaceous of the Swiss Alps affords a Gryphæa limestone, a Caprotina, representing the Scaglia of Italy, the yellow Neuchatel, the Spatangus, and the Aptychus, and a limestone similar to the Biancone of Lombardy   There is, in the environs of Mont Blanc, says Murchison, a complete succession of Cretaceous rocks, passing gradually into Nummulitic beds.

The chief mass of Mount Pilatus is composed of the upper

Neocomian limestone, above which rests the Nummulitic, covered with flysch, a formation comprising limestone, sandstone, and schist, corresponding to the macigno of Italy. It is said that the Neocomian formation on the north side of this mountain, presents one of the finest mural precipices along the whole outer edge of the Alps

The low, undulating country is covered with molasse and nagelfluhe, which are spread over the canton of Lucerne, and form immense deposits on Mount Righi, attaining from six thousand to eight thousand feet in thickness.

The Inoceramus limestone, or Sewer-kalk, encloses on all sides the picturesque canton of Schwytz, and composes the grand, red and white peaks of the Mythen which overlooks the town of Schwytz. This formation differs from all other Alpine limestones, and bears a striking resemblance to the Italian Scaglia.

The Nummulitic limestone, more than ten thousand feet thick, has, in some regions, become crystalline marble. It occurs in the cantons of Lucerne, Underwald, Glarus, Schwytz, Appenzell, and St. Gall, forming an immense zone covered by a vast accumulation of flysch.

The Tertiary rock quarried as Glarus slates is a calcareous flagstone with veins of white spar, and remarkable for fossil scales and teeth of fishes.

The canton of Appenzell has been made classic, writes Murchison, by the investigations of Escher de Linth. Near Lake Wallenstadt is seen the best exhibition in Switzerland of the entire succession of the Cretaceous, Nummulitic, and flysch formations In all portions of the Swiss and Bavarian Alps the flysch, with the Nummulitic limestone, constitutes one of the grandest formations of the chain, equalling, if not surpassing, in thickness the entire Jurassic and Cretaceous limestones

The Grunten in southwest Bavaria is composed of white Neocomian limestone, except on the west slope, which consists of the Inoceramus or Sewer-kalk, of a light-gray or green, passing into the red of the Mythen limestone or the Italian Scaglia. In the environs of the Grunten, the Nummulitic encloses the iron ore of Southofen, in the valley of the Iller, the accompanying flysch, represented by a light-gray sandstone, affords an excellent building-stone similar to the Pietra-forte of Florence.

The limestone formations near the Lake of the Four Cantons, present a curious instance of the foldings and contortions of strata. The upper Jura is seen near the water's edge at Tell's Chapel, while above, the Neocomian, green-sand, Sewer-kalk, Nummulitic limestone, and flysch are all twisted together.

The Tertiary strata form a large and important element in the geology of Switzerland. Besides the great Nummulitic formation, and part of the flysch of the Eocene, the Miocene deposits have a thickness of seven thousand or eight thousand feet, including both fresh-water and marine beds, underlying a great part of the country between the Alps and the Juras, covering the plains, and constituting some of the high mountain summits. This formation, called Molasse, from mol, soft, embraces compact, soft, and often incoherent rocks, of the character of limestones, sandstones, marls, and clays, arranged in three groups, the upper and lower of fresh-water origin, and the middle, marine. The upper series encloses the celebrated Œningen beds; the marine deposits, sometimes found at a considerable elevation, include shells identical with those of the Vienna basin and the faluns of France, in the lower, a large number of fossil plants, including more than five hundred species, are embedded.

Molasse is essentially a Swiss formation, though it has its representatives, with some modifications, in France, Spain, Portugal, Rhenish Germany, Baden, Wurtemberg, and Bavaria. The valleys covered with molasse are very considerable, occupying the great basin between the Jura and the Vosges Mountains.

The limestones of the formation are gray, white, bluish,

brown, or black, sometimes concretionary, and largely lacustrine in origin ; the sandstones are agglutinated by a calcareous
paste, and the clays are serviceable for tiles and pottery.

The marine molasse is made up largely of fossiliferous sandstones, while the fresh-water molasse is more calcareous.
The limestones of the latter hold both fresh-water and land
remains, and are of sombre or lively, variegated colors. The
strata of muddy waters forming a link between the marine and
fresh-water deposits, and partaking of the nature of both, include foliated, marly, bituminous limestones, which burn with
a flame attended by a thick, fetid smoke.

The Tertiary includes a breccia of porphyry pebbles, and
limestone called nagelfluhe, corresponding to the German
Rauch-wacke, a magnesian limestone, and is found interstratified with the molasse A more recent deposit of the nagelfluhe, consisting principally of yellow mud enclosing the bones
of gigantic Mammals, and covered by erratic blocks, occupies
considerable space in the region of the Jura. Modern strata
afford calcareous tufas, which are very abundant in the Jurassic
regions, and are quarried for light masonry work. They are
generally porous and contain innumerable cavities, sometimes
enclosing fossils.

In nearly every country are found vast storehouses of organic
remains, illustrating not only the geology of that region, but
often leading to important results in establishing facts which
have a continental application.

Switzerland affords an example of these deposits so valuable
to the geologist, found in the molasse at Œningen, on the
Rhine, between Constance and Schaffhausen, extending over
an area of about ten miles The river between these places
flows through a depression of this formation, which rises on
both sides into hills from seven hundred to nine hundred feet
in height. .

In this basin, formely the bed of an ancient lake, are found
marls and a cream-colored, fine-grained limestone, exceedingly
rich in fossil plants, shells, Fishes, Reptiles, and Insects.

Plate XIII.

SIENA.

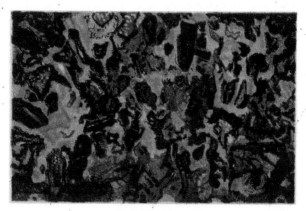

SPANISH BROCATELLO.

ARMSTRONG & CO. LITH. BOSTON.

The place has a celebrity among naturalists, for the discovery in 1700, of a gigantic Salamander, at first supposed to be a human skeleton.

The total thickness of the beds, which are of fresh-water origin, has been estimated to be from thirty to forty feet, but subsequent excavations may have changed this estimate. There are two quarries, including numerous beds, each with its peculiar fossils, from which the remains have been taken, the lower one being five hundred and fifty feet below Lake Constance; in one of the beds, the bones of the Mastodon have been found, in another were enclosed a large number of insects in a remarkably natural state, while the leaves and flowers, with their delicate veins and petals, have found a safe depository in this rocky herbarium   Lyell says these remains give an insight into the state of the animal and vegetable life of the Upper Miocene epoch, such as is found nowhere else in the world.   Between four hundred and five hundred species of plants, and more than eight hundred of insects, had been exhumed from the Œningen strata, to the year 1859   A desiccated lake is supposed to have been fed by springs or streams holding carbonate of lime in solution, which being precipitated to the bottom, formed a calcareous tufa enclosing all substances deposited by the water.

A study of these fossils, especially the plants and insects, is exceedingly interesting, presenting, as it does, to the imagination, a remarkably graphic picture of the flora and fauna of the period.   "We know," remarks one writer, "the character of the trees and flowers that grew on the banks of the lake, and of the insect life that flitted among the branches"

The Jura Mountains, separating Switzerland from France and Germany, extend from Geneva in a northeasterly direction, between one hundred and two hundred miles, covering in breadth an area of about thirty miles   They have a geological interest on account of the important Jurassic system of rocks, named for this chain, and largely developed throughout its course. The Swiss Jura consist of many parallel ridges, with intervening, longitudinal valleys, forming a succession of anticlinals and synclinals, composed of fossiliferous strata, chiefly of the Triassic, Jurassic, Cretaceous, and Tertiary formations.

The Trias of the Swiss Jura, generally covered by the Jurassic formation, comprises three members, the second of the series being the Terraine conchylien, corresponding to the Muschelkalk of Germany and the Calcaire coquillier of France, and sometimes called Rauchgrauer kalkstein. The lower beds of the Terraine conchylien corresponding to the Wellenkalk of the Germans, are composed of a magnesian limestone of a smoke-gray color, full of fossils. This member of the formation is not found in the Swiss Jura, but it covers the vast spaces of the eastern side of the Black Forest in Baden, in the Herzynienne Jura, named for the Isle Herzynienne, supposed to be an island when the formations were deposited in the Triassic-Jurassic ocean, and to cover nearly all the country of Baden. The principal mass of the Terraine conchylien is composed of the Muschelkalk, properly so called, and forms the axis of the great Jurassic chain. The limestone is smoke-gray, quite fine, homogeneous, sometimes granular and sometimes compact This formation reaches an enormous thickness, but compared with the Muschelkalk of Germany and France, it encloses but few organic remains. The characteristic fossils are Crinoids, whose stems sometimes form whole beds, and the Ostrea, Pecten, and Ceratite. Most of the fossils are found in the Black Forest; in the Jura only the remains of the Sea-lily occur, while Fishes and Reptiles, enclosed in the formation in other places, are entirely wanting here. The compact variety of this limestone was used by the Romans for the construction of the more substantial portions of the town of Augusta Rauracorum, on the Rhine. The limestone passes into a compact, granular gypsum of a clear white with gray bands, furnishing a plaster of the best quality, rivalling that of the Paris Basin.

The Terraine conchylien or Muschelkalk is succeeded by the vast series of Jurassic beds, constituting a formation which differs essentially from the Triassic, in fossils and in lithological features.

The formation constitutes the most important element in the Jurassic chain, and holds a prominent place in the geology of Switzerland The diversity in the constitution of the different beds affords evidence of a difference in origin, some being deposited on muddy bottoms, some on shores, others in deep water, but throughout the entire formation are scattered fossil remains in prodigious masses

Gressly divides the Jurassic series into the Lias, the Lower Oolite, the Oxford, and the Upper Oolite, adopting, to a certain extent, the English method. The Lias or Gryphite limestone is abundantly developed in the cantons of Basle, Argau, and in Soleure, but thins out in Berne, and gradually disappears in the southwest cantons. Though variable in details, the formation is characterized in Switzerland, as everywhere else, by the immense quantities of the Gryphæa it holds, which are usually well-preserved The rock is bluish-gray, from twelve to twenty feet thick, and is quarried for building-stone

The Lower Oolite embraces limestones varying in color and texture, some of which are of the nature of lumachelles. One species is called Dogger, and another, La Dalle Nacrée, " slabs of pearly earth," consisting of thin beds from one to six inches but crowded with the shells of the Ostrea

. The Upper Oolite consists largely of limestones, generally of light colors clouded with gray, blue, and yellow ; the group is divided into Coralline limestones and Portland Stone. The Coralline beds are thick, and cover a large area in the northern Jura, where they yield a stone used in art seen in the sculptured statues, crosses, and other decorations of the Burgundian era. The rock can be cut with the facility of ordinary tufa, and resists, to a remarkable degree, atmospheric influences, as is proved by the ruins at Augusta Rauracorum.

The Romans quarried this stone near Delémont, and transported immense blocks to the Rhine, from which they cut the
numerous columns and sculptured capitals used to adorn the
buildings of the ancient city of the Rauraci, the present Augst,
near Basle.

The Portland Stone, classed by Swiss geologists in five
groups, comprises a Coralline variety enclosing fossils and important in determining Jurassic strata, and an impure limestone
loaded with fossils, denominated " Charriages." The Portland
series, called Jurakalk, furnishes excellent building material,
the most celebrated quarries being found in the canton of
Soleure, where it has been used for the fortifications, the
Cathedral, considered the finest in the country, and other
buildings in the city of Soleure.

The Jurassic formation is pre-eminently limestone, and quite
extensively distributed, forming a part of Mont Salève, south
of Geneva, and appearing in Vaud and other regions; but it
has its greatest development in Soleure, Basle, and Argau.
The Nerinæan and the Astarte limestones of this period
afford marble.

The Jura limestones are often fissured, enclosing innumerable caverns remarkable for their peculiar structure. The
walls are often encrusted with calc spar in banded layers, of a
lively red, colored by iron or manganese, which, penetrating
the limestone, imparts to it a dendritic character. These
caves have been explored for precious metals, often to no purpose, though in the Blauenberg chain, mines of silver called
Silberloch, "pits of silver," have been worked in the Coralline
formation.

The Cretaceous rocks, constituting an important part of the
Alps, exist only in a rudimentary state in the Swiss Jura.
The Neocomian, which received its name from Neufchatel,
where it is displayed, includes several varieties of limestones,
sometimes oolitic, and not unfrequently of the nature of lumachelles A yellow, compact, magnesian limestone, holding
an abundance of shells, and a fine, crystalline, red variety with

few fossils, are comprised in the group. The Upper Neocomian constitutes what is termed the zone of the Rudistes, a group of fossils including Hippurites, Radiolites, Spherulites, and a few others, peculiar to the Chalk formation. The Rudistes strata recognized on the north side of Mont Salève extend to Lake Annecy, constituting the entire rock of a hill near by. The chain of Mont Salève in France, reaching more than seven leagues, is divided into four ranges by small, intervening valleys, and is composed of Jurassic and Cretaceous limestones. The Tertiary formation constitutes the small hills and valleys enclosing the groups of the chain, which rise like "islands of limestone in a sea of molasse."

Many species of marbles are derived from the Swiss limestones and dolomites, including those valued for their qualities as an ornamental stone.

A Coralline marble of light-brown, enclosing the Madrepora vermicularis, of pale yellow, glittering spar, exhibiting large stars with a variable number of rays, forms a compact marble receiving a medium polish. Another kind of Madrepore appears like a gray, semi-pellucid flint, resembling the Indian agate; the color varies from ash-gray to grayish-black tinged with red, while the coral consists of white, pentagonal columns crowned with a star. A similar kind is found in England, where it is called "Feather Stone." Vevay on Lake Geneva,. and Doret sent to the Paris Exposition many varieties of beautiful marbles, including a Cipolin of cream-colored ground, shaded with delicate purple and green waves, resembling the antique Cippolino   Another species was similar to the Rosso Levantino of Italy.

For other varieties of Swiss marbles, see Appendix C.

CHAPTER XIII.

LIMESTONES OF THE AUSTRIAN EMPIRE, DENMARK, SCAN-DINAVIA, AND THE POLAR REGIONS.

I. *Austria.* — The calcareous rocks of this large Empire afford a variety of formations, some of them being of great interest to the paleontologist. Each province has its lime-stone series, yielding, to a greater or less extent, marbles suit-able for decoration

The principal formations are the Plànerkalk, Cretaceous, the Zechstein, Permian, found in Germany, and the Nummu-litic, Tertiary, and an Ammonite limestone. The formations of less extensive range include a limestone corresponding to the Italian Biancone, Liassic; another, similar to the Scaglia of Italy, Cretaceous; the limestone of Mythen, near Schwartz, enclosing Corals; and some other fossiliferous species of brown, red, and white colors.

· The Planer limestone is found in Bohemia, Silesia, Poland, Gallicia, and the Carpathian Mountains, showing that these regions are younger than the Chalk period. A variety of limestones and marbles is developed in the Carpathian range, whose highest peaks are nearly ten thousand feet, comprising red and white marble, Encrinital marbles, and a red breccia belonging to the group thought to be analogous to some of the marbles of northern Italy.

Bohemia has attracted the attention of geologists by its rich collection of fossils important to scientific investigation.

By the discoveries of Barrande, who devoted more than ten years to geological researches in this country, it has become the most interesting in Central Europe for its Paleozoic

172

records of the older rocks. The whole Silurian system is represented around Prague, the fossils being identical with those of the same age. in Scandinavia, Russia, Great· Britain, and North America.

The venerable and interesting city of Prague, renowned for its numerous palaces and ·churches, its University, Library, and Museum, is built upon Lower Silurian schists and limestones cut through by the Moldau, while to the south of the city, the Upper Silurian system displays limestones abounding with Corals and other fossils.

No less than eighty-eight species of Trilobites have been found in one variety of limestone marked F by Barrande in his "Primordial Zone," and another denoted by E, enclosing one hundred and eighty-three species, with four hundred species of Cephalopods. The Trilobites were furnished with compound eyes. Barrande counted thirty thousand lenses in a single one, and as their eyes are similar to those of existing Crustaceans and_Insects, the fact is established that the mutual relations of light and the eye were the same in the early geological eras as now. Trilobites reached their climax in this age, and the Silurian rocks became "their grand mausoleum."

The whole number of Silurian species to 1872 is estimated at ten thousand and seventy-two; Barrande found about two thousand eight hundred in Bohemia; one thousand five hundred of them belonged to the Nautilus family, including the Nautilus tyrannus, the oldest species and of huge size. ·The fossils in the basin of Prague, says this geologist, are the oldest mummies ever exhumed.

A limestone with concretions like the "ball-stones" of Wenlock, England, is quarried on the Moldau; in other parts of Bohemia, rocks are found composed of the remains of Cystideans, — Paleozoic Crinoids. The polishing stone of Bilin, used in the preparation of marble works, is a Tertiary freshwater deposit, constituting beds often fourteen feet thick, composed entirely of the siliceous shells of the Gaillonella, a

vegetable fossil so small that a cubic inch of stone, as estimated by Ehrenberg, contains forty-one million of these microscopic organisms. Another deposit of fine, white earth
resembling magnesia, composed of the Campylodiscus, is
developed near Egra ; and other entire strata are known, consisting wholly of similar, minute, diatomaceous shells.

Sprudelstone is the product of the hot springs of Carlesbad,
a city of Bohemia, founded by Charles IV., A. D. 1370. The
stone contains about ninety-seven per-cent of lime, the remainder, of various other products, and presents alternate layers
of white and brown. A hard, fibrous, brown sprudelstone is
used for the manufacture of ornaments.

Limestones with Devonian fossils are met with in the environs of the strong fortress of Olmutz, in Moravia. The
crystalline rocks, extending from the Sudetic Mountains
north of Moravia to the Carpathians, includes saccharoidal
limestones, probably Paleozoic.

A white, compact limestone crossed by red veins, quarried
in Transylvania for marble, is unfossiliferous, but from its
resemblance to a Cretaceous species, enclosing fossils, found
in the southwest part of this province, it is supposed to belong
to that period. The beds of the Alpine ranges of Transylvania have been subjected to many elevations, plications, and
overturnings, and the rocks have been worn more or less by
erosion Mount Negoi, the highest point of the chain, is
nearly eight thousand two hundred feet, and here the Cretaceous limestone affords some grand scenery, having been
cut by deep, long valleys, presenting high escarpments like
the walls of a fortification The valley of the upper Schyle,
a branch of the Danube, is completely isolated from the surrounding regions, with which communication can be had only
by means of frightful mountain roads, impassable except to
pedestrians and beasts of burden.

The "dolomite mountains" of the Tyrol, unlike, in appearance, any others, cover an area of more than seventeen hundred
square miles, and stand like vast obelisks or towers, often with

serrated ridges and peaks, shooting into the air far above the line of perpetual snow, imposing, and sometimes fantastic in appearance. The Sasso di Ranch, one of the obelisks, two hundred and fifty feet high, has been compared to a mountain in ruins, surrounded by immense fragments of rock scattered about in wild confusion No description, says an eye-witness, can portray the effect of these white, solitary columns, streaked with pale orange, as they shoot upwards like needles from the ruins around their base.

The Vienna Basin comprises both marine and fresh-water formations of the Tertiary period, consisting of sands, clays, conglomerates, and limestones, filled with organic remains, including mammalia Some of the Gasteropods and Lamellibranchs are identical with living species of the Mediterranean, Indian, and African seas ; one species of the Cypræa, Buccinum, and Oliva have their representatives on the western coast of Africa.

The Foraminifer Amphistegina is characteristic of the Miocene ; while among Mammals are found the Dinotherium and the Mastodon, enclosed in the Leitha formation, a Tertiary limestone occurring on the Leitha, an affluent of the Danube, and represented by a fossiliferous limestone of Gratz

Nummulitic, Hippurite, and Caprina limestones of the Tertiary and Cretaceous periods are developed in Illyria, Styria, Istria, and Dalmatia, even to the borders of the Adriatic The Nummulite of Istria is composed almost entirely of shells.

Until the discovery of the St Cassian and Hallstatt beds, it was thought that the Trias was of fresh or brackish water origin, and nearly destitute of fossils, therefore when the abundant marine fauna enclosed in these beds were revealed, paleontologists were surprised and delighted at the rich treasure so unexpectedly brought to light

They are the more remarkable for comprising Paleozoic genera not found elsewhere later than the Permian period The beds are exceedingly fossiliferous, enclosing six hundred species of Invertebrates, constituting important links between the Paleozoic and Mesozoic rocks.   St. Cassian is on the south side of the Austrian, or the Carnic Alps, between the Eisach, a branch of the Adige, and the Piava, east of Botzen ; Hallstatt is northeast from St. Cassian in the Noric Alps.   Though the beds of these two localities are at considerable distance from each other, yet their organic remains are similar.   The St. Cassian veins include the Guttenstein limestone ; the St. Cassian, a red, pink, and white limestone, the Drachstein, of a grayish color , and the Koessen or Rhætic limestone, gray and black   A shell limestone found near Hallstatt and the shell marble of Raibel belong to the same period.

Carinthia, in the southwestern part of Austria, yields the remarkably beautiful lumachelle called Fire-marble.   The ground is very dark or black, and the shells, with which it is filled, emit iridescent reflections, due to the pearly lining or nacre of the Ammonite.   This substance exhibits various hues and brilliant, flame-like spots, which impart to the Carinthian marble a resplendent quality, vying with the opal in its beautiful effect.   These chatoyant reflections are seen in some of the shell marbles of other countries, especially in the rich blues of France , but next to the Carinthian in beauty and brilliancy are those obtained near Moscow, Russia

The Hallstatt and St. Cassian beds develop from eight hundred to one thousand feet of red, pink, and white marble, enclosing more than eight hundred species of fossils

A white, granular dolomite called Predazzit, from Predazzo, in the Tyrol, is a very beautiful ornamental stone, and has been regarded by some scientists as a special mineral.

See Appendix C.

II. *Denmark.* — The Cretaceous are the most prevalent rocks of Denmark, forming the chalk cliffs called Terraine Danien, extending along the shores, and a soft, white chalk with black flint, enclosing more than three hundred species of fossils, found in some parts of the peninsula.   The characteristic limestone is the Faxoe, a yellow, coral rock full of Cretaceous fossils, the prevailing type being the Nautilus Daniscus It was named for Faxoe Bay in the Island of Zealand, and forms the sea-cliffs at Stevensklint, on the eastern coast It has been quarried to the depth of more than forty feet, and has been used for buildings at Faxoe; a variety of this formation is polished for marble. Coral limestones are prominent among the rocks in the islands of Zealand and Moen, enclosing many species of Corals, some of which are very rare.

The Denmark limestones resemble the Chalk of England in their fossils; while a Pisolitic limestone is similar to that of the Paris Basin.

III. *Scandinavia.* — The Scandinavian Peninsula forms, geologically, one of the oldest portions of Europe, many of its rocks being Eozoic, and it constitutes one of the European zones of the earliest Silurian life; it has even been claimed that the Eozoon exists in the rocks of Finland. Scandinavia is remarkable for its iron ores, which are interstratified with crystalline rocks, including granular limestones.

The fundamental rock of Sweden is gneiss, but it yields also varieties of limestones, marbles, porphyries, serpentines, granites, and other building and ornamental stones. The Orthoceratite is one of the great representative limestones in Sweden, as it is in Russia, where it is called the Pleta, and is equivalent to the Lower Silurian Landeilo of Great Britain A part of the Gothland limestones have been placed in the Upper and the remainder in the Lower Silurian. They are profusely charged with shells and corals similar to those of the Wenlock or Dudley limestones of England.

The representative rock of Gothland is a limestone of this period, loaded with corals and other fossils, including the Favosite, Syringopora, Tentaculite, Terebratula, Orthis, and others. Some of the corals of the Gothland limestone are very beautiful; among these are a delicate and exquisite species of

Madrepores, called the Porpital or "Shirt-button," formed of perfectly pellucid calc spar, and the Madrepore truncata, a calcareous, cup-shaped fossil, with a stellated surface, embedded in a blue limestone found only in Sweden. Another of the interesting Gothland corals is the Madrepore stellaris, with stars of numerous rays, sometimes as many as sixty, while the Madrepore undulata, resembling the Indian agate, semi-pellucid, and capable of a high polish, with colors varying from ash-gray to grayish black, forms a beautiful ornamental stone.

The Upper Malmo group, including limestones, and named for the fortified seaport at the southern extremity of the Peninsula, corresponds in age to the Lower Helderberg of the Upper Silurian.

Granular limestones are developed in the eastern part of Sweden, near Dannemora and Upsala. The latter city contains one of the most magnificent cathedrals in the country, and the most flourishing university of northern Europe.

The Orthoceratite marbles of Sweden are well-known to commerce in the region of the Baltic; they have been extensively quarried at Borghamm, near Lake Omberg, where the limestone is seen for some distance in cliffs rising from four hundred to five hundred feet.

Sweden develops porphyries and serpentines of rare beauty, and excellence as ornamental stones. The porphyries exhibited in Paris at the Exposition of 1878, included red, green, black, white, and gray varieties, while the collection of serpentines comprised many fine species, one being the Calcaire primitif, similar to the Eozoon Canadense, but the most striking decorative stone was a conglomerate of a light brown paste, with fragments of different bright colors and sizes, and capable of receiving a high polish.

The Silurian rocks of Norway include massive Coralline limestones enclosing the Wenlock fossils, and limestones charged with the Pentamerus oblongus, corresponding to the Woolhope, both of the Upper Silurian of Great Britain The Pentamerus limestone of the southeastern part of Norway,

affords marbles, and the coast limestones contain mineral
veins.   See Appendix C.

IV. *Polar Regions.* — The recent explorations of Norden-
skiold, in the polar regions, have brought to light some interesting geological facts pertaining to these inhospitable climes.
Paleozoic, Jurassic, and Tertiary fossils were found on the
Island of Spitzbergen, while those of the Carboniferous,
Permian, and Jurassic were very abundant in some localities
Though gneiss, granite, and mica schist are predominant, yet
calcareous rocks form a part of the strata, including a limestone with Productæ and other fossils characteristic of the
Carboniferous, a variety without fossils, and a grayish-white
limestone superimposed by one thousand feet of massive
rock "like a wall of basalt."

By dredging, the sea-bottom was found to be covered with
a fine sediment, consisting of comminuted shells of Polythalamia or Rhizopods, Diatoms, and Sponges.   Some of these
were brought up from a depth of eight thousand feet; species
of Annelids occurred at a depth of more than six thousand
feet, — farther below the surface, it is said, than they were
ever found before.   The presence of coal leads to the conclusion that in former geological eras there existed a considerable flora in the Arctic regions.

Jurassic fossils were discovered at Nova Zembla, near the
entrance to the Kara Sea, which is abundant in animal life.
Fossils of the Upper Silurian type, similar to those of Gothland, were found on Waygats Island, between Nova Zembla
and the mainland.   The Islands of New Siberia are rich in
the remains of the Mammoth and other contemporary animals.   Limestones and magnesian schists are developed on
the north coast of Asia, between the Lena River and Behring
Strait, associated with a rock resembling gabbro   Slate, enclosing pyrites, constitutes the rock of Northeast Cape, the
most northern land of the Eastern Hemisphere

Small particles of dust similar to that discovered in snow

at Stockholm, in 1871, containing metallic iron, cobalt, nickel, phosphoric acid, and a colored, jelly-like, organic substance, were thought by Nordenskiold to be of cosmic origin.

The red snow of the Polar lands, as well as that of the Alps, is colored by a microscopic plant, the Protococcus nivalis; and microscopic Crustacea mixed with snow, give out an intense, bluish-white light. One of the most remarkable phenomena of the Arctic regions is the halos, or Northern Lights, occasioned by ice crystals with which the air is filled.

CHAPTER XIV.

I. *Spain and Portugal* — Nearly all Spain consists of an elevated plateau from two thousand to three thousand feet above the level of the sea, traversed by several chains of lofty mountains, some with peaks nearly twelve thousand feet in height, the highest in Europe except the Alps. The longest of these chains, — its eastern portion called the Pyrenees, its western the Cantabrian — connects the Mediterranean with the Atlantic, crossing the entire kingdom in the north, while other ranges reach the ocean through Portugal. The mountain systems of the two countries are thus, to a great extent, identical.

In a region so mountainous as the Spanish Peninsula, where there occurs a large development of different rocks, a variety of limestones would naturally occur among other strata

The Silurian formations are found in the Sierra Morena, where the principal rock is a soft, shelly limestone, and in the mountains of Toledo and Aragon, while Devonian rocks are met with in the Pyrenean chain, and the Carboniferous form the highest points of the Cantabrian range, where there is also a large development of the Mountain limestone.

The Cretaceous group, represented by the Hippurite limestone, is scattered over different parts of the Peninsula, but here, as in other countries of southern Europe, the Nummulitic is the characteristic formation.

Quaternary deposits, in the character of limestones and bone breccias, are found in the environs of Gibraltar.

Dolomite or magnesian limestone is largely developed in the Peninsula, especially about Malaga, constituting the metalliferous beds of Carthage, and was employed for the buildings of Madrid and other Spanish cities.

The Hippurite limestone has been quarried near Alcantara, and was probably used for the bridge across the Tagus at that place, which was constructed by the Emperor Trajan in the first century of the Christian era.

Seville contains many remarkable structures, both ancient and modern, which have made the city one of the most distinguished in the kingdom. The Romans built the famous aqueduct, resting on four hundred and ten arches, which still supplies the city with water; the Moorish kings held their court here in the celebrated palace Alcaza; and here was a magnificent cathedral, the largest and richest in this country of splendid churches, with a lofty tower three hundred and thirty feet in height, surmounted by a bronze statue of Faith. Many of the buildings of Seville were constructed of Hippurite limestone, in which the fossils, especially in the stonework of the Hospital de Sangre, are distinctly visible The Moslems employed the native stones for their buildings, but foreign marbles were used in many of the Christian churches.

The Hippurite formation of Lisbon affords a limestone of variable composition and texture, which furnishes beautiful marbles. A Cretaceous limestone similar to the Scaglia of Italy is called "jasper."

The persistent Nummulitic limestone is found in the north, on the flanks of the Pyrenees, where it covers large areas and yields a compact, crystalline marble; and in the south it forms a portion of the snow-capped Sierra Nevada. Girone, in the northeast, is built upon this limestone, and in the environs of Tarragona, on the Mediterranean, a beautiful Nummulitic marble is quarried, while the yellowish-gray marble of Gualchos, in Grenada, is filled with these fossils of large size, some specimens being more than one inch in diameter.

Plate XIV.

Verde Serpentino.

Granito di Genova.

Armstrong & Co. Lith. Boston.

The picturesque region of the Sierra Nevada is full of wild, romantic scenes, rendered doubly interesting by their historical associations. The vast sierras of Andalusia, destitute of shrubs and trees, writes Irving, but enclosing fertile valleys, are mottled with variegated marbles and granites. The walled towns and villages are built, like eagles' nests, among the cliffs, surrounded by Moorish battlements, while the lofty "Snow Mountains" are the haunts of banditti.

In Grenada the Moors established a colony which became the centre of learning and the arts at a period when ignorance and barbarism pervaded all the rest of Europe. Some of their architectural remains are wonderful for the extent and profusion of their ornamentation. To the antiquary and the romancist, those of the Alhambra, the palace erected by Alhama, are among the most interesting in Europe. This immense pile, built in the ornate Saracenic style, was richly decorated with costly and beautiful stones. The founder, who died in 1272, was buried in his new palace in a sepulchre constructed of rare marbles.

Serpentine as well as marble was used by the Moors as a decorative stone, and that of which the Alhambra was built, obtained from the Sierra Nevada, is exceedingly beautiful, presenting a deep-green base, enclosing bright-green crystals of diallage.

A great variety of limestones and dolomites are displayed throughout the valley of the Guadalquiver, and not in this valley only, but, to a greater or less extent, all over the Peninsula, which yield, in many instances, beautiful marbles.

The city of Almeria, on the sea, rests upon Tertiary rocks, enclosed partly by limestone breccia, possibly of recent origin. A chain of hills near Bajados consists of crystalline dolomitic rocks ; Tarifa, with its lighthouse, is constructed of conglomerate and limestone which extend along the coast to the Fortress of Gibraltar.

Bone breccias, similar in character to those of other places, and enclosing the bones of the same species of animals, are found at Gibraltar; they occur also at Nice, in **Corsica**, in Sardinia and Germany, and in Australia and the adjacent islands.

The Rock of Gibraltar, from thirteen hundred to fourteen hundred feet in height, and three miles in length, is composed of breccia and a compact, bluish-gray limestone The stalactites and stalagmites of St. Michael's Cave are capable of a high polish, and yield a rich marble.

The limestones of the Spanish peninsula afford some varieties of marbles prized in ancient and modern times for their beauty and value for decorative purposes. That the yellow Spanish brocatello was well-known and appreciated by the Romans, is proved by its presence in the ruins of Italian cities. Portugal develops several species which have become articles of commerce. Among these the dove-colored Lisbon, valued for its delicacy and fine polish, is, perhaps, the best-known. Another variety found near Lisbon resembles the Siena of Italy; the block presented by the late king, Don Pedro, for the mausoleum of the prince consort at Frogmore, England, is a species known as " Emperor's Red."

On the testimony of travellers, the marbles of Spain exist in greater variety and afford more beautiful specimens than those of any other country in Europe; and though easily obtainable for commercial purposes they have been almost entirely neglected by the native Spaniards, who have even no knowledge of the existence of many of them. A large and beautiful collection of these desirable stones may be seen in the Cabinets at Madrid.

II. *Italy.* — The great mountain chain branching off from the Maritime Alps, traversing Italy nearly its entire length, passing under the Straits of Messina and culminating in Mount Etna, at nearly eleven thousand feet, belongs to the youngest of the ranges, its formation having been completed after that of the Nummulitic beds.

The rocks which constitute the principal part of the Apennines have been classed with the Mesozoic or Secondary systems, but on both sides of the range Tertiary strata form a line of low hills, called Sub-Apennines, including beds belonging to both the older and the newer members of the formation.

It has been found difficult to determine the age of strata in Italy, especially limestones, in consequence of the deficiency or absence of fossils; consequently geologists have been compelled to abandon their theories on the subject many times, and the absolute accuracy of even their most recent decisions is not unquestioned.

It was once supposed there were no Paleozoic rocks in this country, but subsequent investigations have led to the conclusion that the most important formations belong to that era.

The strata found in Italy have been arranged according to superposition, in three general classes; the lowest consisting of limestones and schist, the middle of sandstones and impure, compact limestones, and the upper of marls, sands, and conglomerates, with outlying strata of the Miocene and the Pliocene epochs This order is not universal, but is subject to frequent interruptions

A pebbly conglomerate called Verricano, a formation of considerable importance, was formerly regarded as the lowest or oldest known sedimentary rock. As it is unfossiliferous its true age is not easily decided, but it has been assigned ·by ·a recent classification to the Permian period, making it younger than many of the marbles hitherto regarded as Jurassic.

The best known limestones of the Apennines, those yielding statuary marble, form parallel ridges along the Mediterranean coast in Tuscany and Emilia, and are now classed as Lower Carboniferous. Besides the white crystalline marble, they include the gray Bardiglio marble, dolomites, and Cippolino or a micaceous limestone. In Tuscany some of the schists are thought to be pre-Silurian.

The Apuan Alps, named for the Apuani, an ancient people of Liguria, are largely calcareous. Here are found dolomites, red limestone, and statuary and ornamental marbles; nearly all these varieties are displayed at the promontory forming the eastern side of the Gulf of Spezia. This body of water, affording one of the best harbors in Europe, and constituting an important naval station, occupies a very deep trough formed of macigno, limestones, and marbles identical with those of the elevated strata on either bank. The fossils at Spezia, including the Ammonite, characteristic of Mesozoic rocks, are enclosed in red and gray limestones superimposed by macigno.

The Red Ammonite limestone, the Ammonitico rosso of the Italian geologists, has shared the variable fortunes of the Carrara marbles, both formations having been assigned to many different places in the geological succession; it has at last found a resting-place in the Middle Lias. The formation, which has its equivalent in the Swiss Jura, is, in some beds, made up to a great extent of the remains of the Ammonite.

The Tertiary occupies a large area in Italy, covering the hilly regions of Lucca, Parma, and Genoa, with limestones and macigno corresponding in age to the flysch of the Alps, and associated with fresh-water deposits. In Piedmont and Tuscany the formation is said to yield coal, which, at Monte Massi, is in places five feet deep. The rock composing this elevation, constituting the foundation for the village of Massi, is a serpentine breccia. The group of hills east of Turin consists of strata closely resembling the Miocene composing the Hill Superga, a high eminence in that city.

From the imperfect condition of fossils it has not been easy to draw the line separating the Jurassic from the Cretaceous strata, and for this reason the Biancone, a formation similar to, if not identical with, the Majolica of Milan has been classed with both. It is nearly everywhere destitute of fossils, but the rare instances in which they occur ally it, in the opinion of Murchison, to the Cretaceous.

The Biancone is generally a white, compact limestone or

marble, with very delicate, blackish veins, and a lustre which renders it conspicuous at a great distance. The Biancone or Majolica marble at Graviate, north of Lake Verese, is very white and of even fracture; in other localities it is often of a yellowish tint, like the Alberese of Tuscany, and sometimes it is greenish shaded with red and yellow.

The basin of the small Lake D'Esco, one thousand feet deep, was excavated in calcareous strata, including Nummulitic, Hippurite, Red Ammonite, and Biancone limestones.

The Venetian Alps yield Cretaceous rocks and others of less doubtful age, including Neocomian and Hippurite limestones, and the Scaglia, the equivalent of chalk. The latter is a red argillaceous limestone, with conchoidal fracture, often enclosing Fucoids, which give the rock a whitish appearance.

A red limestone of Venetia is similar to the Inoceramus limestone of the Mythen, in Schwytz, which is Cretaceous. The Neocomian, or Lower Cretaceous, is not well represented in the north of Italy; in Tuscany it appears as a compact, cream-colored limestone, forming, in the southern part, ridges of considerable length, constituting the principal mountains in the valleys of Umbria, the Sabine Mountains, and the Volscian Hills, reaching to Naples. It includes Hippurite limestone covered by the Nummulitic and macigno formations.

The mountains about Subiaco, where St. Bernard established his famous monastery, are composed of Cretaceous limestones. The Hippurite of this period forms the sea-walls of the promontory of Gaeta, on the Mediterranean, and of Monte Gargano, on the Adriatic, and associated with the Nummulitic limestone, extends along the coast of the latter sea. The Nummulitic limestone is coarse and white, the Hippurite hard and compact. Donati discovered, at the bottom of the Adriatic, a bed of shells one hundred feet thick, which, in places, had been converted into marble.

These two formations, combined with gray Scaglia, and representing the Tertiary and the Cretaceous, form important strata in the Sub-Apennines of Latium, formerly the Roman

States.   The summits of the hills are frequently covered with
Nummulitic capped by macigno, as in the Alps it is capped by
flysch.   The Hippurite affords the marble called Occhio di
Pavone, " Peacock's Eye."

The most elevated Jurassic summits on the western side of
the Apennines are covered with the Cretaceous or the Tertiary limestones.   The lowest strata, in the promontory at
Sorrento, south of the Bay of Naples, considered Jurassic, are
of great thickness.   The Cottanello marble of Latium, and
a conglomerate called the Breccia di Simone, named for the
Sassi di Simone, a lofty range of mountains east of Tuscany,
are considered the representatives of the Ammonitico rosso, of
the Jurassic period   A red limestone at Cesi, near Terni,
resting on one hundred feet of gray limestone, is thought to
have the characteristics of the red limestone of the Venetian
Alps and Spezia ; all probably belong to the same formation.
On account of its fossils the limestone of Cesi is a valuable
landmark.

The mountains between the Maremma and Siena, in Tuscany, are composed of white, yellow, and red marbles with no
traces of fossils, resting under the Scaglia, with which they
form a group scattered along the ridges of the Apennines
towards the south   Ammonites are found in the limestones
east of Assisi, in the mountains east of Perugia, and in the
red marble of Monte Malbe, west of the city; their presence
proves these regions to be, in part at least, Jurassic or Cretaceous.

Some of the terms applied to formations peculiar to Italy
require explanation.   Alberese, used in a general way, designates all light-colored limestones associated with macigno , in
a restricted sense, it means a marly limestone, which forms
one of the characteristic rocks of Tuscany.

Macigno, which is largely employed for a building-stone in
central Italy, is a bluish-gray sandstone, sometimes weathering
to yellow or ash-color, composed of grains of quartz and mica
cemented by calcareous clay.   The rock is known by several

local names, as, Pietra-serena and Pietra-forte at Florence, and
Pietra-morte in the environs of Pisa. It is very abundant in
the valleys of the Arno and the Tiber, and forms the eastern
shores of Lake Thrasymene, memorable for the defeat of the
Roman Consul Flaminius, by Hannibal. Murchison says it
resembles the Upper Silurian rock of Ludlow, Wales, where
Caractacus made his last stand against the Romans. The
macigno, like the flysch of the Alps, is frequently associated
with Nummulitic limestone.

Panchina, used for buildings, is a sandy, shell limestone of
variable character, sometimes compact, at other times tufaceous. It is most fully developed near the seashore, and is
well represented about Civita Vecchia.

Cretone of Alduini, employed for the manufacture of faience
ware, is a soft, pulverulent limestone found in the valley of
the Adige.

To the dolomites and lacustrine limestones, forming a part
of the calcareous strata of Italy, is due much of the variety of
the lovely scenery of this country The picturesque promontory of Bellagio, at Lake Como, the delight of tourists, consists
of dolomite; that of Miemo receives the name of Miemite.

The Hill of Superga, in Turin, between two thousand and
three thousand feet in height, crowned with a royal church
for sepulture, affords, from its summit, magnificent views
of the Alps and the surrounding country. The victory of the
Italians over the French, gained here in the early part of the
eighteenth century, gives it a national interest. Besides its
picturesque beauty and its historical celebrity, the hill is of
importance to the geologist for its Tertiary deposits, including
a great series of strata with some Nummulitic limestone.

In the low valleys about Volterra, in Tuscany, the soil is
composed of argillaceous earth and limestones, enclosing
different soluble salts and hydrogenous substances, and when
the vegetable matter is in a state of decomposition, induced by
the summer and autumn rains, it engenders the malaria so
fatal to the inhabitants of that region. It is in this vicinity

that some of the beautiful marbles and the chalcedony employed in art are found. The marble has become an article
of commerce, and is imported by all dealers in this kind of
merchandise.

Rome, one of the oldest of European cities, occupies a basin
of Tertiary and volcanic deposits, enclosing the remains of
quadrupeds. The most ancient beds, found north and west of
St. Peter's and the Vatican, consist of blue, shelly marls and
clay with calcareous sandstones, while the Campagna is made
up of tuffs, peperino, and volcanic rocks, seen in the hills of
Rome and at the Villa Borghese.

For proficiency in works of art Italy ranks next to Greece
among European nations, as her paintings, statues, and
architectural remains, ancient and mediæval, bear witness.
Under the Empire, the Romans had access to the rich
stores of mineral wealth found among the subjugated nations,
and in later times they developed the abundant resources of
their native country, which, in turn, has supplied material for
the art productions of other races.

The limestones of Italy are remarkable for their beautiful
and valuable marbles so well-known in commerce. A black
marble has been extensively quarried at Vicenza, the native
place of the architect Andrea Palladio, of the sixteenth
century, which contains many palaces of his construction;
and a similar marble occurs at Lake Como and at Varenna.
The latter has been cut through for the celebrated galleries of
the Stelvio passage, nine thousand feet above sea-level; it is
called the highest carriage-road in Europe, and one of the
most remarkable, owing to the difficulties to be overcome in
its construction

A variegated red, black, and smoke-colored limestone is
known by the name of Marmo di Varenna; the black marble of
Bergamo, on account of its excellent polish, receives the name
of "paragone," and another variety is called Panno di Morti,
"robe of death." The Polveroso or "powdered marble" of
Pistoia has the appearance of being covered with fine dust,

and a similar kind, identical, it may be, is seen in some of the sculptured animals of the Vatican Museum. A white marble with black spots, from Lake Maggiore, has been used in the buildings of northern Italy. It is thought the Polsevera green marble was named for a mountain or a small river near Genoa.

A breccia found in the region was used in most of the ancient buildings of Aosta, the Augusta Prætoria, situated at the foot of the Pennine Alps. The remains of the Roman town are still to be seen, especially the triumphal Arch of Augustus.

The marble of Verona has been, probably, the kind most extensively used in the northern provinces, both by the ancient Romans and their successors. It is obtained from the Nummulitic limestone, and affords two varieties, orange combined with red inclining to yellow, of which, it is said, the tomb of Petrarch was made ; and white, with light-yellow and reddish tints, employed by the Romans A brecciated variety was used for the porch and interior columns of the Cathedral of Verona, and for the double row of columns supporting the arches of the cloisters.

Verona, the Roman Veronensis, became under the Empire, one of the most important cities of northern Italy, and was embellished by architectural works, some of whose ruins still exist, proving the magnificence of the buildings of that era. The Verona marble was used in the Amphitheatre supposed to be constructed by the Emperor Diocletian, in the third century ; it has been well preserved, and the fossil shells of the Nummulite may be distinctly seen in some of the blocks

This marble was much used for buildings of the mediæval age, and is specially noticeable in the numerous churches and other public edifices of Venice, the "city of palaces," of which the columns and arches of the two colonnades on the south side of the Doge's Palace, the portal of St. Mark's, the Campanile, and the Academy of Fine Arts, are a few of the many examples.

The Cathedral of Milan, that architectural miracle which

seems like the work of the Divine Master, is of white marble, the only appropriate material for a building so ethereal in aspect, and so pure, noble, and elevating in influence.

The marble is saccharoidal, not perfectly white, but clouded with so delicate a purple that at a short distance it has the appearance of pure white. The stone was taken from a quarry near Lake Como, or, as some say, Mount Candido, in the Tyrol.

The well-known Giallo di Sienà, or Yellow of Siena, is not obtained from that city, but from a place near Volterra; its color is variable, passing from cream-yellow to an Indian yellow, traversed by white veins; and sometimes it forms a breccia with dark-red or purple cement A yellow marble veined with black and a variety of white veined with gray are found near Siena; the latter was used in the public buildings of the city, and, it is said, for the Cathedral of Florence. A limestone ridge near the Siena quarries furnishes a rose-red marble, and in the same neighborhood limestones are developed with Ammonites and Belemnites, which circumstance indicates that they are Secondary, and may be Jurassic or Cretaceous.

The Porta Santa marble, near Caldana, is of a delicate peach-blossom color, but is neither durable nor highly esteemed, therefore it cannot be identical with the antique Porta Santa, which is both durable and highly valued.

Not far from Spezia is quarried the Porto Venere marble, or the " Black and Gold " of commerce. It has been referred to the Lias, but one cannot be sure of the age of Italian limestones. The ground is a beautiful black, crossed by yellow and white veins of dolomite.

The Monte Pisani, a range of hills, east of Pisa, yielded the white marble for the Cathedral, the Leaning Tower, and the Baptistery of that city.

The most celebrated marbles of Italy are the white statuary marbles of Carrara, Massa, and Serravezza, about four miles from the coast, in the province of Emilia, a part of ancient

Liguria. The range of the Apennines in this region is very picturesque, offering a serried outline, writes Jervis, of pale, crystalline limestone and schist, rising to an elevation of from four thousand to five thousand feet, and intersected by deep gorges. The outposts of these bald mountains are ranges of hills covered to their summits with olive orchards, vineyards, and trees.

The age of the marble has been changed by geologists several times: it was at first considered primitive, then secondary, and after occupying several different positions in the chronological scale, it has at last fallen from the Jurassic to the Carboniferous.

Carrara marble was used by the Romans to adorn the imperial capital, though not to any extent before the establishment of the Empire. The mines seem inexhaustible, being scattered over several square miles, and numbering many hundreds in all; but only comparatively very few of the statuary marble quarries are constantly worked.

The white marble is admirably adapted to sculpture, and though held in less esteem than the antique Parian and Pentelic, it has furnished material for some of the noblest creations of modern plastic art. Raphael, Michael Angelo, Canova, and other eminent sculptors, used this marble for their immortal works. The stone is flawed by the presence of foreign substances, so that it is sometimes difficult to obtain a perfect block The quarry of Polvaccio is celebrated for the immense blocks quarried from it for M. Angelo's colossal statues.

These marbles are of four varieties: the translucent white statuary, the veined white, the Bardiglio, and the Ravaccione, which is less known. The Bardiglio is of very fine grain, grayish or bluish-white, crossed by dark veins, and receives different names according to the clouds or the tone of color, as Fiorito, Scuro, etc.

Above the Bardiglio rests the Mischio di Serravezza, or simply Mischio, signifying mingled It is a hard breccia of marble fragments, cemented by amphibole or specular iron ; the cement, when ferruginous, colors the white portions pink. This marble presents an endless variety of tints and patterns, hardly any two blocks being alike, receives a good polish and is very showy, suitable only for the decoration of large interiors. It has been used to cover the walls of one of the rooms of the Pitti Palace, Florence.

A white, saccharoidal marble, crossed with delicate veins, lies above the Mischio. Some of the Serravezza beds, with white ground and purple veins, are called Africano, but the most important variety is a white marble, of a slightly yellow tint, which is thought to rival the Carrara; it is largely developed in Monte Altissimo, a peak more than five thousand feet in height.

A variety of ornamental stones, under the names of serpentine and gabbro, are abundant in some parts of Italy, more especially in Tuscany and Piedmont. The term gabbro has a broad signification, being applied to several species of rocks; it is not properly a serpentine, but sometimes passes into it. Von Cotta designates that rock gabbro which consists of labradorite or saussurite, enclosing green diallage or smaragdite, hypersthene, and some other minerals, and marked by great diversity of composition and texture.

The Italian gabbro is a serpentine, with diallage and some other substances, is generally massive, and from the nature of its constituents forms a beautiful ornamental stone. The distinctions cannot always be drawn between serpentine and gabbro, as they appear in art, nor is this necessary Both often pass into euphotides, presenting a great variety of colors and of combinations, and receive different names determined by these combinations, as gabbro rosso, gabbro diaspro, gabbro galestro, and serpentine amalgam. The different colors are red, green, purple, and yellow; and when brought in contact with granite they are gold color, pearl-white, or bluish-gray. The gabbro rosso is considered a modification of macigno united with serpentine.

The mountains of Tuscany develop a variety of rocks and minerals, embracing serpentines, gabbro, verde antique, granites resembling the serpentines of Elba, and ophite or green antique porphyry, sometimes called prosopyre. The serpentine mass called Gabbro impruneta, near Florence, consists of euphotide, feldspar, and some other minerals The Verde di Pegli, so-called from Pegli on the Mediterranean coast, a few miles west of Genoa, is a serpentine breccia cemented by a light green calc spar. The Verde di Prato is a serpentine obtained from Monteferrato, three miles from Prato, and has been extensively used in Tuscany for architectural decorations, examples of which are seen in the exterior of the Cathedral and Baptistery of Florence. ,

A very hard serpentine, of a clear green color, is found in Piedmont. In the mountains of San Michel, the serpentines enclose brown diallage disseminated in the cement, forming the gabbro of the Italian geologists, and corresponding to the Ophiolite of the French scientist, Brongniart. The mountains formed of these rocks have a red or yellowish tint, and their sterility is due to an excess of magnesia.

Travertine forms large calcareous deposits, and is more compact than the calc tufa of springs; those of Tivoli and Terni are best known. The town of Ascoli, ancient Asculum, considered one of the best-built cities of Italy, was constructed of travertine, which is very abundant in this place. The beds extend to Civitella, not far from Subiaco, a considerable distance from Ascoli, and possess the same character as those of Tivoli. The hot springs of San Filippo, on Monte Amiata, Tuscany, have deposited an entire hill of snow-white calcareous sinter   The water of these springs, charged with lime, in its course down this descent, has been employed in making bas-reliefs by a natural process, by placing moulds of any required pattern in contact with the water which, in a short time, produces beautiful sculptures.

If we may judge from architectural ruins, the ancients regarded travertine, called by them tiburtine, as an excellent building-stone. The walls and temples of Pæstum, the ancient Posidonia, a Greek city famed for its temples, now forming some of the most magnificent ruins of antiquity, were built of travertine. The Doric Temple of Neptune, the best preserved ruin in Italy, is a magnificent example of that order of architecture.

. The gypsum of Italy is generally very pure The agate gypsum or alabaster of Volterra is a fine variety resembling white wax, though red, yellowish, and mottled varieties also · occur. Sculpturing in alabaster is extensively carried on in Italy, an art which dates from ancient Etruscan times, when it was the custom to preserve the remains of distinguished citizens in sarcophagi of alabaster, formed of a single block with elaborate sculptured ornaments and a reclining figure of the deceased.   •

The Temple of Jupiter Serapis at Pozzuoli, near Naples, gives an interesting illustration of the alternate subsidence and elevation of the land at that place.   The roof of this temple was supported by twenty-four granite and twenty-two marble columns, each formed of a single stone ; three of these columns, of Cipóllino marble, are standing, and are forty-two feet in height.   The borings of the Lithodomi began twelve feet from the ground, and extended nine feet.   The changes occurring in the foundations of this structure are supposed to be the following : The temple was built at or near the level of the sea , the ground afterwards subsided, and the sea-water, mixed with the water of the hot spring, still near the ruins, formed a lake of brackish water in the area of the temple, on which an incrustation began ; it was then filled to the depth of several feet with ashes, tufa, and sand, and the walls and columns were covered with a coating of lime deposited by the waters of the hot spring.   The area continued to subside until they were buried twelve feet below sea-level, causing the water to flow in, flooding the temple to the height of nine feet, when the marine borers attaching themselves to the columns perforated them. ·The foundations, after a period of time began to rise, and continued this movement until they regained their original level.

Italy, like many other countries, has its mine of fossil wealth in Monte Bolca not far from Verona, in the province of Venice, where more than one hundred species of fossil fishes were embedded in the strata. Agassiz described one hundred and thirty-three species included in seventy-five genera, twenty of them being peculiar to this locality, all found in the Eocene strata The summit of the hill is covered with basalt, but the principal beds are composed of argillaceous and calcareous strata, including a cream-colored, fissile limestone, abounding in fish in an excellent state of preservation, and of a brown color, contrasting agreeably with the hue of the rock ˙Shoals of fishes of Eocene date are supposed to have been destroyed in a series of submarine volcanic eruptions.

Lyell, who refers to this theory of Murchison, does not account for the formation of the Monte Bolca limestone, or explain how the fishes, *en masse*, became embedded in it ; but another writer suggests that the limestone was erupted into the ocean in a fluid state, and the fish were enveloped in the calcareous mass.

Like Greece and Turkey, Italy has its islands yielding valuable building and ornamental stones. The limestones of Sicily, in the vicinity of Catania, are full of fossils ; those of Iblea are more ancient than many in continental Italy, while others are of recent formation.

The lofty table-land of Sicily, three thousand feet above the sea, is capped by limestones of recent date, containing from seventy to eighty-five per cent of fossils. The limestone was used by the Greeks, who colonized the island, for the ancient temples of Girgenti and Syracuse, whose ruins carry us back to a remote era in human history. Syracuse, on the eastern coast, now partly in ruins, was founded B C. 734, and was at one time one of the most strongly fortified cities of antiquity, as was proved at the siege by the Athenians. There were several quarries in Syracuse whence the stone was taken for the construction of the city, and during the siege they were used as prisons in which to confine Athenian captives. Portions of the Girgenti limestone of Sicily, from seven hundred to eight hundred feet thick, resemble the Calcaire grossier of the Paris Basin, and in other localities it is a compact marble. Girgenti, the ancient Agrigentum, on the south side of the island, built of this limestone, was considered one of the most splendid cities of former times ; its gigantic remains, conspicuous among them the Temple of Jupiter Olympus, are still to be seen.

The low hills rising two hundred feet behind Palermo consist mainly of coarse limestones enclosing shells in admirable perfection, often preserving their natural markings and polish, which belong to species not found in the existing seas   The elegant and picturesque manner in which they are grouped render them objects of peculiar interest and beauty.

At Cape Passaro, white crystalline limestone rests upon ancient volcanic rocks ; some of the beds contain Hippurites, Cretaceous, others are almost entirely made up of Alveolites, a radiate found in the Silurian, and Nummulites, — Tertiary.

Some of the volcanic tufas of Sicily enclose shells, preserving their natural colors, similar to those found in the neighboring seas.   The Madrepore Isis is very abundant in the Sicilian rocks.

Sardinia yields Nummulitic and Hippurite limestones affording marbles, and the islands of Elba, Gorgona, and Giglio, on the coast of Tuscany, contain serpentines, granites, and limestones. The gabbro rosso, or the serpentine of Elba, is penetrated in various directions, by granite, and is intersected by a network of small veins of hydrophane, opal, and other substances, and sometimes veins of copper, the combination forming a beautiful ornamental stone.   Some of the limestones of Elba have been changed into marble.

This island was celebrated for its iron mines in the time of Aristotle, B. C. 384, and of Strabo, in the first century before

Plate XV

GIALLO ANTICO

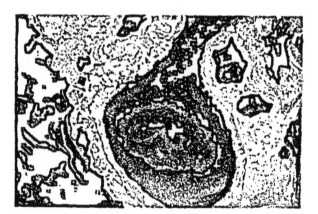

ALGERIAN ONYX.

ARMSTRONG & CO LITH BOSTON

the Christian era; it is mentioned by Virgil under the name of Ilva. The granites of Elba and Giglio were employed by the ancient Romans, and are now seen in many of the antique monuments of Rome.

Gabbro occupies a prominent place in the rocks of Corsica. Serpentine with diallage — gabbro — is rare, but there is an abundance with asbestos. What is called Verde di Corsica contains euphotide, diallage, and often smaragdite, a combination which forms the gabbro of Von Cotta.

Napoleonite, called also granite, porphyry, and orbicular diorite, is a rare and beautiful stone found near Sautina and Ajaccio, in this island. Its mineral constituents are anorthite, greenish hornblende, and quartz, forming concentric layers arranged about a nucleus. Some of the orbs of alternate light and dark colors are from one to three inches in diameter. Corsica, Sardinia, and Malta develop a limestone sometimes called the Mediterranean. The Corsica limestones include a crystalline nearly saccharoidal, a white variety, veined with talc, resembling Cippolino marble, and a Nummulitic similar to that of the Basses Alps.

Malta, whose proximity to Italy classes it geologically with that country, yields fossiliferous and semi-crystalline limestones of light colors, hard and compact, adapted for construction. Of the Tertiary formations, writes T. Fuchs, the upper group corresponds to the Leitha limestone of the Vienna Basin, the lower to deposits found in Italy, France, Bavaria, and Austria. The Malta stone, resembling the Leitha, is very fossiliferous, and has been eroded by atmospheric agencies; the fossils are identical with those of the Vienna Basin. The beds resting beneath this formation enclose Orbitoides of a very large size, measuring, sometimes, four inches in diameter, and form a hard, compact rock. What are called the " Pecten Beds " afford the principal building-stone of the island.

Many of the Italian marbles are antique, and are described with " Antique Stones ; " others are both ancient and modern ;

while a third class is known, so far as we have any authentic history, only to the commerce of more recent times. These marbles present a great variety of colors, but the red and the yellow, either variegated or unicolored, are most abundant. A mixture of green serpentine and light-colored marble, developed in Genoa and Tuscany, passes under the name of Verde antique. A marble of Bergamo (black, ash-white, flesh-red, and bright red), the Green of Prato, and the Ponsevere de Genova, are much used for decoration.

The granular marbles, classed under the general name of Carrara, though they are found in other places in that region, receive different commercial names, according to locality or color.

The best statuary marble is found at Monte Crestola and Monte Sagro, Carrara ; other varieties, distinguished by their colors, are black, violet, red, yellow, and green. Several varieties of breccias may be added to the list of calcareous rocks, found in this region.

For a list of Italian marbles, see Appendix C.

CHAPTER XV.

LIMESTONES OF GREECE. — GREEK ART.

ELIE DE BEAUMONT regarded the Olympian system of mountains in Greece the oldest in Europe, but the most widely-diffused calcareous rocks belong to the Tertiary and Cretaceous periods· A great variety of limestones, which yielded some of the most celebrated marbles of antiquity, are developed in the different mountain ranges traversing every division and island of this small but interesting country.

The northern part of the Morea, the ancient Peloponnesus, is composed of a calcareous conglomerate, forming white, black, blue, yellow, smoke-gray, and wine-colored limestones, enclosing jasper, quartz, and some other minerals. The formation has a wide distribution, being found in the Island of Spezzia in the Gulf of Argos, alternating with soft, marly limestones, and in the Peninsula of Kranidi, the southern part of ancient Argolis, extending to the plains of Argos, where it constitutes the foot-hills of the mountains of Mycene, now Karvata, famous in ancient Greece, and interesting to the antiquary for its modern excavations These conglomerate limestones predominate on the northeastern slope of the mountains which border the Gulf of Corinth, and surround the plains of Nemea, in Argolis ; they appear at an elevation of four thousand five hundred feet, forming the high plateau of the Island of Ægina ; they constitute the highest elevation in the Peloponnesus, Mount Cyllene, in Arcadia, sacred to Mercury, and form the northern slope of the mountains of Achaia.

Besides this conglomerate formation, the upper layers of the Tertiary afford another series of general distribution and economic value, furnishing all Greece with an excellent building-stone called Pierre Poros, also its ancient name, of fine grain, with very few fossils, the homogeneous upper beds forming the Poros marble. The series constitutes the Isthmus of Corinth and Megaris, where it acquires great thickness; it forms elevated patches at Platæa and Eleusis; it is found in the Island of Ægina; in the Peninsula of Argolis as far as Nauplia on the gulf; at the sources of the Eurotas in Laconia; on the western declivity of the wild mountain range of Taygetus, where the formation yields white, green, and rose-colored limestones, and in the valley of the Alphæus, extending to the borders of Elis.

The Tertiary system is represented on the plains of Thebes by a compact, shell limestone, and a brown Hippurite limestone of Cretaceous age, abounding in caverns, occurs in the same region.

What is called the Alpine limestone of southern Europe, has its representative in Greece, in the character of a white or grayish shell limestone, lying in a horizontal position and occupying a surface of great extent.

From the base of the chain of the Citheron, between Attica and Bœotia, to the hills of Thebes, the soil is composed of reddish-gray marls, with soft concretionary limestone, serpentine, and diorite; on the route from Thebes to Chalcis, in Eubœa, the prominent rocks are a pudding-stone, and hard, friable, yellow varieties of limestone, forming elevated mountains. The plains of Marathon afford marly limestones and conglomerates, while the surrounding hills consist of yellowish, granular limestone of the Tertiary, and calcareous pudding-stone. From Marathon to the valley of the Cephissus, pudding-stones, marls, and compact limestones make a part of the system of rocks

Mount Parnassus, the favorite seat of Apollo and the Muses, with its woody flanks and snow-covered summits, its numerous caverns and deep ravines, is represented as composed principally of limestones, including various kinds: as lithographic, marly, Encrinital, of a smoke-gray color, and a greenish-gray limestone from which flows the Castalian Fountain at the foot of Lycorea, the most southern of the two peaks of Parnassus.

The summit consists of reddish, yellowish, or violet limestone, enclosing organic remains, called by the inhabitants "Ox-horns," considered Ammonites by earlier geologists, but which, it is claimed, more recent investigations prove to be Hippurites, a fossil characteristic of the Cretaceous period, and constituting the entire shells south of Chæronea, in Bœotia, showing the predominance of the chalk formation in this region.

Red and black marbles, resembling those of Belgium, are found in the vicinity of Parnassus, and above an ancient chateau of the city of Levadia, southeast of the mountain, there occurs a deep-black limestone veined with white calcareous spar. A black, crystalline limestone, extending from the foot of Mount Helicon, consecrated also to Apollo and the Muses, with its sacred fountains and grove, forms the basin of Lake Copais or Cephissus.

For shell limestones the Nummulitic and the Hippurite are the most conspicuous throughout Greece. Many of the sedimentary limestones are changed into crystalline rocks, and frequently into granular marble.

According to D'Archiac, Attica may be divided, lithologically, into a western and an eastern part, by a line passing through the Piræus. The rocks of the western division are but little metamorphosed, consisting of a thick macigno like that of Tuscany, covered with wine-red schist, gray limestone, and sandstone overlaid by one thousand two hundred or one thousand five hundred feet of Hippurite limestone, all the series supposed to be Cretaceous, forming mountains of considerable height. On the eastern side of the line the beds are crystalline, including the marbles of Hymettus and

Pentelicus of the Chalk era. A blue and gray compact lime-stone, passing into a ferruginous breccia, forms the Lycabettus, and a white or clear-gray, saccharoidal limestone, the Hymettus marble ; the former is obtained from Mount Lycabettus, close to the walls of Athens on the northeast, the latter from Mount Hymettus, three miles south of the city. ·Between Athens and the Piræus, now Porto Dracone, horizontal strata of con-glomerates and yellow limestone occur, and to the south of the city lumachelles are quarried for building-stone.

At the base of Mount Pentelicus, northeast of Athens, lies a mass of white marble superimposed by a variety with lustrous green schists, which, in ascending the mountain, is continually met with, preserving its green zones throughout the entire formation ; the color is varied towards the top, by light, wavy bands of reddish or yellowish tints. It was above these layers the immense quarries were dug which yielded the valuable antique marble called Pentelic. The beds extend from northeast to southwest in a great vein between masses of compact, gray limestone

This celebrated marble has been considered by some geol-ogists contemporary with the limestones of Mount Taygetus, the Tertiary, but Beaumont places it in the Lower Cretaceous. The variety of marbles found at Mount Pentelicus explains the difference between specimens of what is called Pentelic marble, in the Vatican Museum. The statuary marble has a dazzling whiteness and exceedingly fine grain, differing en-tirely from the Hymettus, which is coarse and veined with purple.

The ancient Greeks used for architectural decorations blue and black marbles found at Eleusis, and a yellow marble from Corinth The Lacedemonian stone of Pliny was employed both in Greece and Italy from ancient times ; it is composed of dark-green feldspathic base with embedded light-green crystals of feldspar and augite, containing grains of ferro-titanite It is called by Corsi a Serpentine porphyry, and is used for pave-ments and inlaid work in Italian churches.

The celebrated Verde antique, described with "Antique Marbles," is a serpentine enclosing other minerals, found in Greece, where it was introduced as an ornament in buildings, and was used in the famous luxurious baths of Corinth. A similar stone, occurring in France, has been called mela-phyre.

It has been asserted that the Rosso antico is a Greek marble whose quarries were lost sight of for centuries, but recently brought to light by discoveries made at Cynopolis, Damaris-tica, and Lageia.

Islands of Greece. — The most renowned of these islands yielding marbles is Paros, one of the Cyclades, in the Ægean Sea, from which was taken the unrivalled white marble exten-sively used by ancient sculptors. The quarries have long been abandoned, and this beautiful marble can be seen only in works of ancient art. It is more particularly described as an antique.

The Island of Melo, formerly Melos, also one of the Cyclades, is of volcanic origin, with hot springs, and sulphur and alum mines It has a modern celebrity as the place where the famous statue of Venus di Milo, now in the Louvre, was found in 1820. The island contains granular limestone, with white and yellow marbles, and serpentine, but its chief rock is the Poros lime-stone, enclosing numerous fossils.

The Island of Crete, now Candia, is under the jurisdiction of Turkey, but all its past associations are Greek, and it seems more appropriately classed with the Isles of Greece. It is traversed from east to west by a range of mountains from which, midway, rises Mount Ida, the early home of Jupiter. Homer sings of its hundred cities, here Minos, the judge of Hades, first made laws for the Cretans, and here was the famous Labyrinth of Dædalus, where was offered a yearly sacrifice of Athenian youths and maidens. Though it has been doubted whether the Labyrinth ever existed except in the imagination of the poets and writers of antiquity, it seems probable that it did exist, and that it was one of the natural caverns, many of which are found in the limestones of Crete, enlarged by art and intersected by intricate windings, passages, and galleries, misleading and bewildering to one unacquainted with its entangling mazes. Pliny speaks of this and three other celebrated Labyrinths, the largest of the four being in Egypt, another in the Isle of Lemnos, and the fourth in Italy, all with arched roofs of polished stone. According to the same authority, Parian marble and granite were used in the construction of the Egyptian Labyrinth, three thousand six hundred years before his time, or between five thousand and six thousand years ago. This computation would give an exceedingly great age to Parian marble as known to art. The Labyrinth was nothing less than a subterranean city, divided into different regions called nomes, with their palaces, temples, shrines, pyramids, porticoes, flights of steps, columns, statues, and other objects seen in a city.

Some modern writer has stated that the Cretan Labyrinth was constructed in the Tertiary formation   Oölitic and compact limestones, gypsum, and white marble are found in Crete, but the principal rock is the Cretaceous of the Mediterranean type, and it is possible that the Nummulitic of the Tertiary is included in the rock system of this island.

The bald and misty tops of the mountains of gray limestone seen in Chios, on the coast of Asia Minor, have a sombre appearance, a peculiarity which belongs to the mountains of Greece and Albania, where this rock is abundant. Chios, forming a part of the Turkish Empire, was famous in Greek history, producing many eminent men, and contesting with Smyrna, the honor of having been the birthplace of Homer With less doubtful claims it boasted of the beauty of its women, the excellence of its wines, and the value of its marble and other natural productions.

The Island of Santorin, the ancient Thera, or "Kaliste the Beautiful," is volcanic with the exception of Mounts St. Elias, Stephen, and William, and the monolith of Messaria, which are principally of granular limestone. Santorin, together with the small islands near, has been the theatre of eruptive activity, and in the mass of fragmentary matter forming the island, marine shells are found analogous to those of the sea in the neighborhood, which were thrown up from the deep waters and suddenly buried by showers of ashes Prehistoric cities were overwhelmed by eruptions of the great central volcano, which it is thought must have sunk in the sea seventeen hundred or eighteen hundred years before the Christian era Terra cotta vases have been discovered on the island of Thera, buried under sixty feet of pumice-stone and volcanic ashes

The large Island of Eubœa, the modern Negropont, is traversed through its entire length of ninety miles by a range of mountains of more than seven thousand feet in their greatest elevation, affording limestones of variable character, including hard, granular, sonorous, foliated, and fossiliferous varieties.

In the neighborhood of the ancient city of Chalcis, the mother of colonies, are developed red and black marbles similar to those of Mount Parnassus, which, like the latter, resemble the Belgian.

Cretaceous limestones are developed on the small islands called the Sporades, and the wild, sterile Island of Syme, on the Adriatic coast, affords a variety similar to that of Rhodes, of Tertiary age. Concretionary deposits form, to a great extent, the Island of Cos, sacred to Æsculapius in the early legends of Greece, while to the north lies Samos, at one time the centre of Ionian art and science, with a native school of statuary, divided into two parts by a chain of mountains three thousand six hundred feet high, composed chiefly of lacustrine limestones, similar to those of Chios.

The islands of Standia, Tenos, Naxos, Syros, and Antiparos yield white marble. The last is celebrated for its stalactite cavern, called the Grotto of Antiparos, in the side of a mountain, comprising an apartment of vast height, and walls of pure white marble, with the usual phenomena of columns, pendants, and ornaments, simulating vegetable forms, found in caves of all countries.

A statuary marble nearly equal to that of Paros is native to the Island of Naxos, famous in the legendary history of Bacchus; and Lesbos, the home of Sappho and Arion, once the seat of a school of lyric poetry, is intersected by lofty mountains yielding marble.

The Island of Cyzicus in the Propontis, or Sea of Marmora, was well supplied with marble, and it was, without doubt, partly due to the easily accessible building material that the city of Cyzicus, whose ruins are still to be seen, was so celebrated for the beauty and magnificence of its edifices.

· Scaglia, or the limestone of the Apennines, is the principal rock of the Ionian Isles on the west coast of Greece, therefore it is not improbable that the fortress or palace of Ulysses, which crowned the summit of Eagle's Cliff at the foot of Mount Neium, on the small rocky Island of Ithaca, was built of this limestone, since, from the evidence of recent discoveries, Ulysses and his contemporary heroes cannot be dismissed as mythical characters.

The Island of Cephalonia consists of a white limestone, more or less crystalline, resembling that of Malta   The fossils are rare except in the environs of Argostoli, in the southwestern part of the island, where the Tertiary beds are remarkable for the number and preservation of organic remains. In the island of Zante, the "woody Zacynthus" of Homer, a limestone formation with fossils is largely developed near the city of Zante; it is of a pale-yellow color, and penetrated by caverns.   This island is known for its bituminous wells, which still supply large quantities of pitch.

The excavations of Dr. Schliemann at Mycene and Tiryns, ancient cities of Argolis, prove that limestones and marbles were generally used in construction at an early period in Greece, as they were in other countries. The Cyclopean walls of Mycene were built of the beautiful, hard breccia, with which the mountains abound, and the ancient quarry of Char-

vati is still seen near the ruins. · The wall surrounding the
Acropolis was from thirteen to thirty-five feet high, with an
average thickness of sixteen feet. The blocks of stone are
of different sizes, some very large, and some in the form of
polygons, closely fitted in the joints. These structures, it
is thought, date from 1600 to 1800 B. C. At Tiryns the
immense blocks are rudely put together, but neither here
nor at Mycene do they compare in magnitude with those of
Baalbec.

The most interesting remains of Mycene are those called
the Treasury of Atreus, assigned by tradition to the father of
Agamemnon, which is said to be the only complete historic
monument in Greece. The interior of the Treasury is arched
in the roof and sides to resist both vertical and lateral pressure, showing that the principles of the arch were understood
at a very remote period. A similar structure, called the
Treasury of Minyas, whose ruins are extant, was built of white
marble in a hill of the ancient city of Orchomenus, in Bœotia.
The walls were covered with brazen plates of polished metal
instead of sculpture, a practice of a later date, and fastened by
bronze nails. A large number of similar fastenings were
found at Mycene, where the same fashion was in vogue

Among the materials found in the ruins of ancient Greek
cities used for decoration, vases, ornaments, and articles of
common use, were white, green, red, and blue marbles, alabaster, serpentine, steatite, granite, diorite, basalt, jasper, obsi-
dian, onyx, rock-crystal, amber, fluor-spar, agates, opal, and
gold and silver in great abundance. The specimens of pottery
were remarkable for having preserved their colors fresh for
more than two thousand three hundred years.

A number of the modern Greek marbles exhibited at
the Paris Exposition of 1878 resembled, in appearance, the
antiques, notably the Italian Sette Basi, Pavonezzetto, Rosso
antico, and Verde serpentino. Other varieties are given in
the Appendix, and in the articles on " Antique Marbles."

GREEK ART.

The history of the limestones and marbles of Greece would be incomplete without some notice of a few of the numerous works of art, illustrating the uses made of the abundant material for sculpture and architecture which this country yields

Of all the races of men none have ever surpassed or even equalled the Greeks in their productions in stone. They were the greatest idealists the world ever saw, and marble under their hands assumed forms of beauty, such as could result only from artistic genius of the highest order.

During its most flourishing period, Greek art gave expression to the national religious thought embodied in the sculptured forms of the gods.

Their system of mythology, invented by the poets, was upheld and perpetuated by art ; hence their most beautiful works were the statues of their divinities, and the most magnificent buildings were the temples which enshrined them. The age of Pericles and Phidias, names associated with the most illustrious period in the history of Athens, would, perhaps, afford the best example of the possibilities of the unrivalled Parian and Pentelic marbles under the control of transcendent genius.

As the history of marble cannot be isolated from the history of art, so the name of Phidias cannot be separated from the history of sculpture. Born at a time when Greece was passing through a great national crisis, the struggle with Persian despotism, his youthful genius was inspired by the stirring events of his time to create those wonderful productions which were the admiration of his own age, as the fragments of his works have been of succeeding generations. The temples and shrines of the gods of Greece had been destroyed by the invaders, and it was to their restoration that his great efforts were directed.

Every one at all acquainted with the history of Athens, his

native city, is familiar with some of the more celebrated works by this artist, or those wrought under his supervision, which adorned the Acropolis. Ascending the marble steps on the west side of the hill we enter the Acropolis through the Propylæa, the famous entrances made by Phidias, where the first object of interest was the Parthenon, said to be the most beautiful and artistically perfect structure of its kind of any age, built of Pentelic marble, which was first used in the celebrated sculptures of this temple. Many of them were removed by Lord Elgin, and are now to be found in the British Museum. Lubke, in his History of Sculpture, says of them. "No plastic work has ever again been executed with so elevated power and so graceful beauty. There is a breath of imperishable youth about every figure; nature is conceived with such grandeur and might that one feels as if looking at a race of gods."

Through all her internecine wars Greece held one state, Elis, sacred to peace and friendship. Here the Greeks laid aside their mutual jealousies, and met as brothers of the same noble race; here the national Olympic games were celebrated, and here was the famous grove Altis, the "sanctuary of the arts;" and to this spot, consecrated to Jupiter, the Greek states sent their contributions from their best masters. The wonderful colossal statue of the king of gods, by Phidias, made of gold and ivory, seated on a throne ornamented with precious stones, adorned the sacred grove.

As Phidias was, *par excellence*, the sculptor of the gods, so Polycletus, his fellow-pupil, was the sculptor of men. One of his most celebrated statues was the Spear-bearer, called the "Canon," because it represented the highest ideal of the human form.

Praxiteles appeared at a later period, when art had passed from the region of grand and spiritual representation to one of grace and sensuous beauty. He was the creator of the Cnidian Venus, "which was," says Lubke, "in his day what the Olympian Jove was in the time of Phidias."

Scopas, contemporary with and equal to Praxiteles, produced the sculptures which adorned the famous Mausoleum,
and it has been thought that the Battle of the Amazons,
represented on the frieze, is surpassed only by the sculptures
of the Parthenon.

It is not known whether Praxiteles or Scopas, or some other
artist, gave to the world the celebrated group of Niobe, the
"Mater Dolorosa of antiquity"; but fortunate it was that this
remarkable group was rescued from the destruction which
swept away the larger number of the great masterpieces of
antiquity. Some of the later works of Greek art, inferior in
sublime greatness and spiritual beauty to those of an earlier
period, are the Laocoon, and Apollo Belvedere of the Vatican,
the Venus de Medici at Florence, and the Farnese Bull at
Naples.

The genius of the Greek nation burned with so intense a
glow that it burnt itself out, leaving behind its diminished
lustre, reflected by another people, less gifted in creative and
artistic power.

CHAPTER XV.

I. *The Russian Empire.* — The Eozoic rocks are developed in the regions of the White Sea and the Gulf of Finland in the north, and from the Sea of Azof in the south to the fifty-second degree of latitude, yet they do not afford any of the great limestone formations like the Laurentian series of North America

Paleozoic rocks, including vast beds of limestone, are spread over this extensive empire, where, in some places, they have a remarkable development

The Timan range of mountains, the great western branch of the Ural, reaching to the Arctic, unknown to geologists, says Murchison, writing in 1843, until recent explorations, affords the largest masses of Paleozoic strata, the greater part being unchanged by metamorphism

The Lower Silurian, represented by the Pentamerus limestone, and the Pleta, identical with the Scandinavian Orthoceratite, and characterized by the same species of fossils, covers a large area, and has afforded numerous specimens for collections.

The Pleta limestone of Western Russia prevails in the government of St Petersburg, forming the low hills south of the capital, and extending in cliffs along the Gulf of Bothnia. In the environs of St. Petersburg it is bent into a complete arch, and along the Gulf of Finland, in Esthonia, it sometimes rises in cliffs one hundred and fifty feet high, with buttress-like projections. Lake Peipus, connected with the gulf by the Narva River, precipitates its waters over an escarpment of this limestone south of the old Castle of Narva. In consequence of the disintegration of the lower strata of the cliff, the falls, like those of the Niagara, are receding; the Gulf of Finland has been called, in reference to this geological fact, the Ontario, and Lake Peipus, the Erie, of Esthonia, and of course the Narva River, the Niagara, but the formations of the two cataracts belong to different periods. The Pleta limestone has no rival in its western range to the Baltic, but towards the south it is replaced by those of the Devonian and Carboniferous systems. The Pentamerus limestone is predominant in the government of Kovno, south of St. Petersburg, and is intercalated between two other formations. The Lower Silurian strata, enclosing an abundance of animal organisms, yield marbles and dolomite.

Devonian rocks form one of the most extensive systems in Russia, covering a tract of one hundred and fifty thousand square miles, constituting the Valdai Hills south of St. Petersburg, except the summits, which are Carboniferous, and extend over the region around Lake Ilmen and other large areas. They are, in Russia, le. calcareous than those of the same age in North America, where they yield some of the great limestone formations

In Courland and other Baltic provinces the Devonian series extends to the White Sea, and on the Tchussovaya River, a branch of the Kama, these rocks shoot up to a great height like sharp-pointed needles. The limestones of the series occur in the Urals, and have been quarried on the Polist River south of St. Petersburg. At Lake Ilmen the cliffs, four hundred to five hundred feet high, are composed mostly of these limestones, which attain a great thickness to the south of this region, and several varieties are displayed near the ancient Castle Kircholm, on the Duna, in Livonia, and at the Castle of Selberg, further up the river, where they are more than seventy feet thick.

Plate XVI.

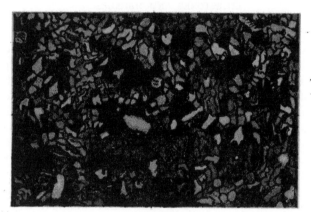

SEME SANTO.

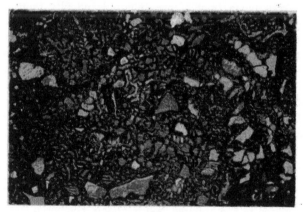

LUMACHELLA PAVONAZZA.

ARMSTRONG & CO. LITH. BOSTON.

The most remarkable specimens of fossil fishes, says Murchison, are found in sand and marl at the cliffs of Dorpat, west of Lake Peipus

In Central Russia Devonian limestones enclose the Producta, a Carboniferous fossil; and at Orel, on the Oka River, where it is extensively quarried, the rock is filled with Serpula, Natica, and Arca, the last forming entire beds.   At Othrada, north of Orel, is found a variety with innumerable minute shells, analogous to the Venus of North America, and still further north occurs a peculiar variety of a magnesian character resembling that of Orel.   The limestones of this period, in Russia, are replete with characteristic fossils identical with those of the Boulonnais of France, the Eifel of Germany, and the Devonshire of England.

The Carboniferous system of this country is very important, and has an enormous distribution, which, through its entire length, has a subsoil of limestone, including several kinds with the typical fossils.

The White Moscow is the representative of the Russian Carboniferous limestones, and covers a vast extent of territory from Moscow to Archangel towards the north, and diverges from Moscow to other places towards the east, south, and west.   It is generally white, of coarse grain, and is distinguished by the fossil Spirifer Mosquensis   At the quarries south of Moscow it has yielded the excellent white stone of which the city is built.

The greatest variety of this formation is observed on the Oka River, where in one locality its outcrop is more than two hundred and fifty feet, and at Kolonma, on the same river, it was used for the buildings of the town; both here and near Moscow it is intercalated with yellow magnesian limestone   Another remarkable display is seen at the ancient Tartar city of Kasinof, on the Oka, combined with a magnesian limestone bearing a close analogy to the Zechstein of Germany, forming a series three hundred feet thick.

The White or Moscow limestone of Archangel, on the

Andoma River, may be called, says the distinguished geologist before quoted, a coral reef largely formed of the Chætetes radians often aggregated in large concretionary masses enclosing caverns. The lime obtained from this rock is used for whitewashing buildings, a prevailing custom in Russia.

The upper member of the Carboniferous group is the Fusilina limestone, which has a large development on the Volga between Simbirsk and Samara, in the form of cliffs two hundred or three hundred feet in height. The peculiar bend in the river at this place, taking the form of a parallelogram, encloses hills of limestone, the lower beds consisting of lithographic stone similar to the Solenhofen, and the upper, of pure Fusilina strata.

The Carboniferous series disappears towards the south but emerges again between the Don and the Dnieper, comprising the richest coal region in Russia, and is spread over a surface of eleven thousand square miles, constituting a part of the Upper Steppes of the Don Cossacks and the New Russias, and some of the strata on the Donetz and the Ural Mountains. The lower beds resemble the Great Scaur of England.

The Permian system, named for the ancient kingdom of Permia, in the east part of Russia, is more fully developed in this country than in any other, extending over a large part of the eastern and central portion, and covering a territory, it is stated, twice as large as France.

The limestones of the period, with few exceptions, are not abundant in fossils, although a zone resembling the Zechstein formation appears near Orenburg, filled with fragments of white shells of the Producta, Orthis, Modiola, and others. Varieties found nowhere else in Russia, occur in the Steppes of the Kirghiz.

Permian limestones stretch towards the west over a considerable portion of the country, and on the Sok, escarpments of white and yellow magnesian strata rise to a height of from one hundred to one hundred and twenty feet, and are the source of the sulphur springs of the Imperial Baths, near

Moscow. In the vicinity of Perm the formation encloses fossils peculiar to the Zechstein

The beautiful city of Kazan, on a branch of the Volga, near the junction of the two rivers, and the seat of a university, is built upon Permian strata, including a white, fossiliferous limestone, affording the foundation-rock of the citadel On the Volga, below the city, the cliffs attain considerable elevation and extend for a long distance The fine town of Arzana on the Tiosho, rises upon an elevated terrace encircled by Permian, fossiliferous limestones ; and to the north, the Piana, like the Tiosho, has cut a channel through this rock, in which are large caverns, occasioned by the subsidences of the gypsum underlying all the limestones of this region. The gypsum, which is also developed on the Pinega River, alternating with limestones, is pure white, and in places is displayed in vertical walls seventy or eighty feet in height The Dwina, three-fourths of a mile wide in the upper part of its course, flows through a long gorge of gypseous alabaster, which produces the effect of a bank of snow, surmounted by a line of dark-green fir-trees. A layer of fossiliferous limestone interstratifies the gypsum cliff, while, a little higher up the river, a pink gypsum, with red and green marls, is displayed on the banks. A pure white, saccharoidal limestone, associated with gypsum, appears on the upper Volga; at the town of Nijni Novgorod, celebrated for its great annual fair, where the Oka unites with this river, the banks display cliffs, from three hundred to four hundred feet high, composed of red and green ribboned marls, limestones, and sandstones The limestone encloses brilliant concretions of gypsum but no fossils. South of Orenburg, on the Ural River, great salt mines with gypsum occur, long known to the nomadic tribes of the country. What is called the Freezing Cavern exists in a hill of gypsum, and has been utilized by the natives for a cellar. It is intensely cold in the hottest weather, but so warm in the cold season that ice is soon reduced to water.

The Great and Little Bogdo are isolated hills or small

mountains on the left bank of the Volga, in the Steppes of the Kirghiz. The Great Bogdo, remarkable for its peculiar fauna and flora, is six hundred feet above the Caspian Sea, the highest point in the Steppes of Astracan. It is an object of religious veneration to the nomadic tribes and of interest to scientific travellers. The base of the hill consists of marl, from which brine springs issue, depositing a solid bank of salt of the depth of a foot in a single year. Other strata cover this marl, but the summit is crowned by a gray limestone, similar to the Muschelkalk, enclosing Ammonites, Gervillia, Perna, and other characteristic fossils. The Little Bogdo has nearly the same composition, but the top is covered with angular fragments, resembling the ruins of buildings, which are believed to be such by the inhabitants. The Steppes of Astracan abound in marine shells.

The Jurassic or Oolitic series of rocks has a more limited distribution in Russia than in most other countries. The strata consist largely of shales and marls in isolated masses, at remote distances, including unimportant limestones displayed at Izium, on the Donetz, and in the steep cliffs of the Crimea.

A white, fossiliferous limestone or Coral Rag, analogous to that on the Donetz, forms the ridge, three hundred feet in height, along the Vistula, near which stands Cracow, the ancient Polish capital, founded nearly twelve centuries ago. About this venerable city cluster many associations of historical and national interest; the sovereigns of a long and proud line, were crowned here, and the Cathedral, regarded the finest in Poland, contains the tombs of the kings and queens, including those of Casimir, Sobieski, Copernicus, Kosciusko, and other distinguished persons.

The Cretaceous rocks, with a large representation, extend in detached masses across the south and south-central portions of the country from east to west, but are not found in the north. One of the finest displays of white chalk in Russia is said to occur on the Donetz, in the Steppes of the Don

Cossacks, where Artesian borings through this formation reach the depth of six hundred and thirty feet.

Cretaceous strata are very abundant in the Caucasus Mountains, and in Kirghiz, in the southwestern part of Siberia, bordering the Caspian and Aral Seas, while shell limestones of this period form the summits of the lofty Caucasus, covering peaks nearly eighteen thousand feet high.

The Tertiary formations are divided by Murchison into three great zones : the Eocene, the Miocene, and the Aralo-Caspian. The Eocene are mostly on the Volga and the Dnieper rivers ; the Miocene, in Bessarabia, Podalia, and Poland ; and the Aralo-Caspian, a brackish water deposit, about the Caspian and the Aral Seas. The last formation, called the Limestone of the Steppes, is spread over a wide area, covering the lower Steppes of Astracan between the Ural Mountains and the Volga, and the Caspian and the Sea of Aral.

The Tertiary strata of the Carpathian Mountains, embracing varieties of marine and fresh-water limestones, are similar to those found in the Apennines and the basins of Vienna, Bordeaux, and Paris.

At Taganrog, on an arm of the Sea of Azof, the limestone is very fossiliferous and yields a rock equal to the Calcaire grossier of the Paris Basin. A whitish, shelly, porous limestone, quarried at Odessa for the buildings of that and other southern cities of Russia, is called the Limestone of Odessa. In places it is valuable, as in the cliffs near the town, including both marine and fresh-water deposits with the bones of elephants, horses, dogs, and other Mammals. Varieties of Tertiary limestones are developed in the Crimea, from Sevastopol in the southwest to Kertch in the east ; at the latter place a shell limestone is quarried identical with the Odessa, composed in the upper beds of masses of corals exhibiting irregular and fantastic forms in imitation of steps and seats ; one of these accumulations, overlooking the city, is called the Throne of Mithridates, the ambitious King of Pontus.

The Aralo-Caspian or Steppe limestone is by far the most important Tertiary limestone in the Russian Empire, covering an immense tract in southeastern Europe and western Asia, forming the largest basin in the world, which was, it is supposed, an early, extensive Mediterranean.   The fossils of this rock include species both of fresh and brackish waters, analogous to, or identical with, the shells now existing in the Caspian, proving, it is thought, that this vast region was once covered by a sea of brackish water, of which the Caspian and the Aral are the "diminished types."   It is probable that this Tertiary sea occupied the wide tracts of Asia constituting the country of the Turcomans and the Kurghiz tribes, and in confirmation of this theory it is argued that the Steppe limestone is almost the only rock found throughout this immense territory, and that the animals enclosed differed as essentially from those of the ocean of that day as those of Australia, at the present time, differ from the animals of all other countries; hence the conclusion is reached that the Aralo-Caspian deposits were accumulated under one vast inland sea.

The limestone of the Taman peninsula, in the Sea of Azof, extends eastward along the northern slope of the Caucasus to the Caspian, and corresponds to that of Daghestan, which forms the low hills on the western shore of this sea; the Paludina, a fresh-water fossil, is abundant in the limestone of Daghestan, while in that of the plateau and Isthmus of Ulst, between the Caspian and the Aral Seas, the Neritina and the Cyclas, salt-water fossils, are combined with the Paludina   Between Astracan and Tzritzin, on the Volga, the Myrtilus is very abundant, forming conglomerates which constitute entire islands.

The Steppe limestone is seen at Derbend and Baku, on the west shore of the Caspian, in the region named the Field of Fire, which emits an inflammable gas called by the natives "sacred fires," and contains mud volcanoes and springs of naphtha.   This formation west of the Aral passes to the south of Khiva, and probably covers the plains of Turkistan.

Some of the Aralo-Caspian fossils have been discovered as far north as latitude fifty-five degrees.

The Steppe limestone is an exceedingly interesting formation, from its great extent and its peculiar and uniform character, affording evidence of a vast interior sea

Limestones form a considerable part of the lofty Elburz Mountains, stretching across the northern part of Persia to the Black Sea, and comprising some celebrated peaks   The Mount Ararat of the present day is volcanic, an eruption having occurred as late as 1785.   It consists of two summits, Great and Little Ararat, the former, ascended in 1829, by Parrot, and in 1876 by Mr. Bryce, is given as a little more than seventeen thousand, and the latter thirteen thousand feet in height.   Mount Alaghez, a peak of the same group, nearly ten thousand feet high, is characterized by four rocky pyramids arranged around the base   Between these mountains, covered with perpetual snow, lies the city of Erivan in the midst of a fruitful region celebrated for its orchards, and interesting to biblical and classical students

A part of the Caucasus Mountains has been referred to the Jurassic period, but the basin of Georgia on the southern declivity, watered by the ancient Cyrus, now the Kur, is Tertiary, including limestone and molasse, in places six hundred or seven hundred feet thick.   In this mass of rock, dwellings are cut, grouped, and terraced in the isolated blocks, which rise one above another, forming gigantic steps to the summit

In the valley of the Aras, the ancient Araxes, the southern boundary of the Russian possessions in southwestern Asia, the hills are composed of different colored clays, in which occur the salt-mines of Akshivan, the Naxuana of the ancients, and, according to tradition, the first city built after the Deluge.

The Nummulitic limestone, and large masses of dolomite, with caverns used by the natives for dwellings, are found in the Likh Mountains.

As the fossils of the Carboniferous period are found in Nova Zembla, it is probable that the Ural range extending under

the Kara Straits, connects this island with the mainland.
This extensive chain, separating two continents, barely attaining the elevation of the lowest mountains, the average height
being from two thousand to three thousand feet, and the
loftiest peaks only about six thousand, yet forms, on account
of its mineral wealth, one of the most important mountain
systems of the globe   Their moderate acclivity renders the
Urals easily accessible, and many flourishing towns are scattered throughout the mining districts. Ekaterinburg has
become famous for the cutting and polishing of gems, porphyries, and jaspers ; and Zlatust for the manufacture of Damas-
cene blades and embossed ornaments.

The Ural Mountains are formed of crystalline rocks, including saccharoidal marble, full of ores and minerals, embracing
those of the Silurian, Devonian, Carboniferous, and Permian
system, best displayed on the western declivity, where they
have not been disturbed, and have undergone but little change ;
on the eastern slope. they have been more displaced, but contain the richest ores

The Jurassic series is developed in the northern Urals, on
the western side, while a light-colored, dolomitic, cavernous
limestone, forming the low hills along the Sylva River, a
tributary to the Tchussovaya, has been referred to the Carboniferous period. Following the latter river south from Perm
to Ekaterinburg, this limestone covers a large extent of surface, and the banks display marbles and greenstone. West of
Ekaterinburg, Carboniferous limestones with fossils are well
developed, but none enclosing organic remains are found
near the axis of the range   At a gorge called Peter's Gate
these limestones, pierced with caverns, rise in picturesque
forms to a height of two hundred feet, while limestones
with Silurian fossils appear at the Demidoff copper-mines
celebrated for immense beds of malachite   To the north
of these mines, rise the Large and Small Blagodat, important for magnetic ores; on the summit, stands a monument of a Vogul chief, burned by his clan for revealing the

site of these ores to the Russians. Murchison, who is very graphic in his descriptions, says that the Tchussovaya, unsurpassed in picturesque beauty of scenery, flows in its way to the sea, through a limestone gorge in which cliffs of every form occur, displaying large caverns, with trees and flowers crowning the top. Rocks, passing through every shade from black to white, contorted into basins and anticlinals, here rising into serrated and broken peaks, there bending into graceful slopes, are brought to sight, delighting the traveller by the variety, beauty, and grandeur of the view; and to enhance the interest of the scene, the romantic incident may be added that these caverns, as well as those on the banks of the Issetz, were the resort of Yarmac, the conqueror of the Siberian Tartars, whose exploits compare favorably with those of the Spanish conquerors of America.

Among the limestones of this picturesque river are black dolomites, said to be unknown in western Europe, white dolomites and a subcrystalline, light-colored limestone of the Carboniferous, called in Russia Stina voi, "the wall," which shoots up like the "Needles" in the Alps. On a tributary of the Tchussovaya, are found limestones of the Silurian and Devonian systems, the latter resembling the Eifel in some of its fossils.

In Siberia, on the Is, a branch of the Tura, a white limestone occurs profusely charged with the Pentamerus, Trilobites, and other Silurian shells; the rocks are horizontal, an unusual condition on the eastern slope. Paleozoic limestones, regarded as Silurian and Devonian, extend towards the north, and at the copper-mines of Turginsk, the limestone, changed to crystalline marble, is associated with fine crystals of garnet. Some of the richest copper-mines and the celebrated gold-mines Peshanka, are found in this formation.

The Kakva River, a branch of the Sylva, passes through a gorge of dark-gray limestone with white veins, in some places changed into granular marble, which crumbles to the touch, in other parts, it is a compact limestone forming grand scenery. The metamorphism was due to the proximity of eruptive rocks, changing limestones into dolomites and marbles.

On the western side of the Urals, the Petchora, flowing north to the Arctic, has its source in a mountain of the same name, three thousand six hundred feet high, consisting of schistose rocks, from which arises another elevation called the Mount of Idols, on account of the eight natural columns of quartz ascending from its summit, the highest being one hundred feet. The tributaries of the upper Petchora are flanked by bands of black, Encrinal limestone, superimposed by gray crystalline marble, the series constituting cliffs rising four hundred feet above the river. The limestone is placed with the Lower Silurian and the marble, enclosing fossils similar to species found in Wales, with the Upper Silurian.

Carboniferous limestones are displayed on the banks of the Iletsk, an affluent of the Petchora, forming escarpments that rise five hundred feet above the bed of the river. Whetstones are obtained from this region, and along the western flanks of the Urals, which supply the Russian market.

The rocks of the Timan range bear none of the characteristics of the Urals, but seem to belong rather to the Scandinavian system. The principal range is Devonian, like the Valdai Hills, while the outer flanks and the southern extremity comprise beds of Carboniferous limestone with the Spirifer Mosquensis.

The White or Moscow limestone, like that of the Timan Mountains, forms capes and high river-banks in the Arctic regions, where the fossil shells, in many instances, are found with the freshness of their original colors preserved and with their valves adhered.

The South Urals, from Perm to Orenburg, develop a great variety of metamorphic rocks, including crystalline limestones. The Sugomac Mountain, with its rocky buttresses of pure white, saccharoidal marble, forms a striking outer defence of the Urals; while on the west flank, extending towards Simsk, red and gray marbles are found. Both the Devonian and Carboniferous systems are represented in this region, the latter encloses the lake at Simsk, with broken masses of limestone, aventurine covering some of the high-pointed rocks. The Siberian aventurine was used for the magnificent vase, now in the Museum of Geology, London, presented to Sir R. I. Murchison by the Emperor Nicholas. Both the material for the vase, and the porphyry column on which it stands, were taken from the hills Bielaretsh and Kargan, and polished at Tomsk, Siberia.

This distinguished geologist, in company with the Grand Duke Alexander, the late emperor, climbed the peak of the Uralskaga, and as he relates, with one foot in Europe and the other in Asia, they sang the national anthem, "Long live the Emperor."

In descending the Ural River, one meets with a saccharoidal marble with Encrinites, similar to that of the Sugomac. The summits of the granite range of the Ilmen, which yields a great variety of minerals, are covered with granular limestone, and the rich metalliferous district between the Miask on the eastern, and the Kara on the western slope of the Urals, develop Encrinital limestones.

Small hills of Carboniferous limestone in the South Ural have yielded a large collection of organic remains, similar to those of the same period found in Belgium, France, and Great Britain; in fact, throughout Russia, the formation is rich in fossils, usually well-preserved. Cephalopods are rare, but Brachiopods are very abundant; the Producta is nearly universal, the Spirifer affords fewer species, the Mosquensis being the most prevalent, while among Corals, the Chætetes, Lithostrotion, Gorgonia, and the Bryozoan Retipora are the most abundant; the Rhizopod Fusilina is peculiar to Carboniferous strata, and constitutes thick masses of rock. Orsk, on the Ural River, near the frontiers of the Kurghiz country, yields a variety of ornamental stones, including marbles, red, gray, and pink porphyries, and ribbon jaspers.

The whole southern portions of the Urals, inhabited by the Bashkirs, is composed of an innumerable number of sharp ridges of Carboniferous limestones, from nine hundred to one thousand feet high, while the central portion develops a great variety of Silurian age   The entire range is exceedingly rich in mineral productions, affording more than one hundred and twenty different species ; among these are found malachites, jaspers, serpentines, porphyries, marbles, iron, gold, emeralds, and diamonds

The extensive iron mines have developed and stimulated native talent to produce some of the best and most beautiful manufactures in iron and steel found in any country ; the etchings and ornaments of Russian swords are most exquisitely finished   Colonel Anossoff, one of the most skilful metallurgists of the age, writes Atkinson, turned his attention to the ancient art of damascening arms, which had long been lost to Europe, and succeeded in rescuing the practice from oblivion. The rich malachite mines of the Demidoffs, whose estates are said to include between three and four millions of acres, are valued at an enormous sum, and develop, besides malachite, iron, copper, platinum, gold, and silver, porphyry, jasper of great beauty, and various colored marbles

Siberia, notwithstanding its inhospitable climate, is, for its mineral productions, one of the richest countries in the world, and considered of great importance by those who have explored it for its animal and vegetable species   The valley of the Yenissee is very fertile ; magnificent pine forests cover regions north of the Arctic Circle, including trees of gigantic size, and it is claimed that one of these forests is the most extensive known. The Altai Range, forming the barrier between the great empires of Russia and China, develops some exceedingly rich silver mines.

II *China* — The Altai Mountains belong, in part, to China, but the geological features of this great empire, however interesting and important they may be, are less understood than those of its powerful neighbor, as in a country whose inhabitants are suspicious of foreigners, scientific explorations are attended with difficulty, if not danger.   Atkinson discovered in Mongolia large veins of beautiful, transparent, rose quartz, and a mountain of red and brown porphyry veined with white. Among the rocks and minerals of the Chinese Altai, he found marbles with purple spots, deep-red aragonite, plum-colored jaspers, agates, chalcedony, sardonyx, olivine, and other gems. The Chinese tablets sold as " rice stones " are made of sparry limestone, while jade is used very extensively for carved ornamental articles, vases, images, and pagodas ; some of the latter are cut in iconite or agalmatolite, and steatite.

One of the most remarkable formations of China is the Loess, consisting of very fine sediment enclosing calcareous nodules and tube-like remains, thought to be the roots and branches of plants.   The Loess forms a striking feature in the north and west, constituting extensive masses, presenting a columnar structure ; in the steep cliffs formed of this deposit, the natives construct their dwellings, which are concealed from the traveller on the plains above.

The rugged and mountainous provinces of Shan-se and Shen-se, west of the Great Plain bordering the Pacific, may be regarded, says Eden, as the mineral districts of China. They abound in coal, copper, gold, iron, cinnabar, jasper, lapis-lazuli, marble, and porphyry.   Granite, marble, and coal are found not far from Peking.

A prospective field of great interest to the geologist lies before him in this vast empire, and it is to be hoped that the government may, in the not far distant future, remove all obstacles in the way of scientific investigation

CHAPTER XVI.

THE extensive domains of the Turkish Empire, including portions of two continents, intersected in every direction by lofty mountains, would, naturally, afford a great variety and abundance of calcareous rocks, embracing, it might be supposed, a wide range of geological time, but a larger part of the limestone formations of this dominion belongs to the younger members.

In European Turkey, the Cretaceous and Tertiary strata are the prevailing types, represented by the Hippurite and Nummulitic formations, which constitute a series of parallel valleys similar to some of those in the Swiss and French Juras. Nearly the entire western part of the peninsula is composed of Tertiary limestones; they are also found in the northern provinces, and it is believed that the vast basin of Bulgaria and Wallachia, on either side of the Danube, was, formerly, a gulf of the ancient Tertiary sea which covered a great part of the shore of the Black Sea. The chain of mountains on the coast of this sea, and in the basin of Thrace, now Rumili, and the northwest provinces of Bosnia and Servia, yield limestones with fossils identical with those of the Tertiary limestone of Gratz and the Leitha of the Vienna Basin. The limestones of Bosnia and Servia may have been employed in the construction of Belgrade, one of the most strongly fortified towns in Europe.

The Tertiary formation includes the steep, isolated, square masses of rock upon which are built the Greek monasteries called Meteores, whose precipitous sides, rising from one hundred and ninety-five to three hundred and ninety feet, can be ascended only by ladders raised and lowered at the pleasure of the monks.

The coast line of the Marmora is composed of Miocene limestones, while ranges of hills extending towards the southwest are covered with Nummulite of Eocene age. This formation, with Coral limestones, is found in the Deposito Dagh, the ancient Rodope Mountains, the highest in Thrace, once sacred to Bacchus.

The celebrated Hæmus range, a name suggestive of cold and snow, now known as the Balkan, has its southern slope composed largely of Cretaceous rocks. It is claimed that Triassic and Jurassic strata, though wanting on the northern side, are found on the south declivity of the chain ; but little is known of the character of the rocks on the western slope of these mountains The Caprotina and Neocomian limestones of the Cretaceous period, with dolomites, are developed in Bulgaria, north of the Balkan The system of rocks on the eastern shores of the Adriatic is regarded as the continuation of the Cretaceous beds of Italy, with a difference in their mineral character, those of Turkey having a preponderance of sandstones, those on the western side, of limestones Serpentines, and a conglomerate resembling the molasse of Thessaly, are very abundant in the Turkish provinces of the Adriatic. In the Danubian provinces many of the limestones are more or less crystalline, and have lost their fossiliferous character. Salonika on the Ægean, the ancient Macedonia, yields limestones enclosing Corals and Crinoids. The Struma River, the Strymon of the ancients, rising in Bulgaria and traversing Macedonia in its passage to the sea, has cut its way through an enormous mass of white and gray limestone and dolomites forming the Golo Brdo Mountains.

Calcareous marls and limestones constitute, in part, the strata in the environs of Adrianople. It may be taken for granted that rock in the neighborhood of a town, if suitable

for the purpose, was used in its construction, therefore there
is not much doubt that limestone, which seemed to be a favorite building material with the architects of former times,
was largely used in this celebrated city. The Emperor Hadrian, at the beginning of the second century, laid the foundation of the town and called it Hadrianopolis; it was a
strongly fortified city, and became the second in importance
in the Eastern Empire. It is situated on the Maritza River,
formerly the Hebrus, a stream made famous in story by the
legends of Orpheus, and was once the seat of the Turkish
Empire in Europe, and the residence of the sultans. Besides
its Roman antiquities, it contains one of the most magnificent mosques in the empire, and other remarkable buildings
erected by the Moslems.

Thessaly, of classic renown, develops marls, molasse,
pudding-stones, and calcareous tufas. The Thessalian plain
was formerly one vast lake, whose waters ran to the sea between Mounts Olympus and Ossa. The beautiful Vale of
Tempe, whose exceeding loveliness poets have celebrated, was
situated between these mountains, and through it flowed the
River Peneus, making a channel for the waters of the plain.

Besides its poetical renown, this region offers some geological features of great interest. The ancient inhabitants believed that the plain of Thessaly formed a vast lake, until a
passage was made through the rocks by some terraqueous
convulsion, when the lake became dry land; and this tradition
was probably founded on fact, though the cause might have
been, in part, the erosive power of water. The Deluge of
Deucalion is easily explained by supposing the outlets of the
lake to have been obstructed by deposits.

Devonian limestones are found on the Bosporus, but the
escarpments of this strait and of the Isles of Cyamus — blue
islands — the movable Planctæ and Symplegades of mythology — are composed of breccias The beautiful harbor of
the Golden Horn is cut through the Tertiary formation at
its junction with ancient schists.

Plate XVII.

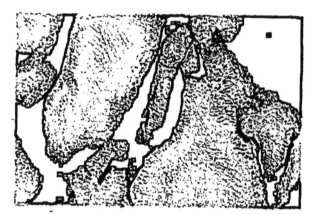

PAVONAZZETTO

SETTE BASI

ARMSTRONG & CO. LITH. BOSTON

To the west of Constantinople, are seen the limestone quarries from which the stone was taken for its bastions, walls, and aqueducts, constructed by the Emperor Justinian, who embellished, with magnificent buildings, the new capital of the Roman Empire, as Augustus had Rome, the old capital, between five and six centuries before   The mosques under Moslem rule were built of the same kind of limestone, which varies in thickness and quality, being sometimes soft and sometimes hard and crystalline, enclosing broken shells, mostly of fresh-water origin   Black marble is quarried at the Sutton mine, on the Asiatic side

The Turkish Empire embraces a territory celebrated in the history and literature of one of the most interesting nations of antiquity, the Greeks, a people that extended their civilization to Western Asia and the neighboring islands.   Like Greece, Asia Minor is rich in associations; every mountain and river, every country and city, is invested with fascinating interest, and here were born many illustrious men, whose genius infused antique art and literature with a "perennial charm and richness," and whose immortal works have been regarded with admiration for thousands of years

The numerous and magnificent cities of Western Asia, with their celebrated architectural monuments, whose ruins are to-day evidences of their former splendor, have a connection with the geological history of this country, once so fruitful and prosperous, so full of memorials of the past and associations with the present, as it became the theatre of the early triumphs of Christianity whose blessings have been transmitted to all succeeding generations

The opposite shores of the Sea of Marmora, says M. Petit-Bois, are widely different in their natural aspects , sandy plains and monotonous hills of recent geological age characterize the European side, while abrupt rocks, rising to a great height, forming mountains, among which the lofty chain of the Mysian Olympas is prominent, constitute the bold outlines of the Asiatic coast ; at the foot of these mountains stands the city of Brussa, formerly Prussa (famed in ancient literature for the festival there celebrated in honor of Hylas), built upon travertine resembling compact limestone. The mountains at this place are more than nine thousand feet in height ; in a deep ravine at their base is deposited calcareous tufa, assuming the form of stalactites and stalagmites.

Here there is little variety in the rocks, but advancing towards the Kara-Sou, an affluent of the Sakaria, the ancient Sangarius, one meets with different colored limestones, while the Kara-Sou itself is enclosed between mountains, with walls of a clear, yellow limestone.   The city of Biledjik is very picturesquely situated in an amphitheatre of conglomerate, while varieties of limestones, forming a group enclosing rare fossils and penetrated by numerous caverns, and very generally disseminated throughout the valley of the Kara-Sou, constitute the high rocks bordering the river in the neighborhood of the city.

Limestones form the high mountain chains between the Black Sea and Persia, and between Armenia and Syria on the Mediterranean.   At Erzerum occurs a beautiful, gypseous alabaster, similar to that of the Euphrates, and for ornamental purposes equal to the Italian alabaster   Madden, or Kebben-Madden, on the upper Euphrates, is celebrated for its silver-mines.   The mountains in which these mines are found, are composed of limestones, including a gray lithographic stone, used for the buildings of Madden, and said to belong to the oldest stratified rocks   The limestone forms a plateau along the river, with magnificent gorges, affording a passage to the water.   At the copper-mines of Arghaneh-Madden it is suitable for construction, and has been employed for building   The plateau of the Tigris develops a beautiful serpentine, with dark-green base, holding crystals of diallage

The eastern branch of the Taurus Mountains is composed of a series of Cretaceous limestones, fifty miles in breadth, covered by Nummulitic strata.   The celebrated Armenian monastery at Arghaneh occupies the summit of a mountain

of Nummulitic limestone two thousand feet above the plain
and four thousand above sea-level. The Cretaceous limestones of this region are similar to those of Europe and the
northern countries of Africa, and the Nummulitic, which is
very prevalent in Asia Minor, sometimes constitutes mountains nearly ten thousand feet in height.

Lacustrine limestones occupy the basin of the ancient
Halys, now the Kirgil Irmak, the largest river of Western
Asia, which formed in early times, the boundary between
states and races, separating the Indo-European from the
Semitic nations   The modern city of Sivas, on this river, is
constructed of travertine, which, with gypsum and limestone,
constitutes the principal rock in the vicinity ; the upper layers
of limestone, with Paludinæ and Cyclades, form an elevated
plateau five miles in width and fifteen in length, cut by deep
ravines.

Vast Tertiary deposits occur throughout the valley of the
Halys, and on the eastern shore of the Black Sea, occupied
by the ancient Colchis, land of the "Golden Fleece," comprising oolitic limestones similar to those of Kertch in the
Crimea

One of the most remarkable features of central Asia Minor
is the presence of lava beds, combined with Tertiary strata,
forming a deposit more than three thousand six hundred feet
thick, extending over a surface of two hundred miles, and .
covering the territory surrounding the ancient city of Philadelphia, called the Burnt Region.

The ancient province of Phrygia yields serpentines and
limestones of various kinds affording marbles, among them
the celebrated Phrygian marbles described in another chapter.
A valley is said to exist in this region containing artificial
grottoes, cut in volcanic tufa, of different forms and sizes, with
broad façades, ornamented with sculpture, and spacious, decorated apartments.   The architectural ornaments belong to
different epochs of art, Greek, Roman, and Byzantine, and on
some of them traces of painting are perceptible , the rooms

have neither stairs nor other artificial means of ascent. These grottoes are numerous, and are found in many different localities, yet no mention is made of them by any ancient or mediæval writer

The remains of Azani, in Phrygia, are considered to be better preserved than those of any other city of Western Asia They comprise a splendid Temple of Jupiter, a theatre two hundred and thirty-two feet in diameter, and other architectural fragments, affording proof of the former magnificence of the city, which occupied a plain surrounded by mountains of schist and marble, at whose base are the quarries whence the stone was taken for the construction of the town.

Sardis, in Lydia, is a very ancient city, and before its decline was one of the most celebrated in Asia Minor. Among its extensive ruins are Ionic columns of white marble, supposed to be from the Temple of Cybele, and the remains of other public buildings; the most memorable relics are found near Lake Gygæa, the burial-place of the Kings of Lydia, which has been called the Place of a Thousand Tombs.

The citadel of Sardis, containing the Palace and Royal Treasury, was built upon a rock projecting from the foot-hills of Mount Tmolus, surrounded by a triple wall, which renders it impregnable to assault, and was taken only by surprise by the Persians under Cyrus The site of the city and the greater part of the basin of Sardis have been denuded and transported by the waters of the Hermus and its tributaries. In this basin fresh-water deposits prevail, while in the vicinity of Troy and the Dardanelles they are wholly marine.

Troy itself was built upon a shelly limestone — Muschelkalk —and the probability is that the same rock was used in the construction of the city of Priam, though there are other kinds of rocks, mostly plutonic, in the neighborhood. Schliemann speaks of a shell limestone used in the buildings, and says that the quarry from which the stone was taken is near the city and was open until a very recent date. The town, rebuilt by the Greeks, must have contained magnificent structures and

works of art, judging from the fragments brought to light.
Triglyphs six and a half· feet in length and two and a half in
width were adapted only for very large buildings. Among
the relics of this ancient city are a metope, with a sculptured
representation of Apollo and the horses of the Sun; idols
carved in very fine marble; a block of marble weighing fifty
tons, bearing an inscription in Greek; a pyramid of striped
black, white, and blue marble; a block striped with white, a
kind of marble not now found in that region, and a block of
Parian with sculptures in high relief, a very interesting relic,
giving evidence of the use of Parian marble for sculpture in
those early ages.

The ruins of Ephesus have been compared to a vast quarry,
furnishing material for the building of many other towns, so
extensive and numerous were the public edifices of this ancient
city; even the famous Temple of Diana, one of the wonders
of the world, has contributed to the embellishment of many of
the churches of modern days   The Emperor Justinian, who
adorned his capital at Constantinople with splendid buildings,
carried off statues and columns of green jasper for the Church
of St Sophia, and other decorations taken from this Temple
are found in Italian churches

Gold and the most precious marbles and woods were
lavishly used in this celebrated building, and some of the most
distinguished artists of the times were employed in its construction   The first temple was two hundred and twenty
years in building, and contained more than a hundred columns,
each one the gift of a king.   It was reduced to ruins eight
times and rebuilt; the final destruction was by the Goths, in
the beginning of the third century of the Christian era.

The only city of ancient renown in Western Asia that has
survived to the present day is Smyrna, which claimed to be
the birthplace of Homer, and contained a magnificent building dedicated to his honor.   Smyrna is called, by its early
historians, a beautiful city, but its present appearance is
attractive only at a distance, made conspicuous by its domes

and minarets.   It is encircled by mountains of compact, gray limestone, enclosing Nummulites and Hippurites, whose slowly accumulated masses of rock material contributed to its beauty and magnificence.   North of Smyrna this limestone rises abruptly from the plain of the Hermus River, on the east side of Mount Spiglas, while on the south lacustrine limestones, varying in texture from lithographic stone to soft chalk, extend for several miles

A red variety of limestone, used at Brussa for marble, has its representative at Mount Olympus and in the Island of Rhodes.

The great plain of Pamphylia, on the Mediterranean, is composed of travertine deposited in the form of cliffs from eighteen to seventy-five feet thick, resting on marine strata; this same deposit constitutes the mountains to the south-west.

Limestones are the prevailing rocks on the shores of the Mediterranean, extending throughout the provinces of Asia Minor, Greece, Malta, Egypt, Arabia, Palestine, and Syria, including the lofty ranges of Lebanon and Anti-Lebanon

Tertiary formations are largely represented in Cilicia, on the Mediterranean, whose chief city was Tarsus, on the Cydnus, a river remarkable for its clear, cold water flowing down from the Taurus Mountains, through valleys composed of Coral limestone and conglomerates   Tertiary strata compose the crest of shell limestones overlooking the ancient ramparts of Antioch, on the Orontes, the capital of Syria, once the chief city of Asia, and famous in the annals of Christianity   The calcareous breccia forming the plains of Antioch furnishes the beautiful marble called Breccia di Aleppo , to the north of this city the Nummulitic limestone is present, and to the south white chalk.

The Libanus Mountains, called by the Hebrews Lebanon or White Mountains, because their highest summits are covered by perpetual snow, and formerly celebrated for their cedars and vines, are mainly composed of limestone and chalk.

The eastern range, called by classic writers Anti-Libanus, develops gray chalk and Jurassic limestones, which, including dolomites, compose Mount Tabor, all the peaks to the east of Libanus, and the region about the Sea of Tiberias.

The limestones of the Lebanon Mountains embrace many varieties, including red, white, black, and yellow; the white constitutes the foundation-rock of the village of Bicherri, just below the cedars of Lebanon, the black is cavernous, and the red is crossed by white veins of quartz.

North of Anti-Libanus, in a plain composed of the same limestone as that used in its construction, stood Baalbec or Heliopolis, whose extensive ruins are full of interest and mystery. The numerous magnificent buildings were erected on an elevated platform, in some places thirty feet above the plain, and surrounded by a wall. After the conquests of Alexander, Baalbec passed successively into the possession of the Greeks, Romans, and Saracens, but neither of these nations built into the wall those huge blocks of limestone that astonish modern travellers. Mr Prime suggests the people who constructed these works may have been contemporary with the builders of the Pyramids. There are twenty of these blocks, some more than sixty feet in length, others from thirty to thirty-two, and all are thirteen feet high and ten and one-half thick. They were cut from a quarry of compact limestone, half a mile south of the town, where can be seen a block left in the mine, probably extracted at the same time, sixty-eight feet long, seventeen feet wide, and fourteen and one-half thick.

On the highest part of the platform, stood a grand temple, extending, with its peristyle, porticoes, and courts, one thousand feet; of its seventy Corinthian columns, seven and one-half feet in diameter, and seventy-six in height, six are left standing. A court four hundred and forty-four feet by three hundred and seventy, was surrounded by small semi-circular temples of Corinthian architecture; but the most celebrated edifice was the Temple of the Sun, ornamented with the most beautiful and elaborate carving; the walls and nine of the columns remain standing.

The beds from which the stone was quarried form a valley between two limestone chains of mountains, and are considered of late formation. It is probable that they yielded.the marble used for the sculptures.

Nearly all Palestine is underlaid by limestones, the greater part Jurassic, of variable character and remarkable for caverns, a fact agreeing with the frequent allusions to caves met with in sacred history; such are the tomb of Abraham, a limestone cavern at Machpelah, the cave of Adullam, and others. The limestones of this country exhibit a great diversity of colors, comprising white, black, rose, red, and yellow. There is some disagreement among writers regarding the Chalk of Palestine, some believe there is no true chalk, while others say that in the region of Jerusalem and the valley of the Jordan, are Jurassic limestones, dolomites, and white chalk, and that a limestone with Cidaris, a Cretaceous fossil, forms the eastern border of the valley.

The celebrated Plain of Sharon, on the Mediterranean, redolent of roses and lilies, is covered by a sandy, marine alluvium; the superimposing beds of limestones are regarded as Tertiary.

Near Jerusalem, more especially about Bethany and the Hill of Ascension, the strata comprise different colored sands, with nodular masses, and yellow limestones veined with red. The mountains about the sacred city are, to a great extent, calcareous, while the rock on which it is built, and which was used in the construction of the Temple, is a very pure limestone, containing more than ninety-eight per cent of carbonate of lime ·

This renowned and interesting city has stood for nearly forty centuries, notwithstanding the devastations of its wars and sieges, unparalleled in history; within its walls and about its precincts there remain evidences of its magnificence in the days of its glory. Under the hill Bezetha is a series of winding passages and immense halls, supported by colossal pillars of pure white marble, which constituted the quarry whence the stone was taken for the buildings. Several columns cut from this Jerusalem marble are seen at the Pool of Siloam.

At the foot of Mount Zion a covered gallery remains, supposed to be a part of the Gymnasium or Forum, and in the ravine below are seen remains of the bridge, connecting the royal palace on this mountain with the Temple on Mount Moriah. Other remains comprise the Tombs of the Judges, a group of sepulchres cut in the native rock, and the Tombs of the Kings, one mile from the walls, both with sculptures, and the latter with columns and pilasters. What are called Zachariah's Tomb and Absalom's Pillar are monoliths with one side still adhering to the native rock, and decorated with Doric and Ionic ornaments

Throughout Palestine and Syria ruins of scattered columns of marble, granite, and porphyry, arches, colonnades, capitals, cornices, adorned with sculptures of classic workmanship, prove the splendor and magnificence of the public buildings of the numerous cities of this once densely populated region

On or near the sea, were Gaza, an important military post, several times captured, destroyed, and rebuilt; Ascalon, adorned by Herod the Great with colonnades, baths, and fountains, and famous in the devastating wars of the Middle Ages; Azotus or Ashdod, memorable for a siege of twenty-nine years, the longest, it is claimed, on record, Cæsarea, the "pride and delight of Roman, Saracen, Templar, and Turk," embellished by Herod the Great, who, in his taste for magnificent structures, was the Augustus of the East, and Tyre, formerly the mart of the eastern world, renowned for its sumptuous temples and tombs.

Samaria, the favorite abode of Herod, was, next to Jerusalem, the most celebrated city for the beauty of its situation and the magnificence of its edifices Glimpses of its ancient splendor are yet seen in the vast colonnades winding from the deep ravine to the highest terraces of the hill, the ruins of temples, and the broken fragments of triumphal arches.

East of the Jordan, the ruined cities are still more numerous, one traveller having counted between three hundred and four hundred in the territory of the ancient Amorites, thus confirming the Biblical statement that there were sixty cities in this region with walls, gates, and bars, besides many unwalled towns   These ruins are on a magnificent scale, . the gates being cut from a single huge, block of stone ; a part of the works antedate the classical era, others belong to the Greek school.

The ruins of Gerasa or Jerash have been thought to equal those of Palmyra, and to resemble, in places, the Colosseum at Rome. They comprise the remains of buildings usually found in Greek and Roman cities, sculptured in the Corinthian and Doric orders. One temple was surrounded by a Corinthian peristyle, and another occupied a large area, enclosed by two hundred columns, while colonnades, bridges, aqueducts, and a necropolis, with sculptured sarcophagi, are all seen in this devastated city.

Bozrah, the capital of the territory, exhibits remains in the Greek, Roman, and Saracenic styles, with columns fifty feet in height, and other architectural marvels.

Palmyra, with its chaotic mass of snow-white marble shafts, capitals, bases, entablatures, all mingled in inextricable confusion, has been called a ruined forest in stone   The great colonnade comprised fifteen hundred columns, in four rows, extending four thousand feet ; but the most remarkable structure was the Temple of the Sun, which occupied a square of seven hundred and forty feet, and was elaborately decorated with exquisite sculptures.

A bituminous limestone of a dark-gray or deep-black, enclosing fossil fishes, is found in the region of the Dead Sea, and is used by the inhabitants of Bethlehem for making small objects for devotional purposes, which are sold to the pilgrims. The rock, which is one-fourth bituminous, burns with a reddish-

yellow flame, and is used by the Bedouins for light. Limestones and basalts are found on both sides of the Dead Sea
for some distance, and the frequent occurrence of lava proves
the region to have been volcanic

Nummulitic limestones are developed on the eastern shore
of the Gulf of Suez, while the interior of Arabia affords chalk
and a yellow limestone, probably Cretaceous. A red sandstone, analogous to the ancient rock of Nubia, covered by
Cretaceous limestone, formed the palaces and tombs of Petra,
of the once flourishing nation of Edom.

From the testimony of travellers, we learn that crystalline
rocks are predominant in the region of Mounts Sinai and
Horeb, that porphyry and sandstone are the chief constituents
of these mountains, that the summit of Mount Sinai is
syenite, traversed by dikes of trap, and that a limestone
thought to be Cretaceous forms the hills in the Desert of
Sinai The opinion that the rock which received the name
syenite came from Syene, in Egypt, is regarded as erroneous,
Mount Sinai being the place where it was found.

Cretaceous beds and Nummulitic limestone extend from Syria
to Kurdistan, and from the Caspian to the Aral The basin
of the Euphrates and the plains of Babylon are covered with
an erratic formation composed of gravel, pebbles, and blocks,
constituting the last deposit before the present epoch; the
region regarded the cradle of the human race is therefore
the youngest in geological history. It is thought that the
formation called the Breccia of Taurus, reaching from the
source to the mouth of the Euphrates, is the result of some
comparatively recent catastrophe. The basin of the river
from the Taurus to Babylon, develops a variety of limestones,
in places forming on the banks escarpments more or less
elevated, while at Bir chalk forms the acclivities and conical
hills from three hundred to three hundred and fifty feet in
height

Orfa, the Edessa of ancient times, supposed to be the Ur
of the Chaldees, stands on the border of the mountain region

adjacent to the rich and fertile plains of Harran, in Mesopotamia, where basalts and dolomites are succeeded by limestones The territory about Orfa abounds in caverns indicating the presence of calcareous rocks, which is very probable, since the city is built of white limestone. Tradition assigns to this region the home of Job and Rebecca's Well.

The most remarkable characteristics of the rocks of Kurdistan, and to some degree of those of Persia, are the compactness and uniform hardness of the limestones in the mountain regions, while on the banks of the Euphrates they become chalky, and on the plains of Mosul they are shelly. At Zenobia, on the Euphrates, a breccia of gypsum sandstone has been found, including quartz pebbles, jasper, serpentine, diallage, and some other rocks, lying under a bone breccia, and combined with various limestones, the whole series constitute the predominant rocks of this region.

The city of Hit, formerly Is, on the Euphrates, above Babylon, is celebrated for bitumen, employed in making the indestructible cement used in building the palaces of the famous capital of the Chaldæan Empire. Limestones and gypsums form the valley of Kasserum, in the basin of the Euphrates, and the limestones constituting the passage of Shapur, are sculptured in antique bas-reliefs.

The Tertiary system is represented in the valley of the Tigris by fossiliferous limestones, and a conglomerate of limestones, diallage, serpentine, quartz, and jasper, one hundred and eighty feet thick, is thought to be of the same age as that on which the walls of ancient Nineveh rested.

Near Mosul, opposite the ruins, beds of compact or granular gypsum, of a bluish-gray or pure white color, are quarried under the name of Marble of Mosul. Above the gypsum is a coarse, friable limestone, full of fossils, commonly used for building-stone, which appears to have been employed in the construction of Nineveh. This city has been considered one of the oldest in the world, having been built, as is supposed, soon after the deluge, by Asshur, who thus laid the foundation

of the Assyrian Empire   It became a very large city, requir-
ing in the time of the Prophet Jonah a three days' journey to
encompass its walls, which are said to have been one hundred
feet in height, with fifteen hundred towers, extending two
hundred feet above them   Some of these sculptured marbles
or alabasters preserved in the British Museum, afford proofs of
the early use of limestones, marbles, and gypsums for carving
and architecture.

Sulphur mines, about eight miles from Mosul, contain a
fine, compact, semi-crystalline sulphur, with beautiful crystals
of citron-yellow and olive-green.   The gypseous limestone, or
Marble of Mosul, is largely developed to the east of Kerkuk,
and southeast of Mosul, while the hills of Kirfir are covered
with limestones enclosing Cyclades, and opposite Ali Dagh
are wells of naphtha and petroleum issuing from calcareous
rocks ; the whole region abounds in a great variety of minerals.
The hills of Bozzan are formed of a hard, compact, fossiliferous limestone resembling the Calcaire grossier of the Paris
Basin.   One hundred and forty miles from the Persian Gulf,
the great rivers Euphrates and Tigris unite to form the Shat-
el-Arab, at a place called Karmah, which the traditions of
those regions assign as the site of the Garden of Eden.

The valleys of these rivers have been, as has been stated,
the graves of nations and cities whose wealth, power, and
magnificence the sculptured records preserved in their ruins
attest   . Nineveh, Babylon, Seleucia, and Ctesiphon represented
great empires which have disappeared from the earth
Travellers bear testimony to the vastness and magnificence of
the remains of these cities, while the carving and inscriptions
on stone confirm the truth of history, both sacred and profane.
It is said that the royal palace of Ctesiphon, the capital of the
Parthian Empire, was a marvel of splendor and magnificence.
The façade was four hundred and fifty feet long and one hundred high, forming a span unequalled in size by any known
architectural structure, and opening into an immense hall one
hundred and sixty feet in height, with walls twenty-two feet

thick at the base.   The palace of Nebuchadnezzar, in Babylon, was six miles in circumference, and surrounded by three walls.

Marbles and alabasters were very liberally used in the more decorative portions of ancient buildings in all the ruined cities of this interesting region, in which alabaster is still very abundant, forming in the territory between Bagdad and Kurdistan entire hills of considerable size.

The palace walls of Nineveh were of brick, covered with sculptured alabaster, and the walls of the Christian churches of the province of Mosul are ornamented with the same material

The modern town of Madin, a fortified place, stands upon a mountain of limestone, between the upper Tigris and the Euphrates   The new town, with its walls, is built on terraces on the side of the mountain, sixteen hundred feet from the plain, of a soft, white limestone similar to that of the Paris Basin   The old town occupied the summit, two thousand one hundred feet from the base.

The Moslems have a tradition that the houris of Paradise come from Madin, and it claims the honor of being the centre of learning at the present day, as it was in ancient times, when it was called Mosius.

The city is so strongly fortified that it was able to resist for three years the attacks of Tamerlane.

CHAPTER XVIII.

I *Arabia* — Though portions of Arabia, consisting of a
strip on the eastern shore of the Red Sea and the northwest coast of the Persian Gulf, belong to Turkey, the great
central and southern districts are controlled by independent
tribes of Arabs, whom conquering nations of antiquity or of
later time have never been able to subdue

This native home of the Bedouin, consisting of barren
deserts interspersed with fertile oases, has its mountains of
limestone, rising in isolated peaks or scattered groups, often
forming the borders of the table-land. The Nummulitic beds,
which are developed on an immense scale to the north and
east of Arabia, appear in the southeast on the Straits of
Ormuz. In this region, writes Carter, there is an extent of
one hundred and twelve miles of white limestone, succeeded
by igneous rocks and every variety of serpentine He classes
the limestones in three groups. 1 A soft breccia, composed
of shells, corals, and igneous rocks of the Quaternary age:
2 A compact, whitish limestone with shells of the Tertiary:
3 A series including a compact shell limestone, a soft shell
variety, and a beautiful white limestone resembling lithographic stone.

Some of the fossils are analogous to those of the earlier
formations, as Alveolites, others to those of a more recent
age, as Orbitoides and Nummulites. The region to the southwest is volcanic. The city of Aden, held by Great Britain, is
built in the centre of a nearly circular crater, one mile and a

half in diameter, surrounded on three sides by a sea of lava, while the walls on the south are washed by the waters of the Gulf of Aden The Island of Perim, a reef in the Straits of Bab-el-Mandeb, one and a half mile in length and half as wide, has become celebrated for the fossil bones of the Mastodon, Rhinoceros, Dinotherium, and other gigantic mammals.

II. *Persia.* — With its eventful history, Persia forms one of the most remarkable countries of the eastern world, having survived alternate periods of extreme prosperity and corresponding degradation for nearly three thousand years ; it has been the scene of foreign invasions and domestic revolution, and the battle-ground of ambitious conquerors for dominion in the East.

Though diversified in climate, its natural features are less interesting than those of many other regions of Asia; it is covered by a network of rocky mountains, valleys destitute of streams, and vast salt or sandy deserts, presenting a scene of indescribable desolation.

The mountains of Persia are largely calcareous, and the same kind of rocks are prevalent in the islands of the Gulf. Kishma, the largest of these, displays rugged cliffs of limestone strata, while the hills of reddish rocks in the Island of Ormuz are covered with snow-white gypsum. The town of Ormuz, under the Portuguese, was a rich city and the centre of eastern trade, until, allured by its wealth, Abbas the Great, assisted by the English fleet, captured and plundered it. A few miles from the ruins, limestone cliffs, eight hundred feet in height, present a bold and striking outline to the coast. The mountainous region from Dalaku to Shiraz, and thence to Ispahan, abounds in limestone and gypsum ; the former is compact, of gray and yellow shades ; the gypsum sometimes constitutes entire hills, or forms masses of fine alabaster. Hippurite limestone is spread out from Teheran towards the west, while Nummulitic limestone, to a greater or less extent, is developed throughout the kingdom.

Plate XVIII.

ALABASTRO FASCIATO.

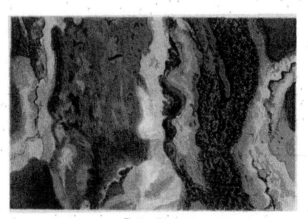

BRECCIA ROSSA.

ARMSTRONG & CO. LITH. BOSTON.

Though Devonian rocks form the axis of the Elburz Mountains, yet on the northern slope, and in the region of the Caspian, the Cretaceous and Tertiary series are displayed, and, united to the contemporary deposits of Arabia by the chain of the Zagros Mountains, near the shores of Lake Urumiah, they extend southeast towards the ancient city of Persepolis.

There are few celebrated empires, says the historian of Persia, so poor in monuments of past greatness as this ancient kingdom, yet the few that remain are remarkable for magnificence and solidity. The absence of architectural relics is, undoubtedly, due to several causes; the principal reasons may have been the sweeping destruction of foreign invaders and the character of the ancient religion. A large part of the monuments of antiquity consisted of the tombs of heroes and rulers, and the temples, idols, and shrines of divinities. The ancient religion of Persia — fire-worship — employed neither images nor temples, properly speaking, which were merely buildings for the preservation of the sacred fire, and neither cremation nor sepulture were sanctioned, though the precepts on this subject were not rigidly followed, as many of the kings and distinguished men were honored with magnificent mausoleums.

The most extensive ruins are those of Persepolis, now Istakhar, which was built at the base of a mountain on an artificial terrace from twenty-five to fifty feet in height, overlooking an extensive plain. The ascent to this platform was by flights of marble steps, cut in huge blocks of sufficient size to contain from ten to fourteen steps in each block. At the upper landing-place stood a gigantic portal, with walls sculptured with colossal animals, while the paving between the walls was of polished marble Several feet from this portal were placed four fluted columns, forty-five feet in height, supporting beautiful capitals, while beyond these was erected a second portal, adorned with carving. The sculptures of the staircases and portals are very profuse, and, in the opinion of modern travellers, correct in design and delicate in finish. The figures are arranged in groups, some representing royal guards and attendants, others the people of different nations in a procession bearing offerings They have been supposed to represent scenes in a religious festival in the time of Cyrus the Great or of Darius.

The most remarkable remains are the "Columns," seventy-two in number, some standing, but the greater part lying prostrate. They belong, says Fraser, to two distinct orders, and are of different heights : some are sixty feet, with a shaft sixteen feet in circumference, fluted in fifty-two divisions ; the pedestals are in the form of the cup and leaf of the lotus, and the capitals are surmounted with the unicorn or double demi-bull ; others are fifty-five feet in height with different capitals. The object of these monuments is a problem ; it has been conjectured that the Hall of Columns was consecrated to some solemn and religious purpose. The rock of the mountain near which the city was built, is a compact, gray marble, identical with that of the ruins, and several half-finished blocks, cut in the same style, are still to be seen in the quarries

The tombs of the kings were cut in the mountain, and here the rulers of the Sassanian dynasty were buried ; a building of white marble near these tombs, thought to be an edifice for the sacred fire, has been called the Kaaba of Zoroaster.

The monuments found at Persepolis have all the inscriptions in the cuneiform character, and are said to show great mechanical skill and exquisite taste. There are remains in the vicinity which prove that this ancient city was once prosperous and magnificent. Strabo speaks of Persepolis and Pasargadæ as places held in honor by the Persians for their palaces, treasure-houses, wealth, and royal tombs The latter city contained the mausoleum of Cyrus, with its gold coffin, gold couch, costly garments ornamented with precious stones, and other relics to attest the magnificence of his final resting-place.

Alexander the Great set fire to the palace after having

plundered its treasures; Antiochus, one hundred and sixty years after, attacked the city; but it was not finally over-thrown until the invasion by the Arabs, whose policy it was to destroy all the existing monuments and institutions of the Persian Empire.

The antiquities in the plains of Mourghab, about fifty miles north of Persepolis, are supposed to be of the same age; they are called by the natives the Mosque of the Mother of Solomon. This structure, surrounded by twenty-four columns, rests on a base of white marble cut into colossal steps, ascending in the form of a pyramid. Near the plain of Keimanshah is an immense piece of sculpture which some antiquaries have considered to be a representation of Semiramis,-the Assyrian heroine. Not far from this relic are fourteen figures representing persons, supposed to be Jews taken captive by the Assyrians.

The remains belonging to the period of the Sassanian dynasty, that preceding the Moslem conquest, are of the Roman-Grecian school, and include the sculptures of Tauk e Bostam, which poetical and popular tradition have connected with the history of the sculptor Ferhaud and the beautiful Shireen.

The remains of Shapoor, a very ancient city northwest of Shiraz, once the capital of Persia, covered a space six miles in circumference. The sculptures representing scenes in the history of the Empire are thought to commemorate the triumph of King Shapoor over the Roman Emperor Valerian. In the neighboring mountain occurs a remarkable prostrate statue, supposed to be that of Shapoor.

The celebrated city of Shiraz, the birthplace of the poets Sadi and Hafiz, contains their tombs, and since the Mahom-medan conquest it has been regarded a sacred place, being embellished with several mosques and tombs of saints. Besides its sanctity, it makes pretensions to superior learning, having been called from early times the "Abiding-place of Science."

Many of the magnificent structures of Ispahan, formerly one of the "noblest capitals of the East," have fallen into decay. Among the existing relics of the glory of former days is a sumptuous palace called Chehel Sittoon, "Hall of Columns," from one of the magnificent apartments in which the columns were inlaid with mirrors, so arranged as to be reflected in a sheet of clear water, while the walls and roof were decorated with mirrors and golden flowers. The remains of Imam Reza and Haroun al Raschid repose at Mushed, in Khorisan, in a magnificent mausoleum, decorated and enriched with gold, silver, marble, and lacquered tiles of the richest colors. A silver gate, the gift of Nadir Shah, opens into the chief apartment, while a branched candlestick of solid silver depends from the dome ; two lofty minarets in gold and azure tower above the splendid structure, and near by stands a very beautiful mosque

The region of Lake Urumiah or Urmiah, in the northwestern part of Persia, is interesting both to the geologist and the historian. This sheet of water, known to the ancients as Lake Spauta or Martiana, is eighty miles long, and in some places thirty wide, with no visible outlet and but few streams flowing into it. Strabo speaks of it as a salt lake, as it is at the present time, but makes no mention of the travertine deposited near. It is elevated four thousand feet above the Black Sea, and every spring it overflows its banks, leaving an extensive salt deposit, which reaches a considerable distance to the east of the lake.

The town of Urumiah, on the west side of the lake, is claimed as the birthplace of Zoroaster, while Tabreez, on the east, was the favorite residence of the celebrated caliph, Haroun al Raschid. The country abounds in picturesque scenery, diversified by mountains and valleys, and it is in this vicinity, at a place called Maraga or Marangha, that the beautiful Tabreez marble or alabaster is deposited by mineral springs The substance is similar, says Hitchcock, to that found at Tivoli, Italy, and resembles statuary marble. The Maraga and the Tivoli springs are the only ones forming marble known to this geologist. He is of the opinion that the Tabreez was deposited beneath deep waters· when the temperature was higher than at present, but others have thought the depositions are constantly going on. It is said that the petrifying pool resembles frozen water, and a stone thrown into it breaks the crust, while the very bubbles on the surface are metamorphosed into marble. The rock contains ninety-six per cent of carbonate of lime, the remainder being iron and magnesia; it is finely laminated, resembling, it has been stated, accumulated sheets of paper, is of a yellowish or light-blue color, perfectly compact, and so translucent, that, cut in thin slices, it is used for windows instead of glass. Immense quantities of this remarkable alabaster have been quarried and exported to various places.

The Elburz Mountains in this part of the kingdom yield turquoise mines, from which the gem so much used in Persia is extracted._ It is found in veins, in small pieces, under beds of limestone.

III. *Afghanistan and Beloochistan.* — These countries occupy a region west of the Indus, known to ancient geographers as Ariana, which was inhabited in the days of Alexander, as it is now, by warlike tribes who have never assimilated with the nations around them. Their country, lying between India, the tempting prize of conquerors, and western Asia and Europe, has frequently been overrun by devastating armies, but the fierce Afghans, with their sturdy independence, have never been found an easy race to subdue

This region, like Persia, has barren deserts, which proved so formidable to Alexander during his march, and mountains with snow-covered peaks; while, in some places, fertile plains yield a great variety and abundance of fruits and vegetables. The mountains of Beloochistan are formed largely of Nummulitic limestones, which are used in construction of various kinds. In certain localities the walls of this formation constitute natural fortifications of great height, presenting a grand appearance. These limestones are generally of a deep-blue color, passing sometimes into gray or pale-yellow, and occasionally schistose with few fossils. The yellow variety often contains nodules of silex, simulating the spots of a tiger's skin, affording a marble suitable for sculpture. This may be the same as the ancient Tigrato, seen in the Vatican Museum. The natives can hardly be supposed to have been skilled in the arts, but it might have been an article of traffic with the Greeks, and possibly the Romans, who used it for sculpture.

Limestones of the Cretaceous period, enclosing fossils allied to Nummulites, are comprised among the calcareous rocks of Beloochistan. They are of great thickness, and include a fine-grained, red variety with white bands, and a dark-blue with lead ore; the banded encloses Foraminifers and is widely disseminated. Geologists have thought that Triassic rocks occur near Kelat, since Ceratites and Orthoceratites have been found in that region.

The Nummulitic formation is developed at Cabool and other places in Afghanistan. The Kandahar and Shah Maksud Ranges, according to Griesbach, are formed of Cretaceous limestone and eruptive rocks, the limestones, folded, and raised into dome-like masses, belong to the Hippurite formation, and are changed in places to crystalline marble. A white crystalline limestone, with red portions, is used at Kandahar for marble, as seen in the shrines and buildings of that city, especially the tomb of Ahmed Shah. The Cretaceous rocks of Kandahar are important in determining the age of the mountain ranges in the region.

The Bolan Pass, separating Sind from the southern part of Afghanistan, is a frightful chasm, seventy miles in length, flanked by lofty rocks, which consist mostly of Nummulitic limestone, presenting in its grandest display eleven thousand feet The lower portion is light-gray; the upper, reddish or reddish-brown. This pass has become memorable in modern history for the terrible calamity which befell the British army during the retreat from Cabool, in 1842, in which more than sixteen thousand persons perished, and only one officer survived. The retreat has been considered the most disastrous and appalling on record

In some parts of Afghanistan, cliffs of perfectly white Nummulitic limestone form escarpments five thousand five hundred feet high, looking like a wall of snow, and at the Maiwand Pass is developed a beautiful, fine-grained, crystalline limestone with red spots, and enclosing granite. The Afghan Tertiary group is said to resemble the flysch of Europe in lithological character. The Gaj group of Sind, in India, principally Eocene, enclosing bright-colored gypsum clays, passes into Beloochistan and Afghanistan, where it covers a large area.

Ghuznee, the famous capital of the "mighty Mahmud," the Napoleon of the East, affords some relics of its former magnificence. It contains the mausoleum of Mahmud, but the Palace of Felicity, the mosque called the Celestial Bride, and the splendid baths, colleges, and other noble buildings with which this conqueror embellished his capital, are now a mass of ruins.

Cabool contains the tomb of Baber, the founder of the Mogul empire of India, whose life has seldom been surpassed in romantic and varied fortunes.

Upon the north slope of the Himalayas, on the high table-land of Thibet, elevated more than ten thousand feet above sea-level, the Nummulitic formation has an extensive development, and it is thought that the Devonian and Jurassic systems are also represented in the country of the Grand Lama.

A gray dolomite without fossils forms a part of the Kuen-Lun Mountains, between Thibet and Turkistan, and in the latter country shell limestones occur. A part of Turkistan or Bokhara, an extensive country occupying the central portion of Northwestern Asia, belongs to China, and a part is governed by independent tribes under the nominal control of Russia It comprises elevated table-lands, interspersed by sandy deserts and crossed by lofty ranges of mountains.

IV. *India* — The rock systems of this very ancient and productive country afford an interesting study to the geologist, and offer an extensive field for the future investigator, as many of its highest mountains have been only partially explored. They embrace deposits of nearly every period, from the earliest to the present epoch, some of which are peculiar to this region.

The great plain in the north, watered by the Indus on the west and the Ganges on the east, with their tributaries, is alluvial, of recent date. Regur, or Black Cotton Clay, is a characteristic deposit of India, covering a third of the southern part, more especially the elevated plateau of Deccan, including Hyderabad, Nagpore, and south of the Mahratta country, forming vast plains in the south-central part of India It is generally black, greenish, or deep-gray, and consists of silica, alumina, lime, magnesia, iron, and water, enclosing fresh-water shells. Clark is of the opinion that Regur is composed mostly of lime and iron; it is probable that it varies in composition It is said to resemble the Nile mud, but more closely the Black Earth of Russia, and is adapted to the cultivation of cotton, whence the name.

Kunker, a typical rock of India, and more ancient than Regur or Black Earth, is a concretionary or tufaceous carbonate of lime, usually occurring in nodules from one-half an inch to three or four inches in diameter, and on the exterior is mixed with clay. It is of a compact structure, like the travertine of Rome, with the interior sometimes cellular, but differs from recent deposits in the absence of fossils ; the color is a clear brown, reddish, or ash-gray, and, owing to the presence of silica, some of it is very hard Both chemical and mechanical agencies were employed in its formation

It is quite generally distributed, and is quarried for building-stone and for the manufacture of lime. The Kunker, near Mysore, in the southern part, is a kind of siliceous breccia, semi-opal, and called by the natives Assuhar.

Laterite, or iron clay, is widely spread throughout India, but nothing like it occurs in Europe It consists, in great part, of peroxide of iron, with some alumina, lime, magnesia, and silica; is soft when first quarried, but hardens after exposure to the air, and sometimes resembles jasper in appearance. The rock is traversed by irregular tubes filled with clay, and presents a reticulated structure, which gave rise to the tradition among the natives that it was composed of an accumulation of giants' bones. It has erroneously been thought to be volcanic, while the presence of paleolithic human implements is evidence of recent origin. The summits of the Raymehal Hills, on the Ganges, is composed of laterite sufficiently compact to be employed for building-stone, of which ancient forts and temples were constructed

Although there is a large development in India, of recent strata, some of the rocks are considered pre-Silurian, or Paleozoic, notwithstanding the absence of all marine fossils in the peninsula, older than the Jurassic, since these may have been obliterated by metamorphism; there are evidences, it is claimed, that this region was free from disturbances during Paleozoic time. In most countries the transition of organic remains from one type to another is gradual, but here, on the contrary, it is abrupt.

The older, unfossiliferous rocks, consisting of gneiss, trap, schist, and certain limestones, have an extensive range; a series with sandstones, shales, and limestones, forming a subordinate member, constitute the Vindhyan Mountains, which separate the central provinces from the northwest, and have given the name to this formation

The rock systems of the peninsula and the extra-peninsula of India are essentially different in character It has been said that there are no traces of marine, Carboniferous strata in the peninsula, but in the northwest the limestones of the Salt Range enclose the characteristic fossils of the period, an evidence that these mountains were under water in the Paleozoic era. Dr. Waagen claims to have found Ammonites and Ceratites, fossils of the Jurassic and Cretaceous periods, in the Carboniferous limestones of India.

In the region of Simla, a town in the northwest, occurs an unfossiliferous limestone, called the Krol formation from the Krol Mountains, formerly referred to the Triassic, but assigned by later examinations to the Carboniferous period; the Blaini group, in the vicinity, includes a magnesian limestone.

Tertiary rocks form the greater part of Sind, on the lower Indus, though the Trias has a limited representation, and in the Laki Range Cretaceous limestone with Hippurites occurs analogous to this formation existing in Persia. Beds of fossiliferous limestone form a part of the Banikot group, but the Kirtha, Nummulitic formation, constitutes the representative limestone of this region, including several varieties known as the Kirtha limestone, with a thickness ranging from a few hundred to two thousand, or three thousand feet, and extending northward into Beloochistan, where it is well displayed near Kelat. A variety with Nummulites, called the Nari limestone, for a river in Sind, constitutes a formation from one to ten miles wide, running parallel with the Kirtha, though differing from it. The fortified town of Hyderabad, the chief city of the principality, is built on a low range of limestone hills forming the east bank of the Indus.

The Gaj group, in the northwestern part of Sind, receives the name from the only river which has cut a channel through the Kirtha Mountains, from Beloochistan; the fossiliferous limestones of the group, considered Eocene, extend to Cutch on the south

Throughout Sind marine and terrestrial deposits alternate; and it is claimed that the Tertiary rocks form, in this principality, a more complete series than in any other place in northwest India The Salt Range affords a remarkable series of formations, from the older Paleozoic to the later Tertiary, embracing, under the general term of Hill limestone, varieties of different periods, including a fossiliferous limestone of the Jurassic, another enclosing Ceratites, of the Triassic, a magnesian, Carboniferous, and a Nummulitic variety of the Ter-

tiary, with the Para and Teling limestones.. The Carboniferous is full of Cephalopods, Brachiopods, Bryozoans, and
Crinoids, resembling in its general features the Mountain
limestone of Great Britain. The Para or Rhætic formation
is a black dolomite, strongly bituminous, enclosing fossils similar to those of the St. Cassiăn series; above this formation
rests the Teling limestone, two thousand feet thick, of dark
colors, often bituminous, enclosing remains like those of the
Para, among which the Avicula contorta is the most charac-
acteristic fossil; both these formations occur in the upper
Trias, or between the Trias and the Lias. It is said that
there are found in the Teling, Liassic fossils not known to
exist in any other formation in India.

The Jurassic series occurs in the Punjab, in the western
Himalayas, and in Thibet. The Punjab, watered by the upper
Indus, was formerly the dominion of the powerful Sheik,
Runjeet Singh, but, like Sind, it is now under the jurisdiction
of Great Britain. Including the Nummulitic limestone, the
Tertiary rocks of this country have been estimated to com-
prise twenty-five thousand feet of strata, but only two thou-
sand or three thousand of the lowest contain marine fossils.
In the northern part of the province, an eminence called the
Hill of Nummulitic Limestone is composed of a dark, massive
rock with nodular bands.

The Valley of Cashmere, immortalized by the poet for its
roses and fountains, its temples and grottoes, is elevated from
six thousand to seven thousand feet above the sea, and is
formed of limestones and dolomites, representing the Silurian,
Carboniferous, and Triassic periods.

The upper Tertiary, called the Siwalik group, claimed to
be chiefly a fresh-water deposit, distributed over an extensive
area, affords, in the Himalayas, an interesting collection of
fossil mammalia, analogous to those found in some parts of
Greece; forty-five genera and eighty-four species had been
discovered up to the time of the Geological Survey by Medlicott and Blanford, 1879 The shells of land and fresh-water

origin are all represented by living species. By far the greater part of the collections were obtained from the lower Siwalik, called the Nahan group, and on this account great importance is attached to the Nahan area.

It is thought that the foldings and contortions of the Himalayas were effected since the lower Tertiary, though the area of this range was land at a much earlier period, and the frequent occurrence of earthquakes in this region is regarded as evidence that the interior forces which produced these stupendous results are still active. Owing to the difficulty of exploring them, scientific knowledge of the Himalayas is, at present, meagre; but so far as is known they exhibit, says Medlicott, more regularity of structure than the Alps.

The Sub-Himalayas, forming the southern belt, is composed of a soft, Tertiary sandstone of the same age as the molasse of the Alps. Between this low range and the great snow-capped chain, there lies an area fifty miles in width, consisting of irregular ranges from five thousand to twelve thousand feet in height, largely made up of crystalline, metamorphic rocks, while the lofty Himalayas are composed, to a great extent, of gneiss and fossiliferous strata, the latter presenting an instance of the wonderful rock-producing power of organized beings.

Silurian, Carboniferous, Permian, Jurassic, and Triassic fossils are said to exist in the central Himalayas, but it is a question whether the Nummulitic formation was ever developed along the southern slope, since geologists have found no vestige of this well-nigh universal limestone in the Sub-Himalayas of the middle region. The discovery of the Siwalik fossils places this chain in the Tertiary rather than the Secondary era, to which it had been previously assigned.

Nummulitic beds are found in the Assam Range, in the northeastern part of India, extending through Burmah and Tenasserim to Sumatra, Java, and other islands of the Malay Archipelago. The impenetrable forests of Burmah and Assam seriously obstruct geological investigations in those

countries, while the metamorphic character of the strata
renders it difficult to assign them to their proper eras; the
same impediments are met with east and north of the Bay of
Bengal. The upper Tertiary of Burmah and Assam are all,
with few exceptions, fresh-water deposits, but the lower Tertiary are marine, represented by the Nummulitic limestone,
which, in Maulmain, is thought to be not less than ten thousand feet thick; Cretaceous and Carboniferous limestones are
less abundant The most valuable and productive ruby mines
known are found in the Shan States, northeast of Ava Burmah is rich in mineral productions, including a variety of
rocks, fossil-wood, and gems of great value. It yields a
beautiful dark serpentine, with bronzite and veins of gold-
colored crysotile, resembling the gabbro of Europe; the rock
passes into green stone, forming hills covered with luxuriant
forests. A fine, white or greenish sandstone, containing
fossils, and called by the natives Image Stone, is used for
carving images of Buddha. The beds of fossil-wood found in
Pegu are considered the remains of a formation which covered
an extensive area, and which still covers a large part of
northern Prome.

Tertiary rocks surround the extinct volcano Puppa, three
thousand feet in height, with a summit of ash-breccia, and the
sides marked by streams of lava enclosing fine crystals of
pyroxene and porphyry. The mud volcanoes of Arracan and
Burmah are numerous; the best known are on the Irrawadi
and the islands of the coast; those of Rami eject stones,
flames, and sometimes inflammable gas, which often takes fire
and lights up the country for miles.

The Karmul formation of the lower Vindhyan Mountains includes a fine crystalline limestone, and a sandstone
quarried for diamonds; above the diamond-bearing strata
rests the Planad limestone, taking the name of the district
where it is found. The province of Bundelkund, in north-
central India, yields limestones of variable composition.
The Kaimer conglomerate is everwhere conspicuous for its

bright-red jasper pebbles, "which present the appearance of a tulip-bed."

None of the rocks of Cutch and the adjoining islands are older than the Jurassic; the limestones include a variety with Trigonia The Golden Oolite, resembling gold-colored mica, belongs to the Chari beds of Cutch; it is composed of calcareous particles coated with a thin, ferruginous layer cemented by carbonate of lime. Jurassic beds are found in the great desert north of Cutch, called the Run of Cutch, including the Jesalmir limestones, forming the escarpment near the town of Jesalmir. The Nummulitic and Gaj limestones of Sind penetrate this province; Miliolite beds, resembling those of the Paris Basin, are developed in Kattywar, south of Sind.

The geologists of India have noticed a remarkable deficiency of marine fossils of the Paleozoic and Mesozoic formations in the Indian peninsula; with few exceptions, there are no marine deposits older than the Cretaceous, and these are found only in two areas widely separated, one in the neighborhood of Pondicherry and Trichinopoly in the south, and the other in the Nerbudda valley in the west, both yielding fine specimens of fossils. The Pondicherry formation includes the Utatur coral limestone, enclosing nearly three hundred species of invertebrates; the Trichinopoly limestones, filled with the remains of Gasteropods and Lamellibranchs remarkably well preserved, with their original polish and sometimes color, extensively quarried for ornamental uses under the name of Trichinopoly; and the Arialur group in which the remains of a Megalosaurus have been found.

The city of Pondicherry, belonging to the French, is, like Madras, built upon movable sand filled with shells, used for the manufacture of lime, and environed, in part, by diamond-bearing limestones. Trichinopoly is an inland fortified town, on the river Cauvery, near which was erected the largest and most splendid pagoda of all India.

A large part of the presidency of Madras rests upon marine clay, filled with shells, quarried for decoration, in imitation of the beautiful marbles found in temples and other buildings.

There is, it is said, a striking resemblance between the fauna of the Cretaceous beds of Trichinopoly and some other parts of India, with those of South Africa, but a marked difference between those of South India and the Nerbudda valley on the northwest coast, which develops the Bagh group, inclosing most of the fossils. The discovery of Cretaceous fossils in this region was due to the blocks of limestone containing analogous remains found in the ruins of a town near by. The Bagh series includes a coralline limestone, employed for buildings, composed mainly of shells and fragments of Bryozoa, giving it a mottled appearance, and several other varieties, including a nodular limestone of considerable extent   The Bagh fossils are very imperfect, and resemble those found in Arabia   Nummulitic limestone occurs at Serat, south of the Cretaceous groups of the Nerbudda valley.

The volcanic series is one of the most prominent and widespread of all the rock systems of the Indian peninsula; it is called the Deccan trap, a term of broad significance, including a great variety of igneous rocks. This great central region, called the Deccan, is distinguished for peculiar scenery, represented as composed of great undulating plains intersected by flat-topped hills and elevated terraces, often presenting escarpments four thousand feet high. Vegetation partakes of the same exceptional character, indicated by long grass and very few trees   From November to June nearly all plants are dry, and the country presents a desolate picture of black soil, bare rocks, and withered trees, but when the rainy season begins vegetation springs into life, clothing the barren earth with a vesture of green, that forms an agreeable contrast with the dark-colored rocks   Combined with the rocks of the Deccan is a small group of calcareous eruptive strata, called the Lameta limestone.

South of the Deccan area crystalline limestones, mostly

magnesian, form beds of great thickness, seen in projecting cliffs standing out in bold outline and displaying the
grandest scenes in the prospect. The old hill fort, east of
Goa, one of the numerous strongholds of the Mahratta tribes,
stands on one of the most prominent masses of these limestones ; the neighboring cliffs, with the huge blocks detached
from the mass and precipitated into the valley below, render
the site of this fortress one of great wildness and picturesque
beauty

Tertiary rocks cover but a small part of the peninsula, and
are mostly confined to a narrow strip on the coast ; they
are different from those of Western Asia or Europe. Human
implements, supposed to belong to the Pleistocene period,
have been found in the valleys of this part of India.

The Bhima formation consists chiefly of unfossiliferous limestones of different colors, largely used in building. It was employed exclusively for the ancient fortified city of Ferozabad,
of the fourteenth century, for buildings in other places, sometimes for windows, and for stone implements, by the early inhabitants.

The Talikot limestones of the Bhima series are largely
lithographic, of fine texture and waxy lustre, and display nearly
all the colors found in limestones, including cream-color, gray,
buff, pink, purple, and varieties banded with pink, purple, and
cream-color. The formation reaches a thickness of six hundred feet, and is liable to subsidences and landslides, which,
disrupting the rocks, afford material for the remarkable tufa-
breccias and conglomerates found near it. · The limestone is
extensively quarried, and was used for buildings in the city of
Talikot.

Limestones, jasper conglomerates of a great variety of colors, and breccias composed of jasper and hematite schist in a
purple cement, are met with between the Krishna and Mal-
prabha rivers. The limestones of the Ghatpralha valley display as great a variety of colors as the Talikot group ; some
of the beds enclose spar, used for carving ornaments.

Plate XIX.

Lisbon.

Rosso Brecciato.

Armstrong & Co. Lith. Boston.

The Yadward valley is especially prolific in limestones, the best varieties being found in the vicinity of Warrutsgul. They are of different colors, comprising a species of delicate veins of malachite, and a breccia with crystals of red feldspar embedded in a purple ground, yielding a beautiful stone.

Many of the limestones of the Lower Kaladgi are capable of a high polish, forming marbles of great beauty and value. The mountain slopes east of Goa afford dolomites, which may have furnished some of the marbles for the Portuguese churches and monasteries of this small province. The limestones of Travancore, a British dependency in the south, belong to the Tertiary, and are full of fossils later than the Nummulitic formation.

India, developing so many limestone formations, contains some noted caverns, either natural or artificial; the most celebrated are those of Ellora and Elephanta. The latter occurs on a small island near Bombay, named for a huge figure of an elephant carved in stone, and consists of Hindoo temples cut in the rock, with roofs supported by columns, and filled with numerous sculptures. The cavern of Billa Soorgum, in the south, opening into a diamond-yielding limestone, is capable of being converted into a genuine Aladdin's Cave.

Ancient Jain temples, excavated in reddish-yellow sandstone, with elaborate carving, are found at Aiholi and other places

The rulers of this venerable country, the mother of eastern civilization, embellished their capitals with magnificent temples for the numerous divinities recognized in their religious system. Asaca, one of the kings of Magada, the birthplace of Buddha, erected what are called the Edict Columns at Delhi, upon which are inscribed his orders for establishing hospitals and dispensaries, and for planting trees and digging wells along the highways, thus showing the advanced civilization of this kingdom long before the Christian era. These inscriptions, with those on other pillars, caves, and rocks, were not understood, either by natives or Europeans, until recently; they are now considered to be in the Pali language.

Ruins east of Nepaul indicate the site of the ancient city of Panchola, whose magnificence has been the admiration of both Mahommedan and native writers

Elphinstone, in his History of India, mentions the splendor and magnitude of Buddhist temples; of these the cave temples, especially at Ellora, are specimens, but the finest is at Carla, between Puna and Bombay; these structures, for length, height, colonnades, and vaulted and ribbed roofs strongly resemble Gothic cathedrals.

The temples of the Jains, one of the Hindoo sects, are, writes this author, generally large and handsome, with courts, colonnades, and statues of saints, marble altars, sculptures in relief, and walls painted with legendary scenes. The finest specimens of Jain temples are seen in the remains of white marble on the mountain of Abu, to the north of Guzerat. The Jains have their cave temples on a grand scale in various places, and at Chinrapatan, in Mysore, there exists the statue of one of their saints variously estimated at from fifty-four to seventy feet in height. The Sultan Mahmud of Guznee, in his conquests in India, destroyed or pillaged many of the rich and splendid Hindoo temples, carrying off immense treasures to enrich his capital. The fortified temple of Nargarcot, on the Himalayas, regarded with peculiar veneration, enriched by the offerings of kings and princes, and the repository of immense riches, was robbed by this conqueror in one of his numerous expeditions, of a vast amount of silver, gold, pearls, and precious stones. The most celebrated temple was Somnat, in the peninsula of Guzerat, which Mahmud plundered in the beginning of the eleventh century. It is said that there were from two hundred thousand to three hundred thousand native offerings presented in this temple during every eclipse, and that two thousand priests, three hundred musicians, and five hundred dancing women were employed in the service of Somnat; the golden chain attached to the bell used in worship has been valued at one hundred thousand pounds. The ruthless invaders were struck with awe at the grandeur of the interior, whose lofty roof was supported by fifty-six pillars curiously carved, and decorated with precious stones. Immense treasures, far exceeding those taken from any other temple, were carried off.

Ahmedabad owes its magnificent buildings to Ahmed Shah, whose zeal prompted him to pull down the temples and erect mosques in their places. Delhi, the favorite capital of the greater part of the Mogul emperors, was, from time to time, embellished by these magnificent rulers. Firuz built a splendid mosque of polished marble on the Jumna, while other rulers, before and since his reign, in the fourteenth century, added to the beauty of this city; but many of the buildings are in ruins. Akber, perhaps the most celebrated of the Mogul rulers, took great pleasure in constructing grand works at Agra, Allahabad, and Futtehpur, the remains of the latter are among the most splendid in India He adorned Agra with a beautiful mosque and palace of white marble, and many other structures; but none of the emperors exceeded Shah Jehan in his passion for splendid buildings. The grandeur of the cities during his prosperous reign, and the pomp and magnificence of his court, were the admiration of travellers from all countries.

The Hindoos seem, says Elphinstone, to have had an early acquaintance with the principles of architecture. They used twelve kinds of mouldings, some of which are employed at the present time, and sixty-four sorts of bases, but they had no fixed orders Their style resembled the Egyptian only in its massiveness and profusion of sculpture, but, unlike the Egyptian, their columns were generally high, slender, delicate, and thickly set; clustered columns and pilasters were of frequent occurrence Architectural embellishments were employed, and the walls of buildings were covered with sculptures in relief, representing the wars of the gods and other legends.

CHAPTER XIX.

I. *Japan.* — The Empire of Japan, with a length of nine hundred miles, and an area of less than two hundred thousand square miles, comprises between three thousand and four thousand islands, some large and others exceedingly small. It is very mountainous, being traversed its entire length by a lofty range crossed by steep passes elevated from one thousand to five thousand feet above sea-level. In the deep ravines and valleys of the range, nestle numerous small villages, secluded from the rest of the world. Many of the highest peaks are volcanoes, either active, or extinct; Fuji-yama, in the Island of Hondo, the most conspicuous of these, is thirteen thousand feet high, with a crater five hundred feet deep, and is overspread nearly to the summit with cultivated tracts and a belt of prairie land, while above them there lies a vast region covered with a great variety of forest trees.

Calcareous rocks are more or less abundant throughout the islands, though the granitic and volcanic series are the most prevalent. Granite was used in the construction of some of the fortresses of the Empire, and furnished the huge blocks of the castle-walls of Osaka, which are nearly, if not quite equal to the largest in the great pyramid of Cheops, measuring, according to the judgment of Sir E. J. Reed, forty feet in length and twenty in height.

The Island of Yesso, or Yezo, is traversed from north to south, through the centre, by the Hamaikotan group, supposed to contain the oldest rocks on the island. They are crystalline and metamorphic, embracing limestones with Carboniferous fossils, grayish-white marbles, and dark-green, brown, and black serpentines; the group is rich in precious metals, and quartz crystals. The coal-beds of Yesso, over which are scattered nodules or balls of limestones, enclosing the fossils of the Carboniferous period, have an enormous development. The volcanoes rest on strata including limestones, and in the western part of the island the rocks are largely made up of tufa conglomerates. It is the opinion of geologists that both this island and Niphon or Hondo were elevated at a late period, and that volcanic action took place before the upheaval.

A large development of metamorphic limestones occurs on a small stream in the southeast, forming cliffs on both sides, six hundred feet above the water, extending for miles. The formation yields dark-blue and light-gray limestones, enclosing beds of marble. East of Hakodate a limestone cliff of less height presents a front of eight hundred feet, and limestone forms the coast strata of this part of the island. Fossils, supposed to be Jurassic or Cretaceous, have been discovered in eastern Yesso.

Marbles for ornamental purposes are quarried at different places, and a breccia of dark-red, deep-yellow, grayish-white, and black, constituting a marble resembling a Sicilian variety, is cut into large balls and polished.

The famous limpid quartz crystals of Japan are found in the veins of a decomposing granite near the village of Mitke, where they are quarried. The ball exhibited at the Vienna Exposition is claimed to be the largest ever made from these quarries.

Japan, like other countries which sanction the worship of numerous divinities, contains a great many temples, shrines, and pagodas, but wood was largely employed in their construction, and the palaces of earlier times were rude structures without any architectural merits. In later years, however,

the emperors built immense and splendid edifices, which may
become durable monuments of the magnificence and glory of
their reigns.   The power and audacity of the priests of the
Buddhist temples, which were marvels of wealth and splendor,
led to the destruction of their vast monastery near Lake Biwa,
with its five hundred temples, shrines, and priestly dwellings.
The celebrated Tokugawa temples and shrines were begun
in the time of one of the Shoguns, who flourished at the beginning of the seventeenth century.   Miss Bird, in "Travels in
Japan," mentions a Buddhist town with two streets of temples
adorned with grand gateways and paved courts.   More ancient
and more renowned for sanctity are the Shinto temples of Isé,
built in the fifth century, but, like all the sacred buildings of
this sect, they are very plain.

The Loo Choo, a group of small islands south of Japan, and
a dependency of the Chinese Empire, develop a limestone
formation which appears as belts or dykes crossing the islands,
and rising into peaks with castellated forms, sometimes seventy or eighty feet above the ridge, constituting a marked
feature in the landscape.   The limestone is sometimes fossiliferous, and on account of its cellular structure has frequently
been taken for lava ; a recent formation, comprising pebbles
and fragments of corals in a lime cement, constitutes a compact breccia.   These islands yield the precious and many of
the common metals, coal, jaspers, agates, corals, and pearls.

II. *Australia.* — Australia, the El Dorado of the Southern
Hemisphere, though nearly of the size of Europe, is histor-
ically the youngest of the continents, and portions of its
territory still await the investigations of the geologist.   It is
supposed to have a mean elevation of about five hundred feet
less than any other grand division, while the arid plains of the
central region attain no greater height than two hundred
feet.

Its highest mountains, the Australian Alps, on the southeastern coast, vary from five thousand to six thousand five

hundred feet, while the height of the elevations on the western and southern borders is much less. The northeastern shores, on the Coral Sea, are guarded by the Great Barrier Reefs.

The rock systems are believed to include nearly every formation above the Cambrian. The Silurian strata, the most important for their mines of wealth, cover a very large area, and are found in all the colonies except West Australia; they are intersected by auriferous quartz veins, and have supplied immense quantities of the precious metal. Since the discovery of these deposits, Australian geologists have estimated the yield to be more than one billion of dollars worth of gold, besides other metalliferous ores and diamonds. In Victoria they include several limestone formations, and are highly fossiliferous, but in the other colonies they contain few organic remains

In the Waratah Bay district, limestones and marble destitute of fossils have been found, either Lower Devonian or Upper Silurian, probably the latter; the marble is black and white, mottled or veined, and suitable for ornamental work. The limestone, occupying massive beds, is called the purest and finest in Victoria.

The limestones of Buchan and Bindi form scattered patches varying in extent from some miles to only a few acres, deposited in the hollows of porphyry. As they enclose fossils identical with those of the Eifel of Germany, they are supposed to belong to the Devonian The Buchan formation, named for the place where it is more especially developed with the Snowy River porphyry, yields a dark, compact limestone, penetrated by numerous caverns or "sink holes," as at a place called the Pyramids, where the Murendel River disappears, and then reappears at some distance off.

The Bindi limestone occupies an area of ten square miles, and is second in extent to the Buchan The Bindi Basin is said to present one of the most charming views of mountain scenery in Gippsland, where the rock has been sculptured into gently-swelling hills with smooth, green slopes, enclosed by mountains of granite, quartz, porphyries, and slates, with rugged peaks and bold escarpments.

The Tertiary of Gippsland develops the Bairnsdale lime-stone, displayed in precipitous banks on Mitchell River, and spread over a wide area west of this river, reaching a thickness of two hundred and fifty feet. A limestone of this period, called the Portland stone (Jurassic), resembles a formation in New Zealand used for architectural carving.

Several varieties of limestones are found among the Coal Measures of the Cape Otway district, in the southern part of Victoria; and in New South Wales the coal-beds rest on a limestone with fossils supposed to be Carboniferous A fresh-water limestone of Victoria is called the Geelong formation.

It is estimated that this colony contains not less than two hundred and sixty square miles covered by volcanic rocks; the northeastern portion, it is thought, was once overspread with a continuous sheet of lava, but the process of denuda-tion has left mountains nearly six thousand feet high, ruins of a former great plateau, standing out in solitary grandeur like the isolated castles and fortresses of mediæval Europe.

Victoria, which has been more thoroughly explored than the other colonies, develops a great variety of rocks, includ-ing several valuable building-stones, and numerous species of minerals; one indefatigable collector · gathered in a single year between five hundred and six hundred different species. Nearly a dozen varieties of limestones have been analyzed, and their economic value established, though the auriferous, Silurian rocks surpass all others in this respect on account of their rich deposits.

Cretaceous rocks are spread over the vast areas of Queens-land in the east, and West Australia in the west regions of the Continent. What is called the Desert Sandstone, believed to be Tertiary, and to have covered at one time the larger part of Australia, has an extensive development in Queens-land, and, perhaps, in other colonies. Within a few years an exploring party, starting from the western coast and penetrating to the centre of the Continent, found granite to be almost the only rock, with few scattered patches of recent strata similar to those on the eastern coast, the remains of the great masses of stratified deposits eroded and borne away by denudation

The Quaternary formation is represented by a reddish breccia similar to the bone breccias of the Mediterranean, enclosing organic remains of quadrupeds, mostly marsupials of gigantic size.

Miocene fossils are found in strata on the islands between Australia and the Continent of Asia, which has suggested the idea that there might have been an extensive Tertiary sea in this region. The limestone formations of all the East India Islands are thick, and extend around the base of mountains, giving them a tabular form like modern coral islands.

The oldest-rocks of Sumatra, says Verbeck, are granitic, but limestones and schist form mountain ranges in the highland districts. Tertiary limestones occur filled with Corals, Orbitoides, and other shells, while strata are found enclosing fossil fish similar to the Glarus slates of the Alps and Monte Bolca, Italy.

Tasmania and the neighboring islands display their limestone formations, which, in Borneo, includes the Nummulitic; while Java and the Madura consist largely of Coral limestones. Calcareous deposits, rising eighteen hundred feet above the sea, characterize the coast-line of the Sandalwood and Sumbawa Islands, and Coralline limestone form the hills seven hundred or eight hundred feet high.

The Tertiary of New Guinea includes a limestone similar to the Geelong of Australia, and in New Zealand it is very prolific in fossils. F. W Hutton found in this formation three hundred and seventy-five species of true Mollusks, twelve of Brachiopods, and eighteen of Echinoderms.

III. *Africa.* — The Cretaceous or Chalk formation is very largely developed in Africa, extending from Sennaar, on the Blue Nile, northward to Nubia, through Egypt, and along the Mediterranean coast, overspreading Tripoli, Tunis, Algiers, Morocco, Fezzan of the Great Desert, and appearing also in South Africa   The Cretaceous beds are nearly always superimposed by the Nummulitic series, the two formations affording a great abundance and variety of limestones.

In the mountain regions of the fertile country of Abyssinia, very ancient marine beds have been deposited, and the surface of the soil is scattered over with marine shells in a perfect state of preservation.   The islands of the Red Sea bear marks of the same age, while the shores display shell limestones and gypsums; and a siliceous limestone occurs in the Desert of Adel, southwest from the Straits of Babel-Man-del.   The Blue Nile, whose sources are in the cool mountains of Abyssinia, flows through fresh-water beds of the nature of ancient alluvium, while below these beds rests a blackish-gray, sonorous limestone, with a tendency to a crystalline structure, containing vegetable and animal remains, the latter being analogous to those living in the surrounding waters.

The strata covering the great plateau of the Libyan Desert, extending from the north to the Oasis of Ammon, contain Tertiary organic remains.   The series of rocks include salt-beds, with carbonate of lime and sulphate of lime (limestone and gypsum), and furnish the chemical products for the Natron Lakes in that region.   The most celebrated of these lakes is on the eastern side of the valley called the Waterless River, fifty miles south of Alexandria

Of all the countries of the globe known to the ancients but few equal Egypt for the interest and importance of its civilization, its institutions, its science and art.   Besides its contributions to learning, it has been an inexhaustible mine for architectural decoration, yielding treasures of ornamental stones for the embellishment of the cities and magnificent structures of younger nations:

Egypt comprises four geological districts, consisting, respectively, of granites or similar crystalline rocks, sandstones, limestones, and modern deposits. The granites, extending from the mountains of Nubia to Assouan, the ancient Syene, where the Nile passes the first cataract, occupy only a small part of the surface of Egypt, but they furnished the material for many of the monuments of Lower Egypt. The celebrated quarries of Syene, which, it has been claimed, gave rise to the name syenite as applied to a rock, were cut into a coarse-grained stone composed of large crystals of rose feldspar, hyalin quartz, black mica, and hornblende. This rock was employed for the most colossal monuments of Egypt, and is said to have formed the covering of the Pyramids, and to have been used for the temples of Karnak and Luxor, near ancient Thebes, the obelisks, and other works of antiquity.

The Cretaceous sandstones of Egypt extend north from Assouan, on the east of the Nile, to Esneh, on the west bank, a little below Thebes. This sandstone afforded material for the Temples of Isis at Dendera and other magnificent buildings of this remarkable country. The rock is white, crystalline, and either coarse or fine-grained. In the vicinity of the Cataracts it passes to a breccia, enclosing agates, and was employed in the Statue of Memnon, many of the Sphinxes, and the Temples of Karnak. The limestones of Egypt are variable in color, hard, compact, and yield an abundance of marble, often crossed with green veins. The region between the Nile and the Red Sea constitutes the Blad Recam, or "Marble Country," celebrated for the great variety and abundance of its marbles with fossils, and of different colors, green, rose, white, ash, and other hues. The valley of the Nile affords an extensive development of the Nummulitic formation. The compact limestones of Upper Egypt, extending far into the Desert of Sahara on the west, and Arabia on the east, are composed of masses of Polythalamia, identical with those of the European Chalk.

Cairo El Kahira, "the victorious," containing the tombs of the caliphs, is on the right bank of the Nile, where two ranges of mountains separate, one branching to the east, called the Arabian, the other to the west, the Libyan; the rocks which constitute these chains were used for the tombs of the ancient kings in Thebes. The summits of the hills behind the citadel of Cairo comprise the White Beds, a concretionary limestone, the Red Beds, a coarse shell limestone, and some other varieties enclosing Nummulites and Echini.

Many of the magnificent Temples of Egypt, the Great Sphinx, and the Pyramids, the wonder of the world for more than forty centuries, were constructed of limestone. It is due to the warm and dry climate of this country that the Great Pyramid, a miracle of the constructive power of its ancient people, erected, it is supposed, before the time of Abraham, has been preserved from the eroding influence of atmospheric agencies. The immense pile consists of two hundred and sixty layers of large blocks of stone, rising to a vertical height of four hundred and eighty feet, and resting on a base of more than thirteen square acres. It is built of Nummulitic limestone, on the native rock, with its four sides facing exactly the four cardinal points, and it has been estimated that it required for its construction more than eighty million cubic feet of stone, sufficient to build a wall five feet high and one foot thick, of more than three thousand miles in length. Much of the stone was taken from an eminence near, called Pyramid Hill, and on the eastern escarpment are seen in abundance fossil Nummulites about the size of a pea, which are called Strabo's Beans.

To the west of Cairo the rocks are gently sloping, but to the east they form abrupt escarpments, which are bathed by the waters of the Nile. Not far from this city exists a sterile plateau, elevated above the river, called the Petrified Forest. Wood, containing fragments of jasper and quartz, is scattered about, and trunks of trees sixty feet in length are lying one upon another, like a prostrate forest. Some trees are horizontal, others vertical, but destitute of knots, branches, or roots, and appear to be conifers. The interior of the trunks is frequently filled with sandstone, while the petrified portions pass to agates and quartz of different colors. Limestones are found in the region, and at Red Mountain a marine limestone and conglomerates are quarried, penetrated by caverns, which afford shelter for wild beasts

The Lunettes of Dendera, found in a limestone, are spheroidal stones of various dimensions, depressed in the centre, sometimes double or twins, surrounded with concentric prominences resembling a cushion, and simulating eyes, whence the name.

The rock called Egyptian breccia is a conglomerate of rounded and angular pieces of diorite, gneiss, porphyry, argillaceous and siliceous schists, serpentines, flint, compact feldspar of a clear green, and marble, the whole cemented by a calcareous paste of various tints from green to purple-red. This breccia, found in the region of the Gebel Ghareb, two hundred feet above the level of the desert, was quarried to a considerable extent by the Egyptians and Romans, as is proved by its use in the ancient temples and palaces of Egypt, in many of the churches in Italy, obtained from ruined buildings, and in the mosques of Constantinople The sarcophagus supposed to be that of Alexander the Great was cut in this conglomerate, which is called in Italy, Breccia di Egitto, Egyptian breccia; its age is not known, but it does not indicate a very great antiquity

The great Nummulitic formation, occupying the largest part of the kingdoms of the Pharaohs, extending from the Nile to the vast plains of the Libyan Desert on the west, forming the base of the deserts, and to the Red Sea on the east, includes beds of limestone varying in color, structure, and composition.

The celebrated Egyptian alabaster marble was quarried in a hill six hundred or seven hundred feet above the valley of

the Sanmur, twelve hours from the Nile; the base of the hill
is composed of layers of alabaster, the upper part of cavernous limestone.   The hills along the river are composed
of limestone, forming immense beds, which extend far beyond
the valley.   Hitchcock says that a beautiful, translucent
alabaster, consisting of pure carbonate of lime, evidently
deposited by springs, and similar to the Tabreez marble of
Persia, was employed by the Pasha of Egypt in building
one of his numerous palaces in Cairo.

At some hours from Ghemir, limestone hills comprise beds
of compact, rose-white marble, and the deep valley of the
Arabah, in the region of the Red Sea, constitutes a depository
of marbles of white, rose, and green colors, with a granular,
shell marble of a red tint, passing to an obscure white, the
series resting under a Nummulitic limestone   Large beds of
marble are developed in the chain of Gelaleh, whence were
obtained many of the beautiful antique marbles so highly
prized by ancient nations, and so eagerly sought in modern
times.

The ancient quarries of red, antique porphyry were re-dis-
covered by Burton and Wilkinson, in a district east of the
Nile, in the mountains of Djebel Dakhan, twenty-five miles
from the Red Sea   This porphyry, identical with that of the
ancient monuments, is composed of a feldspathic paste, enclosing different crystals of clear, red, violet-red, wine-red or reddish-brown.   The chemical composition is as follows · Silica,
58 92; alumina, 22 49; calcite, 5 53; the remaining parts,
iron, magnesia, and some other substances.   From its chemical composition it is easy to see that it is not properly a
marble, yet, strange to say, it has been styled the Rosso
antico of the ancients, which is a pure limestone; nor
is there such a similarity between the two substances that
they need be confounded.   Sometimes the antique porphyry
has a deep-violet base with brown, resembling certain
varieties of the Elfdalen of Sweden.

The Egyptians did not employ the antique porphyry for

sculpture, but the Romans, after the reign of Claudius, A. D. 54, began to quarry the stone, which they used extensively, as may be seen in the works of Rome and other cities of Italy. For the sacred scarabæ and other objects of small size, the Egyptians employed serpentine, basalt, trap, and Verde antique. Large statues of basalt are rare, but some of the most remarkable are found in the ruins of Karnak. Antiquaries have often taken a deep-colored granite with black mica, and also a dark diorite for basalt.

The Nummulitic limestones of Algeria are widely disseminated, forming a great part of the mountains of this region. In this province are found representatives of the macigno of Italy, the flysch of the Alps, and the sandstones of Vienna. The Cretaceous formation is developed at the city of Algiers, including many varieties of limestones, gray, and yellow, like those of Constantine, limestones with fossils, like the Jurassic, lithographic, and black limestones, a white saccharoidal, which is quarried, dolomites, ancient travertines, and solid calcareous breccias. Salt, lead, and copper mines, worked by the Arabs for a long time, have been found in these rocks. The beautiful onyx marble of Algeria is, without doubt, a calcareous deposit of springs.

The city of Constantine, in Algeria, the ancient Certa, is built upon a square rock at an elevation of more than two thousand feet, surrounded by abrupt escarpments, at the foot of which flows the Roumel, formerly the Ampsaga, and presents a thick mass of compact limestones of fine grain, generally without fossils, except the upper layers, which contain Hippurites, Ammonites, and Caprotina. The Hippurite and black limestones extend a long distance ; the former constitutes, with reddish-yellow dolomites, some of the mountains.

The species of the Constantine limestones are numerous, affording gray, black, red, brown, and rose as regards colors, and fossiliferous, oolitic, lithographic, lumachelles, as regards origin and texture ; some beds of a bright color are quarried

as marble. In Constantine and Bona, sheets of calcareous
tufa cover the hills and plateaus ; at the former place they are
compact and crystalline, of a rose color, and have been used
for marble in many ancient monuments. In some localities
the tufa passes to a ferruginous sandstone, used for building.
Between Algeria and Constantine are an innumerable number of dazzlingly white, calcareous pyramids, assuming fantastic shapes, formed by the deposits of hot springs

To the preceding limestones of Algeria may be added the
compact, fossiliferous, rose-colored limestone of Oran, a limestone with Madrepores, and a breccia enclosing sparry shells.
The quarries called Du Genn yield a bluish-green porphyry,
with fine grain, penetrated with veins of calcite.

The ubiquitous Nummulitic formation, with its remarkably
uniform characteristics, appears in Morocco. There is little
variation in the limestones of this country from those of the
others on the western Mediterranean, except that they are
less numerous than the Algerian. The southern side of the
Atlas Mountains consists of limestones and sandstones, with a
great variety of fossils ; some of the rocks are analogous to
the macigno and alberese of Italy.

The limestones of Tunis and Fezzan are destitute of fossils ;
those comprising the hills of Tripoli include a great variety
with dolomites. Near the ruins of Carthage, one of the most
celebrated cities of antiquity, occurs a conglomerate of sandstone and limestone, which may have been employed in its
construction. Of this city, which filled so large a place in
history, nothing remains except some of its cisterns and an
aqueduct, though we are told that it contained many magnificent buildings.

The limestone of Red Hill, in West Africa, encloses fragments of scoriæ, which has associated it with igneous
agency ; a variety, forming cliffs east of the mouth of the
Congo, or Livingston River, is filled with the Ostrea, while
Jurassic strata, with Ammonites, are developed on the east
coast of the Continent.

Plate XX.

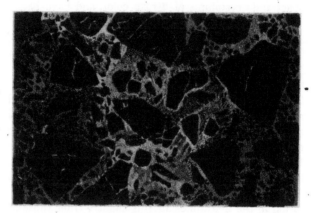

BRECCIA VILLA ADRIANA.

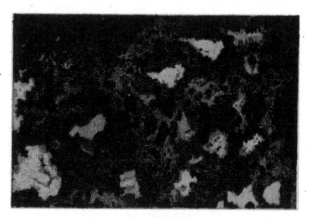

VERDE PLASMA.

ARMSTRONG & CO. LITH. BOSTON.

The Island of St. Louis, on the coast of Western Africa, is composed entirely of marine, shelly sand, enclosing the Arca, a Lamellibranch found in the rocks from the Silurian to the Tertiary. St. Helena yields a calcareous rock composed of the débris of shells, while porphyries and aragonites are found on the Azores.

The Island of Santiago, one of the Cape Verde Islands, is volcanic, but at Porta Praya the sea is bordered for many miles by a white band of solid, shell limestone, in some places passing to a perfectly pure, crystalline marble, resembling aragonite. Like the rocks on the west coast of Africa, it is Tertiary.

CHAPTER XX.

I. *Antique White Marbles — Marmor Parium: Greco Duro, or Parian Marble.* — Certain stones, including marbles, serpentines, porphyries, basalts, granites, or any other rocks capable of receiving a polish and suitable for decoration, were early used for architecture and sculpture, as is proved by the ruins of cities, inscriptions, and the writings of ancient chroniclers. On account of their superior beauty, their great variety, and capacity for being easily worked, marbles were more frequently used for art purposes than any other stone.

Although some of these marbles are still quarried, and must be considered both ancient and modern, the mines to a great extent are either exhausted or forgotten, and their valuable productions can be seen only in fragments found in the ruins of old buildings, or in the churches and palaces of mediæval times which have been decorated by the spoils of antiquity.

According to an estimate made by Corsi, there are more than seven thousand antique columns in modern Rome, made from nearly seventy-five different species or varieties of stones, obtained from the ruins of the old city.

Antique marbles may be arranged in two general classes : White or statuary, and Colored. Ancient sculptors sometimes employed the latter, but white was generally preferred, especially before the decline of art. Among all the varieties of

280

white marble used for sculpture, Parian held the first rank.
The island of Paros, in the Ægean Sea, is thirty-six miles in
circumference, and though small in extent became noted in
Greek history and Greek art The marble for which it was
celebrated was principally obtained from Mount Marpressa,
near the centre of the island, whose quarries were worked
many centuries before the Christian era Some translators
have thought that Parian marble was referred to in the Book
of Esther, though that rendering has had opponents. In the
Vulgate and the Septuagint versions of the Bible, it is said
that David procured Parian marble to be used in the construction of the Temple in Jerusalem. If this is a correct
understanding of the text, it proves that this marble was extensively known and used before the age of Homer. It has
been found in the ruins of Troy, but it might have been
brought thither by the Greeks at a period subsequent to the
foundation of the Homeric Troy.

Parian has always taken precedence of all other marbles,
and by way of eminence has been called Marble or Parian, as
if these were names for what was most beautiful and excellent among decorative stones.

Pliny says it was called Lychnites, on account of its having
been quarried by lamplight, but modern travellers believe that
the marble was taken from the side of the mountain open to
daylight, and that the name was given on account of its
brilliancy. Pinkerton thinks the name Lychnites may have
been applied to a calcareous alabaster in the form of stalactites, found with the marbles of Paros

It is a nearly pure carbonate of lime, with a crystalline,
granular structure, and when freshly broken presents a
brilliant play of light peculiar to it. A delicate rose tint and a
velvety appearance have been ascribed to this unrivalled
marble, but, as seen in antique statues, it inclines to a yellowish hue, peculiarly adapted to represent flesh-tints. It is hard,
and consists of rather large, glistening scales, unlike the Pentelic or Carrara.

The ancients considered Parian 'peculiarly agreeable to the gods on account of its whiteness and purity, and its virtues have been widely celebrated by classic writers.

The Parian Chronicles, as they are called, found in the Island of Paros, now in England, are inscriptions cut in a block of this marble giving an account of the principal events of Greek history from Cecrops, 1582 B. C., to Diagnotus, 264 B. C., a period of one thousand three hundred and eighteen years.

It is related by Herodotus that the Alcmæonidæ, a noble family of Athens, 750 – 400 B. C., having been banished from their native city, contracted to rebuild the Temple of Delphi, which had been burned 548 B C, of Porinum, a marble of less value, but they used the more costly and beautiful Parian instead for the exterior front walls, and this act of generosity made the family very popular in Greece.

Parian was employed in the construction of the Mausoleum of Hadrian, now the Castle of St Angelo, Rome, and the sculptures which adorned it were of the same material   One of the statues, the Barbarini Faun, taken from this monument, is now in the gallery of Munich.   The antique marbles called Pavonazzetto and Giallo antico were used, in combination with Parian, for the decoration of this sumptuous tomb. Many of the antique sculptures in the Vatican Museum were carved in Parian, as in the Minerva Medica, in which it resembles a very fine alabaster, remarkably translucent, and tending to a yellowish tint, and in the Ariadne and the Venus, of a bluish-white, unlike the Minerva, but with the large lustrous scales of the Parian.   The Mercury of the Belvedere is said to be of this marble, while the Apollo Belvedere has been considered by some connoisseurs to be Parian, and by others, with less probability, Luni or Carrara.

Marmor Porinum: Grechetto Duro of the Italians — This marble is similar in hardness and whiteness to the Parian and ranks next to it, but has smaller scales and a lighter texture, whence the name " porous."   It was called by the ancients Chernites, from its resemblance to ivory, and was much used for sarcophagi on account of its supposed preservative qualities. Pausanias says the Porinum marble was found near Olympia, in the Peloponnesus, and that it was used in the famous Temple of Jupiter Olympus. Doubtless many other sacred edifices found in this region, consecrated to peace and art, were constructed, wholly or in part, of this variety of marble.

Many of the celebrated sculptures of the Vatican Museum were made of Grechetto duro or Porinum, including the Torso of Hercules, erroneously catalogued as Pentelic; the Amazon, in the Gallery of the Statues, considered the finest in existence; and the Apollo Cytharædus, in the Hall of the Biga.

Marmor Pentelicum : Greco Fino, or Pentelic Marble — This marble is described with the "Limestones of Greece," but a mistake as to the place whence it was taken has caused some confusion among writers about Pentelic marble which requires explanation.

Mount Pentelicus proper is a branch of Mount Parnes, between Athens and Marathon, extending to the coast northeast of the former city. It has been described as close to the walls of Athens and very near Mount Hymettus, but it is probable that Mount Lycabettus, one of the Pentelic range, near the city, was meant Another cause of perplexity is the want of uniformity in the marble; the fact is that Mount Pentelicus yields different kinds, one variety veined, and another pure white, which furnishes the true, antique Pentelic, both are seen in the Vatican Museum. The marble of Mount Hymettus has sometimes been mentioned in a way which might leave a doubt as to whether it was not identical with the Pentelic, but the two marbles are radically different

Xenophon writes that there is developed near Athens an abundance of marble, from which the most beautiful temples, altars, and statues of the gods are made, and which is much prized by the Greeks and the Barbarians.

It was used in the time of Pericles for columns and other parts of buildings, and, though Parian was generally preferred for sculpture, yet Praxiteles, and Scopas, who was a native of

Paros, employed it, to a considerable extent, for statuary.
The antique has a remarkably fine grain, and a dazzling whiteness, which distinguish it from most other marbles.

The statue of the Young Augustus, in the Vatican, Corsi
regards as Pentelic, though it is said to be Parian in the catalogue.   The marble has the dead whiteness of the former
rather than the flesh-tint of the latter.   A statue of Commodus larger than life, of Venus Anadyomene, of Posidippus and
Menander (in the last two, the marble is veined with bluish-
gray), a Bacchante, life-size, the Laocoon, and some other
works of less note, are said to be sculptured in this marble.

Marmor Hymettus: Imezio, or Cipollo. — Mount Hymettus,
about three miles southeast from Athens, was celebrated in
ancient times for its marble and honey.   The quarries yielded
an abundance of an obscure white marble, tending to a yellowish tint, marked by long veins of deep bluish-gray schists,
giving it a ribboned appearance.   It is called Cipollo by Italian
marble-workers, from the odor emitted when struck, similar
to that of the onion.   It is greatly inferior to the Pentelic,
and was principally used for columns, architraves and other
architectural members   On the authority of Corsi, the first
foreign columns ever brought to Rome were of Hymettus
marble, and the number found in that city at the present time,
is very large.   Forty-six columns were saved from the con-
flagration of St Paul's Church outside the walls, while forty-
two sustain the nave of the Church of St. Maria Maggiore, and
twenty are found in the Church of San Pietro in Vincoli ; it is
seen in so many churches and other buildings that it cannot
be mistaken for any other.   The Hymettus was so generally
used for architraves, that it is said when a painter wished to
represent this member he always painted it in imitation of
this marble.   The Meleager and the Diana Lucifera of the
Vatican are claimed to be in the Imezio or Hymettus; in the
latter statue the marble is white and compact.

Marmor Thasium: Greco Livido, or Tarsio. — The island
of Thasos, now Tasso, in the Ægean, near the coast of Thrace,

attracted, on account of its gold, the enterprising Phœnicians, who also discovered there mines of marbles which were afterwards used by Greek sculptors. It is called by Italians Tarsio, from its native island, and Livido on account of its tendency to a dark tint. The texture is rather compact, and, like the Parian and the Hymettus, it has a brilliant fracture. The reputation of this marble has been variable ; sometimes it was not popular enough to be introduced into architecture, but was degraded to the use of fish-ponds, while, at other times, it was held in highest estimation by the Greeks, and employed to some extent in sculpture. It was used for the Euripides in the Braccio Nuovo, and for covering the Pyramid of Caius Cestus outside the walls of Rome. According to Pausanias two statues of the Emperor Hadrian, made of this marble, were placed in the Temple of Jupiter Olympus, at Olympia.

Marmor Lesbium : Greco Giallognolo, or Yellowish Marble. — Lesbos, "where burning Sappho loved and sung," the largest and most important island of the Ægean, near the coast of Asia Minor, and intersected by lofty mountains, one of which bore the classic name of Olympus, was the native region of the Æolian school of lyric poetry, and the birthplace of many distinguished characters. The high mountains which form so grand a feature in the scenery of the island afforded the Lesbian marble used in the production of antique art.

Its brilliancy and tendency to a clear yellow rendered it desirable to represent flesh tints, and it was preferred to any other for sepulchral monuments. Corsi says this marble was used for the statue of Julia Pia in the Museum of the Vatican. There is a bust of Julia Pia in the Braccio Nuovo, and a portrait statue, life-size, of Julia, the daughter of Titus, catalogued as of Luni marble, but with the characteristics of the Lesbian ; perhaps this is the one intended. This antiquary says the celebrated Venus of the Capitol was sculptured in the same variety.

Marmor Tyrium ; Greco Turchiniccio, or Bluish marble.— There is sometimes found an antique marble in the ruins of

Rome called Greco Turchiniccio, Greek bluish marble, from a tendency to a blue color, though it is not thought to be Greek.

Its ancient name has not been transmitted with the stone, but from its resemblance to the marble of the Scala Santa, a flight of twenty-eight steps supposed to be taken from the palace of Pilate at Jerusalem, and brought to Rome by the Empress Helen, A. D. 326, it has been considered Tyrian marble from Mount Libanus, and, in confirmation of this opinion, Statius says that a white marble quarried at Mount Lebanon was called Tyrian and Sidonian indiscriminately, because the quarries were not far from these cities, and that it was an article of commerce to the Tyrians. Josephus records that the Temple was partly constructed of the white marble of Mount Lebanon, and in our version of the Bible we read that large hewn stones were brought from Lebanon for the foundation of the Temple.

The identity of the marble of the Scala Santa and that of Mount Lebanon is based on slight proof, since it is doubtful whether the Scala Santa was brought from Pilate's Palace, and, provided it was, whether it was made of the marble in question, since Jerusalem is in a limestone region, is even built upon this rock, some of which yields marble.

Marmor Lunense: Marmo di Carrara. — This variety, known to the ancients as Lunense, celebrated in modern times as Carrara marble, was obtained near the Etruscan town of Luna, now Luni, which gives the name to this valuable stone.

Strabo informs us that near Luna were quarries of marbles of different shades of blue and white, furnishing blocks of sufficient size for columns. The Carrara or Luni marble was not probably used by the Romans before the time of Julius Cæsar, but from that date it was extensively employed to embellish Rome, and superseded most other kinds, on account of its excellence and the facility and cheapness of transportation from the quarries by the sea and the Tiber. At the close of the dictatorship of Cæsar it was most highly valued for sculpture, a rank it has held ever since. The bluish marble called Bardiglio, from the same region, was less prized by the ancients than the Bathium.

The columns and architrave of the Dogana di Terra, the Custom-House at Rome, erroneously called the Temple of Antoninus Pius, shows in what great masses it was used. The immense size of the blocks, and the danger to which the populace were exposed in their transportation through the narrow streets, have afforded themes for the verses of Juvenal. The Luni marble has a fine grain and a white color approaching that of majolica, but it is often marred by the presence of specks of metallic substances.

Marmor Coraliticum: Palombino — Pliny being authority, this marble was found on the banks of the Coraliticus or San-garius, a river in Phrygia, Asia Minor; hence it was called both Coraliticum and Sangarium. Ajasson is of the opinion that the ancient milk-white marble still found in Italy, and known as Palombino, may have been the Coraliticum of Pliny, but there is some reason for supposing the latter to have been a gypseous alabaster, or the fine, white marble called Gre-chetto. Corsi is persuaded that Palombino is identical with the Coraliticum, since it answers to the description of the Roman naturalist. This marble is white, of a clear grayish or yellowish tint, simulating the color of a white dove, which gained for it the name of Palombino, with very fine grain, said to be the finest among marbles, compact texture, fracture without lustre, and bears some resemblance to ivory.

Ancient writers agree that Coraliticum was never found in blocks exceeding two cubits in size. In the Vatican Museum are two cinerary urns of Palombino, not more than one foot in height, bearing the inscription of T. Claudius Succèssus. The life-size bust of Annius Verus Cæsar, son of M. Aure-lius, was sculptured in Coraliticum or Palombino, if the iden-tity of the two marbles has been established; an altar said to be Palombino is probably travertine. The Coraliticum was used in antique pavements of rooms and courts, in small pieces forming squares and rhomboids.

Other white statuary marbles without specific names or distinctive qualities, have been classed under the titles of Trojan, Mylasian and Ephesian. Limestones and marbles are very abundant near the site of the ancient city of Ephesus, which supplied the material for the celebrated Temple of Diana and other magnificent buildings of this the chief of the twelve Ionian cities. Strabo says that the city of Mylasa, in Caria, was built on a plain, under the projecting brow of a mountain of very beautiful marble, and, as a consequence, no city surpassed it in the magnificence of its buildings. It was adorned with porticoes and temples, including the national Temple of Jupiter Carius, and other splendid buildings, whose ruins are very extensive.

Statius speaks of a white marble called Trojan, found at Mount Ida, near Troy, which may have been used in the construction of Ilium.

II. *Antique Colored Marbles.* — The varieties of white antique marbles are few in comparison with those that are colored, the latter, though sometimes used for statues, were more frequently and with more taste employed for architectural work, and as such they were exceedingly beautiful and appropriate.

The wide extent of the Roman dominions under the Empire, and the wealth, power, and resources of the emperors, placed within their reach all the mineral products of those countries subjected to their authority. The rarest and most costly stones were brought from every province where the Roman legions had penetrated, to adorn the temples, palaces, and villas of Italy, and to gratify the luxurious tastes of her rulers Asia, Africa, Greece, and the islands of the Mediterranean yielded up their subterranean treasures to enhance the splendor of Roman cities, and to minister to the sumptuous habits of the Roman people.

Many of the foreign decorative stones introduced into Italy were obtained from quarries that had been worked by the subjugated nations themselves; others were discovered and first used by the Romans; but most of them are abandoned, and were it not for the extensive ruins of Rome and other Italian cities, we should have no other acquaintance with these beautiful and valuable marbles than what can be obtained from ancient writings.

These buried treasures, taken from the old palaces and temples, are rapidly disappearing, being used for various kinds of ornamental mosaic work, and but for the churches, which are more or less adorned with them, they would eventually be entirely lost to the public.

Marmor Numidicum: Giallo Antico. — This beautiful marble, unsurpassed for the splendor of its hues and the fine quality of its grain, was obtained from Numidia, in northern Africa, a region made historic by the wars between Jugurtha and the Romans. It is said that the quarries were on the side of Mount Maurasidus; and, from the near neighborhood of Libya, the marble has been called Libyan. M. Lepidus, a Roman consul, 78 B. C., according to Pliny, was the first to bring it to Rome, and was censured for using so beautiful a marble for the common use of lintels and thresholds of doors.

To distinguish this marble from the modern yellows of Siena and Verona, it has been called Giallo antico, though a tolerable familiarity with the latter would prevent any confusion of the two   The texture is compact and the grain very fine, consequently it receives a high polish. The base of the color is always yellow or yellowish, but of many shades, from deep yellow to nearly white, including ivory, canary, gold, saffron, and orange. The different varieties have received different names to indicate the shades of color, — as Dorato, golden; Cupo, deep orange; Paglia, straw color; Carnigione, flesh color. The ancients compared it to ivory, to the rays of the sun, to purple, from the color of its veins, and to saffron. Some varieties are brecciated, others are veined with different shades of yellow or purple; the variety which presents a single tint is considered the most valuable, and of unicolored species the rose-yellow is the rarest. There are several antique yellow breccias, but they differ in many points from the Giallo antico.

The extraordinary quantities of the Marmor Numidicum or Giallo antico found in Rome proves that it was very abundant in its native quarries, and was extensively exported. Some of the largest columns are seen in the Pantheon, the Church of St. John Lateran, and the Arch of Constantine; two very large columns in St. Peter's of the Vatican were taken from Trajan's Forum.

Marmor Luculleum: Bigio Morato. — The Luculleum received its ancient name from L. Lucullus, the distinguished Roman consul whose wars with Mithridates fill so large a place in history, but who is equally well known for the luxurious tastes he so freely gratified in the latter part of his life. He constructed many magnificent palaces for his own use, employing this marble, for which he had a predilection, in their decoration. Pliny says he was the first to introduce it into Rome, and that it was black, and brought from the island of Melos, according to the English translation published by Bohn, which is probably an error, Melas, the Greek name for Nile, being intended.

Corsi thinks the marble was obtained from Meroe, in Abyssinia, which seems very probable, as Lucullus was at one time governor of Africa. It is black, with very fine spots like dust, and is slightly varied; that of a deep color is called Bigio morato scuro; that less tinted, chiaro. The most highly-prized variety has spots of deep black. It was found in large masses, since there were three hundred and sixty columns thirty-eight feet high brought to Rome by Scaurus, to be used in a temporary theatre, many of which were subsequently appropriated for his own house. There are two columns of Bigio morato or Lucullian marble in the Church of S. Maria Maggiore.

Marmor Iassense: Porta Santa. — This marble was obtained from Iasus, a small island in the gulf of the same name, on the coast of Caria, and is sometimes called Carian; the ruins of the town of Iasus, now Asyn Kalessi, are still to be seen. The modern name Porta Santa was given because it was used about the entrance to St. Peter's, called Porta Santa.

The Emperor Claudius, A. D. 41–54, who embellished Rome by several public works, had a great admiration for this marble; consequently it is sometimes called Claudian stone. There is a great diversity in the tints, though the general tone is red or reddish; it presents none of the pure, primitive colors except orange, but ranges through many varieties, from pure white to black, and from delicate red to its darkest shades; green is seldom seen. The veins are irregular, — now wide, now narrow, sometimes wavy, sometimes articulated. It is difficult to determine the color of the ground, which is covered with red, pink, orange, or some other colored veins, and there is no harmony, though the hues are quite vivid in some varieties; the rarest and most beautiful has purple spots. The fountain in the Piazza Colonna, Rome, affords an example, and it is so plentiful that there are few churches or other public buildings not adorned with it.

The Emperors Gordiani, who flourished in the third century of the Christian era, had a villa on the Via Praenestina leading from Rome to Preneste, now Palestrina, which was embellished with two hundred marble columns; fifty of Giallo antico, fifty of Pavonazzetto, a purple and white marble, fifty of Cippolino, a green and white, and fifty of Porta Santa. These columns formed the exterior decoration, and give some hint of the magnificence of the interior.

Marmor Carystium: Cipollino. — The chain of mountains which traverse the island of Euboea, on the eastern shore of Greece, terminates at the southeastern extremity, in Mount Ocha. On its western slope were the quarries of the ancient Carystium marble, named for the town Carystus, on the

coast, at a convenient distance for the exportation of the stone
from the quarries.   The marble was used in the Temple of
Jupiter Marmarius, built on the side of Mount Ocha.   The
Carystium presents a foundation generally of an obscure or
pinkish white, with green or bluish veins of talc or mica,
which causes the layers to peel off like the coats of an onion,
whence the name Cipollino ; sometimes red is found among
the colors, but it is not common.   It has been compared to
the waves of the sea, and very appropriately, both for the
color and the form of the veins or clouds.

It is said that the large columns of Cipollino, belonging to
the celebrated portico of the Temple of Neptune, built by
Agrippa, who consecrated a marble which so well represents
the waves, to the god of the sea, were placed in the Curia
Innocenziana.   Ten columns of this marble, forty-six feet
high, support the façade of the Temple of Antoninus and
Faustina, now the Church of San Lorenzo in Miranda, near
the Roman Forum.

The Cipollino admits of great variations; when green
spots assume an elliptical form, the species is called Mandolato verde, green almond ; when both base and spots are of
different shades of red, Mandolato rosso, which is very rare
and valuable ; another rare variety shows parallel bands of
white on a green base; two others, one with yellow foundation and the other with rose color, both covered with bright
green waves, are seldom found.   The kind displaying compact white and lively green clouds is called Cipollino marino,
seen in the Villa Albani; another variety occurs of a red tint
bearing some resemblance to the Rosso antico   One of the
most beautiful forms of this changeable marble is seen in the
magnificent columns of the Braccio Nuovo, in the Vatican
Museum.   The foundation color is white, covered with light
and dark purple waves, displaying occasional delicate yellow
tints, which assume the forms of circles and ellipses

Cipollino is not generally used except for columns, but
unfortunately it does not weather well.   It was extensively

employed by the ancients, and is found in many mediæval buildings, and sometimes in recent monuments, as in that of the Immaculate Conception, in the Piazza di Spagna, Rome.

Marmor Synadicum: Pavonazzetto, or Phrygian — Phrygia occupied the western part of the great table-land of Asia Minor, between the chain of the Olympus on the north and the Taurus on the south, a region celebrated in the fabulous ages for the worship of Bacchus, its mountains yielded gold and marbles.

Synnada was a town in the interior of Phrygia, near which was quarried the Synnadic marble, a name given to it by the Romans, but called by the natives Docimite, from Docimea, a small village near the mine. Strabo states that to gratify the extravagance of the Romans, pillars of large size and surpassing beauty, quarried at this mine, were transported a long distance to the sea, whence they were conveyed to Rome.

The marble resembles alabaster in its translucent quality, and in the form and direction of the veins. The base is sometimes opal and sometimes a creamy white, marked with veins of purple ranging from very dark to quite red, often blended with rose color. The clouds have considerable regularity, frequently passing into a soft, translucent white, and occasionally presenting pink and yellow hues, affording a very beautiful variety. When the purple and white are about equal in proportion it is called a brecciato, on account of the deep red (pavonazzo) exhibited in some varieties, the name pavonazzetto has been given to it, the termination being a diminutive. The most valuable specimens exhibit a lively crimson.

The Emperor Hadrian had a special liking for Synnadic marble, and employed it for the decoration of his tomb, now known as the Castle of St. Angelo, while the Temples of Jupiter and Juno were embellished by one hundred and twenty columns of this beautiful species. It always commanded a great price, and ancient writers were accustomed to compare anything valuable to Phrygian marble. From the large quantities found in the ruins, it must have been very generally used by the ancient Romans, and it seems to be a great favorite with their successors, as it has been so generally appropriated for the decoration of modern edifices. A few of the many buildings where this elegant marble is seen are the churches of S. Maria in Ara Cœli, S. Maria Maggiore, St. John Lateran, and S. Clemente. The High Altar of S. Prassede is made of the Pavonazzetto breccia, and a large vase is found in the Vatican Museum.

Marmor Chium: Marmo Africano. — One of the largest and most celebrated of the Ægean islands is Chios, a competitor for the fame of having given birth to Homer, and, like most islands of the Grecian Archipelago, it is traversed by a chain of rocky mountains, whose highest peak is Mount Pelinæus, now Elias; Chios, the chief city, stood at the foot of this mountain, while a Temple of Jupiter crowned its summit. Pliny informs us that variegated marbles were first discovered in Chios, and employed by the natives for the walls of the town, of which they boasted as being very magnificent. This vaunt led Cicero to reply that they would have been equally valuable had they been made of travertine, since in his day it was customary to paint common stones for walls of buildings.

If the blocks of Chium marble used in their walls were polished the inhabitants could make good their pretensions, as the Africano is one of the most showy of the antique marbles, and whether the walls around the city or the walls of the buildings were intended the effect must have been striking. The Italian name Africano is misleading; Africa not being the place from which it was obtained.

The colors, though very positive, are greatly diversified. The white is clear and the black very deep; the different shades of greens are lively, while the reds vary from a delicate rose to a vivid purple, often assuming the tints of the coral and sometimes the brightness of flowers; the varieties containing green, crimson, and yellow are rare. It is a shell marble, though the fossils are not always recognized, and is

Plate XXI.

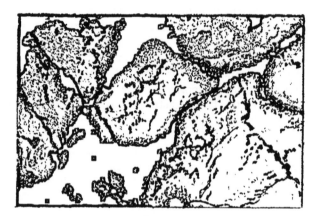

AFRICANO

CIPOLLINO

sometimes veined and sometimes brecciated. The Africano is very abundant, being found in most of the churches and other public buildings, where it is used with good effect in covering large spaces. The columns of the central door of St. Peter's afford one of the numerous examples of the use made of it.

Rosso Antico: Ancient Red. — This marble, though frequently seen in Italy, has not authentically been traced to its source, nor has the name by which it was known to the ancients been transmitted to us, says Corsi. Some writers have endeavored to identify it with Giallo antico, but the absurdity of the attempt is evident when the two species are compared. Others have seen in the Rosso antico the Alabandic stone of Pliny, which he says was obtained from a mine near Alabanda, in Asia Minor Perhaps there is no antique marble which has caused so much ambiguity among writers as this. The Red porphyry of Egypt has unfortunately been called Rosso antico, a fact that has led some persons astray in regard to the marble called by that name, making the two species of stones identical; but there ought to be no confusion, since their chemical constituents, texture, and color are different. It is possible that Rosso antico was found in Africa, but it is more likely that Greece was its native place, since it is claimed that the quarries have been rediscovered in the latter country A block of red marble, exhibited at the Universal Exposition, was claimed to be the genuine Rosso antico, taken from an old Greek quarry recently brought to light. There are modern red marbles in France and some other countries, which bear a striking resemblance to the antique.

The grain of the Rosso antico is very fine, the color red, from deep blood to rose, sometimes passing to a purple, and not unfrequently different shades of red are found in the same specimen When clouded at all, it is usually with white, either in veins or brecciated form, and occasionally with small black or purple lines, which give it depth and richness of color. The ancients imitated this marble in terra-cotta so well that it was difficult to distinguish between the true and the false.

The Faun of the Capitol, the steps of the High Altar of the Church of St. Prassede, and the two Columns in the Casino of the Rospigliosi Palace, containing Guido's Aurora, are specimens of this species.

Marmor Tænarium: Nero Antico —Laconia, in the Peloponnesus, whose capital was Sparta, is crossed from north to south by the Taÿgetus, a wild and lofty range of mountains, ending in the promontory of Tænarium, the most southern point of Greece. It was from this projection that the Nero antico, highly prized for its lustre, was quarried.

The grain is fine, the texture compact, and the color deep black, sometimes with fine, short, broken lines of white. Examples of this marble may be seen in the Museum of the Capitol and other places. Some of the modern black marbles surpass the antiques in beauty; notably the Belgian Black, whose color and lustre are unrivalled.

Marmor Molossium: Fior di Persico. —The ancient tribe of the Molossi inhabited the region of Epirus, now Albania, on the eastern coast of the Ægean, the country of Pyrrhus, whose history was one of the most romantic and eventful of former times.

Near the source of the river Acheron, which communicated with the "lower regions," was quarried a beautiful marble named by the Romans Molossium, for the tribe originally occupying the country Modern stone-workers call it Fior di Persico, from the resemblance of its color to the peach-blossom.

The base is white, always more or less covered with veins and clouds of a beautiful purple, passing frequently into red and crimson; the shading sometimes occurring in parallel lines and sometimes reticulated A fine display of this marble is seen in the magnificent Corsini Chapel, in the Church of St John Lateran; it is also used in the Casino of the Rospigliosi Palace, and in many churches.

Marmor Phengite: Bianco e Giallo. — Pliny says that the Phengite was found in Cappadocia, a mountainous country of Asia Minor, celebrated in early times for its horses. It was probably a volcanic region, as Strabo writes that in some parts flames issued from the ground, and that the hidden pits of fire became dangerous to the incautious traveller and to cattle Its mineral productions were considerable, including gypsum, a red earth called Sinopic, an article of traffic; building-stone; a white stone resembling ivory in color, found in small pieces; and a transparent stone for windows, yielding large masses and forming an article of export. It is possible that the "transparent stone," giving a broad significance to the word transparent, may have been the Phengite—"bright stone"— of Pliny, similar to some of the calcareous alabasters, as the Tabreez marble, used for windows.

The ancient Phengite received so high a polish, says the chronicler Suetonius, that it reflected images like a mirror, and was employed by the Emperor Domitian, whose cruelties had rendered him suspicious, for lining a portico in which he was accustomed to walk, that he might see the images of any secret foe reflected by the polished surface. According to one interpretation of Pliny, the walls of Nero's Golden Palace were covered with Phengite, while another represents him as saying that Nero built the Temple of Fortune, enclosed in this palace, of Phengite, which, from its brilliancy, partially lighted the interior. Corsi identifies the Phengite with the Bianco e Giallo—white and yellow—and says it is very rare. It has only two colors, white ground and yellow veins, is opaque and of unequal fracture. Its opacity does not correspond to the "transparent stone," but would render it suitable for reflecting images

Marmor Corinthium: Giallo Tigrato. — "Tigrato" is a misnomer; the spots on the marble resemble those of the leopard, and not the stripes of the tiger: it should have been called Leopardo

Corinth, one of the most famous cities of ancient Greece,

was built on the side of the Acrocorinthus, a mountain rising
one thousand nine hundred feet above the plain, on the Isthmus of Corinth   It was near this city, and probably from this
mountain, that the rare and beautiful Corinthium or Giallo
tigrato was quarried   At the time Corinth was captured by
the Roman Consul Mummius, B. C. 145, it contained a large
number of the most beautiful works of art found in Greece,
which were either destroyed or carried off to Rome ; and it is
probable that then, or subsequently, this Corinthian marble
found its way thither.   The ground is tawny yellow, with
orbicular pieces of deeper yellow, resembling the spots of the
leopard ; it takes a fine polish, and is admirably adapted for
the sculpture of that animal.   Examples of the Giallo tigrato are
found in the Vaticum Museum, in the Church of S. Andrea
della Valle, and in the tomb of Cardinal Toledo, in the Church
of S. Maria Maggiore.

Marmor Batthium: Bigio Antico.   Ancient Gray — Corsi
says it is not known where this marble was quarried ; the
name possibly may ·have been derived from the Battiadæ, a
succession of kings of Cyrene, in the northern part of Africa.
The first king of the line emigrated from Greece B C. 631,
and founded Cyrene, which became a flourishing city.   Its
ruins are extensive, comprising a great variety of works of
Greek art, and an examination of these remains might throw
some light upon the subject.

The Bigio antico is gray, as the name implies, with spots,
waves, and bands of commingled black and white.   When the
spots are all black or all white it receives the name of Bigio
brecciato ; when it contains fossil shells, it is Bigio luma-
chellato ; when the veins are bluish-white, it is called Bigio
venato, as in the large Lion in the Gallery of Animals.   The
massive columns near the door of the Church of Santa Croce,
in Gerusalemme, were cut from this marble.

Marmor Proconnesium: Bianco e Nero. — There are four
species of antique black and white marbles, obtained from
different countries, bearing the name of Bianco e Nero, found

in the ruins of ancient buildings. One of these localities is an island in the Sea of Marmora, so called from the marble it yields, and known to the ancients as Proconnesus — Fawn Island. It is mentioned by Strabo that large quantities of excellent white marble were found in this island, and that the most beautiful works in the cities of that region, particularly Cyzacus, a Greek town celebrated for its magnificent buildings, were made of it. The black and white marble of Proconnesus, sometimes called Marmor Cyzicum, was used in the decoration of the palace, and, probably, the tomb of Mausolus at Halicarnassus.

The Bianco e Nero antico, found in Italy, and identified by Corsi with the Proconnesium, contains fossil shells, often distinctly visible. There are four columns of this marble in the High Altar of the Church of S. Cecilia in Trastevere, Rome.

Marmor Celticum: Bianco e Nero di Francia. — As the name indicates, this species of marble was obtained from France, whence the Romans brought many ornamental stones The black ground is interspersed with small reticulated veins and spots of a milky white; the colors have less vigor and lustre than the Proconnesium.

Marmo Bianco e Nero d'Egitto. — This marble is known only by its modern name of White and Black of Egypt, but it is supposed to belong to that country, or some adjacent region, from the fact that many of the sculptured Egyptian idols and animals in the Museum of the Capitol were cut in this antique stone; the white shells, retaining their natural form, constitute the small spots exhibited in a very black cement, and, like all the other black and white marbles, it receives a beautiful polish.

Marmo Bianco e Nero Tigrato. — The name of this marble gives no clue to the place where it was quarried, nor the title by which it was called in ancient times, but as it has been found among the ruins it is considered antique The name Tigrato is due to the form and arrangement of the spots;

marble-workers call it Granito tenero, soft granite; the colors tend to reddish and greenish tints. It may be seen in the Villa Borghese as blocks for columns.

Occhio di Pernice: Eye of the Partridge. — This species, though found in excavations of buried structures, has not preserved its ancient name or the place of its native mines. The ground color is generally a tawny or yellowish-brown, with spots inclining to amaranth, sometimes without regularity, and at others, arranged in circles bearing some resemblance to the eye of a partridge. One variety has a base of deep peach-blossom, with light-gray spots sprinkled with red, and another displays white parallel lines. The High Altar of the Church of San Lorenzo in Lucina displays this marble to advantage.

The Occhio di Pernice (Œil de Perdrix), or white garnet, from Vesuvius, the Leucite of Dana, is a volcanic substance, entirely different from the antique marble of this name.

Marmor Rhodium: Giallo e Nero. — The island of Rhodes, on the coast of Asia Minor, admired for its beauty, fertility, and agreeable climate, was the native place of this marble. The city of Rhodes, celebrated for its magnificent buildings and numerous statues, became the seat of different schools of Greek art and oratory. In the harbor was placed the famous Statue of the Sun, called the Colossus of Rhodes, sculptured by Chares, which, in its brief existence of a little more than half a century, acquired the reputation of being one of the Wonders of the World. Pliny says that there were one hundred and five other colossal statues in the city; he also mentions a black marble called Rhodium, with gold-colored veins, which corresponds to the Giallo e Nero It has a compact texture and exceedingly brilliant lustre, and though rare, may be seen in the mask of the monument of Paul III. in St. Peter's.

Marmo di Cotanello — This stone is both ancient and modern, and is now obtained from Cotanello, north of Rome. It was used by the old Romans, as is known by its presence in the ruins, specimens having been found in the villa of Lucullus, near the ancient city of Torracino. It is employed in the churches of modern Rome, and one of the most conspicuous examples of this use is the immense columns in St. Peter's of the Vatican. The marble displays several colors, red, purple, gray, and yellow, none of them very vivid; sometimes it presents the appearance of a large breccia.

III. *Lumachellas: Shell marbles.* — Many of the most beautiful marbles, both ancient and modern, belong to this class, but only two species of antiques have preserved their earlier names. The first of these is the

Marmor Megarense: Lumachella Bianca Antica. — Megaris, whose chief city was Megara, constituted a territory of ancient Greece, on a strip of land between the Corinthian and Saronic Gulfs. The marble called Megarense was quarried near the city, and undoubtedly was used in the construction of the public buildings, of which there were many. The black and white ground, delicately shaded, is studded with extremely small shells. Cicero is said to allude to statues of this marble, but there is no mention made of any work of art that has been preserved sculptured in Megarense, and it is very rarely found in the ruins.

Marmor Schistos: Broccatello Antico. — The antique name Schistos, "split stone," was given to this marble on account of its laminated structure. Ajasson thinks the Schistos of Pliny was the mineral called limonite, a hydrous oxide, bearing no resemblance in composition to marble. Its modern name, Brocatello, from broccato, brocade, a fabric woven with gold, is in allusion to its prevailing color. This rich marble was and still is quarried near Tortosa, Catalonia, in the northern part of Spain. The ancient Romans used it in great abundance, judging from the quantities found in the excavations, and it is employed in the modern buildings of Italy, as may be seen in the decorations of the Vatican Museum and other places.

The Brocatello is composed of fragments of shells of different shades of lively yellow, embedded in a calcareous cement, passing from light yellow to violet or crimson. When the colors are all yellows the marble is called Orientale, a name of no significance, as it did not come from the east; when mixed with violet it is named Broccatello di Spagna. The characteristic fossil is said to be the Anomia, a Mollusk found in the Cretaceous and Tertiary periods

Lumachella d'Egitto. — This marble is found in ruins in the form of paving-stones, but the place where it was quarried is not known; a very large mass was discovered in a vineyard near Testaccio. There is no reason for calling it Egyptian, since there is no proof that it was brought from Egypt. The ground is white with embedded oyster-shells of blue-gray or black, the shells varying in size but always uniform in color. Two rare varieties are sometimes found, one with yellow base, and the other with coral red. The crown of the bust of the Gordian Juno, in the Capitol Museum, is considered to be sculptured in this species.

Lumachella d'Astracane — The original place of the Astracane is not well established, though the name suggests Astracan, celebrated in the romances of the middle ages, a Russian territory, with its capital of the same name, on the Volga, near the Caspian. Ancient authors make no mention of this place, though Albania, a country south of it, came under Roman jurisdiction. Some writers have supposed that this marble came from the region of the Ganges, but that does not explain the origin of the name. Corsi does not pretend to have any knowledge on the subject other than that it was found in the ruins of Rome. He probably had not seen Pinkerton on Rocks, who says the name Astracan is a mistake; it should be Costrican, the name of mountains in Syria from which the marble was obtained. He mentions a variety of a deep brown color, with shells of gold or orange-yellow of a circular form. Pinkerton's Costrican marble may be identical with the Astracan, though there is room for doubt.

The two principal varieties have been classed by marble-cutters as masculine and feminine; the latter of a light-yellow, the former deep-yellow, tending to green and sometimes with red spots. Examples of this marble are seen in the balustrades around the High Altar of the Church of S. Andrea della Valle and the two columns in the garden of the Corsini Palace. A very rare and beautiful variety is of a flesh-color.

Astracane Dorato. — This marble has been claimed as a variety of the former, but Corsi thinks they have nothing in common, and form separate species The characteristic fossils are the Ostrea and the Turbo, the latter producing very beautiful effects; the rarest and most valued varieties have crimson or purple ground with gold shadings. A fine instance is seen in the Church of S. Maria della Scala, in Trastevere, forming the steps of the third altar on the left; and another in the Fountain of Borghese.

Lumachellone Antico. — A paving-stone found in the excavations, a kind of Lumachella, which, from the large size of the pieces, is called Lumachellone. The bluish-gray cement contains small shells resembling Ionic volutes; probably they are Ammonites.

The Lumachella Nera has a deep-black ground with very small fragments of the Anomia and the Tellina, and is found in the Church of S Augustino, last altar on the right; and in the presbytery of S. Maria in Via Lata.

Lumachella Rossa. — It is said that among the paving-stones of Rome there was found a small block of lumachella differing from all others, presenting a deep-red base, covered with small, white circles, arranged in regular order, which may have been Encrinites. The graceful form of the fossils and the harmony of the colors render this species one of the most beautiful of shell marbles.

Lumachella Rosea is the name of a species with rose-colored ground, and small, whitish shells, similar in form to melon-seeds. It is rare, only two examples being mentioned, one in the large columns on the ground floor of the Sciarra Palace, Rome, and the other in the Oxford Collection made by Corsi.

There are several other species of antique shell marbles with modern names to designate the color: Lumachella bigia, with ash-colored ground and white shells resembling the Anomia, a rare variety; Lumachella gialla, pale-yellow, often with crimson spots, found only in the fragment of a column; Lumachella pavonazza, composed of Encrinites, Belemnites, and Sea-stars, of white or rose color, in a violet cement, forming a very beautiful marble but exceedingly rare. Another species of lumachella, yielding more specimens, is the Occhio di Pavone.

The fossil Anomia is characteristic of this marble, and presents a circular form in whatever way it is cut. This uniformity has given rise to the name Peacock's Eye, with additional epithets to designate the prevailing color; as, rosso, when this ground is deep-red with white shells, a rare and beautiful variety; bianco, when the cement is grayish-white; nero, black ground and white fossils, a rare variety; roseo, rose-colored shells in white cement; pavonazzo, purple ground with obscure white fossils. The most highly-valued variety is seen in two large columns in the Vatican Library.

Under the title Stellaria are classed those fossiliferous marbles presenting the appearance of stars arranged about a centre; the ground is generally whitish, and the stars ivory-white, passing to brighter yellow; sometimes the base is red and the fossils grayish-white.

Shell marbles were valued less in ancient than in modern times, and this may be the reason why their antique names, if they had any, and a knowledge of the places from which they were obtained, have not been communicated to us by ancient writers. The fact that they are generally found only in fragments is evidence that they were not extensively employed by the Romans.

IV. *Breccie Antiche: Antique Breccias.* — Breccias, as is well known, are formed of broken fragments of rocks, sometimes entirely of marble, sometimes of other stones, and frequently of several species combined, held together by a cementing substance, usually carbonate of lime. These conglomerates, when admitting of a polish, often form very beautiful ornamental stones. They differ from the clouded and veined marbles, not only in the manner of their formation, but in the disposition of the colored portions, being without regular order, and the size of the spots varying from very small fragments to very large.

They were known to the ancients under the name of the marble of Scyros, one of the Sporades, celebrated in the mythical ages of Greece, and for its quarries of variegated marble; they were also called the marble of Hierapolis, the name of a city in Phrygia and of another in Syria. Strabo relates that the public and private buildings of Rome are ornamented with beautiful and variegated stones from Chios and Aleppo, so that columns and tablets are formed of different marbles united in one and the same marble; this description answers to the character of breccias. The specific names of antique breccias, known to the Romans, are lost, but the substance, being less perishable, has been preserved in the ruins of their buildings.

Marmor Lydium: Rosso Brecciato. — This is the only species of breccia, according to the Roman archæologist so often quoted, to which its corresponding Latin name can be assigned with any certainty. Lydia, a province of Asia Minor, was the seat of several eminent ancient cities, — Philadelphia, Ephesus, Smyrna, Sardis, and Thyatira, all more or less renowned for their public buildings and works of art; but all have perished except Smyrna. Mount Tmolus, near which Sardis was built, extends under the sea to the Island of Chios, from which the marble called Chium or Africano was obtained; and it is probable the range yielded breccias.

The Lydium is composed of white fragments of different

sizes, cemented by a lively red paste, forming a species of which there are but few specimens.

Breccia di Aleppo. — This is the modern name of a stone which has caused considerable doubt among antiquaries as to its native place.   Some have referred it to Aleppo, in Syria, a very ancient city, if, as is supposed, it is the same as the Hebah mentioned in the book of Judges, and the Helbon of Ezekiel ; but it is said there is not satisfactory proof that the breccia was obtained from Syria, though perhaps it is as likely to have been found there as anywhere else, as breccias are very abundant in that country.

Another place claiming to be the original source of the Breccia di Aleppo, is Aix in France ; this is on the authority of Brongniart, who says that the Brêche d'Aleppe did not come from Syria, and should be called Brêche d'Alert, from the place whence it was found.   As there is so much uncer-'tainty about its origin a change of name seems unadvisable.

It is composed of gray, red, brown, and black fragments, commingled with a predominance of yellow.   In the Gallery of the Candelabri there is a small column of this rare and beautiful species of marble.

Breccia Dorata. — The name "golden" was given to this variety on account of the clear yellow, passing from orange to oil tints, which characterizes the marble.   The cement is purple, of variable shades, sometimes passing to flesh-color, but considerably marked by small yellow fragments ; in a rare variety these pieces are encircled by fine, red lines, or are dotted with purple.   This breccia is highly prized for its exceeding beauty, but it is seldom seen in any collection.

Other yellow breccias, differing in some respects from the Dorata, are found in two columns of an atlar, in the Church of S. Maria della Vittoria ; and it is said a very rare specimen is preserved in the Villa Godoy or the Palace Mattei

Breccia Corallina. — The Corallina receives its name from the color of its cement, which is frequently of a coral red, sometimes vivid, but often pale, when it is less beautiful and less valued; the fragments are a clear, obscure, or yellowish-white, varying in size from very small to very large   It is quite abundant, though it is not known where it was quarried. Fine examples are seen in the four columns of the portico in the Casino of the Rospigliosi Palace and in the Church of S. Prisca

An extremely rare breccia of flesh-tinted ground and rose-red fragments, called Breccia Color di Rosa, has been found in the ruins, but only in very small pieces

Breccia Gialla e Nera. — Black and gray fragments in a cement of brilliant yellow resembling gold, sometimes passing to light-green, with spots distinct or reticulated, constitutes this beautiful marble, which may be studied in two columns of a chapel in the Church of S. Andrea della Valle, and in the Basin for Holy Water in the Church of S Carlo à Catinari

Breccia della Villa Adriana — The Emperor Hadrian distinguished his reign by the erection of magnificent public works in the cities of his extensive empire, and splendid structures for his private use; of the latter were his mausoleum (the Castle of St. Angelo), and his celebrated villa at Tibur, now Tivoli   In the grounds of this villa, embracing many square miles, various buildings were constructed, meeting the wants of a large town, including palaces, academies, and theatres; while to diversify the scenery there were representations of the Elysium, Tartarus, Alpheus, Vale of Tempe, and other places of Greek celebrity.   Innumerable works of art adorned the buildings and grounds, many of which are seen in the churches and museums of modern times   In this valuable treasury of antiques was found the beautiful breccia called by the name of this famous villa   It is also known as Breccia Quintilina, from the Villa Quintilius Varus, near Hadrian's, and it has been inappropriately called English breccia.

· Many of the fragments of this marble are of the color of burnt coffee, while others are of a lively red, yellow, green,

purple, and sometimes white and black, the whole producing
an agreeable harmony. Examples of this stone, which exists
only in small pieces, are seen in the Churches of S. Andrea
della Valle, S.S. Domenico e Sisto, and S. Pudenziana.

Breccia Traccagnina. — A small column in the room of the
Dying Gaul, in the Museum of the Capitol, was cut from a
marble bearing this fantastic name. It was so called from its
fancied resemblance to the mask of an actor, and for the
same reason it has also been styled Arlechina, "harlequin."
The breccias known by these names enclose fragments of
different and opposite colors, though each variety is characterized by some prevailing tint, for which it receives a distinctive
title, as nera, when black predominates; persichina, when
the pieces are yellowish-gray; and cenerine, when they are
ash-color. A brick-red, enclosing red, gray, and black pieces,
constitutes a rare variety, but the most valued has white, red,
and bluish fragments in a gold-yellow cement.

Breccia Pavonazza. — Purple is the prevailing tint of the
paste, though it admits of many shades, while the fragments
vary in color, and sometimes the entire mass is of different
shades of purple.

An urn in a chapel of S Antonio dé Portuguese is cut in
a variety displaying white clouds on a purple ground Sometimes this breccia is distinguished for red and gray, or yellow
and green fragments, while not unfrequently the same marble
unites all these hues, but for harmony and delicacy of coloring
a clear purple with red and white surpasses all others Two
columns in the Church of S. Maria in Via afford specimens of
this variously colored breccia

Breccia a Seme Santo. — This whimsical name, "sacred
seeds," has been given to a peculiar variety of breccia, from an
imaginary likeness it bears to a kind of confectionery of different colors, resembling seeds, and used to disguise medicine
for children. The ground is dark-purple, chocolate, or yellowish, scattered over with small white, yellow, or gray fragments,
looking somewhat like the seeds of plants. It is thought the

quarries were in Egypt, from the fact that an Egyptian idol, found in the Vatican, was sculptured in this marble.

Breccia Bianca e Nera. — This stone is not identical with the White and Black marble previously described, but forms a species by itself. The white fragments in a black or gray-ish brown paste assume regular figures, constituting a rare variety

A beautiful marble of a clear red cement enclosing the Ostrea, with fragments of delicate red, green, gray, and gold-color, of an elliptical form, constitutes what is called Breccia rossa

Breccia di Sette Basi. — Accepting the opinion of Corsi, this marble was found in the ruins of the Villa of Septimius Bassus, near Roma Vecchia, on the Via Appia, and the term Sette Basi is a corruption of the old Roman name.

There were several persons known by the patronymic Bas-sus, one of whom was destroyed with his villa by an eruption of Vesuvius, and could not have been the one intended. There are extensive ruins at Roma Vecchia, said to be those of the Villa of the Quintilii, near the town of Sette Bassi. However the marble received its name, the probability is quite strong that it was obtained from this region.

The principal colors are deep-red, yellow, and purple, well covered by oblong fragments, which, from their arrangement, give the breccia a peculiar character The pieces are yellowish or opal white, and sometimes other colors, like Seme Santo; the most beautiful variety displays red spots inclining to rose. When the colors are intermingled, it is called fiarita, "flowered;" when circular, mendolata, "almond" Near Mount Testaccio, an artificial mound within the walls of Rome, composed of rubbish, great quantities of this breccia have been found, and named Semesantone di Testaccio, or a large kind of Seme Santo. A good specimen is seen in the Room of the Dying Gaul, Capitol Museum. Breccia verde, or green breccias, are very rare, unless the African green marble and the Verde antique are classed with them.

Eight columns in the Church of S Maria in Ara Cœli, Rome, are made of Broccatellone, a kind of large brocatello, with delicate purple ground and canary-yellow fragments.

Breccia Verde d'Egitto. — Among the ancient conglomerates was the highly-prized Egyptian stone quarried in Upper Egypt, called "universal breccia" on account of the great number of species of rocks it encloses. The ground color is nearly always green, while the fragments of porphyry, granite, basalt, and quartz, of medium size, are of different colors, including shades of green, passing to yellowish or reddish tints. Specimens of this remarkable breccia are seen in the Palace of the Conservatori, at the Capitol; in an elegant vase with a band of white quartz, in the Vatican Museum, and in the Villa Albani.

The antique breccias bearing modern names were all known, it is presumed, to the ancient Romans, and employed in their buildings, since they have been found in the excavations, but their Latin names and native quarries have not yet been discovered.

Marmor Lunense: Bardiglio. — Strabo says that the Lunense marbles used by the Romans included white statuary and other varieties, marked with blue tending to clear gray, not green, as it is rendered by some translators. The Bardiglio is compact, fine-grained, of pure flesh-white or gray, covered with veins, spots, or clouds of very deep purple tending to black Specimens of the antique are numerous in mediæval buildings, while the modern, which is identical, may be seen in any of the establishments of foreign marble importers.

Marmor Argillosus: Pisana. — Tradition assigns to Pisa a very great antiquity, accounting it as founded by Greeks from Pisa in Elis, the companions of Nestor, on their return from the Trojan war. After it was incorporated with the Roman Empire it was embellished with triumphal arches, theatres, and temples, but few vestiges of its ancient glory remain, and it is better known for its marble quarries.

Plate XXII.

Fior di Persico

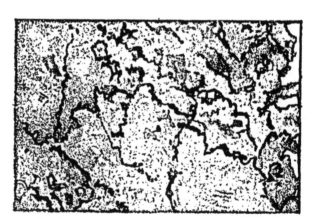

Porta Santa.

The modern argillaceous marble of Pisa, called Lithomarge, is supposed to be identical with the antique. Though soft and easily cut, it is very compact and takes a fine polish. The small fissures, filled with a ferruginous substance, often assume fantastic· forms representing various objects; when trees, plants, or vegetable masses are simulated it is called Dendrite, if rocks, walls, and ruined castles are imitated, it becomes Ruin-marble, when the lines represent doubtful forms, it is said to be Varioform , and when unicolored, or simply veined, it is merely Lithomarge. The latter variety, used by the ancients and still found in the quarries of Tuscany, yields a marble of different shades of vivacious green; the dendritic displays nearly always a yellow ground with black herbage, and is thought to be the same as the Ciottoli d' Arno, "pebbles of the Arno," so much used in Florentine mosaics.

Dendrite, being found only in small masses, was not much used by the ancients, though specimens have been discovered in the Villa of Hadrian, but Ruin-marble, existing in larger pieces, was in great demand for the pavements of buildings. A variety with red ground and bluish-gray veins was employed by the Romans in the Baths of Titus, cut in the form of rhomboids, and used with Palombino marble, producing a fine effect.

The poet Statius is said to be the only classical writer who mentions the marbles of Liguria or Genoa. This region abounds in green stones, called serpentines, and it is thought one species of green and white serpentine, styled granite, from Liguria, was included among the antiques, as the term marble was formerly, and is at the present time, frequently applied to all stones capable of a polish and used for architectural decoration.

Lapis Ligusticus: Granito di Genova. — This stone is known by so many different names that it is in danger of losing its identity entirely, Verde Serpentino, Granito di Genova, Serpentino di Genova, Verde Plasmatico Granito, Polcevera or Polsevera Green, have all been assigned to the Lapis Ligusticus.

It is composed of deep-green serpentine, white feldspar, and chatoyant diallage, approaching the color of brass, and on account of its hardness has been called by artisans granite. Vases of this stone, which has been pronounced identical with the modern serpentines of Liguria, are seen in the Gallery of the Candelabri, in the Vatican.

Marmor Tauromenium: Diaspro Tenero di Sicilia, "Soft Sicilian Jasper." — The city of Taormina, ancient Tauromenium, in Sicily, was named for Mount Taurus, on which it was built about four centuries before the Christian era. It was celebrated for its splendid theatre, cut out of the natural rock, and said to be capable of holding from thirty thousand to forty thousand spectators.

Sicily has yielded, both in ancient and modern times, an abundance of colored stones for architecture, but the best known is the Taormina marble, or Sicilian jasper, found near the city from which it received its name. The form and color of the bands found in this marble resemble those of jasper, which is abundant in the island, and for this reason it is called Sicilian or soft jasper. It is fine, compact, and easy to cut, and is distinguished from all other veined marbles by the variety of the clouding and the want of harmony in the colors. A green band is often next to a yellow, and both crossed by red veins; other extravagances occur which render it a showy, but not a pleasing ornamental stone; the veins are not well disposed and the colors are deficient in vivacity.

This marble was very generally used in mediæval architecture, and is seen also in many of the churches of a later period. It is not clear that the ancient Romans employed this variety, though it is evident that they used the siliceous jaspers, and perhaps the Sicilian marble, with purple ground and grayish, triangular figures, seen in S. Dionigi and other churches.

CHAPTER XXI.

ANTIQUE ALABASTERS, SERPENTINES, BASALTS, GRANITES, AND PORPHYRIES.

I. *Alabasters.* — Among the decorative stones of antiquity remarkable for beauty and elegance, vivacity of color, variety and precision of spots, translucency and brilliancy of lustre, oriental alabasters are entitled to a pre-eminent rank. The ancient Romans regarded them worthy to be used for the statues of gods and emperors.

Calcareous alabasters, those formed of carbonate of lime, having the same constituents as marble, are very properly classed with them, though they differ from them in some respects.

The antique, oriental alabasters of Asia and Africa are more beautiful and varied than those of Europe, consequently they were more sought after for art purposes   They are mentioned by the earliest writers, showing that their value as a decorative stone was understood by the most ancient nations. The onyx mentioned in Genesis ii : 12 has been considered by some Biblical scholars to mean alabaster ; and the old classic writers use the word onyx when speaking of alabaster, and say it was found in Egypt, Arabia, Syria, and other places   Near the city of Thebes, in Egypt, according to Pliny, there was a castle called Alabaster in the neighborhood of the quarries, from which the onyx first took the name alabaster.

A savant, M Jomard, who accompanied the French expeition into Egypt, relates the following: The ruins of the

313

city of Alabaster are still seen near Gebel Khaly, upon the road to the Monastery of S. Antonio, in the desert between the Nile and the Red Sea, near quarries of marble called alabaster. So large a number of carts were used to transport the stone that one of the cities near the desert was named A'rabah, meaning cart. Upon the road leading to A'rabah are scattered many fragments of alabaster and other precious marbles of different colors. This was probably the "Marble Country," Blad Recam of modern Egypt.

The Arabian and the Egyptian alabasters were used in the manufacture of vases for holding unguents, balsams, and other articles of perfumery, because this stone was thought to possess peculiar qualities for keeping these substances incorrupt. From the constant practice of using alabaster for this purpose, by a figure of rhetoric, the name of the material of which it was made was applied to the vessel; hence the expression "an alabaster," or "an onyx," used by ancient writers, meant an alabaster vase of balsam or some other precious substance. Horace speaks of an alabaster of nard, another writer of an alabaster of unguents, or alabaster unguents, and in designating different kinds of vases, one is styled an alabaster, and sometimes the name was applied to vases made of other materials. Upon the head of our Saviour was poured an alabaster box of precious balm of spikenard.

This beautiful stone, at first used only for vases, was subsequently used for other articles, and for columns. Assuming that the ancients were correct in using onyx and alabaster as interchangeable terms, when speaking of this marble, we find an early recognition of its value in the enumeration made of the costly materials collected by King David for the building of the Temple at Jerusalem. In 1 Chronicles xxix: 2, we read of onyx stones, glistering stones, and of divers colors, and all manner of precious stones and marbles in abundance.

At first alabaster was very rare in ancient Rome, but as wealth, and consequently the desire for luxuries increased, the Romans sought the most beautiful and costly alabasters to ornament their public and private buildings. Cornelius Balbus, a contemporary with Julius Cæsar, placed in his theatre, as something remarkable, four small columns·of alabaster; but in Pliny's time, the first century of the Christian era, there were thirty large columns of alabaster in the hall built by Callistus, in the reign of Claudius. That there must have been large quantities of this stone introduced into Rome during the Empire, seems certain from its frequent use in mediæval architecture. The largest, most rare, and most beautiful mass of alabaster seen in this city, says Corsi, is a fluted column, twenty-seven palms in height, in the Villa Albani.

The varieties of alabaster are very numerous, and their names are due to some peculiarity of formation, veins, or color, often fanciful, sometimes striking; as in allusion to color, Cotognino, Sardonico; to the arrangements of clouds, Fortezzino, Tartaruga, Pecorella; to the formation, Giaccone, Pomato.

The colors are greatly diversified, passing from a clear white to a deep black, and, though rarely, these extremes are sometimes united in the same variety, an example of which occurs in the pavement of a chapel in S Andrea della Valle. Yellow, purple, green, red, blue, in all their gradations, are found in alabasters A particular description is given of the more important species.

Alabastro Bianco. — This variety surpasses in whiteness all other stones, even statuary marble Pliny says it was quarried near Damascus, and that the most valuable came from Carmania, the next in quality from India, while the least valued was from Cappadocia, Asia Minor. It is stated that the white alabaster was also obtained from Thebes, in Egypt, while another species, known to the ancients, and used for windows, was found in Arabia and in the.Taurus Mountains, which may have been the same as the Tabreez marble now obtained from Persia. The white opaque and the diophanous varieties are sometimes found in the same marble, and one or the other is banded. The finest example of white alabaster is seen in a column in the Vatican Library.

The alabaster stone was found near Damascus, mentioned in the history of Abraham, and near Thebes, called No in the Scriptures, and considered one of the oldest cities in the world, having reached the height of its splendor sixteen centuries before the Christian era; it is possible, therefore, that those extremely ancient cities may have been embellished by the same kind of stones seen to-day in the buildings of Rome and other Italian towns.

Alabastro Cotognino.—A semi-transparent alabaster of white inclining to yellow is called Cotognino from its resemblance to the color of the quince. When the color and texture is uniform it is called schietto, "pure," and venato when it has opaque bands. All alabasters not of a clear white, but inclining to gray or green, are sometimes called Cotognino. An example of this kind is seen in the six columns of the Basilica of St. Paul.

A variety of Cotognino, formed of small, round particles resembling ice, of a honey-yellow, is called Pomato, a corruption, it is said, of pomellato, which may signify dappled, like an apple; it forms a very beautiful stone, and resembles the alabaster called Sardonyx.

Alabastro a Giaccione.—This variety was formed by the aggregation of conical or triangular crystals united by adhesion among themselves, from which it receives the name Giaccione, from giaccio, ice. The colors are generally grayish-white, honey-yellow, deep red, or violet, sometimes similar to quartz amethyst, but it is not easily cut, as the crystals often separate under the chisel. There is a cup of this species in the Museum of the Vatican.

Alabastro a Onice: Onyx.—Although the term onyx was formerly used to designate all calcareous alabasters, it is specifically applied to a kind with white, gray, yellowish, or reddish bands, either curved or straight, occasionally square or triangular.

Alabastro a Nuvole: Clouded. — In the Confessio of St. Peter's, of the Vatican, are four columns of this variety. The ground is one color, passing to red, yellow, or peach-blossom, covered with round spots of a different color, white or gray, and sometimes blended.

Alabastro a Occhi — This species receives its name from the circular or elliptical spots, thought to resemble eyes, arranged upon a base of one color, generally yellow, though sometimes gray. The spots are white or gray, disposed without regularity; and not unfrequently the entire surface is crossed by bands of the same color.

Alabastro a Tartaruga. — In the Capitoline Museum there is a bust of Julius Cæsar sculptured in this species of alabaster, but it has never been found in the excavations, except in small pieces. The colors are of different shades of yellow and very deep red, passing to nearly black, mingled without order, representing no particular figure, but having one color or the other quite prominent. From its resemblance to the shell of a tortoise it is called Tartaruga.

The *Alabastro Sadonico* is not inappropriately compared to the oriental sardonyx, since the color and form of the bands in these two stones, unlike in composition, are very similar. The alabaster has a saccharoidal structure, with the ground of one color and bands of another. A vase in the Vatican Museum and a bust of Faustina in the Museum of the Capitol, are said to be cut in this variety.

Alabastro a Pecorella. — This peculiar name, "flock of sheep," was given to a species of alabaster of a deep-red, with thick masses of white of nearly the same size, regularly disposed, which a lively fancy might compare to sheep; each spot representing one of these animals is enclosed by three white, separate lines, as if constituting a fold. This variety of the Pecorella differs from all others, and never varies in color or the form of the clouds.

There are other varieties, called Pecorella, differing from the red and white, as white ground and purple clouds, both base and spots consisting of different shades of red, and yellow ground with clouds of a delicate shade. An example of the last is afforded in the bust of Tiberias, Capitol Museum.

The red and white Pecorella frequently simulates natural objects; sometimes representing animal, at other times vegetable forms, as certain grasses and mosses; and when the colors are blended it is called "flowered." In the collection of marbles made by Corsi for the University of Oxford, he says that in one specimen there was a representation of a peacock as faithful as the pencil could delineate. The rarest and most beautiful variety presents a clear white ground, with small, round spots of rich purple, the whole resembling shell marble. Examples are seen in large masses in a court of the Vatican.

Alabastro Fortezzino. — One of the caprices of Nature is to anticipate works of art, and this she has done in a certain way by the production of what is called Fortification marble, or alabaster, representing walls, ramparts, towers, turrets, parapets, embrasures, and other features of a fortress. A variety of this species is called "fasciato" when the colors form straight bands.

Alabastro Fiorito, "flowered," does not indicate the arrangement of the clouds; "striped" or "veined" would better express their appearance; the size of the stripe varies, some being very narrow, while others are of considerable breadth. The species has many and beautiful varieties; the kind called Melleo, highly prized by the ancients, displays tints of honey-yellow, while all the primitive colors, with many gradations, are seen in the Listato, "striped," variety. A clear white alabaster crossed by obscure white lines, forms a column placed in the Room of the Dying Gaul, and two large columns of the Fiorito, with green, are in the Palace of Altemps. A small statue in the Chiaramonti displays a ground of red crossed by bands of rose, green, and white, while the Leopard, in the Room of the Animals, is sculptured in a stone said to be alabaster, presenting a coffee-colored base with red and white bands; while a rare and beautiful specimen forms the block for a column in the Etruscan Room The Fiorito affords a great variety of colors, including white, gray, black, red, blue, orange, yellow, and purple.

Alabastro a Rosa — The name sufficiently indicates the form of the clouds, — that of the rose, often of the natural size, — while the foundation color is generally purple, with the rose delineated in fine lines of .various hues, forming one of the most beautiful species of alabaster. The varieties are quite numerous, comprising red ground with lighter red flowers; yellow, with red roses, white, with black; and other combinations forming varieties. The large Stag in the Vatican affords an example

Alabastro Dorato — The lively golden tint of this alabaster has won for it the appropriate name of "Dorato," but it is the color only that distinguishes it from the Rosa, since the form of the spots is similar to those of the latter. It is properly called Dorato only when both base and clouds are yellow, which is very rare, but the name has been applied to varieties, as, Dorato a Rosa, a Nuvole, a Giaccione, according as it resembles these species. A base supporting a head in the Chiaramonti, and a foot of a colossal statue in the Gallery of the Candelabri, are sculptured in Dorato.

Alabastro di Palombara. — Palombara is situated at the foot of Monte Gennaro, one of the highest peaks of the Sabine Mountains, about twenty miles northeast from Rome; in the ruins of a villa at this place was found this alabaster. It differs from. all other species in its uniform opacity, its compact fracture, and stratified texture. The basal color is white or uniform yellow, the spots are variable in form and color, but it more commonly presents chestnut bands upon a clear ground; the colors are gray, white, yellow, coffee-color, and purple, often passing to the deepest shades of the Rosso antico It is very hard and takes a fine polish, and was used largely for ancient pavements The bust of Hadrian in the Capitol Museum has erroneously been called Palombara.

II. *Serpentines.* — *Lapis Ophites: Verde Ranocchia.* — Serpentines were not extensively employed in ancient art; the best-known species is the Ophites, named from its imitation of the serpent's skin, which modern artisans call Ranocchia, in allusion to its mottled appearance, like that of the frog. This variety is dark-green, with veins and spots of red, purple, and green, passing to yellow. Pliny affirms there was but little of this serpentine in Rome, and only in the smallest columns; and, in describing the magnificent baths of Etruria, Statius observes there was wanting the much-sought Ophites, a statement corroborated by Corsi, who writes that it is never found except in small pieces among the ruins, and that at the Villa of Lucullus, near Frascati, he was able to obtain only the lip of a cup no larger than a common salt-cellar.

Lucan, in his Pharsalia, alludes to the Ophites, and calls it Thebais, from a province of Egypt; and as there is a small idol of Egyptian sculpture in this stone, in the Vatican, the evidence seems to be in favor of Africa as its native place.

The Lapis Ophites comprises several varieties, including a serpentine entirely green like emerald, one of different greens, a third of green with white spots, and others with yellow spots; of the last kind is a vase in the Vatican Museum. Two large vases in the same collection were made from a garnetiferous serpentine found at Smyrna, and brought to Rome in the pontificate of Pius VI., 1775-1800. The Roman mineralogists have given it the title of Braschia, in honor of Pius VI., whose name was Braschi, but the stonecutters call it Granata, for the garnets it holds. Two other kinds of serpentine were known to the ancients, under the names of Stone of Augustus and Stone of Tiberius.

The *Lapis Augusteus,* or the Italian Verde Ranocchia Ondato, "waved," is described by Pliny, who says it was first found in Egypt under the rule of Augustus, and was remarkable for the beauty of its color. It exhibits a very deep-green base with lighter green spots blended with yellow, in the form of waves and circles.

The *Lapis Tiberianus*, or Verde Ranocchia Fiorito, has been described by the same naturalist, who places it in the same rank, and refers it to a similar origin as the Lapis Augusteus. It differs from it in appearance, having a green foundation with gray bands, or more properly small light-colored lines like reticulated work, over a dark ground, constituting a rock similar to the Gabbro of Impruneta, of Tuscany. There is a small Egyptian idol in the Museum of the Kircheriano, in the Collegio Romano, said to be carved in this stone.

Lapis Atracius: Verde Antico. — This celebrated antique, highly valued by the Romans for decoration, has been classed both with marbles and serpentines. It was quarried near Atrax, on the River Peneus, in Thessaly, from which it received the names Atracius and Thessalian stone. One variety has a foundation of lively green with spots of deeper shade passing to blue, while another exhibits marks of snow-white or clear black; from the union of these colors there results a beautiful combination. Examples of this stone are numerous in Rome and other Italian cities, but for special reference the following may be cited: twenty-four columns forming the niches of the Apostles in the Church of St. John Lateran; columns of the High Altar of St. Agnese; and two large tables in the Vatican Museum.

The Verde antique so nearly resembles a green stone in Piedmont that it is difficult to distinguish the ancient from the modern.

Lapis Amiantus: Amianto. — Some mineralogists class Amianthus among serpentines, while Dana considers only Chrysotile a variety of the Serpentine, and asbestos, the amianthus of the Greeks and Latins, a variety of Amphibole.

The amianthus is indestructible by fire, and its flexible, silky fibres can be woven into cloth. It is related by Pliny that a people of India used it for garments, which were cleansed by casting them into the fire; and among the Romans the bodies of the deceased were folded in this kind of fabric for cremation, that their ashes might not commingle with those of the funeral pile. A shroud of this kind, found in a sarcophagus with human bones on the Via Prænestina, in 1703, is preserved in the Vatican Library.

On account of its peculiar qualities the amianthus has been called "incombustible flax;" "wool of the salamander;" "pens of the Holy Spirit;" and "wood of the Holy Cross."

The mineral was found in various places: Dioscorides says it was obtained from the Island of Cyprus, and Byzantius relates that near the city of Carystus, in the Island of Euboea, besides Cippolino marble, there was a stone whose fibres were made into cloth, and that garments made of it were cleansed by fire.

Lapis Æquipondus: Pietra Nefritica, or Nephrite.—A hard, compact stone used by the Romans, of dark-green color inclining to black, and unctuous to the touch, has been classed both with jades and serpentines. It received different names according to its different uses; when employed for weights and balances it was called Marmor Æquipondus, and the manner of its use has been described in a treatise on the weights and measures of the Romans by Lucus Petus. He says the ancients formed weights of certain black stones marked with veins of deep-green; to the largest weight of one hundred pounds were attached two hooks or rings, to those of less weight, only one hook; the weight, varying from one hundred to four or five pounds, and even one ounce, was sculptured upon the stone, the ounces being indicated by points or small circles. When the size of the stone was sufficient, there was inscribed upon it the name of the questor, to whose charge was committed the care of the public weights. Sometimes the name of the prefect was inscribed, as is seen in many of these antique weights in the Museum Kircheriano.

In the persecutions of the Christians these weights were employed as instruments of martyrdom, and were subsequently called Lapis Martyrum. After being used for this purpose they were held in great veneration, and many of them are embedded in the walls of the churches, being found in S. Sabina, S. Clemente, S Prassede, S Nicolo of the Tullian Prison, and others in Rome.

III. *Basalts.* — *Lapis Basanites : Basalti.* — Basalts, though not to be compared with marbles and serpentines for variety, beauty, and elegance were, nevertheless, extensively used by the ancients for sculpture. Writers do not agree as to the use or the origin of the word Basanites, some maintaining that it was derived from the Greek Basanos, "touchstone," and others, from Basal, signifying "iron," in the language of Æthiopia. This difference of etymology has led to a difference of opinion in regard to the character of the rock Pliny speaks of a stone found in Æthiopia of the color and hardness of iron, whence the name Basanites, called also Stone of Æthiopia, understood by some authors to be basalt, and by others the Lydian stone. The latter is found only in small pieces, while the former must have occurred in large masses, judging from the size of the groups of figures sculptured in it.

Basalt is of volcanic origin, hard, compact, tenacious, and well-adapted to resist the disintegrating influences of time and the atmosphere It is of dark colors, often black, as in the large antique urn of the High Altar in S Croce in Gerusalemme. That it was found in large blocks is evident from the group of the River Nile, placed in the Temple of Peace dedicated by the Emperor Vespasian, a copy of which sculptured in white marble is now in the Vatican Museum. Though black is the predominating color, yet green and coffee-colored varieties are met with, seen in a small Bacchus sculptured in coffee-colored basalt, with the restorations in a green variety, in the Gallery of the Candelabri. Green basalts vary in tint from apple-green to greenish-bronze: the green and coffee-colored are sometimes united in parallel bands. A large and rare bath of green basalt is placed in the Court of the Octagon. That this stone was used extensively for antique sculpture is evident from the great number of statues, busts, and hermes in the Museums of the Vatican and the Capitol.

Lapis Lydius: Pietra di Paragone. — This hard, black stone is not identical with the Basanites of Pliny, if we adopt the opinions of Corsi and some others. It had various names derived from the places where it was found, or from its uses; as Lydian stone, from a province of Asia Minor; the Stone of Heraclea or Hercules, a city near where it was found; and the Index stone, from its use to detect alloy in metals. As it was used to test the value of gold more frequently than that of any other metal, it received the name of Chrysites, and when cut into small pieces, Corticula, "hard stone." Ovid says that Bacchus was once transformed into the Lapis Lydius for revealing the theft of oxen made by Mercury. Its modern name "paragon" refers to its excellence as a test-stone.

IV. *Granites.* — Four kinds of antique granites are found in the ruins of Rome: Red or Pyropœcilos; Gray or Syenite, commonly called Granitello; White or Granite of the Forum; Black or Æthiopian. The red was obtained near the city of Syene, on the Nile, the quarries being on the side of the mountain from which the stone was extracted for colossi, obelisks, and pyramids, of extraordinary size. It received the name pyropœcilos, "like fire," from the red tint of the feldspar, which displays all the gradations from pale-rose to blood-red. It is referred to by ancient writers as the stone from which the great obelisks were made, consecrated to the sun, by a king of Heliopolis.

There are in Rome twelve of these red granite obelisks brought from Africa; that of Aurelian on the Pincio is of a very deep-red similar to the great columns of the Church of S. Maria degli Angeli, near the baths of Diocletian; the granite basin of the fountain in the Piazza di Venezia is of the same species. When mica predominates the rock has a dark tint, as occurs in one of the Egyptian idols of the Vatican, and when quartz prevails it is light, as seen in another statue. A valuable variety presents deep-red feldspar and clear-red quartz, while the rarest exhibits a copper-color.

The *Lapis Syenites:* Granito Bigio, is called by the stone-masons Granitello antico. It was supposed to be obtained from Syene, near the mines of the Red granite, and was called Syenite, which later mineralogists refer to Mt. Sinai. It was frequently employed by the Romans, and afforded more examples than any other kind. It contains but little mica, and displays white and gray crystals; but the most beautiful kind encloses copper-colored mica, with a dark-colored ground, traversed by short, fine, black lines, forming a remarkably rare and elegant stone, seen in a vase of the Vatican Museum, and in two columns of the Farnese Palace.

Lapis Psaronius: Granito del Foro. — It is said that the quarries were near Syene, a region remarkable for granites, and was called the granite of the Forum because the columns of Trajan's Forum were cut from it, and Psaronius, from its fancied resemblance to the feathers of the starling, "psaros," in Greek The rock is composed of white quartz and black mica, but no feldspar.

Lapis Hethiopicus: Granito Nero. — Syene, from which much of the Egyptian granite was taken, was situated not far from the frontiers of Æthiopia, which accounts for the ancient name of this species. It is entirely, or for the most part, black, and has been sometimes confounded with basalt, that the Egyptians employed it for sculpture is proved by idols found in collections of African specimens. Veins, bands, and spots of a different colored granite often occur in this species, like those of the Lions on the steps of the Capitol Two rare columns in the Braccio Nuovo are conspicuous for light-colored bands passing around the shafts. The dark crystals are occasionally inclined to violet, seen in one of the Egyptian images, and with white spots tending to red, like the two Sphinxes in the Room of the Vases. A black granite, with long crystals of feldspar, is sometimes called the "Granite of the Column" because the small column, which tradition connects with the scourging of our Saviour, placed in the Church of S. Prassede, is made of this variety. Another kind of white and black granite furnishes many specimens in this church and in the Villa Albani.

Granito Verde, or green granite, has not been mentioned by any ancient writer, and in consequence of this silence it has been classed with serpentines and porphyries. One variety of the antique, with green base and irregular spots, sometimes articulated with veins or threads of white quartz, is called Granito della Sedia, because it ornaments the pedestal of the Chair of St. Peter. A kind with deep-green, covered with fine intersecting lines of light-green, is called Theban granite. A small vase in the Villa Albani affords an example of the Granito Verde; the Oxford Collection is said to contain a rare specimen, if not the only one, of a green granite flowered with gray.

The varieties entirely green, resemble serpentines, porphyries, and green basalts, from which it is difficult to distinguish them. The rarest and most highly valued green granite has the misfortune of bearing an unpleasantly suggestive name, — Pediculare, "lousy." Over a base of greenish quartz are scattered the smallest crystals of white feldspar and black mica, which nearly obscure the ground color, so that it appears a mass of minute green, black, and white spots of equal size. A specimen is afforded by a column in the Vatican Museum, and another in the Villa Godoy.

In an account of the Island of Giglio, on the Tuscan coast, written in the sixteenth century, it is reported that a cave of reddish granite was discovered containing detached columns, and sketches upon stone, indicating that the rock had been quarried before that time. In the early part of the present century the excavations were visited, and previous statements corroborated; the quarries are convenient for the embarkation of the stone, and showed indications of having been worked. A large part of the island consists of a gray granite, combined to a greater or less extent with small masses of a

Plate XXIII.

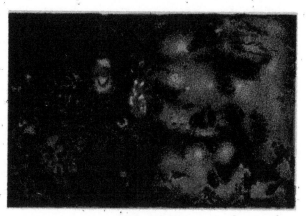

BRECCIA DI ALEPPO.

EGYPTIAN BRECCIA.

ARMSTRONG & CO. LITH. BOSTON.

deep-green mineral, probably either hornblende or serpentine, which enhances the beauty of the stone.

Two columns of the granite from the Island of Giglio, known in Italy as Granito dell' Isola del Giglio, in the Church of S. Croce in Gerusalemme, are grayish-white, tending to pale red. This granite was used in the churches built in the first centuries of the Christian era.

Granito dell' Elba. — That this species of granite was used by the ancients is evident from their monuments, but not from their authors, since it is not mentioned by any chronicler of the times. Immense quantities of rubbish, usually seen about quarries, have been found at different localities on the Island of Elba, and in several places large columns with drawings have been abandoned in a half-finished state, showing that it had been used in earlier times

The rock is grayish-white, covered with particles of black mica, and a grain varying from very small to quite large.

V. *Porphyries* — *Lapis Porphyrites: Porfido* — The term Porphyrites was given to this species of rock because some varieties displayed a purple color. Porphyries were known by several names; Purple stone, from the color; Thebaicus, from the place in Upper Egypt where it was quarried; and Leucostictos, from the white spots it exhibits Later writers have given it the name Pietra Romana, or Romana, *par excellence*, in consequence of the large quantities found in Rome. Fine examples of porphyry are seen in the sarcophagi of the Hall of the Greek Cross, Vatican Museum, said to be those of the mother and daughter of Constantine the Great. Eight columns of Pietra Romana, taken from the Temple of the Sun, erected at Rome by the Emperor Valerian, were carried to Constantinople for the decoration of the Church of St Sophia

The source of antique porphyry has been ascribed both to Egypt and Arabia; the apparent contradiction is explained by the fact that the city and Mount Porphyrites, from which it was quarried, were on the frontiers of both countries. On a small temple at Beylet-kebye, in Egypt, a notice is seen that Marcus Ulpius was qualified to superintend the mines of porphyry near, proving that the ancient Romans obtained some of their supplies from this region.

The Porfido rosso, red porphyry, considered the most valuable, has generally a lively red ground, spotted with clear white crystals, seen in the large bath in the Vatican Museum, and in columns of the churches of SS. Giovanni in Fronte and Crisogono in Trastevere; or deep-red inclining to purple, with obscure white crystals. Differing from these is a variety with purple base enclosing large black masses spotted with white, and another with gray foundation covered with greenish, purple, and rose crystals, like a column of the Octagon, in the same Museum.

Two columns of a window in the Room of the Urns, and a small cup in the Room of the Candelabra are cut in the Porfido nero, with black ground and white or gray crystals. Porfido verde, green porphyry, is composed of a very deep-green paste, enclosing light-green crystals tending to yellow, of which the finest example occurs in the great urn of the High Altar of St. Niccolo in Carcere. A variety of pea-green, with very delicate green crystals, is generally called Porfido Vitelli, for its discoverer, who found a mass in the excavations from which several interesting objects of art have been sculptured. A light-gray porphyry obtained from the modern quarries near Frejus, France, has been proved to be identical with that found in Roman remains. Stone-workers have given it the name of Granito a Morviglione, or "granite with measles." Large columns of this variety are seen in the Altar of St. Gregory, in St. Peter's Church.

Lapis Memphites. — The stones called Lapis Memphites have been named by the ancients Ophites, "serpent stones," and Tephrites, "ash-colored stones;" by moderns they have been classed with serpentines, but Corsi says they are porphyry; the term Memphites suggests that Memphis, Egypt, was the place from which it was obtained. The colors are white, black, and gray, and on account of its hardness it was used for mortuary urns. Two beautiful vases in the Vatican Museum, and one of the columns in the Church of St. Prassede, which sustains the architrave to the door of the Santa Capella, were cut in this species.

Lapis Lacedæmonius : Porfido detto Serpentino. — It would be difficult to class this stone scientifically, since it has been ranked with marbles, serpentines, and porphyries; the preponderance of evidence is perhaps for serpentines   Pliny speaks of the green Lacedæmonian stone as being more brilliant in color than any other marble, a character which can hardly be ascribed to serpentines. Strabo says Laconia, Greece, where it was found, contains quarries of valuable marble, and that they have been opened in Mt. Taÿgetus; and Pausanias mentions a stone found in Laconia used to decorate the temples of the gods. The serpentine of these mountains was disclosed by a natural phenomenon, as related by the ancient writers   A portion of Taÿgetus was shattered by an earthquake as had been predicted by Anaximander of Miletus, who warned the Spartans of the catastrophe; by the falling of the mountain the city of Sparta was partially destroyed, but the disaster revealed a rich mine of valuable stone.

The Lapis Lacedæmonius, named for Lacedæmon, the chief city of Laconia, was not employed by the Romans for sculpture or for large architectural works, but for paving dwellings, temples, piazzas, and roads.   Nibby states that the Grotto of Egeria was paved with serpentine, and that the piazzas or courts of Heliogabalus, on the Palatine, were paved with Lacedæmonian stone and porphyry.   The practice was adopted by Alexander Severus, from whom it took the name of Opus Alexandrinum.   It is said in our version of the Scriptures, that a court in the palace of Ahasuerus of Shushan, was paved with red, blue, white, and black marble; in other versions it has been rendered Parian marble and serpentine, called Smaraldine stone.

After the decline of art, serpentine was employed in the temples as a decorative stone, and in the oldest churches it is found in pavements. An example occurs of its use for columns in the Church of St. John and St. Paul on Mt. Celio, a work of the fourth century, and another in the High Altar of St. Paul's, beyond the walls of Rome.

The Lapis Lacedæmonius received the name of Sassus Spartanus, Spartan stone; Taÿgeta, from the mountains; Teneria, from the southern promontory of Laconia; Croceatus, from the Castle Croces, near which it was quarried; and Sassus Smaraldinus, from its emerald green. There are many varieties, including different shades of green and other colors. The name poryhyry applies to the form and disposition of the crystals, and not to its chemical properties.

CHAPTER XXII.

ANTIQUE marbles and other ornamental stones, seen at the present time in the museums, churches, and palaces of Italy, often in considerable masses, either as architectural decorations or sculptured ornaments and statuary, were obtained from the ruined structures of a former period and transferred entire, as in the case of columns and statues, or used for various modern works of art with which many of the collections are enriched. These relics of the past convey an idea of the magnificence of the ancient Roman villas, which, Strabo says, resembled in gorgeousness Persian palaces, and the richness and splendor of the public buildings of Roman cities under the emperors.

The celebrity of the Vatican Museum is world-wide, and many of its masterpieces are known from observation, description, or reproduction; therefore it was not intended by the author to describe these celebrated sculptures as works of art, but only to mention, as far as is known, the character and name of the principal stones in which they were carved.

It is generally understood that the Museum containing the largest and most valuable collection of statuary in the world, made at different times, and under the patronage of different popes, occupies a great number of rooms in the papal palace, whose numerous apartments, aside from the collections they hold, are exceedingly interesting for their magnificent architectural decorations. In the following descriptions, made from personal observation, Professor Massi, who quotes from the antiquary Visconti, the first director and principal arranger of the Museum, and Professor Corsi, a Roman archæologist, are cited as authority, though there are some discrepancies in their statements.

The Braccio Nuovo, or " New Arm," in which are arranged some of the most celebrated statues and masterpieces of Greek art, is a splendid hall two hundred and sixty-one feet long and fifty-five broad, with a decorated vaulted ceiling and cupola supported by eight Cippolino columns, a rare and beautiful variety of light-purple, white, and yellowish veins or waves, with similar columns placed at both ends of the hall. The jambs about the doors are made of Sicilian jasper, or the marble of Taormina, a rich and showy stone of dark-red, orange, light-yellow, and light-green. In this room are columns of granite with black ground, enclosing reddish and greenish crystals, one of which has a broad elliptical band of reddish-brown ; a column of light-brown granite ; other columns of what is called Granito persichino, of light-purple, black, and whitish crystals ; red granites of different shades, some called oriental, others African; two columns of Giallo antico, a very beautiful variety of light-pink and yellow with dark reticulated veins ; and two columns of Alabastro bianco, white alabaster, with alternate opaque and translucent layers, similar to the Cotognino. Among other marbles for decoration occurs the rich Spanish brocotello of variegated colors of red, purple, orange, gray, and white.

The sculptures of the Braccio Nuovo afford examples of many species of stones, including a variety of green basalt with minute particles like dust, and a black Egyptian basalt ; oriental alabasters, resembling Pomato and Giaccione, the latter translucent, of a greenish tint, looking like petrified water; white marbles of various kinds, as Parian, Pentelic, Grechetto, Tarsio, Lesbio, Carrara, and many others.

The statue of Commodus is of Pentelic, while that of the great tragic poet Euripides is Tarsio, like the Venus of the Capitol,

with a brilliancy and yellowish color finely representing flesh
tints.   A statue in the room of the large Pavonazzetto vase is
cut in a marble similar to that of the Euripides. · The figure
of Julia is claimed by Massi to be of Carrara, but Corsi says
it is Lesbian, a Greek marble.   The stone has a remarkable
translucent appearance, is of a yellowish tint, with the purple
veins and brilliant scales of Tarsio.   The Parian of the magnificent statue of Minerva Medica is diaphanous and of a
yellowish hue resembling a very fine alabaster; while a Mercury larger than life is in Pentelic.

The Chiaramonti Corridor is a long gallery containing more
than seven hundred marble sculptures, arranged on both sides,
and embracing a great variety of subjects   This hall is separated from the Corridor of Inscriptions by an iron grating between columns of Lumachella bigia, or gray shell marble,
resting on bases of Sassio or Pietra Santa marble.   The columns are of a deep-purple, with grayish or white masses
crossed by fine lines, while the bases consist of a large, modern
breccia of dark and light-red and white, resembling the
antique Porta Santa, and is obtained from Sasso, in the western
part of Tuscany, or from Pietra Santa, in Liguria, perhaps
from both places.

The larger number of sculptures in this gallery are of
white marble, the exceptional colored stones being an altar in
Pavonazzetto or Phrygian ; a female figure in Pietra di Monti,
a hard, light-colored stone; a plinth of Alabaster of Tivoli,
probably modern, of white, yellow, and brown, with distinct
crystalline structure, bust in Nero antico; Jupiter Serapis
in Marmo bigio; Fallen Gladiator on a plinth of Alabaster
of Tivoli, Tiger in black Egyptian granite, displaying large
purplish-white and black crystals; Captive King in Phrygian ;
the tunic of a torso in Alabaster fiorito, of yellow, red, purple,
and white bands; a base for a figure, consisting of a beautiful alabaster with yellow and brown curved lines; a head of
Bacchus in a variety of Giallo antico, called Carnagione, flesh-
color ; and a faun in green basalt.

The white marble of the Young Augustus has a peculiar fineness, compactness, and whiteness, nothing like the warm, living tints or brilliancy of Parian. The marble of two busts near the Augustus resemble it, but differ in translucency and apparently in texture. The heads of Ariadne and Venus, called Parian by Massi, are bluish-white, with large, brilliant crystals, resembling that of Ganymede, in the Cabinet of Masks. There is in this corridor an Isis and a Neptune, said to be Pentelic; a sarcophagus, not a pure white, in Luni; a Silenus in what is catalogued as Salino marble, from a villa near Lake Albano, a white, compact stone; and a Hercules in Porinum, a Greek marble.

From the Vestibule of the Belvidere a fine view of the city is afforded, a prospect which suggested the name, but its renown is derived from the famous Torso Belvidere, sculptured, it is supposed, by the Athenian artist Apollonius, and regarded by art critics as representing Hercules deified. This celebrated statue is considered by Massi to be in Pentelic marble, but Corsi, who seems to be the better authority in such questions, says it is Grechetto duro, or the antique Porinum, found at Olympia, Greece; it has fine grain and brilliant scales, and differs from other examples of Pentelic. The centre of the Round Vestibule is occupied by a vase of Pavonazzetto marble which measures twenty-five palms in circumference. The Meleager is said to be sculptured in Imezio or Greek Hymettus marble, with the blue veins of other specimens of this variety.

The Court of the Belvedere is surrounded by a portico supported by sixteen columns of Corallina breccia and gray and white marbles, with capitals of Verde serpentino, Giallo antico, and Porfido rosso, or red porphyry; the cabinets at the four corners contain, respectively, the Apollo Belvedere, the Mercury, the Laocoön, and the Perseus and the two Boxers by Canova. One of the columns consists of very rare pink, brown, and gray granite, called Morviglione, and among the interesting specimens of antique art occupying the portico are a bath of black Egyptian basalt; a basin of beautiful Egyptian granite of fine grain, resembling basalt; a column of rare gray and pink African breccia; a cornice in Rosso antico; a large bath of a rare variety of Porta Santa of pale colors, pinkish-brown, white, and some others, an altar of Pentelic; and two columns of rare and beautiful porphyry. The porphyry columns are remarkable; the ground color of one of them is deep purple with large, greenish-yellow spots, giving it the appearance of a breccia, the whole overspread with greenish and pinkish-white particles. The ground of the other is light-gray, enclosing dark-gray and white spots

The Mercury of the Belvedere, called by some critics the most nearly faultless example of ancient sculpture, is in Parian, which has the yellowish tint and brilliancy of this marble seen in other examples, while Pentelic was employed for the group of the Laocoon, and Parian for the beautiful statue of Isis; the large bath, regarded as Egyptian porphyry, resembles granite The celebrated Apollo Belvedere is said to be sculptured in Parian by some critics, and in Carrara by others; but if the statue was brought from Greece, as is generally conceded, it was undoubtedly made of Greek marble; the stone has a slightly bluish tint, but is lustrous. The Perseus and the Boxers, being modern works, were of course sculptured in marble used by modern artists, undoubtedly the Carrara. Among other articles of this court are a bath of dark-green basalt of fine texture, sprinkled with very small specks like dust, and large blocks of red and white alabaster, called Pecorella.

The Hall of the Animals, appropriated to sculptures representing the lower orders of creation, has been very properly called a "marble menagerie" It contains a great variety of subjects and of material used in sculpture, and from the numerous specimens, illustrating the use of the different ornamental stones, the following have been selected:—

A Griffon in Alabastro fiorito, "flowered alabaster," presenting different arrangements of the various colors; a Stork in Rosso antico; a Dog in Pavonazzetto; a small group in a marble of different shades of brown; a Stag in two species of alabaster, the body of Alabastro a rosa, of deep-red, orange, yellow, purple, and white in forms simulating a full-blown rose, and the horns of a yellow and white alabaster called Cotognino; a small Lion in a very rare orange and brown marble called Pietra Carnagione, covered with minute, bluish particles resembling dust, with the tongue and teeth in their natural colors, and the base on which the figure rests of a beautiful granite, consisting of small crystals of light and dark green and black; and a Lobster in a green stone called in the catalogue Verde di Carrara, but not recognized as an antique under that name. The species of green stones are quite numerous, including marbles, serpentines, granites, porphyries, and basalts, bearing some resemblance to one another. In the Lobster the ground color is dark green, covered by thin yellowish-green clouds, while a vase in another room, called Verde di Carrara, displays yellowish-green spots, with fine white lines on a dark-green base.

Other examples in colored stones are a Wolf in Phrygian or Pavonazetto marble; a Sphinx in Giallo antico; a Tiger of pink and white Egyptian granite; a Lion said to be Giallo antico; a breccia of large fragments of buff, yellow and yellowish-white, resembling the columns in the Hall of the Statues; a Panther or Leopard in Alabastro fiorito, which differs from that of the Griffon, the stripes being in different shades of yellowish-brown, while the black and yellow spots, in imitation of the natural colors of the animal, were undoubtedly the work of art.

In this "menagerie" are seen a Tiger sculptured in a beautiful variety of Egyptian granite, composed of crystals arranged in delicate clouds of light-purple or slate, covering a dark ground; a Lion in Bigio venato antico marble, presenting a dark-gray foundation crossed with light-gray veins; a small Lion in Bigio, a very peculiar marble of dark-gray base sprinkled with fine particles of bluish-white like dust, — the

deception is perfect ; a Cow in Pavonazzetto; the pedestal of
a vase in Alabastro fiorito, similar to that of the Griffon; a
Horse in a marble resembling the Bianco e Nero d'Egitto,
called by Massi, erroneously there is little doubt, Lydian stone.
In this hall are placed two large tables of Verde antico, named
Morato, the most valuable variety, composed of large fragments of black, dark-green, and white, overspread, as with a
veil, by light green clouds, the white portions being encircled
by green lines or narrow bands.

A Dolphin affords a specimen of delicate yellow and brown
alabaster, it may be Sardonico ; a Cow of dark-brown marble,
similar to that of the Lion, but covered by dust particles of a
different color, and supposed to be a copy of one in bronze
by Myron; a Crawfish, of rare green porphyry, with dark-
green base and yellowish-green crystals, inclined to a circular
form; a Tripod of Serpentino Tiberiano, according to Corsi,
but catalogued as Polsevera Green, displaying a ground of
dark-green, reticulated by light-green, white, and pinkish
veins, waves, and circles. A red breccia is quite generally
used for the bases and pedestals of figures.

Gallery of Statues. — The fine columns supporting this Gallery are of Giallo antico, similar to that of the Lion in the
Hall of the Animals, while the pilasters are of Sette Basi,
both marbles affording a very rich and appropriate decoration
for a room devoted to sculptures in white marble.

The large Bath, made of the elegant yellow and white
Alabastro cotognino, occupies the centre of the room. The
statue called the Genius of the Vatican, or the Vatican
Cupid, supposed to be the work of Praxiteles, is said to be
Parian, but its identity with that marble is not assured ; it resembles the Triton and a Bacchus in the same room. The
Penelope, from its style, supposed to belong to the Greek
school before Phidias, is sculptured in a marble like the Pentelic, which was not used for art until about his time. The
Amazon in Grechetto duro, ancient Porinum, is of fine grain,
bluish tint and purple veins ; the sitting statues of Posidippus

and Menander are executed in the variety of Pentelic, veined with blue and purple. A green, translucent variety of the Alabastro cotognino, forms the drapery and armor of the bust of the Emperor Otho, while Vespasian is invested with a chlamys or mantle of Verde antico and armor of Porta Santa.

A fluted column supporting a mask of Rosso antico, designated in the catalogue as Nero antico Africano, is simply Nero antico, a Greek marble, and a rich variety of Alabastro fiorito is seen in a bust with the chlamys. The vase called Breccia Africano, on a base of Porta Santa, is called by Corsi Traccagnina, but differs entirely from other specimens of this breccia, displaying a black ground covered with reddish-gray and white fragments in the form of small veins and light clouds, sometimes blended and sometimes clear and distinct. A modern alabaster, called Civita Vecchia, of reddish-brown, combined with various other colors, forms a vase, resting on a column of Alabastro giaccione, of yellow and white.

A bust of Annius Verus Cæsar is made of fine, white Palombino, ancient Coraliticum; a bust of Julia, of Porta Santa; a cuirasse, of the Alabaster of Orte, said to be the rarest kind, obtained from the quarries, now extinct, at Orte, a small town on the route from Florence to Rome. This exceedingly beautiful alabaster might be easily mistaken for a deep, rich amber, which it strikingly resembles in color; there are two small columns of this stone in the Confessio of St. Peter's, and a vase in the Museum. The reclining statue of Ariadne, so called, is said to be in Parian, and it seems to answer to the descriptions of that stone; while the marble of the supposed statue of Bacchus resembles Grechetto or Porinum. A vase of alabaster called Agatino, supported by a column of Verde antico, with orange and yellow, is identical, probably, with the antique Sardonico.

The Cabinet of Masks is decorated with eight splendid columns and pilasters of a white and yellowish-brown alabaster, called, by Corsi, Alabastro a giaccione, but in the catalogue it is written Alabaster Monte Circeo. In this cabinet are

seen several statues ; a Bacchante in Pentelic marble ; Diana
Lucifera in a white, compact marble called by Massi Cipollo,
which is the Imezio or Hymettus, a variety with large crystals
of rather obscure white and purple veins or bands, employed
generally for columns, but different from that of another Diana
in the same apartment   The Ganymede resembles examples
in the Hall of the Statues, said to be Parian, while the Adonis,
claimed to be of the best kind of Greek marble. which is
Parian, is carved in a clear, white marble of fine texture.   A
Faun, basin, and seat of Rosso antico are found here

The Hall of the Muses is supported by sixteen columns
of Carrara, and a large part of the statues and busts in
this hall, found near Tivoli, are sculptured in white statuary
marble, but only one is referred to any particular species,
the Euterpe, in Pentelic.   Of the magnificent works in the
Rotunda in white marble, the Ceres and the Hadrian are said
to be in Pentelic, the immense basin, sixty palms in circumference, found in the Baths of Titus, is sculptured in red
porphyry

At one entrance to the Hall of the Greek Cross are seen
two statues in Egyptian red granite, and on either side of the
room stands two large Sarcophagi of red porphyry, supposed
to be those of Constantia and Helena, the daughter and the
mother of Constantine the Great.   In this room is the Venus
of Cnidos, considered the best copy of the original of Praxiteles, but it is not certain what kind of marble was used for
the statue

The Sala Regia, or Royal Staircase, consists of four flights,
adorned with columns of marble, porphyry, and granite, found
in the ruins of Præneste or Palestrina, with balustrades of
bronze, entablatures, etc   Corsi makes the following enumeration of the columns · six of Granito persichino ; two of
Granito del Foro ; eight of Granito bigio ; four of Granito
rosso ; two of Porfido nero ; four of Breccia corallina.   There
are eight of the latter, as every one can see ; but four of
these, which Massi classes as Breccia di Cori, Corsi has

omitted from his list. The name Cori suggests the ruins of ancient Cora, a town in the Volsian Mountains, existing several centuries before the Christian era, as the place where the marble or the columns were found; the ruins of this town include the remains of walls and temples. The Breccia corallina composing these columns has large fragments of red, pink, white, and yellow; and the four called Breccia di Cori are similar, but with pieces more distinct, and are probably varieties of the same species. The two rare columns of black porphyry, Porfido nero, presenting a black ground with small yellowish or greenish-white crystals, were found near the Porta San Paolo, and are considered the only examples of the kind.

The granite columns are of different varieties: a red, or reddish-brown and black; one with light purple, enclosing black, white, and pinkish crystals, called Persichino; the light-colored granite named the Granite of the Forum, and a gray granite with light brown crystals. A vase called Plasmatico granito, with a ground of a rich, clear green, enclosing bluish-green and a gray feldspar, stands near a balcony of the staircase. The name Plasma has been given to a vase in the Gallery of Vases as synonymous with Serpentine of Genoa; the two vases differ in appearance, but the difference may be only of variety.

The eight fluted columns supporting the cupola of the Hall of the Biga cannot be of Carystium or Cippolino, as stated by Massi; they are white, with delicate purple veins, and resemble the columns in the Rotunda, which he calls Carrara. In this room is placed the statue of a Roman in Pentelic marble, and a fine statue of Apollo in Grechetto or Porinum. The centre of the hall is occupied by the Biga, a Roman chariot in white antique marble, though large portions of the group are restorations, consequently in modern stone.

The Gallery of Vases and Candelabra contains the largest collection of rare and beautiful colored stones found in the Museum. The gallery is divided into six compartments

by columns of elegant gray marble; in the first compart-
ment are placed pillars of alabaster called Civita Vecchia, of
red, brown, and white waves.

As the specimens in this apartment are so numerous, and
many of them of small size, they will be designated by numbers corresponding to the catalogue   No. 1. Affords an example of Egyptian Green breccia of black, green, yellow, and
gray fragments crossed with lines of other colors, in a cement
of very dark green or black dotted with yellow, seen in the
handles of a vase standing on a column of red porphyry.   No.
14. A vase of porphyry with purple-red crystals in a black
and white ground.   Nos. 17 and 18 Two vases of remarkable
oriental granite of black ground and light-bluish green spots,
producing the effect of dark-green with light-green crystals
No 21. Cinerary vase in Alabastro a rosa, on a base of Verde
antico.   No 40 A torso in Alabastro di Montalto, of a yellowish color with reddish veins.   Montalto is an eminence on the
southern slope of the Alps in the northwestern part of Italy,
crowned with the ruins of a castle.   No 41 A foot and
buskin in Alabastro fiorito dorato, of deep orange and red,
with light colors and dark spots   Nos 46 and 56. Two vases of
Serpentino di Genova, or Verde plasma, sometimes called
Polsevera green, but classed by Corsi with granite, resting
on columns of a granite called Morviglione, displaying light
crystals in a reddish-brown foundation.   No. 48 Cinerary
vase of Egyptian granite of very small black and white
crystals, on a block of deep-green granite flowered with light-
green spots, both supported by a column of Giallo antico.
No. 50 Vase of gray serpentine porphyry, said to be rare
No. 52. Faun in green basalt.   No. 69 Vase of Lisimico
jasper, a very rare and beautiful stone, displaying a black
ground covered with large spots of deep-orange and light-
yellow, dotted by small red particles, seen under transparent
livid-white clouds crossed by fine lines.   It would be interesting to know from what place this remarkable species was
obtained.   Pliny speaks of the Lysimachos, an ornamental

stone resembling Rhodian marble, with golden veins; it is possible it came from Lysimachia, a town in Thrace, founded by Lysimachus, or from Etolia, near a lake of the same name, and identical with that in the Museum. The column on which this elegant vase stands is called Breccia di Aleppo by Corsi, and Traccagnina by Massi. No. 70. Vase of serpentine porphyry with black ground and bluish-green crystals over-spread with light-yellow waves and spots of reddish tints. No. 82. Two vases of Serpentino granito, deep and light-green and white crossed by fine reticulated lines, called also Polse-vera green. No. 87. A vase said to be in Phrygian or Pavon-azzetto marble of very delicate purple and white, differing from most other examples of the kind. No. 92. Vase in Serpentino di Genova, or, as it is sometimes called, green plasma granite, of green, purple, and white crystals embedded in a green base crossed by fine, straight lines, giving it the appearance of having been scratched. No. 96. Vase of Theban granite, a rare species of reddish purple overspread by light-green, brick-red, and white clouds. No. 107. Cinerary vase in Pietra di Monte, a compact white stone like travertine. No. 112. Vase of Polsevera of the same species as No. 82. The ground is coffee-colored, well-marked by light-yellow, green, and white veins, and large purple spots, with a clear white border; also a cup of Tigrato marble, presenting a speckled appearance, quite peculiar and rare, produced by a mingling of white, brown, yellow, and orange colors, in clusters resembling small flowers. No. 120. Tripod in Alabastro sadonico, of rich and beautiful colors, red and yellow pre-dominating, arranged in layers similar to those of the Sardonyx. No. 123. Vase of Porfido nero serpentino, similar to No. 70, with dark-green and bluish or greenish-white crystals placed on a column of Bigio morato marble. No. 133. Column of Ala-bastro fiorito, found in the Roman Forum, of very rich colors of deep orange, red, yellow, and white, with a base of a handsome yellow, brown, and white breccia. On the top of the column stands a vase of orange and white alabaster called Cotognino.

Plate XXIV.

ALABASTRO A TARTARUGA.

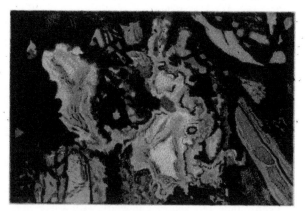

BROCCATELLONE.

ARMSTRONG & CO. LITH. BOSTON.

The columns supporting the Gallery of Vases are made of very light-gray marble, covered with graceful-waves of white light-purple, and yellow tints, the stone bearing some resemblance to jasper   No. 156. Vase in Verde di Polsevera, similar to No 82, with some variations.   No 159 Vase of the same stone, called by various names, standing on a block of lustrous yellow and white alabaster, said to be Giaccione, but unlike other specimens of that variety.   No. 173. Cinerary urn on a column of Pavonazzetto; an urn of Palombino of chalky whiteness, resembling porcelain; a vase said to be Rosso Levantino, but this must be a mistake, as it resembles No. 112; it is probably Polsevera.   No. 185. A vase called Verde di Carrara, of dark green foundation, covered with yellowish-green spots and fine white lines enclosing crystals, resembling feldspar, which, in their interesting play of colors, produce the effect of labradorite.   No 188. Vase of the exquisite, gem-like alabaster of Orte supported by a column of Cippolino marble.   No. 189. A column of Giallo antico, of the variety called Carnagione, supporting a vase of rare jasper with a red ground similar to Rosso antico, covered by reticulated blue, purple, and white veins.   No. 192. Vase called by Massi Nero antico Africano, which is probably Nero e Bianco d'Egitto, since it resembles specimens of that marble in the Museum of the Capitol. This vase has a black ground with obscure-white clouds, and clear-white veins.   No. 220. Vase of exceedingly rich Polsevera green standing atop a Cippolino column.

Fifth Division of the Gallery: No 221. A cup of Rosso antico in a base of red breccia   No. 227 Vase of Alabastro a rosa, which does not mean rose-colored alabaster, as expressed in the catalogue, but a kind in which the various colors assume a figure resembling a rose.   Nos. 235 and 236 Two splendid vases cut in a stone called by Massi Garnetiferous serpentine, and by Corsi granite, named Pietra Braschi, in honor of Pius VI.   The ground of dark-gray, enclosing purple-red garnets, is scattered over with thin, light-yellow clouds blended with green, exhibiting something of the chatoyant nature of labradorite. This extraordinary granite was found at Civita Castalana, between Rome and Florence, near the place which yielded the rare alabaster of Orte. No. 239 Cup said to be of white marble, is of green serpentine porphyry on a base of Sicilian jasper or Taormina marble. No 247. Cup of red granite of the smallest grain, called red oriental Granitello; the minute crystals are of light-red and dark colors. No. 249. Cup of Porfido nero, a rare species of porphyry. No. 268. Vase of Egyptian gray granite with very fine crystals

In the Etruscan Room are some sculptures in Nemphro, or volcanic tufa What is called a crater in sculpture is a vase for mixing wine and water, of which there are several in the Museum.

Egyptian Room. — This collection was partly gathered from Egypt and partly from the museums of Rome. Those works brought from Egypt were, of course, sculptured in the stones of that country. One statue, which strikingly resembles Polsevera green, was probably a copy; another, carved in a native stone, the character of which is not perfectly clear, displays a ground of dark and light purple with white and yellow spots; it may be a breccia marble or a granite; there is no other example of it in the Museum, but a specimen resembling this variety is seen with darker purple, finer crystals, and white spots like flakes of snow There is an idol sculptured in a peculiar marble covered with small, brown specks, called Palombino, which may have been a copy, as that marble was not found in Africa; and an idol in Verde Rannochio ondato, or Serpentino Augusteo, of delicate purple, light yellowish-green, and grayish-white.

The basalts used for Egyptian coffins were of different kinds; one variety might be taken for bronze, it so ·closely resembles it, while another is of a coffee-color. The Egyptian alabasters are mostly white or whitish, and of no special beauty, but the granites are of many species, including red, black, gray, and purple, and some with crystals so large as to give the stone a brecciated appearance. A marble called

Seme Santo pallido is a cream-colored stone with small particles of other colors scattered in the cement like seeds.   Purple and white marbles, a Bigio morato, very peculiar and
beautiful, and a black breccia marble with very large yellowish-white fragments, are all found in this department.   A
summary of the principal works of art in the Egyptian Room
are thus given by Corsi: Fifteen statues in black granite;
three statues in red granite; an urn in green basalt from
Memphis; an urn in black basalt; two lions in black granite;
an idol in gray breccia à Seme Santo; an idol in Palombino;
an idol in green and white granite; an idol in Serpentino
Augusteo; a vase in Alabastro giaccione; two mummy-cases
in Lumachella bianca; a statue of the Nile in gray marble; a
statue in coffee-colored basalt.

In the Museo Kircheriano, in the Collegio Romano, is a
small Egyptian idol in Serpentino Tiberiano, or Verde Rano-
chio fiorito, of deeper green than the Augusteo; another idol
of a dark green with light yellow veins, and a column of
gray marble.

This Museum, established in the first part of the seventeenth century, by Kircher, contains fewer sculptures in
marble, more especially in colored antiques, than are found in
many other collections.

The Capitoline Museum, begun by Innocent X. about the
middle of the seventeenth century, and completed by Pius VI.
in the last part of the eighteenth, has a much less extensive
collection than that of the Vatican, but it contains several masterpieces of statuary.   The Room of the Dying Gaul, usually
styled the Dying Gladiator, contains two immortal works —
the statue of the wounded Gaul, a Greek sculpture in a marble
resembling Parian, and a copy of the famous Satyr of Praxiteles, considered the best extant.   In this room is an interesting column of Breccia traccagnina, composed of a cement
of reddish-yellow, enclosing fragments of various colors and
sizes, none of which are entirely of one color but variegated,
displaying a mixture of black, red, brown, gray, and yellow,

with a gradual blending of tints, crossed by fine lines, or thin clouds.

In this Museum is seen a beautiful specimen of Nero e Bianco d' Egitto, or Egyptian gray marble, with light purplish-white veins and clouds, sometimes tending to yellow, on a black ground, similar to some of this species in the Vatican Museum. There are two half columns of Sette Basi of a lighter color than that seen in the Vatican, consisting of yellowish-white, reddish-purple, and violet, with small fragments arranged near together. The Rosso antico of the Faun of the Capitol, found at Hadrian's Villa, is veined with black and white; the two Centaurs from the same place, said to be sculptured in Bigio morato, have also been classed under the Black and White marble of Egypt, and the Jupiter and Æsculapius, called Nero antico, are of the same marble as the Centaurs.

The varieties of alabasters include a specimen of the Tartaruga, displaying wavy bands of shades of yellow, on a deep-red ground; the Fiorito, of light-yellow, orange, and red; a bust in Palombara, striped with delicate yellow, orange, purple, and white; specimens of Giaccione, of Banded, and Onyx alabasters; a column of Pecorella; another of Alabastro bianco, and two others of different kinds.

Further illustrations of colored marbles are comprised in a deep-red and obscure white Bigia lumachella; a column of gray marble; half columns of Granito persichino; a grayish-white and orange marble; rare Verde antico containing red; a rare variety of Lumachella d'Egitto seen in the crown of Juno; and Cippolino with green base covered with purple and white clouds or waves. The marble of the Venus of the Capitol, said to be Lesbian or Grecco giallognolo, is of a yellowish tint and large brilliant scales.

The numerous sculptures of the Capitol Museum are, to a great extent, in white statuary marble, probably some of it native to Italy.

CHAPTER XXIII.

ANTIQUE STONES USED TO DECORATE ROMAN CHURCHES.

It is in these structures the antique stones can best be studied, since they are often seen in large masses, as in columns, or covering extensive areas, as on walls, where the colors and cloudings are displayed to advantage.

✓ Church of S. Maria Sopra Minerva. — This edifice, erected on the ruins of the Temple of Minerva in 1285, the only Gothic church in Rome, contains a great variety of antique marbles, some of the most notable being: Two columns of Giallo brecciato — yellow breccia — with bases of Lumachella gialla; two columns of Breccia corallina; a column of rare Breccia dorata — golden breccia; two columns of Fior di Persico; two columns of Nero e Bianco; two columns of Occhio di Pavone; a column of Breccia rossa; columns of a rare variety of Porta Santa; specimens of Africano, Verde antico, and other species.

Church of the Gesu. — This is the principal church of the Jesuits, and one of the most georgeously decorated in Rome. Though built in the latter part of the sixteenth century, some of its decorations are recent; the walls having been covered with marble by Prince Torlonia in 1860. Among antiques are Verde antico, Africano, Breccia corallina, Giallo antico, and Porta Santa, with a great variety of beautiful alabasters. There are two large columns near the entrance resembling Cippolino, and two columns in the second altar, of an elegant red and gray breccia. This church contains a globe of lapis lazuli made of a single piece, said to be the largest mass óf the kind known.

CHURCH OF S. MARIA IN ARA CŒLI — A very old building, with numerous antique columns in Cippolino, Pavonazzetto, Tarsio, Breccia dorata, Breccia corallina, Giallo antico, Breccia traccagnina, Porta Santa, Broccatellone, Red granite, Green granite, Granite of the Forum, Red porphyry, Green porphyry, and some other species including Gialla e Nera, Sette Basi, Seme Santo, and a marble resembling Fior di Persico, all used for decoration in some form

S. ANDREA DELLA VALLE — A church with some precious antiques, including Gialla e Nera, seen in a pilaster, Breccia pavonazza, Breccia of Hadrian's Villa, a very rare marble, and Giallo tigrato. The balustrades of the High Altar are of Lumachella d' Astracane; while four columns in the Barberini Chapel resemble Giallo antico; and other columns are of rare Verde antico Porta Santa, Brocatello, Bianco e Nero, Sicilian jasper, and rich alabasters have been effectively used for embellishment.

The most interesting examples of antique marbles in SS. Trinita di Monti are seen in the beautiful columns of Porta Santa, displaying a variety with rich and vivid colors

S MARIA LIBERATRICE — This church occupies the site of the Temple of Vesta, near the Palatine Hill, and contains columns of Breccia corallina and Breccia traccagnina; while two columns of purple, with yellowish spots, resemble the small columns and base of the High Altar in S Maria in Ara Cœli

S MARIA IN TRASTEVERE. — One of the most ancient churches in Rome, founded, it is said, in the beginning of the third century, in the reign of Alexander Severus, but restored several times since it was first built. It is a basilica, richly ornamented with mosaics and marbles, both on the exterior and in the interior. Inside are placed twenty-eight large columns of antique red and gray granite, some with Ionic, others with Corinithan capitals and bases, besides four large Corinthian pilasters, encased in Cippolino marble, two columns of Broccatellone, two of Pentelic marble, a fluted column of Hymettus, two of red and black granite, several columns of Africano, and several of beautiful and variegated alabasters and red porphyry The High Altar is supported by four columns of the latter, and enriched by four others of a rare and elegant variety of Nero e Bianco, gorgeous alabasters, gems, lapis lazuli, and other ornaments The chapels display a great number of antiques, while the Tribune is ornamented with mosaics of different periods, the oldest dating from the twelfth century The walls are covered with paintings on gold, and the centre of the ceiling is occupied by Domenichino's Madonna on copper. The church, according to tradition, was the house of St Cecilia, who suffered martyrdom during one of the persecutions of the Christians, and contains the reclining statue of the saint sculptured by Maderno, near the close of the sixteenth century, after the opening of the sarcophagus, where the remains were found in a state of pres-preservation. The walls of the porticoes are covered with numerous inscriptions

S. Maria Maggiore. — Of the great number of churches dedicated to Mary this one is regarded the largest and one of the oldest in Rome, if not in Christendom. The façade consists of a porch resting on four red and four antique gray granite columns ; the architrave of the nave is supported by forty-two Ionic columns, thirty-three of these being in Hymettus marble taken from the ancient Temple of Juno Lucina, and the remainder are of gray granite. Columns of Nero e Bianco display white waving lines encircling the shaft, producing an effect altogether unique. Numerous species of alabasters, marbles, and gems seen in other churches, some of them rare and peculiar, are profusely used in this church. The High Altar consists of an ancient porphyry sarcophagus, in front of which is the richly decorated Confessio, enclosed by balustrades of Bigia lumachella, while ten porphyry columns decorate the Capella del Presepe or the Chapel with the boards taken from the manger of the infant Redeemer.

S. PRASSEDE. ——This church, first erected at the beginning of the ninth century, contains the Chapel of the Column, where may be seen a small column claimed to be the identical one at which Christ was scourged. Two rare and beautiful columns, one of black and white granite, and the other of serpentine porphyry, stand at the entrance to this chapel, while the interior is covered with mosaic with gold ground. The nave is supported by twenty-eight columns of gray granite, seventeen of them being enclosed, forming pilasters

The High Altar is furnished with columns of red porphyry and white Pentelic marble carved in leaf ornaments, and ascended by steps of Rosso antico. The fine columns of Giallo e Nero are black, with yellow and white spots, and the two of Broccatellone are light-yellow and light-purple.

SAN GIOVANNI IN LATERANO. — St. John Lateran dates from the time of Constantine the Great, and has passed through many vicissitudes, having once been destroyed by an earthquake and twice by fire, but has since been rebuilt, altered, and modernized   The nave is sustained by twelve pillars, enclosing, in part, twenty-four columns of Verde antico, and forming niches for the white marble statutes of the Apostles. The most remarkable chapels are those of the Torlonia and the Corsini families, both literally covered with rich ornamental stones, including many varieties of antiques. The Corsini Chapel is conspicuous for its beautiful Fior di Persico and its elegant alabasters. Magnificent columns of Giallo antico, two of them taken from Trajan's Forum, are placed in the right transept , those of Sicilian jasper occur in the Sacristy, while the Choir is embellished by a large number in granite, Pavonazzetto, Cippolino, Bigio, and Hymettus marbles.

Eight large porphyry columns in the Baptistery support an antique marble architrave, said to be the gift of Constantine the Great ; and two of the splendid Breccia gialla dorata ornament the Oratorio   Jerusalem marbles, including columns from the Temple of Solomon, may be seen in the Cloisters.

S. CLEMENTE. — Recent excavations made below the present edifice, built in 1108, have laid bare three different layers of masonry belonging to different periods, — the early Christian, the Imperial, and beneath these, the Republican, the early Christian forms the crypt of the present church, called the lower church. The nave of the upper church contains sixteen antique columns, of which five are in Hymettus marble, six of Cippolino, one of them resembling those of the Braccio Nuovo, the others green and white, and five granite columns. Corsi calls the purple marble, covered with yellowish, reddish, and grayish fragments, seen in two columns of this church, the rare Breccia pavonazza; the one he refers to as Lesbian may be the small spiral column near the High Altar.

Eight columns of Cotinello, and four of Verde antico, taken from the Arch of M Aurelius, decorate the Church of S Agnese. The four columns of the High Altar of the Church of S Pantaleo, said to be Porta Santa, are different from other varieties of that marble, and bear some likeness to Sicilian jasper; there are two like them found in the Church SS. Domenico e Sisto A specimen of the rare and elegant marble called Breccia della Villa Adriana, found at Hadrian's Villa, is encrusted in the walls of this church, and among the antiques ornamenting the Confessio, occur some remakably beautiful varietes.

S MARIA DELL' ANIMA is the German National Church, containing the monument of Pope Hadrian VI, in which a very high nave is supported by six large pillars. Several columns of antique marbles, including a rare variety of Africano, have been introduced into this edifice, but neither here nor in S Luigi de' Francesi, the French National Church, are the decorations so rich in valuable marbles as in most of the Italian churches. The pilasters of the showy Sicilian jasper give to this edifice a gaudy appearance, which is somewhat modified by columns of Verde antico, gray, and other antique marbles; the specimen of Lumachella gialla displays large and distinct shells.

S. Maria in Vallicella. — This church, though com-
paratively modern, is one of the most richly decorated in
Rome, and, perhaps, exhibits as many species of antique stones
as can be found in any building of the kind   The list includes
Brocatello, Giallo antico, Sette Basi, rare varieties of Porta
Santa, Rosso antico, Bigio morato, Gialla e Nera, a beautiful
variety of Pavonazzetto, Fior di Persico, rare kinds of Africano,
Nero e Bianco, Verde antico, Breccia rossa, Occhio di Pavoni
rosso, Breccia Traccagnina, and many species of alabaster.
The pilasters of Gialla e Nera, a very elegant marble seen in
one of the chapels, exhibits small veins of vivaceous yellow,
orange, and white on a black ground   The seventh chapel on
the left is excessively decorated with marbles, alabasters,
gems, gilding, paintings, and other ornaments

San Marco was founded about the time of Constantine, and
is notable for the Roman and Christian inscriptions built into
the walls of the vestibule.   The nave is sustained by twenty
columns of Sicilian jasper and pilasters of Hymettus marble;
near the High Altar stands a fine column of Breccia pavonazza, of deep and light purple and white, affording a remarkable instance of one side of a column being in the light and
the opposite side in the dark tints of the marble.

Another example of Breccia pavonazza, exceeding in beauty
that of San Marco, is seen in four columns near the High
Altar of the Church of S Maria Madelina; while a third
variety of this purple breccia occurs in S. Maria in Aquiro, a
church ornamented with gems, alabasters, marbles, gilt, and
mosaics

S. Agustino — This building, said to be the first Roman
church covered with a dome, is approached by a broad flight
of steps made of travertine taken from the Colosseum   It is
profusely ornamented with gems, antique stones, statues,
monuments, and paintings, including Raphael's Prophet
Isaiah.   The columns claiming to be Fior di Persico differ
from specimens in the Corsini Chapel in St. John Lateran;
they exhibit purple and yellow instead of white, with colors

well blended, and seem to be of the same kind of marble as ·
those of the first altar on the left. Near the High Altar
are four columns of Nero e Bianco, and a small one of gray
marble.

S. LORENZO IN LUCINA — This church is celebrated for
the great painting of Guido Reni, one of the most impressive
representations of the Crucifixion ever placed upon canvas.
The most remarkable specimen of antique marble in this
edifice is the High Altar, made of the very rare Occhio di
Pernice, "eye of the partridge."

SAN PIETRO IN VATICANO. — This celebrated church attracts
more by its grandeur than by its beauty ; its immense columns, expansive walls, and gigantic monuments impress one
with an overpowering sense of magnitude. For objects and
spaces so large vast masses of marble would be required,
therefore the rarest specimens of antiques should not be
sought here, yet many of the most abundant species found
in ancient ruins, and many of the most valued alabasters have
been employed in the construction of this edifice.

The portico is supported by immense columns of Africano,
Cippolino, Pavonazzetto, red granite, and the gray granite of
the Forum. The casements of the Porta Santa, opened only
once in twenty-five years, are made of the marble which
received its name from this door. The nave is lined by forty-
four immense columns of Cotanello, while columns of Bigio,
Tyrian, Porta Santa, Cippolino, Africano, Verde antico, Giallo
antico taken from Trajan's Forum, Hymettus, Bigio morato,
Nero e Bianco, Bigia lumachella, found near Hadrian's Villa,
granites, and porphyries are arranged throughout the body of
the church and Sacristy.

Exquisite alabasters, remarkable for their rich colors, are
very profusely used in the Confessio and other parts of the
building, while among granites, perhaps the most elegant is
the Granito persichino, with pink, white, and black crystals on
a purple ground, if we except the rare green granite in the
pedestal of the statue of St Peter.

The number of churches selected as illustrations bear only a small proportion to the whole number found in Italy, still they are enough to show what vast quantities of ornamental stones were used by the ancients for architectural decoration; but no description can convey an adequate idea of their beauty, elegance, and richness.

APPENDIX A.

AGE AND LOCALITY OF THE PRINCIPAL LIMESTONES.

LOWER SILURIAN, OR CAMBRIAN LIMESTONES.

Western Hemisphere.

Paleozoic Era, including the Cambrian, Silurian, Devonian, and Carboniferous Ages	Auroral and Martinal (of Rogers) .	United States. Some formations found in British America
	Bellerophon	
	Bird's Eye	
	Black River	
	Blue of Kentucky	
	Burnet Marble	
	Calciferous	
	Cape Girardeau	
	Chazy	
	Cincinnati	
	Galena	
	Leptaena	
	Marbles of Tennessee (in part) . .	
	Maclurea	
	Murchisonia Marble . . .	
	Quebec	
	Receptaculite	
	St. Peter's	
	Trenton	
	Ute Pogonip	
	Utica	
	Magnesian Limestones . .	
Lower Silurian . .	Anticosti and Mingan Islands (in part) .	British America.
	Orthoceratite of Point Levis . .	

Eastern Hemisphere.

Bala, Hirnant, Caradoc .	England and Wales,	Europe.
Wrea . .	Scotland . .	
Connemara Marble. .	Ireland . . .	
Grauwacke (probably)	Germany . .	
Aphrite L. or U Sil.		
Orthoceratite . .	Scandanavia . .	
Gothland (in part)		
Pentamerus .	Russia . . .	
Pleta . . .		

355

Upper Silurian Limestones.

Western Hemisphere.

Paleozoic Era . .

Catskill	
Clear Creek	
Cliff	
Clinton	
Crinoidal	
Delthyris or Spirifer	
Le Clair or Waukesha . . .	
Lower Helderberg	United States. A
Maysville	part found in
Meniscus	British Amer-
Niagara	ica.
Oriskany	
Pre-Meridian (of Rogers) . . .	
Pentamerus	
Racine	
Scalent (of Rogers)	
Water-lime or Tentaculite . . .	
Magnesian Limestones	

Upper Silurian . .

Guelph or Gault (found in United States) .	
Anticosti and Cape Gaspé (doubtful) . .	British America.
Hudson's Bay (Magnesian)	

Eastern Hemisphere.

Woolhope or Barr	
Wenlock or Dudley	Great Britain.
Aymestry or Ludlow	
Gothland (in part)	
Upper Malmö	Sweden.
Waratah Bay (doubtful)	Australia.

Devonian Limestones.

Western Hemisphere.

Devonian . . . .

Coralline or Falls	
Corniferous or Upper Helderberg . . .	
Cadent (of Rogers)	
Crinoidal of New Hampshire	United States.
Hamilton	
Onondaga	
Past-Meridian (of Rogers)	
Tully, Magnesian Limestones	

DEVONIAN LIMESTONES (*concluded*).

Eastern Hemisphere.

Paleozoic Era . .	Devon or Plymouth .	} England.
	Ilfracombe, Comb Martin .	
	Babbicombe, Torbay	
	Ipplepen, Torquay .	
	Birdiehouse (fresh-water formation) .	Scotland.
	Cornstone .	Wales.
	Clymenian Kalk (Devonian or Carboniferous) .	} Germany.
Devonian. . . .	Eifel, Cypridinæ	
	Stringocephalus	
	Givet .	{ France and Belgium.
	Griotte Marbles (possibly Carboniferous) .	France.
	Buchan .	} Australia.
	Bindi .	

CARBONIFEROUS LIMESTONES.

Western Hemisphere.

Carboniferous Age includes Sub-carboniferous, Carboniferous, and Permian Periods,	Archimedes or Kaskaskia	
	Burlington	
	Chaetetes .	
	Chester .	
	Chouteau .	
	Humboldt Mountains	
	Kinderhook .	
	Keokuk .	
Carboniferous Period	Lithostrotion or Barren	} United States.
	Lithographic .	
	Maxville .	
	Pittsburg .	
	St. Louis .	
	Warsaw .	
	Wahsatch Mountains	
	Magnesian Limestones	
	Hermosillo .	} Mexico.

CARBONIFEROUS LIMESTONES (concluded).

Eastern Hemisphere.

Paleozoic Era . .	Mountain Limestone	Great Britain and Ireland
	Great Scaur . . . . Marbles of Derby and Stafford . .	England.
	Black Marble	Isle of Man and Anglesey.
Sub-carboniferous Period	Armagh . . . . . "Ekers," and part of the Irish Marbles .	Ireland.
	Visé	France and Belgium
	Tournay, Hainault, Petit Granit . . Marbles of Gobzienne and Dinant .	Belgium.
	Culm	Germany.
	White Moscow or Spirifer . . Fusilina, Producta, "Stina voi" .	Russia.
	Carrara (Statuary) and Bardiglio Marbles .	Italy
	Krol	India.

PERMIAN LIMESTONES.

Western Hemisphere.

	Interior Continental Basin . . . Kansas, Black Hills. . . . . Indian Territory	United States.

Eastern Hemisphere

Permian Period .	Magnesian Limestones .	Great Britain and Ireland.
	Zechstein, including Rauch-wacke . . Rauhkalk, Plattendolomit, Fetid Limestone .	Germany.
	Magnesian, Modiola, Spitzbergen . .	Russia
	Verricano (the latest classification) . .	Italy.
	Australian Limestones	Australia.

TRIASSIC LIMESTONES.

Western Hemisphere.

Mesozoic Era includes the Triassic, Jurassic, and Cretaceous Periods	Distinctions between the Triassic and Jurassic strata in the United States not yet clear The two systems found in the Western Interior, the Rocky Mountains, and the Pacific Border . . .	United States.
	Probably in British Columbia	British America.

TRIASSIC LIMESTONES (*concluded*).

Eastern Hemisphere.

Mesozoic Era . . | Penarth Beds, including the Avicula Contorta Beds . . . . England.
Calcaire Coquillier . . . . France.
Muschelkalk, including Encrinital and Tere- bratula Limestones, and Wellenkalk . . } Germany
Terraine Conchylien, or Rauch-grauer Kalk- stein . . . . } Switzerland.
St Cassian Beds, including Guttenstein . .
St Cassian and Hallstatt Red and White Marble . . . .
Triassic . . . . | Dachstein White and Gray Marble . . } Austria
Koessen, or Rhaetic Gray and Black Marble
Fire Marble of Carinthia . . . .
Predazzit (Dolomite) . . . . . The Tyrol.
Para and Teling (probably) . . . India.

JURASSIC LIMESTONES.

Western Hemisphere.

Idaho and other Rocky Mountain Regions . United States

Eastern Hemisphere.

Jurassic Period, in- cluding Liassic, Oolitic, and Wealden Epochs, | Lower or Bath Oolite, Middle or Oxford Oolite, Upper or Portland Oolite . .
Lower Oolite comprises: | Inferior Oolite, a Calcareous Free- stone . . . .
Stonesfield and Collyweston Cal- careous Slates . .
Great or Bath Oolite . .
Cornbrash and Forest Marble . | England.
Middle Oolite comprises | Kelloway Rock, Coral Rag or Coralline Limestones .
Upper Oolite Portland Stone, Purbec Beds .
Wealden Beds (Jurassic or Cretaceous) .
Sussex or Petworth Marbles . . .
Glyphite Limestone (Liassic) . . . } Continental Eu- rope.
Calcaire a Nérinées . . . . The Jura.
Caen Stone, Calcaire Marbre of Caen . .
Calcaire Polypier, Marble of Argonne . .
"Blue Stone," "White Stone," "Pierre Rouge," } France.
Marbles of Montbard and Nancy . .
Nerinaen Limestone . . . . . Russia.
Alpine Limestone (?) . . . . . Both Continents.

JURASSIC LIMESTONES (concluded).

Eastern Hemisphere (concluded).

Mesozoic Era . .	Solenhofen or Lithographic Stone . .	Germany.
	"Dogger," La Dall Nacreé . . .	Switzerland.
Middle Lias . . .	Ammonitico Rosso	
	Cotanello Marble	
	Biancone, identical with the Majolica of Milan	
	(Jurassic or Cretaceous) . . .	Italy.
	Porto Venere Marble (Jurassic or Cretaceous)	
Lower Lias . . .	Mischio di Serravazza (?) . . .	
	Marbles of Siena (?)	
	Jesalmir and Golden Oolite . . .	India.

CRETACEOUS LIMESTONES.

Western Hemisphere.

	Chalk (very little if any)	
	Rotten Limestones	
	Caprina, Caprotina, Exogyra . . .	United States.
	Turritella, Trigonia, Hydraulic . .	
	Austin, Washita, and Ripley Limestones	
	Suisun Marble of California . . .	
	Limestone of Cerro de las Chonchas . .	Mexico.
	Hippurite	Island of Jamaica.

Eastern Hemisphere.

Cretaceous Period.	White Chalk	Great Britain, Continents of Europe, Asia, and Africa.
	Neocomian of Neuchâtel	Switzerland.
	Inoceramus or Sewer-kalk . . .	
	Maestricht Beds	Netherlands.
	Hils-Conglomerate	Hanover.
	Faxoë, Terraine Danien . . .	Denmark.
	Pläner-kalk, Mittlequader . .	Germany.
	Spatangus, Serpulite, Aptychus . .	
	Hippurite, Calcaire Pisolitique . .	France.
	Marbre Napoleon	
	Zone of the Rudistes belong to this Period .	Switzerland.
	Occhio di Pavone, Scaglia . . .	Italy.
	Hymettus and Pentelic Marbles . . .	Greece.
	Bagh, Utatur, Trichinopoly, Arialur . .	India.

TERTIARY LIMESTONES.

Western Hemisphere.

Cenozoic Era . .	Orbitoides or Vicksburg	
	Clayborne Beds, Bluffs on the Tombigbee	
Tertiary and Qua- ternary Periods .	Cardita Beds, Tampa Bay Limestone . .	} United States.
	White and Cheyenne Limestones . . .	
	White, Coast, and Yellow Limestones .	West Indies.
	Tosca, of Brazil, Patagonia Limestones .	South America

Eastern Hemisphere.

Tertiary includes	Nummulitic (the most characteristic) .	{ In most countries { of E Hemisphere
Eocene, Miocene,	Headen and Bembridge Series .	
and Pliocene	White Crag and Red Crag .	} England.
Epochs . .	Calcaire Grossier, Calcaire Siliceux	
	Calcaire de la Beauce, Lits Coquillier	
	Miliolite, Indusial (fresh-water)	} France.
	Travertines of Auvergne .	
	Molasse and Falun	
	Rupelian, Bolderberg, Coralline Crag of Ant- werp, Yprisian, Tongrian .	} Belgium
	Kleyn Spawen Beds, Rupelmond Strata	
	Flysch, Nagelflue, Glarus Slates .	} Switzerland.
	Œningen Deposits . . .	
	Mayence Basin, Litorinella . .	Germany.
	Tripoli, or Polishing Stone of Bilin, Beds of Croatia	} Austria
	Gratz and Leitha Limestones, Vienna Basin .	
	Alberese, Macigno, Verona Marble .	
	The Superga in Turin, Hills of Rome .	
	Lacustrine Strata of Val d'Arno .	
	Calcareous Tufa, Panchino (doubtful) .	
	Eastern Base of Mount Etna (Sicily)	
Tertiary . .	Girgenti Limestone (Sicily)	
	Pierre Poros and Conglomerate Deposits of Pikermé	Greece
	Aralo-Caspian, or Limestone of the Steppes, Limestone of Odessa . .	} Russian Empire.
	Kirtha, Siwalik, Travancore . .	} India
	Nahan (enclosing mammals) . .	
	Bairnsdale	Australia.
	Limestones of the Madeira, Azores, and Canary Islands.	

QUATERNARY FORMATIONS.

Cenozoic Era . .	Recent Formations, Tufas, Travertines, Bone Breccias	
	Sprudelstone of Carlsbad . . .	Austria
	Regur, or Black Coton Clay . .	India
	Laterite, Kunker . .	
Quaternary Period.	Red and White Conglomerate . . .	Cuba.
	Breccia of Taurus . .	Turkish Empire.
	Tabreez Marble . .	Persia.
	Loess Formation	China.
	Probably the Onyx Marbles of Mexico and Algeria.	

APPENDIX B.

FRENCH MARBLES.

Decorative Stones exhibited at the Paris Exposition of 1878, comprising Marbles, Serpentines, Porpyhries, and Granites collected from the different Departments of France.

Department of Ardennes
1 Charlemagne — Black, with white and gray spots.
2. Florence. — Reddish-brown, with gray clouds.
3 Rancennes (St Anne) — Black, with white and gray shells.
4. Rancennes (Florence) — Black, brown, and white

Department of Aude
1. Griotte d'Italie — Black, tending to purple, and deep-red veins
2 Griotte Rouge — Red, like Rosso antico, with small purple and white spots
3. Griotte Rouge Fleuri — Same base as the preceding, crossed with distinct, compact, white veins.
4. Griotte Rouge Vert — Red base, with greenish-gray spots
5 Griotte Grand Jaspé — Red, with large spots of lighter red
6 Griotte Rose Isabelle. — Light-red, tints languid
7 Griotte Gris Flambré — Delicate pink and gray in clouds
8. Felines-Incanot. — Light-red, with gray clouds.
9. Incanot-Dit-Languedoc — Similar, with obscure white
10 Rouge-Antique-Villerembert — Resembles Griotte
11 Languedoc-Rouge Turquin — Light red, white, and gray
12 Gris-Agathe de Caunes — Very dark gray or black base, with light-gray, yellow, red, and white clouds
13 Gris Agathe — Rose de Caunes — Dark and light-red, with white, tints languid.
14 Rose-de-Vif de Caunes. — Similar to the preceding

Department of Ariège
1. Noire-Grand-Antique. — Black and white, crossed with very fine, yellow lines.
2. Griotte de Pyrenées — Dull-red, with greenish-gray clouds
3 Vert de Moulin — Light dull-green, shades blended.
4 Rose de l'Ariège — Yellowish-red and white.
5 Sarencolin — Red, brown, gray, purple, and yellow
6. Violette D'Arbessoit (breccia) — Purple, green, and white, tints languid
7. Isabelle de Seix — Similar, with colors more distinct
8. Marbre de Moulis — Black, with light-brown and white shells.
Vert-Claire (locality not certain) displays delicate tints of green, blended with white; resembles Cippolino
Bleu d'Aulis. — Delicate bluish-green in clouds

363

FRENCH MARBLES (*continued*).

Department of }
Allier . . . }

Marbre de Dion. — Light brown, with white shells.

Department of }
Côte-d'Or . . }

Marbre de Fadonée. — Delicate yellow and red in clouds.

Department of
Basses Alpes.

1. Brèche de Rouviret. — Black, brown, gray, a little red, with fragments distinct; resembles antique Traccagnina.
2. Marbre de Pourcieu. — Light-red and grayish-white in clouds.
3. Marbre de Condèron. — Light yellow, with pink and white veins.
4. Pierre de Pompignan. — Light brown, with some white.
5. Pierre de St. Ambroix. — Black, with small yellowish-white crystals; resembles granite.

Department of
Hautes Pyre-
nées . . .

1. Campan Vert Mélangé. — Red, brown, green, and pink.
2. Campan Hortense Mélangé. — Light-red, green, with grayish-white crystals.
3. Campan Rouge. — Dark red, light-red, with green spots and white veins.
4. Campan Rouge Mélangé. — Similar to the Vert.
5. Campan Vert Foncé. — Light and dark-green, with clear white veins.
6. Campan Vert Rouge de Moulins. — Very dark green and red, with rose-white veins.
7. Griotte de Sost. — Dark shades of red, with white spots.
8. D'Hérechêde. — Languid reddish colors blended.
9. Brèche Portor Degers. — Black, with orange, yellow, and white.
10. Brèche Infernale de Regaude. — Black, with dark brown and white clouds.
11. Beyrède a Nervure. — Red, gray, and yellow in clouds.
12. Beyrède Rubané. — Bright red, with yellow.
13. Beyrède Rouge Vif. — Same colors, with deeper red.
14. Sarencolin Doré. — Deep-red, gray, and yellow. Other varieties with nearly the same colors. The Sarencolin marbles display lively and delicate reds, grays, browns, and yellows. Sometimes the fragments of this breccia are large.
15. Lumachelle de Lourdes. — Grays, red, white, and yellow.
16. Turquin D'Ossen. — Gray and white.
17. Montgaillard. — Light gray, with white and black spots.
18. Noire D'Aspin. — Black and gray, in lines and spots.

Department of
Haute Ga-
ronne . . .

1. Nankin de Mancioux. — Shades of yellow, purple, pink, and white.
2. Brèche de Bouchire. — Black, with deep yellow and grayish-white fragments.
3. Rouge Acajou de Cierp. — Red like the Rosso Antico, with fine, black veins, the whole covered with small particles like dust.
4. Vielle Brun. — Large spots of light and dark red, some white.
5. Brèche de Lez. — Base of grays, with red covered with small, dark spots.
6. Blanche Jaunette de Lez. — Clear white, with pink and yellow clouds. A very delicate marble.
7. Marbre de Labarth. — Gray, with white veins.

FRENCH MARBLES (*continued*).

Department of Hautes Alpes.

1. Cipolin de St. Maurice. — Light tints of pink, green, and grayish-white in veins.
2. Vert de Ceillar. — Black, covered with thin, light-green clouds.

Department of Haute Saône.

Porphyry of St. Barthelemy. — Shades of green and reddish brown.

Department of Haute Savoie,

1. Gris de Pouilly. — White and light-brown.
2. Marbre de Taninges. — White, with shades of brown and yellow.
3. Jaspé de St. Gervais. — Red, green, some white.

Department of Herault . .

1. Griotte Rouge et Bleu. — Dark-brown, deep red spots, and white veins. Colors less distinct than in some other varieties.
2. Griotte Œil de Perdrix. — Black, with dark-red and white spots. Often used in ornamental work.
3. Griotte Verte de Felines. — Dark-green, with red and white spots.
4. Marbres de St. Pons. — Clear opal white, with yellowish and gray clouds. Very delicate and beautiful.
5. Froide de Frontignan. — Reddish-brown, with small white veins.

Department of the Jura . .

Marbles of Sampons present three varieties : —
1. Drab, with fine yellow lines, the whole dotted with purple.
2. Yellowish base, with small brown spots of different shades.
3. Similar to the second, except the base is reddish.
4. Jaune Verni. — Light yellow, crossed by red and purple lines.
5. Jaune Dit Lamartine. — Light-yellow, with red lines.

Brocatelle Violette de Chassel. — Red, white, brown, and yellow.

Department of Lot-et-Garonne,

1. Marbre Clairæ. — Light yellow, with small, dark spots.
2. Marbre L'Argenais. — Rose-yellow, with veins of a deeper tint.

Department of Saone-et-Loire,

1. Rouge de Flaci. — Reddish-brown, with small yellowish-white spots.
2. Nante Jaune Rosé. — Light-red and yellow, in clouds.

The Napoleon Gris Grande Mélangé is a delicate and pleasing marble, offering shades of brown, with white, red, and yellow.

Island of Corsica . . . .

1. Vert Antique D'Orezza. — Different shades of purple, with green spots.
2. Marbre de Maltifeo. — Black, red, and white, blended.
3. Marbre de San Garving. — White, with pink, and black veins.

French Marbles (*concluded*).

In the collection from Marseilles were varieties of modern marbles remarkable for their resemblance to some of the antiques. Of these were a small column of Verde antique precisely like that seen at Rome and Naples, a yellow marble similar to the Giallo antico in some of its varieties, and a deep-red marble, which might be taken for the Rosso antico

In the fine collection of L'Ecole des Mines are many varieties of marbles, alabasters and serpentines of rich and vivid colors and rare excellence

· The onyx marble, so called, from Algiers, is extensively used in France since its rediscovery.

The serpentines of France present many varieties, they are generally green, and many of them very beautiful   The variety called Serpentine D'Estrival, Department Lot-et-Garonne, is very rich and elegant   It presents a deep-green base overspread with gauze-like clouds of a lighter green   A variety from Corsica, called Vert-de-Mer, is a sea-green, as the name signifies, on whose surface appear to float light-green clouds   The Serpentine des Quarrades is of the deepest green, seen through transparent yellow clouds

Some of the varieties contain red colors like the English serpentines, while others present the rare combinations of purple and yellow

APPENDIX C.

Marbles of Great Britain and Ireland, Germany, Austria, Switzerland, Scandinavia, Italy, and Greece.[*]

GREAT BRITAIN AND IRELAND.

Derbyshire and Staffordshire.
- Variegated white, gray, dove, blue, black, and russet.
- Dark, with different colored shells.
- Deep-red, with small dark and yellow spots.
- Black, with small white shells.
- Light-buff, light-brown, russet and black, with yellow shells.
- Rosewood.

Devonshire . .
- Deep orange and red; yellow and red; pink and white.
- Shades of brown; red, orange, and yellow; white and black.
- Dark and light reds; orange and gray; red and brown.
- Reddish, with brown, red, yellow, and gray shells.

Somerset. . . Dark-brown, with light-yellow shells of Ammonites.

Isle of Man. . . Black; dark, and light breccias.

Wales . . . .
- Mumbles marble; dark, with light-yellow spots.
- Brown, yellow, and purple breccia.

Scotland . . .
Hebrides . . .
- Aberdeen greens; Glen Tilt; white and dark.
- Tiree marble, light pink, or yellowish, with green spots.

Ireland . . .
- Irish green or Connemara; yellowish, with light and dark-green; light-browns and yellows; light-green and white.
- Greens, with pink and white.
- Kilkenny. — Black, with white corals; red and white.
- "Irish Sienna," mottled.
- Limerick. — Pink and white; brown and gray.
- Clonomy. — Browns, with veins or spots.
- Cork. — Black and white.
- Kenmare Islands. — Black and white; purple, white, and yellow.
- Galway. — Black.

Serpentines . .
- Lizard's Point. — Red, green, white, pink, purple, gray, and yellow, forming many varieties.
- Potsoy. — Red and white.

[*] It is not supposed that this list comprises all the varieties of marbles of any given country, or that it may not include some not now used for the purposes of art.

367

GERMAN EMPIRE.

Badra Marbles of Schwarzburg ... } Dark-red; gray and red, dark-red, with white, ash, and yellow spots.

Saxon Marbles.
{ Dark-gray, with yellow spots, an elegant marble.
Ash color, with green and red.
Pale-red ground, with white, light-green and sometimes purple, forming a beautiful variety.
Dark-red, found at Pirna Other varieties combining different colors.

Bavaria, Baireuth ...
Hof . . .
{ Varieties of Baireuth marbles display a fine, light-yellow, with snow-white spots, highly valued in art
Reddish-gray, with black clouds.
Marble similar to the Italian Breccia di Sarravezza
Light and dark gray, white and black, with red spots
Pale red, an elegant, glossy marble.
Gray with black veins, gray veined with pale green
Yellow, with small, red spots, brown and blue with black clouds; dark brown, with gray and light-red.

Other Bavarian Marbles . .
{ Elegant varieties of yellow; yellow striped with gray and red.
Flesh-color with gray, gray with veins and spots of red.
Nuremberg marble, yellow, and other colors
Black marble, and dark with green veins from Ratisbon.

Marbles of Silesia . . . .
{ Black marble of Frankenstein, green with dark veins; green with white veins, used as a common building-stone; black, with green spots.
Greenish-yellow, used in the city of Breslau.
Cipolin at Brieg on the Oder, used for walls.

Prussia, Blankenburg . .
{ The Blankenburg marbles afford a great variety veined and spotted with brown, red, yellow, gray, white, and other colors
Entrochal marble of variable colors, some blocks being veined with red and yellow, others with white, green, and brown
The Blankenburg marbles generally exhibit bright colors, a smooth, compact, and uniform texture, and are susceptible of a high polish. It is said the quarries were opened in 1721

Hanover . . .
{ Compact shell marbles of gray and white, spotted with orange.
Variegated marble of brown, red, purple, yellow, and ash-color.
Black marble.

Brunswick . . Ash-color, with red and purple veins.

Hartz Mountains ... } Red, with black and white spots.

AUSTRIAN EMPIRE.

Carniola . . . Black; black and yellow varieties.

St. Cassian and Hallstadt . . } Pink and white.

Bohemia . . . Ash-gray, with black spots.

Salzburg . . . Variegated gray and white.

Lenburg . . . Black variegated.

Hall . . . . Deep-green and deep-brown.

Carinthia . . Fire marble.

Tyrol . . . . Predazzit.

SWITZERLAND.

Found in the Cantons of Berne, Geneva, Grissons, and other places . . .
- Ash-brown; saffron-red; yellow; green; black; reddish purple; black, and white brocatelle; black and yellow; gray with white veins; iron-gray with black spots; gray and yellow; purple with white spots; Cipolin marble; Dendritic marble.
- Fiery red; red with white and black.
- Red, with cinnabar spots and black veins.
- Ash-gray; blood-red, with black and white veins.
- White, with small black spots.

SCANDINAVIA.

Sweden and Norway . . .
- Green; white and green; lucid white with light-green spots; pale-green with deep-green veins; gray with black veins, from Gothland.
- Deep-green mottled with white, opaque spar and black spots, a beautiful marble from Ostergothland, similar to a variety of Great Britain and Austria.
- White with dark and red spots.

ITALY.

Italy . . . .
- White statuary of Carrara; black of Vicenza, Como, Varenna, and Bergamo.
- Dust-brown, called Polveroso of Pistoia.
- Red, black, and white of Varenna.
- White with black spots from Maggiore.
- Orange and red; white with yellow and red, both from Verona.
- Yellow variegated, from Siena.
- Peach-blossom, near Caldana.
- Black and gold, from Porto Venere.
- White, with dark clouds, the Bardiglio of Carrara.
- Marbles with black, violet, red, yellow and green colors, from Carrara.
- Mischio, a breccia of white, brown, ash, yellow, purple, green, and other colors, of Sarravezza.
- Marbles with black, ash-white, flesh-red, and bright-red, from Bergamo.
- Green, called Green of Prato; dove-colored.
- Green of Piedmont, called Ponsevera.
- Deep-red with white spar; rose-red; flesh-color.
- Cinnabar color with white spar, called Peacock's eye.

Modern Greece.

Greece . . .

Yellow base with brown clouds; dark-red with dark veins.
White and black; dark ground, with fine white and yellow veins.
White, red, and yellow, colors mixed.
Grayish-white covered with black, like shells.
Deep-red and gray breccia; light pink with white veins; varieties in browns.

INDEX.

A

371

X.

Y.

Z.

Lightning Source UK Ltd.
Milton Keynes UK
UKHW020757290421
382834UK00004B/379